DRAGON GATE

Competitive Examinations and their Consequences

Kangmin Zeng

D0002108

CASSELL

FRONTIERS OF INTERNATIONAL EDUCATION

Series Editor: Colin Brock

Already published:

Gonzalo Retamal and Ruth Aedo-Richmond (eds): *Education as a Humanitarian Response*

Kangmin Zeng: *Dragon Gate: Competitive Examinations and their Consequences*

Forthcoming:

Gillian Squirrel: *Education and Change within Penal Settings*

Cassell
Wellington House
125 Strand
London WC2R 0BB

www.cassell.co.uk

Cassell & Continuum
370 Lexington Avenue
New York
NY 10017-6503

First published 1999

British Library Cataloguing-in-Publication Data
A catalogue record for this book is available from the British Library.

ISBN   0–304–70015–0 (hardback)

Typeset by Annette Abel
Printed and bound in Great Britain by T. J. International Ltd, Padstow, Cornwall

Contents

Preface

In Japan, Korea and Taiwan, the entrance exam systems are the centrepiece of the educational structure, shaping both the intellectual profile of the future élite and the general population. The main questions that this book addresses are: First, to what degree do Japan, Korea and Taiwan share the same history in the formation and development of their entrance exam systems? Second, did the three systems originate in the common experience of Japanese administration of education before World War II? Third, what kind of knowledge is tested? Fourth, what role do the subcultures of the exam system play in the larger society?

To answer the first question, the exam systems in East Asia incorporate both cultural continuity and the structure of modern education. The 'prime mover' of that fusion is mainly attributed to the Meiji Restoration, which initiated the modern system of merit selection in East Asia. The parallels among the exam systems of Japan, Taiwan and Korea are closely associated with that legacy.

As for the second question, the exam systems of Taiwan and Korea were the corollary of Japanese colonial expansionism, and the legacy of Japanese education was profoundly felt in the two countries. It planted the seed of meritocratic idealism at an age perhaps the darkest in modern history. Once emancipated from colonialism, the Taiwanese and Korea aspire to the ideals that Japanese education left behind.

To answer the third main question, the primary commonality among the exams of Japan, Korea and Taiwan is that they are the achievement test assessing competency rather than qualification. This results in high quality, although their immediate utilitarian purpose seems to have been blurred. They measure not only intelligence, but also character, determination, and the will to succeed.

To pursue the fourth question, the formal entrance exam system's competitive pressures have engendered at least two major spin-off enterprises: the ever-growing cram industry and interest in evoking the help of a supernatural power. Both demonstrate the compelling impact of the exams on the students and their parents. Entrance exams have always symbolized upward social mobility, in folklore, imagination, and to a degree reality. The competition for the prize of educational high status has driven people in East Asia to invest enormous time, effort, and money in preparing for exams.

Youth suicide and cheating are two negative phenomena related to exams that draw much media attention. Comparative data on suicide rates, however, do not substantiate the assertion that exam pressures are a major cause of youth suicide. Despite continual intellectual critique and the amplification of the dark side of the exam system, its high degree of internalization within East Asian society is a fact.

East Asian entrance exams are seen by East Asians as measures not only of achievement and intelligence, but also of character, determination, and the drive to succeed. One symbolic message they send is: learning is a long journey of ordeal. Without pain, one can hardly attain it, and there is no shortcut.

Acknowledgements

I wish, at the outset, to acknowledge the initial interest, insights, enthusiasm and firm support of Professor Colin Brock, Oxford University, who has patiently and impeccably transformed my book script into this book, to be published in the Frontiers of International Education series.

I am very grateful to Cassell for publishing this volume. I am indebted primarily to Ruth McCurry for her editorial industry and wisdom in supervising its publication.

As the penultimate draft of my book was coming out, my memory jogged back in time to many people whose generosity and goodwill have made this work possible. First and foremost, a very special note of thanks goes to my adviser, Professor Thomas P. Rohlen. Way before the gestation of this book, he artfully let my mind play around the ideas, and later, guided me through the many phases that led to the final draft. 'Every step is painful', he metaphorizes for me, 'and you have many steps ahead. You may have to continue your search for the answer in your lifetime.' This metaphor has been my cynosure. Professor Rohlen scrupulously went through my numerous drafts, editing, questioning, and challenging many of my points at different angles. His insightful teaching and suggestions, his heartfelt help, his unwavering generosity and his good sense of humour enabled me to weather my writing of the past years with joy. And I enjoyed the freedom he gave me to develop my own interests and ideas from the very outset.

I would also like to express my deep gratitude to other members of my committee: Professor Francisco O. Ramirez, Professor Raymond Mc-Dermott, Professor Daniel I. Okimoto, and Professor Myra H. Strober, who have always been willing to read, discuss, and share their knowledge and critical thoughts with me. I have benefited greatly from the breadth and depth of knowledge all five scholars have brought to this study, and I thank them for the guidance they have provided.

I gratefully acknowledge Stanford University Asia/Pacific Research Center and Stanford University Institute for International Studies, for their support of my book-related fieldwork, data collection and archival research in Japan, Korea and Taiwan during 1993 and 1994. Particular thanks in this regard are owed to Professor Daniel I. Okimoto and Mrs Nancy Okimoto for their appreciation and great support. My acknowledgement is also due to the Spencer Foundation for its Dissertation Fellowship Award, which enabled me to concentrate on writing and finalizing my work.

In East Asia, I was assisted by many people in the course of my research, and I only wish that my book could repay their friendship and generosity. In Japan, I am indebted to Masami Kajita, of Nagoya University, for his ample assistance and arrangements; Ikuo Amano, of Tokyo University, for his advice and guidance; Akiyoshi Yonezawa, of the Administrative Headquarters of Tokyo University, for his friendly and incessant help; Takashi Sakamoto, Norio Suzuki, and Tabuchi Akihiro, of Japan's National Center for University Entrance Examinations, for their intellectual insight and hospitality; Katsuhito Tsuboi of Kawaijuku for his cordiality and corporation; Jiping Li and Chuanxün He, for their considerate arrangements at different cities in Japan, which greatly facilitated my work.

In Korea, my earnest gratitude goes to Chong Jae Lee, of Seoul National University, for his consistent support; Hyung Kee Sun, of the Korean National Board of Educational Evaluation, for his kindness in providing me with valuable information; Carl Porter, for his selfless help, studious library search, and voluntary translation work. I want also to give my special thanks to Rick L. Chu, whose assistance is exceptionally appreciated.

In Taiwan, I am first of all grateful to Doris S. C. Wu of Fu Jen University for her kindly support and arrangements that not only made my fieldwork in Taiwan possible but fruitful. I also owe thanks to Ping-huang Huang, of the College Entrance Examination Center, for his valuable comments and encouragement; and Maw-Fa Chien, of National Taiwan Normal University, for his assistance.

I want also to extend my thanks to the staff of the following institutions who assisted my search for material: in Japan, the Japanese Ministry of Education, Obunsha, Nagoya University, Tokyo University, and the National Center for University Entrance Examinations; in Korea, the National Board of Educational Evaluation, the Korean National Commission for UNESCO, the Korea Educational Development Institute, and Seoul National University; in Taiwan, the College Entrance Examination Center, National Taiwan Normal University, National Chengchi University, Fu Jen University. I gratefully appreciate the cooperation offered by schools of various types that I visited in East Asia.

I would like to thank Jeannette Colyvas particularly for her excellent editorial work, encouragement, and many suggestions concerning my book, which is infested with foreign phrases and festooned with footnotes, tables and figures.

The people who offered me a helping hand or shared their valuable thoughts with me are too numerous to list by name, and I give my sincerest tribute to each and every one who is not mentioned here. None of these people, however, should be held accountable for the text's deficiencies or errors of fact, judgment and translation, which are wholly my responsibility.

I conclude with my thanks to my wife Zhiping Li, who has shared with me the vicissitudes of my academic life at Stanford. My son, Bin Zeng, also helped me with my writing in some unique way. This book is dedicated with filial affection to my parents, Shixi Liu and Hesheng Zeng, who educated me with great love, wisdom, and self-sacrifice.

Notes

For the transcription of Chinese terms, there are two systems in use. Hanyü Pinyin, the system adopted by the People's Republic of China, is generally employed by newspapers and magazines as well as in many scholarly books, especially those on modern and contemporary China. The other is the traditional Wade-Giles system. The practice in this text is to use the Pinyin transcription, except for those terms that have entered the English language, such as 'Confucius', 'Sun Yat-sen' or 'Chiang Kai-shek', which conform to neither Wade-Giles nor Pinyin.[1]

Japanese terms are romanized using the Hepburn system. The tendency of Japanese to build words into longer units by compounding and the addition of prefixes and suffixes sometimes makes it difficult to do the dividing without separating elements that really go together logically. Here, longer Japanese sense units have been divided into smaller units by spacing, except when it was felt that doing so might obscure the overall meaning. Macrons are used to indicate long vowels, except that macrons have been omitted for some commonly accepted spellings, like 'Tokyo' (Tokyô), or *'yobiko'* (*yobikô*). The same principle is applied to Chinese romanization. To follow the custom, the spelling of *'keju'*, for example, is used instead of *kejü*.

To avoid confusion, I generally follow the name sequence of the English language, whereby given names precede surnames for Chinese, Japanese, and Korean.

All dates, except in a few particular circumstances, are expressed in the Gregorian calendar.

All translations from Japanese and Chinese texts are my own except where indicated.

---

[1] The conversion between Pinyin and Wade-Giles is given by *People's Republic of China: Administrative Atlas* (Washington, DC: Central Intelligence Agency, 1975), 46–7.

List of tables

List of figures

CHAPTER 1

Introduction

The unexamined life is not worth living.
– *Socrates*

Everything possible to be believed is an image of truth.
– *William Blake,* The Marriage of Heaven and Hell, *1790*

The metamorphosis from a humble carp fish to a sacred dragon is conjured up by the Chinese legend of the 'Dragon Gate', a cultural image which refers to the imperial examinations. The Dragon Gate is a geographical reference to a steep gorge of the Yellow River, located at Hejing, Shanxi Province. Carp, a fish well known for swimming against powerful currents, regularly gather there. The place owes its name to the belief that the carp which can surmount waterfalls will go on to soar into the sky, thus transforming itself into a dragon, a divine creature of imperial majesty or greatness.[1] '*Liyü tiao longmen*', or 'Carp jumping over the Dragon Gate', is commonly used as an allusion to a candidate who succeeds due to enormous effort.

In imperial China, the 'Dragon Gate' also was the actual name of the front doorway of the civil service exam hall (*Shichang zhengmen*). As was true of so many other images in ancient China, this imagery found its way to Korea and Japan, where the Dragon Gate is known as *Deung-yongmun* and *Tô-ryûmon* respectively, a literal translation from the Chinese word *Deng-longmen*, meaning 'ascending the Dragon Gate'. This image is now

---

[1] Contrary to the symbolism in the West, *long* (dragon) in the Sinic culture does not have any negative association with the satanic monster to be overcome by Saint George. However, the exact meaning of *long* depends on the connotation. In general, it refers to the emperor or things that are regal. In the Chinese phrase '*Wangzi chenglong*', or 'expecting a child to become a dragon', *long* stands for a person who earns his success through education.

thoroughly embedded in the concept of meritocracy in both national cultures.[2]

The first Dragon-Gate tale I read when I was in elementary school was different. It was a burlesque of that legend. The plot was witty but bitterly sardonic. I recollect it was contained in a slim book printed in the 1930s, a time when China was experiencing a kind of renaissance of Western influence. In the story, the Gate appeared insurmountable. But some carp candidates decided to pass it anyway, by whatever means necessary. After some long and hard thinking, they hit on a brilliant idea. Each fixed a coil-spring on his tail as a special propulsion mechanism. At the time of the 'exams', the powerful springs propelled them like pogo-sticks, sending them over the Gate in a marvellous but improper way.

Before long, the story continued, these successful candidates became high officials, thus 'dragons' in Chinese symbology. There was only one tiny problem: they could not remove those springs. This did not bother them much, as their long official gowns concealed them well. One day, however, they went to a wine party at the imperial court and all got drunk. Intoxicated, they exposed their 'gadgets' one after another. At that moment, they all changed back to carp again. The burlesque of this story thus confirmed the stereotype of the examinations as profoundly difficult, as tied to the dignity of high status, and as serious business indeed.

Of course, this story also serves as an example of the Chinese intellectual tradition, one inclined to critique, caricature and denounce exams as a system.[3] However, the tale, for all its wisdom, cannot compare to the original image of the Gate, etched deeply in the collective memory. It catches on a set of meanings and related behavioural patterns that were at the core of Chinese culture for several thousand years.

The classic image of the Gate is used in my introduction to symbolize the modern 'Gates' – the systems of higher education entrance exams in East Asia.[4] Today, in Japan, the national entrance examination system is the centrepiece of the educational system. It shapes the overall structure of schooling. It also shapes the intellectual profile of the future élite as well as the overall Japanese population. Finally, it governs access to the bureaucratic and corporate worlds (Rohlen, 1983; Amano, 1983; Spaulding, 1967).

---

[2] In his study of Imperial Japan's higher civil service exams, for instance, Robert Spaulding (1967) cites the Dragon Gate as the main metaphor commonly shared by Japan and China.

[3] The exemplary mockery of the imperial exams is found in a satirical novel, *Rulin Waishi* (The scholars) by Wu Jingzi (1701–54). Its modern versions abound, represented by such noted writers as Lu Xün in his stories *Kong Yiji* (Confucius Himself) or *Baiguang* (The white light). See, among others, Miyazaki (1976) in English, or Guo (1994) in Chinese, for a more detailed discussion.

[4] The designation employed and the presentation of material in this book do not imply the expression of any opinion whatsoever concerning the legal status of the areas or their authorities.

These features match the traditional Chinese Dragon Gate. Thomas Rohlen (1983) states:

> Exams have been a major aspect of the Japanese popular imagination since Meiji, nearly synonymous with social success. They epitomize the excesses of the world's most advanced meritocracy. (82)

In this regard, there is also substantial resemblance to the central role of entrance exams in Taiwan and Korea, where the merit-based, highly competitive systems provide access to the pathways to success in many fields (Thomas and Postlethwaite, 1983; Jayasuriya, 1983; TMOE, 1992; KMOE, 1992).[5]

From the outset, this study of the three examination systems is largely motivated by a worldwide assessment of student academic performance across various curriculum subject areas. The level of educational achievement in Japan has long been known, and well discussed (Rohlen, 1983; Lynn, 1988; Stevenson and Stigler, 1992; Medrich and Griffith, 1992). On international tests in both science and maths, for instance, Japanese mean scores are higher than those of any other country. The degree of variation in ability among Japanese students is also shown to be very low, meaning that equality of achievement is notable (Rohlen, 1983: 3).

The achievements of Taiwanese and Korean children, however, are much less known, and less researched. For that reason, I reproduce some relevant statistics in Figure 1.1. The data here are based on the 1991 International Assessment of Educational Progress (IAEP) Tests, in which fifteen countries, mostly Western, participated. Among 13-year-olds, Koreans and Taiwanese tied for first place in maths. In science, Koreans were placed first, followed by Taiwanese. Among 9-year-olds, South Koreans were placed first in maths, with Taiwanese in third place. In science, South Koreans were again placed first, followed by Taiwanese.[6]

From the series of assessments sponsored by various sources, a common factor in Japan, Korea and Taiwan appears to be the great similarity in their world rankings. It indicates that the salient achievement is not limited to Japan alone: it is an 'East Asian phenomenon'. Japan, Korea and Taiwan are noted for their common cultural heritage, geographical proximity, and many parallels in cultural and educational values, concepts and practices.

---

[5] In this book, 'JMOE' stands for Japanese Ministry of Education, 'TMOE' for Taiwanese Ministry of Education and 'KMOE' for Korean Ministry of Education.

[6] For the relevant data and interpretation of the international comparisons of educational achievements, see US Department of Education (1992) and (1993). There has been an expanding literature on the validity or reliability of these comparative studies. For a confirmative discussion of these assessments, see, for instance, Bracey (1996). For a sceptical and challenging study, see Rotberg (1992). A meta-theoretical critique of the methodology of comparison is given by Theisen, Achola and Boakari: 'The underachievement of cross-national studies of achievement', in Altbach and Kelly (1986).

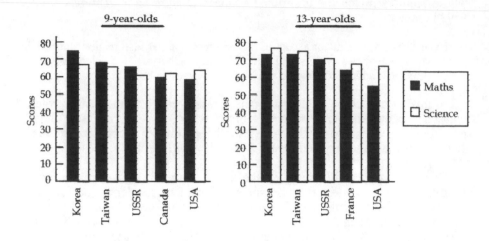

Figure 1.1 Maths and science test scores of 9- and 13-year-olds for selected countries in the International Assessment of Educational Progress, 1991. *Source*: US Department of Education, National Center for Education Statistics, International Assessment of Educational Progress, *Digest of Education Statistics* (Washington, DC: US Department of Education, 1993), 412–14.

In this larger context, their close rankings strongly suggest that, while the causes of their good performance may have some local characteristics, a set of commonly shared explanatory factors are at work, underlying their comparable configurations.

One important implication here is that we may 'test' the existing hypotheses – especially those concerning Japan – by moving them into a Japan–Korea–Taiwan comparative frame and examining their applicability, replicability and explanatory power.

In this comparison, the great resemblances between the exam systems of Japan, Korea and Taiwan warrant our particular attention. As previously cited, these exam systems have become deeply rooted, because they are seen as raising levels of knowledge and because of their impartiality in allocating scarce places in higher education (Young, 1958; Eckstein and Noah, 1993). As a consequence, on the one hand, the European model for modern education in the world cultural frame is a dominating and indispensable feature of local educational systems (Ramirez and Boli, 1987; DiMaggio and Powell, 1983). On the other hand, however, a comparative study of the pattern of parallels, non-parallels, and convergence of the examination systems in the three East Asian countries points to the effects of an array of factors that are embedded in their common cultural root and historical legacy.

THE MAIN QUESTIONS

The essential questions this study attempts to answer are four:

1. To what degree do Japan, Korea and Taiwan share the same history in the formation and development of their entrance exam systems?
2. Have they or do they use the same rationale?
3. Did the three systems originate in the common experience of Japanese administration of education before WWII?
4. The exam systems have given rise to the academically oriented cram industries as a subculture: *juku* in Japan, *hakwon* in Korea, and *buxiban* in Taiwan. Are they so isomorphic, and what role does this subculture play in the larger society? [7]

The archetypal image of the Dragon Gate reflects a coherent set of mental and behaviour patterns. This classical image refers to a general cultural context and history, a context shared by all three countries and thus the context in which this research will be pursued. It does not apply to all people, nor is it determinative in time. In fact, there has been, as noted, a history of intellectual scepticism and castigation of the exams in China dating back to when the imperial system was founded. Today, the system of exams, while highly developed, faces its strongest criticisms from the intelligentsia and the media. The burlesque image mentioned above is a useful reminder of this criticism and dissatisfaction with a system that allocates status and power and pits aspiring youth in a competition that is demanding and limiting. It is a reminder for all of the scepticism, censure and reforming efforts that have run throughout the history of exam systems in East Asia.

Ancient, but still very much alive, the Dragon Gate is perhaps the most central image defining the cultural continuity of East Asian education. This cannot, however, be something simply taken for granted. In their study of the importance of the role of the French examination system, for instance, Bourdieu and Passeron claim that one must not 'impute the most salient features of the system to the unexplained legacy of a national tradition' (1994: 141). While their argument might be proper for France, it is not necessarily applicable universally. The history of exams in the early Meiji Era, as will be discussed in Chapters 2 and 3, provides abundant evidence that the system was a cultural and historical outcome.

AN AUTOBIOGRAPHICAL NOTE

For me, a Chinese student, the entrance exams have been both a literary theme from which I read in the classics and also a personal experience. From 1949 until 1977, when the fury of the Cultural Revolution faded away, birth, not exams, determined one's educational opportunities and social status. Birth into the wrong class meant a child whose parents were classified into one of the 'Black Nine Categories' (*Heijiulei*): former landlords, former rich peasants, reactionaries, 'bad elements', rightists, 'Capitalist Roaders' (a special term referring to the Communists generally in high positions who

---

[7] The use of terms in this book, such as 'country', 'government', etc., to refer to economies makes no judgement or implication about the legal or other status of a territory.

were criticized as following capitalist policies) ... and intellectuals.[8] The despicable label for intellectuals was, incidentally, the 'Stinky Old Ninth Category'. Not included in this blacklist, but often treated in an even worse manner, were former capitalists and former entrepreneurs. Then there were a host of categories less disgraceful but earnestly untrusted, children whose parents were middle-level peasants, administrative staff and generic clerks. A doggerel, very popular in Communist China, put it well:

> Dragons produce dragons,
> And phoenixes bear phoenixes,
> As for the despicable rats, what can
>   they produce but baby hole-diggers? [9]

Implied here is predestination by birth, ironic perhaps in a Communist system, yet very real. The weight of the 'privileged' new class élites crushed the 'pariah' classes. Children were locked into the stratification, and there was no way out. But this stifling societal structure was ultimately shaken loose by the anarchy of the Cultural Revolution (1966–76).

The milestone that marked the gradual alleviation of a class birth determinism policy and the spell of status reproduction in China was the new system of university entrance exams started in 1977. It was the very first of a series of daring reforms in the post-Mao era. Equal chances for all children became true for the first time since the Communist takeover. While the system is now in some ways corroded, at the outset it was a meritocratic one, pure and simple. It cut through the Communist caste system, giving millions of people a fair chance of university; I was one of them. This was a dream I had never dared to dream: a son of an accountant, a *petite bourgeoisie*, was not supposed to get an advanced education. In retrospect, I see there was no other channel of social mobility for a person of my non-privileged birth.

Thus, the research topic I chose explores a system that I keenly experienced. The difference that experience might make is germane not only to the formation of one's viewpoint, but also in shaping one's method of approach:

> If the purpose of a piece of qualitative work is *emic*, that is, if the intent is to give an account of how the participants in a situation see it, then checking the account with the participant is a vital step. On the other hand, if the intent is *etic*, that is, if the purpose is not to describe a situation from a participant's viewpoint but from, say, an Eisnerian connoisseur's outside perspective, then getting the imprimatur of the participants is beside the point – their judgments about 'credibility' are irrelevant. (Phillips, 1987: 20)

---

[8] The word 'former' means the status prior to 1949 when the Communist Party took power.

[9] The original Chinese is: '*Long sheng long / Feng sheng feng / Laoshu shenger da didong.*'

For me, the '*emic*' and '*etic*' are intermingled. My prior experience was a starting point, one consciously and I suppose subconsciously reinvoked. Meanwhile, my own training and fieldwork cast new light on my experience. While this might be helpful in a way, the reader should also take heed of my strong feeling about the subject, which sometimes creates a tension between a descriptive reconstruction of history and a prescriptive tendency and value judgement.

This unrepentant memory of mine followed me, and accounted for my confusion when I stumbled into the American academic field, taking the East Asian exam system as my focus. It may be true, as Allan Hanson (1993: 1) claims, 'America is awash in tests.' It is equally true that America is also especially critical of tests and exam systems (Eckstein and Noah, 1992). In that country the 'balance sheet' of pluses and minuses seen in exams and tests, as given in Table 1.1, is heavily tilted to the negative side. The points listed only serve to give a general idea of the very complex and active conflict of opinion that tests and exam systems raise in America.

Nor is the United States alone. There is no question that the same general perspectives can be found throughout the Western world, within the liberal orthodoxy, and certainly in most of the dominant thinking in education circles, especially schools of education. We are thus faced with a major difference in world views – globally dominant Western liberalism and entrenched ancient East Asian meritocracy of little universal recognition.

Table 1.1 A balance sheet of pluses and minuses of exams. *Source*: Max A. Eckstein and Harold J. Noah, *Examinations: Comparative and International Studies* (Oxford: Pergamon Press, 1992), 149.

Pluses	*Minuses*
They [examinations] have earned praise because, it is claimed, they provide objective, fair, public criteria for selection; they supply valuable educational data; and they establish and maintain a *de facto* canon of knowledge to be learned and norms of achievement, stimulating student learning and teacher effort. Furthermore, 'where educational deficiencies are identified, it is asserted that examinations can be used to assist in the remedy. In this way, examinations are seen as potentially useful levers of changes.'	'... Examinations have been roundly accused of being inherently, if not deliberately, biased. They are charged with overloading students with work, raising anxieties in students and their families, depersonalizing schooling, discouraging creativity, and supporting credentialism and "the diploma disease". The examinations are said to hinder school- and teacher-initiated innovations, restrict teachers' professional autonomy, and act as barriers to correction of all these alleged defects. In fact, some consider examinations to be inherently hostile to educational reform and therefore to be necessary instruments of the status quo.'

EAST ASIA AND THE EXAMINATION SYSTEMS

A historical overview

The idea that the king should be served by a group of advisers known for their moral integrity and wisdom has deep roots in Chinese history. It comes from Confucius' insistence on rule by moral men of talents, and it was transmitted in history through the writings of the Confucian school. The genesis of the exam system, or *keju*, in imperial China can be traced to the Han dynasty (201 BC–8 AD), when an attempt was made by the imperial house to regain control of society. The emperor asked the feudal princes to send men of quality to the court to be appointed as civil servants. These men, in the latter part of the Han, would compete with each other through tests of various sorts, for the better positions in government. Later on, exams were used to supplement recommendations as a measure of talent (Smith, 1991; Menzel, 1963).

After several centuries, the Sui (581–618 AD) and Tang (618–906 AD) dynasties saw in the training and recruitment of a centralized civil service the best means of overcoming the powers of regionalism and hereditary aristocracy. To train such an élite, the Tang organized a regular system of exams and began to recruit a substantial number of its officials from those who passed. The following dynasties, the Song (960–1279), Ming (1368–1644) and Qing (1644–1912), relied heavily on a series of public, competitive exams to recruit state officials. By Ming times, exams at three levels – prefectural, provincial and metropolitan – led to three successive degrees which have often been identified with the Western sequence of Bachelor, Master and Doctor degrees. For the most part, only a degree qualified a man for service in officialdom (Menzel, 1963).

The civil service examination of ancient China, *keju*, has been generally recognized as the original source of the examination system, which was not found in the civilizations of Europe, Egypt, Babylonia-Assyria and Persia. It has also been shown to have had a direct influence on the adoption of the examination system in England, France, the US and Japan (Williams, 1848; Monroe, 1931; Têng, 1968; Miyazaki, 1976; Huang, 1992; Eckstein and Noah, 1993). Japanese scholars acknowledge that the examination system Japan adopted from Europe in the nineteenth century was originally based on the imperial *keju* from China. Miyazaki (1976) systematically studies the lineage of the so-called 'Examination Hell' (*shiken jigoku*) in Japan and China.

In Korea, during the Koryô (919–1392), the Chinese civil service exams were adopted in 958 and a hierarchical bureaucracy of civil and military officials, known as the *yangban*, was instituted. During the Mongol domination of Koryô, the Yüan (1206–1368) dynasty resumed the civil service exams in 1314; the Koryô exams came to serve as the provincial exams for the Mongolians. Unlike in China, the exams in Korea never came to function as a means through which power was widely dispersed. Yet, the meritocratic ideal intrinsic in the exams left some room for newcomers. An analysis of 14,600 people who passed the exams during the Chosôn (1392–1910) dynasty reveals that 750 lineages were represented among those who passed, but that 21 lineages produced 40 per cent of the degree holders, while 560 lineages produced 10 per cent. This shows that, while power was concentrated and perpetuated within a small élite, minor lineages were not completely excluded (Haboush, in Rozman, 1991).

In the early eighth century, Japan tried an exam system, *kôkyo*, modelled after the Chinese civil service exam system. According to the Taihô Code, which outlines the *kôkyo*, to take the examinations one was first required to study Chinese classics at the government's college (*daigakuryô*) established in the capital, or at a local school. These colleges were founded around 670 AD, and their teachers were Confucian scholars from Korea. The *kôkyo* differed in several respects from the *keju* system. The examination's relationship to employment was perhaps the most important difference. In China, those who succeeded in the exam were almost always given a high-ranking civil service position. In Japan, the main route to the highest positions was hereditary privilege, based on the *on'i* system. In this system, the male children of aristocrats of the fifth rank or higher were automatically given an official rank at the age of 21 (Amano, 1990: 21–3).

Western observers had early identified the civil service as one of the unique marks of Chinese culture and politics. Matteo Ricci, architect and early chronicler of the Jesuit mission to China, gave a detailed and admiring description of the contents and procedure of the exam system.[10] Later on, during the seventeenth and eighteenth centuries, reports about the civil service recruited on the basis of virtue and ability drew the warm admiration of philosophers. Voltaire, Turgot and many others, through their writings, helped to fix the image of the Chinese civil service as a career open to talent, and used such information as they possessed to attack the forces of privilege and heredity in the Europe of their day.

The histories of modern education in East Asian societies have been intertwined. The apogee of this relationship was the Japanese colonial empire, where Japan forced its influence on Taiwan and Korea. Meyers and Peattie (1984) describe these colonial structures as an 'anomaly', as the cultural heritage that Japan shared with its subject peoples was unique among the imperialist powers. In Meiji Japan, the imperial exam system, emphasizes Thomas Rohlen (1983), is a grand solution to a dilemma between Eurocentric modernity and national culture. In Korea and Taiwan, the earliest systems of modern exams were the reproduction of the Japanese ones during the colonial era, a vestige indelible even today.

After World War II, the Western impact, especially through the American presence, was notable in East Asia. Due to this influence, there was a rapid expansion of enrolments, the implantation of democratization, and some decentralization of education in the three countries. This change can be described as part of a process of Eurocentric globalization, the sweeping tendency to isomorphism that has ritualized many aspects of education worldwide (Ramirez and Boli, 1987; DiMaggio and Powell, 1983). Before long, however, in East Asia, the examination systems, very much contradictory to the many features of the new direction, re-emerged, justified by a broadly felt need to regulate quality, weed out corruption and give more chance to bright, low income students (McGinn *et al.*, 1980). In a word, meritocracy was valued despite Westernizing trends and this was embodied in exam systems. This re-emergence occasioned two forces, which I define as a 'pulling force' and a 'pushing force'. By 'pulling force', I mean the

---

[10] Matteo Ricci (1552–1610), Italian missionary to China. He was a student of law, mathematics and science, and he was also knowledgeable about astronomy, cartography and practical mechanics. In China, he made few converts, but brought Christianity into good repute. Ricci sent back to Europe a comprehensive report on Chinese civilization.

expanding governmental control of the system surrounding the entrance exams *per se* since the 1950s. The institutional climax of this was marked by the nationalization of key elements of the entrance exams by the governments: 1954 in Taiwan, 1969 in Korea, and 1979 in Japan. My term 'pushing force' refers to the '*juku* phenomenon', a growing proportion of students sent by parents to cram schools in an educational 'arms race' (Rohlen, 1980). In Tokyo, 94 per cent of students attending *juku* came from public schools, demonstrating the limited capability of public schools to prepare them fully for the competition of entrance exams (Kagayama, 1990). In all of East Asia, while the exam systems are subjected to growing centralization, the sources of preparation have become more decentralized and privatized, manifested in the proliferation of *juku* in Japan, *buxiban* in Taiwan, and, to a lesser extent, *hakwons* in Korea.

A review of research on exam systems, especially in Japan

The first Western theoretical critique of competitive entrance examinations may have come from Emile Durkheim (1938). In his study of the Jesuit college, Durkheim notes the drastic changes in schooling due to competitive testing adopted by the Jesuits as a result of a report by Matteo Ricci on the Chinese exam system. The Jesuits aimed to reward achievement, to induce effort by personal honour, and to evaluate students' progress. Durkheim was stunned by the unprecedented intensity created by the development of such a system, one which he saw as making education 'a totally different system'.

Durkheim's criticism of the competitiveness exhibits marked ambivalence. On the one hand, he denounces the value of rivalry which made students become warring foes of one another. On the other, he does not regard testing as a mire into which students were sucked passively. It is, to the contrary, seen as a device that maintains self-esteem in a constant state of 'extreme excitation'. Using the German word for 'self-awakening', he describes test competitiveness as one basis for the emergence of a new modern personality after the Renaissance.

In the course of their formation, examination systems have been heavily criticized in many sources (see Coleman *et al.*, 1966; Jencks *et al.*, 1973; Dore, 1975; Ishida, 1993). Noteworthy here is the monumental work of Christopher Jencks *et al.*, *Inequality: A Reassessment of the Effect of Family and Schooling in America* (1972). Based on their research, Jencks *et al.* regress educational achievement statistically on genotypical, environmental, demographical, socioeconomic and occupational inequalities. The result of the study shattered unqualified optimism in the meritocratic myth. It serves as a sobering revelation that examinations may well be inherently, if not deliberately, biased, because of the many sources of inherent inequality in the educational process. When applied in the US, or in other countries, however, the theory has encountered some corroborative problems.[11]

---

[11] For example, see Sewell and Straus (1957, 1970) and Sewell and Hauser (1980) for the Afro-American community; E. Elliott (1993) for Asian-American students; Hansen *et al.* (1989) for Indonesia. For a more general discussion of the inconsistent findings in the application of SES model in the international context, see Theisen *et al.* in Altbach and Kelly (1986: 27–49).

The exam systems in Taiwan, Korea and Japan can all be traced to a common Sinocentric world a millennium ago, and the hypothesis on meritocracy is most researched and tested in the context of the ancient Chinese civil service examinations. In 1938, based on his preliminary research on the imperial dynasties, K. Wittfogel concluded that the ruling officialdom largely reproduced itself through the civil examination system. Along this line of enquiry, P. T. Ho (1964) collected statistical data on the educational and economic backgrounds of the 40,000 Ming–Qing examination graduates. The findings of his research, however, argued for the civil exams as a channel of mobility and as a politically and socially stabilizing factor. This line of study was further pursued by E. Kracke Jr (1968), I. Y. Chen (1972), K. T. Sun (1980) and T. Lee (1985). What can be generalized from this exhaustive inquiry is that a number of people from non-official and poor commoners' family backgrounds were capable of moving up through the civil exam channel. Researchers also found a downward mobility pattern to accompany this phenomenon. Although many families of wealth and power still managed to maintain their loci in the social hierarchy through generations, the exams did not guarantee their status in terms of official position by any means.

The modern entrance examination systems in Japan, Taiwan and Korea have become the focus of much interest, largely on the part of policy-makers and social leaders due to the success of East Asian economies. This preoccupation has not been accompanied by substantive research on either the exams themselves, the system or its administrative process. Nor has the multitude of exam-takers been studied carefully. Whenever there is literature, it is often considerably outdated. A classic treatment of the issue is given by Ronald Dore in his study of credentialism (1975). Dore's comparative study, especially his postulation of the Late Development Effect, notes that the global trend towards credentialism may help late developer nations absorb foreign knowledge. In the developing nations, because modern technology and knowledge are imported, people learn them via an education process that diffuses foreign knowledge to the entire population. Dore theorizes that the later the national development starts, the more intense effort must be, and this means greater control over the formal exam qualification system. He does not favour such a system, because it cannot supply a genuine education beneficial to the national growth. For Dore, test culture is a malady.

In comparison, Thomas Rohlen (1983) provides us with a more rounded portrait of the Japanese national obsession with entrance examinations. While mindful of the infirmities of the system, Rohlen, unlike Dore, likens entrance examinations to a 'cryptographic code' by which social structure and personal ambition are translated into the imperatives of educational preparation. Equally significant is the popular dream of almost all parents for their children to attend university. Based on his anthropological scrutiny, Rohlen implies that the achievements of Japanese education rest on the central function of the entrance exam system, as it shapes a national consciousness, motivates enormous effort and maintains high standards. While exams push the future élite to work harder, they also keep most other students on their toes. Rohlen and others also contextualize Japanese education in social and educational structures: a merit-based class consciousness; a solid base of relatively equal opportunity in public primary and middle

schools (also see Cummings, 1980); the high standards set by the centralized educational system; and finally, a long and intense school calendar.
Many writers also relate Japanese schooling to family and policy support for
educational achievement (White, 1987; Rohlen, 1983), to unique child-
rearing and pre-school socialization (White, 1987; Peak, 1988), and to
efficient classroom instruction and time spent on work (Stevenson and
Stigler, 1992; Lynn, 1988).

THE ANALYTICAL FRAMEWORK

This book attempts to reconstruct the evolving formation and changes in the
university entrance exam systems in Japan, Korea and Taiwan. In my study,
these systems are treated as a sequence of historical outcomes in their
cultural context. Meanwhile, it is vitally important for me to portray the
examination systems as they are now, since much of what I am going to
write about has not been much documented. Therefore, the essential
methods of approach that I employ are both historical and descriptive. Here,
what I need to reiterate is that my study is not designed to search for an
answer in the framework of causality.

The central role of exams in a larger number of institutions, stated
previously, needs now to be substantiated. What is implied is the
relationship between the system of exams at the centre, and its ancillary
exam cultures. The exam system becomes an occasion for many social and
institutional factors, such as the emergence of a vast number of cram
schools; the emergence of meritocratic churches and religious services, such
as Shinto Temmangu shrines in Japan and Taiwanese Wenchanggong
temples; and the social patterns of academic behaviours, including: exam-
defined school curriculum, parental support and pressure, expensive investment by families in education, students' long hours spent on study, and the
historical phenomenon of '*rônin*' in Japan (exam repeaters), which has its
counterparts of '*Jai su saeng*' in Korea, and '*Chongkao Sheng*' in Taiwan.
This core–peripheral relationship is schematized in Figure 1.2.

**First and foremost, as shown in the diagram in Figure 1.2, entrance
exams have come to be a significant part of the legitimating norm for
education and quality.** The exam system functions as a criterion of how
regular schooling should be operated, manifested in the exam-focused
pedagogy and curriculum. The dominating role of university entrance exams
reaches its pinnacle at the high school level. As Thomas Rohlen identifies:

> The popular preoccupation with entrance exams also shapes Japanese definitions
> of education. Despite the continuing public policy goals of developing
> democratic education, this intention at the high school level is largely
> overwhelmed by the more powerful pull of exam-oriented concerns. The
> criterion of efficiency in preparation, of meeting competition by gearing
> education to the examinations, reaches deep into nearly every corner of high
> school education. (1983: 108)

As a result, this normative criterion eventually asserts itself at the higher
macro-level. Exams and acceptance ratios of certain universities have long
been the arbiter of school prestige, and have ranked schools almost
everywhere in a linear hierarchical order.

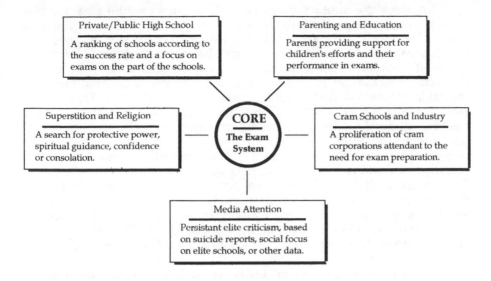

Figure 1.2 The core role of the university entrance exam system and its corollary culture, in both the behavioural and institutional dimensions.

Second, the competitive nature of exams in the three countries compels students to grind away at absorbing knowledge of possible use in passing exams. Much of this knowledge has been canonized by the nation-state as 'basic'. The goal of achieving this compulsory education extracts great sacrifice, investment and perseverance from both parents and students. Underpinning the massive study behaviour is the Confucian belief in effort as the key to scholarly virtue, which forms a folk cognitive theory in all three societies. I see this emphasis as less debilitating and less passive than an index such as IQ, which carries a lifetime stigma and seems to undermine motivation.

Third, a 'Public/Private' dialectic in education is dramatically demonstrated in East Asian cram industries. The teaching methods in these cram schools may be unappealing to Western theorists and short-term in their emphasis on teaching to the test, but they inspire and focus student energy. Cram schools are not a recent phenomenon: two of the three largest cram corporations in Japan, Sundai and Kawaijuku, for instance, date way back to 1919 and 1933 respectively. What has drawn growing public concern is their high degree of institutionalization, their expanding relevance to most families and their children, and the ever-increasing competitiveness of the exam wars, to which they contribute what amounts to advanced weaponry.

Fourth, in Japan, Taiwan and Korea, invoking scholarship deities for help in passing exams is a notable religious activity. Exams generate dreams and hopefulness as well as great anxiety, for which religion can provide solace and spiritual power. It is interesting to note that religious services and cram services converge in the exam system. If *juku* represents the extreme example of a rationalized approach, religion is its opposite and most candidates take out both kinds of insurance policies.

Fifth, since the public is so interested, the news media play a major 'muckraking' role persistently critical of the system. The exam system is not only extremely vulnerable as ideology since it creates winners and losers and dominates the lives of so many youths, but it is not supported within the circles of professional educators either. As a result, exams easily fall prey to the media which excel in manipulating and amplifying bits and pieces of critical information to feed curiosity and shock the public. The 'Examination Hell' (*shiken jigoku*) is a typical example. Issues such as student suicide, bullying, corporal punishment, lack of creativity, poor physical health, and undue stress on élitism and school ranking, etc., are all diagnosed as products of the exam system. There is, however, often a gap between the empirical evidence and the stereotyped critiques.

A better evaluation of the exam system, therefore, demands a more descriptive, more empirical, and more holistic picture than the facile generalization and abstract theorization found in the media. This is, comments Rohlen (1983), essential in understanding the dynamics of Japan, and in understanding the dynamics of Korea and Taiwan as well, I think:

> If history has provided a set of contrasting ideals and legacies, contemporary Japanese society has come to constitute an environment for education that establishes entrance examinations as the key to understanding its dynamic. (76)

The forming of this 'environment' – a culture that gives high priority to high-standard education – is the product of at least two reciprocal factors: one is the value-and-belief system, the other is the mechanics of the system. The former is largely a matter of cultural legacy, and the latter is part of modern social structure. The value system is historically relatively constant and latent, embedded in the culture's language, truisms, mythology and so forth. The actual system of exams, on the other hand, is a highly regularized set of practices, reifying and actualizing the values of meritocracy. These two factors tend to confirm and reinforce each other. For this reason, the 'exam syndrome' is often noted as self-perpetuating and intractable to reform efforts. Entrance exams play a pivotal role in the close articulation between education and the social ladder, a role that is remarkably powerful in East Asia as reflected in the fact that such an extensive syndrome has evolved around it.

METHODS OF APPROACH

The basic methods I employ are (1) comparison, (2) historical perspective, and (3) an emphasis on the transition between micro- and macro-level analyses.

Comparative framework

The essential technique for my study is comparison. All social scientific methods can be described as comparative: 'Thinking without comparison is unthinkable. And, in the absence of comparison so is all scientific thought and scientific research' (Swanson, 1971: 145). Our Japan–Korea–Taiwan comparative study is a specific kind, concerning similarities and differences between 'macrosocial units' (Easthope, 1974). In emphasizing the multiple-country case study, Emile Durkheim (1958) states:

Only comparison affords explanation. A scientific investigation can thus be achieved only if it deals with comparable facts, and it is the more likely to succeed the more certainly it has combined all those that can be usefully compared. (41)

Comparison provides a basis for making statements about empirical regularities and for evaluating and interpreting cases relative to substantive and theoretical criteria (Ragin, 1987: 1). The comparative method attends to configurations of conditions. It is used to determine the different combinations of conditions associated with specific outcomes or processes. It uses relevant data to find the preconditions of a specific outcome and, by examining the correspondences and differences between relevant instances, 'elucidate its causes' (Ragin, 1987: 15). The cross-societal comparative work, as an inductive inquiry, is more powerful than argument based on the one-country case study. With qualitative approaches, especially when causation is explored, the absence or presence of a potential contributing factor in two or more cases (societies) is important evidence for an explanatory theory.

Nevertheless, comparison still has its limits. Educational phenomena are inordinately complicated, especially when causal effects are under scrutiny. Causation is complex because many variables are involved. As Lévi-Strauss argues, scientific explanation does not consist in the reduction of the complex to the simple. Rather, it consists in a substitution of a more intelligible complexity for one which is less (Geertz, 1973). In this regard, the achievement issue is a typical and relevant case in point. Study shows that the application of such established models as social economic status (SES) or Educational Production Function (EPF) generated serious inconsistency in some findings (Theisen et al., 1986). As Theisen et al. deplore: 'In short, not only do the measured causal determinants of achievement vary by level of education and subject matter; the impact of the same variables appears to be positive in some countries and negative in others!' (in Altbach and Kelly, 1986: 27–49). This may result from the failure to include differences in sociocultural context or other factors like educational policies (ibid.: 33). The fact of the matter is, simplifying our assumptions cannot do justice to the causal complexity. By the same token, this study will not and cannot 'prove' that the exam system functions as a key determinant of educational achievement in East Asia. To reach such a conclusion, we have to study with statistical or qualitative sophistication each variable of the complex, combinatorial explanations. That goes far beyond the scope here.

The historical perspective

In my study, the exam systems are treated as a sequence of historical outcomes in cultural context. I compare the three countries not only in general terms, but for the different periods in search of their possible divergence or convergence. For the present, it is vitally important for me to portray the core systems of examinations and their peripheral culture as they are now, since much of what I am going to write about has not been documented before. To that end, I consider a micro-level descriptive approach is indispensable.

To write history is not just an impulse to produce a chronological table. History, I hope, may tell us something about today and tomorrow. In linking history to the present, Ernst Breisach (1983) writes:

They [psychologists] have found that the span of time which we actually experience as 'now,' the 'mental' present, is only about one-fiftieth of a second long. ... Every important new discovery about the past changes how we think about the present and what we expect of the future; on the other hand, every change in the conditions of the present and in the expectations for the future revises our perception of the past. (2)

In that sense, the importance of the contemporary historian's approach lies in the reality that life 'flows' through time. Although 'past', 'now' and 'future' are separate concepts, we experience them as inextricably linked. I do not think we can understand such things as tradition and modernity, constants and variables, reforms and inertia, without a knowledge of how they affected all three exam systems in the past.

The micro-to-macro transition

Implicitly or explicitly, a comparative work proceeds at two levels simultaneously – the level of systems (or macrosocial level) and the within-system level. Any analysis that is based only on macrosocial similarities and differences is not truly comparative. The system-level variable should be used to explain variation across systems in within-system relationships (Rokkan, 1966: 19–20; Przeworski and Teune, 1970: 50–1). What often occurs, however, is the wide gap that splits the system-level hypothesization and micro-level empirical research. For that reason, the 'micro-to-macro transition' is necessary (Coleman, 1990: 6–10, 19–21). To wit, whenever possible, I approach a phenomenon related to the exam system (for instance, the cram schools) by questioning: (1) What does it look like? To answer it, I present the 'reality' through ethnographic data as *prima facie* evidence. (2) How typical is the 'reality' I presented? To answer it, I show its frequency by statistical data. (3) What is the point? To answer it, I hypothesize. This step-by-step inference is used to bridge the micro-to-macro transition.

To illustrate, let us again take the cram schools. One of my propositions, for instance, is: 'The high-stake exam system generates the continued growth of cram schools.' For an explanation of why, I go to the within-system level, especially family and individual level. Afterwards, I produce statistical information to back up what I observed at the micro-level. This micro-to-macro transition is diagrammed in Figure 1.3.

Figure 1.3 shows a two-level system of proposition. The upper horizontal arrow represents the macro-level proposition. The three connected arrows represent the three linked propositions. Starting from the left, the exam system creates the competition and test anxiety at the individual and parental level. To successfully pass the high-stake exams, students find it necessary to spend extra hours preparing for them. As statistics show, many of them have to go to cram schools as a result. Data also indicate that the *juku* attendance ratio among students is on the rise. Because of that expanding market demand, the cram schools are gradually growing.

One more point I need to make about the method is that the exam culture reaches into many aspects of social life. As a result, this study will touch on a number of areas. Interdisciplinary forays are thus almost regular, and boundary crossing is essential rather than marginal. If that causes some kind of unevenness in the writing, it is perhaps inevitable.

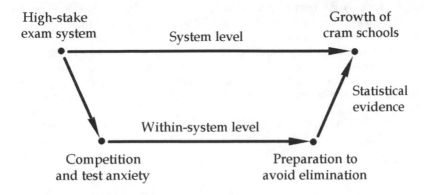

Figure 1.3 The micro-to-macro transition: the example of the relationship between the exam system and the cram industry.

ORGANIZATION OF CHAPTERS

The chapters that follow are composed of a mass of dates and events, snapshots, tables, graphics and case studies. To chart a course through them, I need to explain briefly the organization and themes of the chapters. Digressively, this study was highly inquisitive and exploratory in its proposed form. Instead of revamping it, I will just keep that *ad hoc* 'legacy' in organizing the chapters. As a result, questions are always posed first. While this introduction asks the basic questions for the entire study, each of the following chapters will start with its own questions, and the chapter will be woven around them.

In Chapter 2, the question is: how did (1) Confucianism, (2) Japanese imperialism and (3) the European models contribute to the formation of the modern exam system? In answering it, I attempt to reconstruct how the bond between merit and status was initiated constitutionally, and explain why the system has been so intractable despite various reform efforts.

Chapter 3 examines (1) the course of postwar reform in Japan, Korea and Taiwan and (2) the dissimilarities among the three systems.

Chapter 4 scrutinizes the tested knowledge. This will help us to learn what factors compose the intellectual profile of the future generation and set the criteria for educational quality. It defines what 'knowledge' is for students preparing for the exams.

Chapter 5, perhaps more exploratory than the other chapters, tries to answer such questions as: What is going on inside cram schools? How have these enterprises changed over the years? Who attends them? What effects does the cram experience exercise on children?

Chapter 6 explores the religious dimensions of examination life. For students to invoke supernatural forces in their pursuit of success is an ancient practice that has only become more popular.

Chapter 7 attempts to pursue these questions: (1) Is there more time and money invested in East Asia than in other countries? (2) Is this due to the exam system? (3) What can money buy? (4) How much money and time are 'wasted'? (5) What combination of time, money, ability and location is optimal? The overall framework used is similar to the educational production model except for the addition of the 'labour' factor that incorporates the variable of individual effort.

Chapter 8 contains two major case studies, investigating (1) the cause–effect relationship between adolescent suicide and exam pressures in East Asia, and (2) cheating practices in exams. They try to measure the gravity of the problems caused by the exam systems and their sociological meaning.

The final chapter recapitulates the major points in each chapter and summarizes the findings with reference to university entrance examinations and their subcultures in Japan, Korea and Taiwan.

CHAPTER 2

A comparative history of university entrance examinations: to the end of the Japanese Empire

Those who excel in their study should become officials.
– *Confucius:* Analects, *19:13*

Mounting atop a white horse of gilded saddle,
He was the focus of a thousand admirers.
Everyone asked: 'Whose son is he
   that became such a glorious official?'

In the morn, he was still a rustic farmer in the field;
In the eve, exams brought him to the Heaven Son's Palace.
Behold, generals and premiers have no breeds,
My little boys, you only have to work hard!

– Mingxian Ji, *a child primer in ancient China*

'The present', says Stefan Tanaka (1993) in his discussion of the Oriental world, 'was both the child of the "maternal" past and the architect of a "paternal" future.' Modern exam systems arise in history. They are formed of many influences working in time. We tend to view them as a mechanical system born *sui generis*, but we are wrong in this naive perception.

This chapter attempts to reconstruct the history of the exam systems in Japan, Korea and Taiwan, and to search for major formative influences. The three systems can be traced back to ancient China, but their modern versions came into being only around the turn of the twentieth century, rooted in the Japanese colonial empire. They are all visibly chained to modern events like the Meiji Restoration, Japanese colonialism, Westernization and postwar development. Even these key influences themselves were in fact the interactions of two dynamics: tradition and modernization.

In order to sort out the dynamics of this long tradition and complex recent history, this chapter focuses on the following questions: What was the traditional heritage? How did European models contribute to the formation of the Japanese colonial exam system? How did this system initiate the modern relationship between merit and status? What have been the commonalities and dissimilarities among the exam systems of Japan, Korea and Taiwan up to the end of World War II? Has the fact that the three systems originated in the common experience of Japanese imperial administration before WWII been of overriding significance in shaping all three? In the next chapter, we will examine the course of postwar reform in Japan, Korea and Taiwan, asking how similar the three systems have remained.

CONFUCIANIZATION AND THE CHINESE IMPERIAL MODEL

> I looked up to them [the ancient Confucian doctrines], they seemed to grow in stature; I tried to penetrate them, and they seemed to become more impenetrable; I looked at them before me, and suddenly they seemed to be behind. The Master, by orderly method, skillfully leads people on.
> – *Comment on Confucius made by Yan Yuan, cited from* Analects

Confucius was born in 551 BC and died in 479 BC, a period roughly contemporary with Gautama Siddhartha, the founder of Buddhism. Through his teaching and interpretation of the tradition, Confucius gradually made himself known as the inheritor *par excellence* of the ancient virtues. In the Han Dynasty (206 BC–25 AD), the Chinese state and the ruling class of literati developed a strong commitment to the values labelled 'Confucian'. As the state orthodoxy of that era, Confucianism had, among many, two impacts of particular relevance to our study of East Asian society. First, it helped to establish a social order based on a cosmology centring on an ethic of filiality. Filiality was essentially the state's rationale for social hierarchy and inequality. Hierarchy, properly constructed, was the key to social stability. Second, Confucianism connected moral virtue to knowledge. It then ordered a meritocratic order via rewarding scholarship (virtue and merit) with official position (prestige and power). In this way, the Han imperial house subdued the power of aristocrats and sought to rejuvenate the civil service. Its ideal became one of educational opportunity without class discrimination.[1] The pivot of this system in practice was the exam system. It related merit to power and put learning at the heart of the élite subculture. It focused ambition on the task of passing government exams.

Korea was the first 'relay station' for the east-bound transmission of Confucianism in East Asia. Confucian texts were introduced in the fourth century into Korea and in the fifth century into Japan via Korea. Because of the absence of Confucian proselytizers (unlike Buddhism), and with the exception of migrants who moved about the region, Confucianism remained largely confined to the north-east part of the Asian region (Rozman, 1991). In Korea, the influence of Confucianism changed an originally matrilineal society into a patrilinear one (Kendall, 1992; Deuchler, 1992). The historical

---

[1] The prototypical ideal of schooling without class discrimination is found in a quotation of Confucius, '*You jiao wu lei*', or 'In teaching, there should be no distinction of classes' (*Analects*: 15.39, in Legge, 1991: 214).

transformation generated in Korea by Confucianism had a paradoxical impact. On the one hand, Confucianism reframed Korean society into a more hierarchical order. On the other, it also instituted the principle of meritocratic promotion, one that helped undermine the traditional social order. In Japan, imported Confucianism did not have as far-reaching an impact. But there is no doubt about the very great influence of Confucian ideals on Japan, then only a remote tributary of the culturally dynamic Chinese empire. In both Korea and Japan, the process of social reform touched off by Confucianism initiated profound trends towards a social order built on a patrilinear structure and universal ethical laws, and a bureaucracy meritocratic in theory. Korea became far more Confucian in practice than did Japan until the seventeenth century when Japan too made its tenets the official orthodoxy.

The influence of Confucianism on education in East Asia can hardly be emphasized enough. That legacy is encapsulated in quotations of Confucius and his disciples and in many enduring phrases passing down through centuries. These can be grouped into at least three basic notions. First, Confucius believed in the importance and sincerity of study. That men are not born equal in intelligence and capacity was taken for granted by Confucius (Ho, 1964). It is equally true that he laid great stress on *xüe er zhi zhi*, or 'Knowing through learning' (*The Doctrine of the Mean*, in Legge, 1991: 42). While it is possible that one might possess transcendental knowledge, Confucius never acknowledged anyone in real life as acquiring knowledge in that way (Chen, 1957). Confucius also believed that knowledge was identical in its content regardless of the learner.[2] His earnest attitude was expressed in his unique way of defining knowledge: 'When you know a thing, hold that you know it; and when you do not know a thing, allow that you do not know it; – this is knowledge' (*Analects*, Book II, 2.17, in Legge, 1991: 75). To him, study was not only useful, but a source of endless joy: 'Is it not pleasant to learn with a constant perseverance and application?' (*Analects*, Book I, 1.1, in Legge, 1991: 64). In Confucianism, knowledge is the accumulated crystallization of exhausting effort.

Second, Confucianism rationalizes the hierarchical nature of society by selecting members of the ruling class on the basis of individual merit. Confucius regards rule by merit as the very foundation of good government (Ho, 1964). Confucianism did not demand that hereditary rulers give up their thrones, but it insisted that they should turn over the administration of their governments to men chosen from the entire population, on the basis of virtue and capacity. This is shown in an oft-quoted sentence in the classics: 'Those who excel in their study should become officials' (*Analects*, Book

---

[2] The idea that the composition of knowledge content is identical regardless of accesses to it is expressed in the following passage: 'Some are born with the knowledge of those duties; some know them by study; and some acquire the knowledge after a painful feeling of their ignorance. But the knowledge being possessed, it comes to the same thing.' See *The Doctrine of the Mean*, in Legge (1991: 42).

XIX, 19.13, in Legge, 1991).[3] This meritocratic guidance had its para-
phrases in ancient primers as well. One common example was in the popular
Mingxian Ji (The Quotations of the Fame):

> Tens of thousands walks of life would be inferior,
> When compared to book-reading.
> Look at those dignitaries in the imperial court,
> Who is not but a scholar (*dushu-ren*)?[4]

One major question arising from this system is: how to obtain for the
government the intellectually and morally superior? The Confucian ideal of
educational policy emphasized 'education for all'. The prototype of that
ideal was found in a quotation from Confucius, '*You jiao wu lei*', or 'In
teaching, there should be no distinction of classes' (*Analects*: 15.39, in
Legge, 1991: 214). This is perhaps the only sentence of the kind in Confucian classics. However, his disregard of birth and wealth in education has
been a fundamentalist ideology amazingly retained, at least in words, as the
central principle of egalitarianism.

The epistemology that stresses learning, the veneration for knowledge
and an articulation of academic achievement with social status, all form the
components of the essentials of Confucian meritocracy. It embraces and
defines a complex pattern of social, ethical and academic behaviour.

The late nineteenth century was in every way a *fin de siècle* for East Asia.
The region was shaken by external impact and internal tumult. In the midst
of foreign intrusion and surging nationalism, Confucianism was denounced
as an inferior, outmoded mindset. The 'scapegoating' of Confucianism
started with Japanese intellectual thinkers prior to the Meiji Reformation. As
Western influence began to pour into Japan from the 1860s, it looked for a
time that Confucian values would be 'swept aside as remnants of a discredited feudal past' (Collcutt, in Rozman, 1991: 146–7).

After a brief eclipse in the 1870s, Confucianism found new respectability
and a place for itself among the mix of influences shaping the development
of modern Japan. Shiratori Kurakichi, a famous historian who laid great
stress on the uniqueness of Japanese history, explains the rationality behind
the renaissance of Confucianism:

> When we research [the subject of Confucianism] coolly and calmly, contrary to
> expectations the true, priceless aspects emerge from the background and the
> value of Confucianism is demonstrated. Then for the first time the spirit of
> Confucianism comes to life. (In Tanaka, 1993: 130)

---

[3] This sentence is sometimes mistaken as the quotation of Confucius, although it
belongs to his disciple, Zixia.

[4] For more examples in ancient child readers of China signalling the importance of
learning as a social ladder, see Guo (1994).

This revival took place in the realm of Japanese education through a series of Imperial Rescripts. Within a decade of the Meiji Restoration, Confucianism was making a comeback among intellectuals and in government circles. One influential spokesman was Motoda Eifu (1818–91), lecturer to the Meiji emperor, and the drafter of the major Imperial Rescripts that emphasized Confucian values. In 1879, 'The Great Principles of Education (*Kyôgaku Taishi*)' was issued as an Imperial Rescript, which accentuated significance in Confucianism:

> For morality, the study of Confucius is the best guide. People should cultivate sincerity and moral conduct, and after that they should turn to the cultivation of the various subjects of learning in accordance with their ability. (Passin, 1965: 227)

This document led to the landmark Imperial Rescript on Education (*Kyôiku chokugo*) issued on 30 October 1890, which blended notions of the divine ancestry of the imperial line with Confucian notions of the duties of subjects. The Rescript was literally 'memorized by millions of teachers and schoolchildren and read aloud in every schoolroom'. It was a 'powerful document in shaping political, social and educational attitudes in subsequent decades' (Collcutt, in Rozman, 1991: 150). The 're-Confucianization', symbolized by the Imperial Rescripts of 1879 and 1890, had lasting impacts upon at least three aspects of society: (1) moral rectitude, (2) the principle of meritocracy, and later on, (3) the assimilationism policy in colonial Taiwan and Korea.

First of all, priority was given to 'moral training' in schools which took Confucianism as its foundation (Hall, 1973; Nakauchi *et al.*, 1986). Tanaka comments:

> The Imperial Rescript of Education of 1890, the centerpiece of the Confucian revival, highlighted the morals and ethics – not the system of thought – necessary to unify Japan. (1993: 131)

Shiratori Kurakichi, the historian mentioned earlier, predicted that the 1890 Imperial Rescript on Education was a moral canon of Confucianism that would control Japanese and their children (Tanaka, 1993: 150). While this turned into a fact in prewar Japan, there is perhaps still a grain of truth in that prediction even today.

Second, re-Confucianization consolidated the merit system that bound the link between education and the centralized system of government. The merit principle is, in Confucianism, a principle of virtues, such as a strong work ethic, a strong drive to learn, etc. The 1890 Imperial Rescript, for instance, stressed the fusion of 'intellectual faculties and perfect moral powers', and the pursuit of learning and cultivating arts (in Beauchamp and Vardaman, 1994: 37). In the Rescripts, moral and intellectual values were not the antithesis of each other, unlike the self-contradiction found in the 'Red-or-Expert' dilemma in Communist China in the 1950s and 1960s. The reason for that harmony lies in the nature of moral value in the Rescript: it was centred on filiality, a natural embodiment of humanity. The crux of it is 'modesty and moderation' rather than certain demand of extreme behaviour (ibid.). The significance of the selection system of exams in the Confucian order is stated in the following words:

> Entrance exams play a central role in the Confucian tradition. They channel career aspirations, produce a meritocratic élite that can be further shaped through the sponsorship of the existing élite, lead to the dissemination of the national culture to local élites, set the standard for discipline and motivation, and bolster an ethic of fair competition. ... Despite its own weak examination tradition, in the 1880s Japan quickly grasped the merits of rigorous entrance examinations and made this the cornerstone of its recruitment of officials and reshaping of sponsored social mobility. (Rozman, 1991: 179).

Third, the impact of 're-Confucianization' was also reflected in Japanese colonial policy, particularly 'assimilationism', a peculiarly Japanese ideology of international education. Assimilationism was the ideology that every subject was equal before the emperor.[5] According to this dictum, even in the case of Japanese colonialism, peoples should not be separated and discriminated against but united and given equal education. This ideology was adopted when Taiwan and Korea were annexed by Japan (Nakauchi *et al.*, 1986). Scholars like Martin Collcutt argue that:

> [The Japanese attempted to] use Confucianism to take some of the edge off Japanese colonial aggression. In Korea, Manchukuo and China the Japanese actively promoted Confucianism and presented themselves as the restorers of a Confucian cultural tradition. (In Rozman, 1991: 152)

In the colonies, as in Japan, the Japanese inculcated Chinese or Korean children with Confucian values through the Japanese written syllabary and pronunciation system. 'Confucian ethics were presented as Japanese ideals or universal principles shared by but not unique to the Chinese people' (Tsurumi, in Myers and Peattie, 1984: 293–8). It is ironic to note that, in history, the Japanese were the last among the three countries to learn Confucianism, and in the modern era, they were the first to strike it down; and yet, they were the first to pull it up again.

---

[5] The idea of equality among all before the supreme rule was probably first found in *Shi-jing* (Classic poems), an anthology of the earliest poems in China (circa 1100–256 BC):

> Nowhere under the heaven, is not the soil of the Kingdom;
> In this kingdom, everyone is a subject of the King.

For an analysis of the ecumenism in Confucian concepts, see, for instance, Fairbank (1968).

THE NEW EDUCATION SYSTEM IN IMPERIAL JAPAN

Ye, our subjects, be filial to your parents, affectionate to your brothers and sisters; as husbands and wives be harmonious, as friends true; bear yourselves in modesty and moderation; extend your benevolence to all; pursue learning and cultivate arts; and thereby develop intellectual faculties and perfect moral powers.
– 'Imperial Rescript on Education', 1890

In Japan, the year of 1872 was marked by an avalanche of remarkable events. The solar Gregorian calendar was adopted in place of the lunar one; Sunday became a holiday; Buddhist priests were permitted to consume meat, grow their hair, and get married; post offices were erected, which, together with newspapers, gas lamps, steam-driven ships, photography and holding a world fair were proclaimed as the 'Seven Essentials' of 'Civilization and Enlightenment (*Bunmei kaika*)' (Suzuki, 1968). Life was rushing forward with a speed and exhilaration that gave people little time to stop and think.

Amid these kaleidoscopic changes, a less flamboyant and novel event is especially noteworthy. The Fundamental Code of Education (*Gakusei*) was issued by the Ministry of Education, which itself was founded only a year before. Article 49 of the Code provided for a 'Grand Test (*Daishiken*)', a new device for gate-keeping at the transition point from elementary school to middle school and from middle school to university (Masuda *et al.*, 1961). The Code began the institutionalization of a new educational age, 'an age of freedom and competition, in other words, the age of examinations' (Amano, 1990). A Preamble which the Japanese Cabinet attached to the Code stated: 'it is only by studying hard according to the best of his ability that a person may make his way in the world. ... Learning is the key to success in life, and no one can afford to neglect it.' The very optimistic faith in education was unprecedented for the time, an attitude attributed to the first Minister of Education Oki Takato, who partook in the formulation of the 1872 Code (Kurasawa, 1973). Other than an idealist, it appears he was an exceptionally realistic and thoughtful administrator, but one committed, as were many other young leaders of the Meiji Restoration, to the principle of 'ability first' (Amano, 1990). Yet, the Code only outlined the philosophy of a merit-based system and provided guidelines for an exam system. It had yet to be coupled to power and status, to be institutionalized and made part of children's lives.

Legalization of examinations: Coupling merit with status

There had been a recent precedent of coupling power and status, the so-called 'Kanda's Chinese Plan' of 1869.[6] In 1869, the national assembly asked the government to institute annual competitive examinations for the government office on the Chinese model. The Vice Chairman of the national

---

[6] This part is based substantially on Spaulding (1967) and Amano (1990).

assembly, Kanda Takahira (1830–98), was a famous scholar of both Western 'Dutch' studies and the Chinese classics. He claimed that the Chinese civil service examinations and the Western parliaments are 'the twin glories of East and West, and Japan should adopt both'. The proposal was approved in the Japanese Parliament by a landslide: 146 of the 188 attending members approved, 9 opposed, and 33 abstained (Amano, 1990). To the majority from small domains and even the formerly great Tokugawa houses, the exam system would hopefully weaken the centralized power under the control of Satsuma and Choshu, the domains that had played the essential role in overthrowing the shogunal rule and founding the Meiji regime (Jansen and Rozman, 1986). Nevertheless, the proposal was not put into effect, because it did not have the support from these leaders of the few domains that controlled the new regime. They were prepared to admit a few men of the former lower classes (merchants, farmers and artisans) to higher education and government, but they were not ready to have 'merit' or ability measured by universalistic criteria.

The 'Chinese Plan' was put on the back burner, until, fifteen years later, the need for a meritocratic system of civil service selection again surfaced. This time the model came from Prussian Germany. The two models, Chinese and German, have a basic common denominator: both were an impersonal system based on measured achievement, and both deterred hereditary access to bureaucracy. However, at the end of the nineteenth century, the German Model was more legitimate, especially since in the nineteenth century the Chinese exam system was in the process of being discredited and destroyed in China itself. Another difference between the two was that the German system was more attuned to the priorities of the modern era.

Japan faced the need to create courts and laws that would stand on an equal footing with the Western powers, a *sine qua non* for eradicating their unequal extra-territoriality imposed on Japan by these powers (Spaulding, 1967; Amano, 1990). In order to attain full judicial sovereignty, Ito Hirobumi (1841–1909), later a Prime Minister, was asked to plan Japan's constitution. In 1882–3, Ito went to Europe in search of legal models. In the course of ten months, Ito listened to 44 lectures by German scholars, such as Albert Moss (1846–1925) and Lorenz von Stein (1815–90). Von Stein made a profound impression on Ito, and had an influential impact on the Meiji constitution. Von Stein reaffirmed that 'the men appointed [to the civil service] must by all means first have received the education necessary for their positions, and must then have passed examination'. Stein's firm emphasis on examinations preordained a comprehensive and ultimately dominant position for this sorting device in the larger sociopolitical structure of Japan. This affirmation from Europe also mollified the scepticism of the power holders. This was another step towards the coupling of education to a vast and intricate system of military and civil service. In 1884, an examination for judicial office was promulgated, which marked the first acceptance of examinations by the Meiji leaders (Spaulding, 1967).

The coupling of education to social status was realized and tightened up through a number of other similar measures. First, the 1886 Middle School Ordinance was issued, which ended the muddled passage from compulsory to 'higher' education, and established the higher school as a clearly demarcated university prep school (Roden, 1980). Soon afterwards, in 1887 a general examination ordinance was adopted and went into force which extended exams from the judiciary to all parts of the government. Japan's leaders had eventually concluded that governmental stability depended in large part on a career bureaucracy and that such a bureaucracy could not be maintained without examinations for its career fields (Spaulding, 1967).

A close examination of the 'higher' schools is in order here, since, as the structural gateway to tertiary education, admission to them was virtually a sure ticket into university. In fact, Japan's 'higher' schools were the *de facto* élite academies of the country. Their status was equivalent to universities today. And like Japan's contemporary universities they were characterized as scholastically carefree, once the harsh competition at the gateway was overcome (Roden, 1980). Competition ratios in 1936 at the élite higher schools illustrate the severity of the entrance contest (see Table 2.1).[7]

Table 2.1 Competition ratios of selected élite higher schools in Japan, 1938. *Source*: Obunsha, '1938 Senkoku Jôkyû Gakkô Kakuteki Nyûshi Kyôsôriritsu Sôran (An overview of the competition rate for the higher-level schools in Japan)', in NSMS (Tokyo: Obunsha, 1938), 1–5.

Name of school	Number of applicants	Number accepted	Competition ratio[†]
First Higher School	2573	300	8.6
Second Higher School	1644	210	6.7
Third Higher School	1658	240	5.9
Fourth Higher School	1479	210	5.9
Fifth Higher School	1588	240	5.8

Note: † Competition ratio = number of applicants ÷ number accepted.

It is argued by Ikuo Amano (1990) that the concept of competition was not socially acceptable prior to the Meiji Restoration. He goes on to discuss the distinction of '*tôsô* (fighting)' and '*kyôsô* (competition)'. If true then the establishment of universalistic rules creating such competition was a major shift for Japanese society. Competitive entrance examinations thereafter would always be the primary standard of judgement in determining who would enter the higher educational track (Roden, 1980). This is manifested in the following application information for the First Higher School:

---

[7] The 'higher schools' refer to the preparatory schools for imperial universities. They are also called 'number schools', as they were ranked with order numbers, such as the First Higher School. All the number schools were converted into universities after the Occupation, such as the First Higher School: Tokyo University; the Second: Sendai University; the Third: Kyoto University; the Fourth: Kanazawa University; and the Fifth: Kumamoto University, etc.

Information of Application to First Higher School, 1936 (excerpt)
...
Names of disciplinary areas. Human science, Types A, B and C. Natural science: Types A and B.

Entrance requirement. (1) Examinations; (2) Completion of four-year middle schooling, or graduation of the Type A vocational school, or persons who have obtained permission for higher education or prep school of the university.

Number of vacancies. Human science: Types A – 90, B – 30 and C – 30. Natural science: Types A – 90 and B – 60.

Date of application. From 16 January to 31 January.
Application requirement. Application form, two photos, and ¥5 application fee.

Subjects and Dates of Examinations.
17 March 9:00 a.m. – 11:30 a.m. Japanese and Chinese (composition), botany and biology.
18 March 9:00 a.m. – 11:30 a.m. Japanese and Chinese (Japanese paraphrasing, Chinese paraphrasing, Japanese grammar).
19 March 9:00 a.m. – 11:30 a.m. Mathematics.
20 March 9:00 a.m. – 11:30 a.m. Foreign languages (paraphrasing, English, German, French, grammar).
Interview and physical check-up will be held after all examinations are completed.

Date of notification. 5 April.

Venue of examination. First Higher School Main Campus, Komaba, Meguro-ku, Tokyo City.

Tuition and fees. Tuition: ¥240 (¥80 per year). Alumni fee: ¥41 (membership ¥5). ... Total: approx. ¥1700.

Dormitory accommodation. Three-year boarding system, all inclusive. Rent: ¥1 and ç50 per month (¥1 per month for four consecutive months, and ç80 for seven months)....

Future orientation. Tokyo university as the first priority.

Special remarks. Off-campus residency was absolutely forbidden. A candidate will be eligible regardless of [his or her] *rônin* status or age.[8] Although the lowest scores of acceptance will not be publicized, the acceptance cut-off line is

---

[8] *Rônin* is an applicant to the university who, having failed to pass the entrance exams, plans to take them again. In the course of this book, the issue of the '*rônin* phenomenon' will be examined in further detail at the relevant juncture.

70 percentage points for human science majors, and 75 percentage points for natural science majors.[9]

The openness and transparency of the system are obvious in this sample. The timeline was clear; the entrance procedures and requirements were expressly open; and the minimum scores for acceptance were categorically disclosed, although the precise score necessary was not subsequently announced. The reason for choosing the First Higher School here and subsequently is that the school was earmarked by Japan's Ministry of Education as the model institution whose policies would be emulated by the other higher schools in terms of curriculum, student regulations, etc. No other school had garnered as much respect within society (DIKG, 1939; Roden, 1980). This is evidenced in the entrance requirements and procedures of most other higher schools at the time. The student culture in the First Higher School of the late 1880s was portrayed in minute detail by Roden (1980), who claims that they were 'a group of petty-bourgeois achievers with the traditional values and ethos of the dying aristocracy'. Roden in the meantime maintains that 'achievement had in fact been a disguise for status'. The Meiji leaders crafted a school system which by the turn of the century allowed for limited social mobility while reaffirming the legitimacy of a stratified society. This argument is highly germane to our study of entrance examinations in which we find many tendencies: the seeds of a meritocratic order and a crypto-graphic code for social mobility (Rohlen, 1983); a ladder of success (Passin, 1965); and a linchpin of the entire educational system, including curriculum, textbooks, pedagogy, and the organization of classes (Brereton, 1944). The issue before us in assessing the prewar Japanese system is just how much real social mobility or opportunity was created by the new arrangement. One approach is to look at stratification trends. Table 2.2 presents what data are available. It is a register of the changing ratios of *kazoku* (nobility), *shizoku* (former samurai), and *heimin* (commoner) in the higher schools.

That studious commoners gradually rose in this academic milieu and that a degree of mobility was created is beyond question. It is helpful to note that estimates put the samurai class at roughly 5–6 per cent of the population in 1870. It is also clear that this class very actively competed to retain its hold on higher status via education (Nakauchi *et al.*, 1986). The shift towards greater commoner participation is also illustrated in data given in Table 2.3 on the social origins of students at Tokyo University.

During the period under review, the students with privileged samurai (warrior) status fell by 22.2 per cent, whereas the commoner class more than doubled in Tokyo University.[10] The mobility is also reflected in the

---

[9] Obunsha, 'Showa 11-nen Jôkyû Gakkô Seito Bôshû Yôkô' (1936 information on admission into the higher-level schools), in NSMS (Tokyo: Obunsha, 1936), Appendix, pp. 2–3.

[10] Statistics provided by Ikuo Amano (1990) about imperial universities and higher schools in general also confirmed a clear decline in the student ratio for samurai, and a rise for commoners, 1890–1900. However, for national government professional

screening effect of civil service examinations, which illustrates the eventual coupling between education and élite positions, as indicated in Table 2.4.

Table 2.2 The class background of higher school students by percentage, 1878–85, 1890–2. *Sources*: For data of 1878–85, Yoshiro Shimizu, *Shiken (Examinations)*, (Tokyo: Iwanami Shoten, 1957), 108–9; for data of 1890–2, JMOE, ed., *Monbushô Daijûhachi Nenpô* (Tokyo, 1967), quoted from Donald Roden, *Schooldays in Imperial Japan: A Study in the Culture of a Student Élite* (Berkeley: University of California Press, 1980), 68–9, note 79.

Year	Nobles	Samurai	Commoners
1878	0.48	81.82	17.70
1879	0.55	86.31	13.12
1880	1.00	77.25	20.37
1881	1.59	72.74	25.49
1882	1.15	70.05	28.34
1883	0.48	64.31	35.22
1884	0.35	59.61	40.05
1885	0.17	61.70	38.13
...			
1890	0.34	51.46	48.37
1891	0.11	51.40	48.49
1892	0.18	51.61	48.21

Table 2.3 The social status of Tokyo University students by percentage, 1878–85. *Source*: JMOE, *Japan's Growth and Education* (Tokyo: JMOE, 1963), 34.

Year	Nobles	Samurai	Commoners
1878	0.6	73.9	25.5
1879	0.5	77.7	21.8
1880	0.9	73.6	25.5
1881	0.0	51.8	48.2
1882	0.1	49.1	50.8
1883	0.1	52.9	47.0
1884	0.2	50.2	49.6
1885	0.2	51.7	48.1

Note: Figures from 1878 to 1880 refer to the students of law, science and literature. Figures from 1881 to 1885 refer to the students of law, science, medicine and literature.

schools, such as medicine and agriculture, the samurai class increased their representation (191–95). This more complex picture is perhaps a manifestation of the shift during a historical period of the samurai class from their domination in the core class to certain specialized professions.

Table 2.4 The social class of men passing administrative examinations. *Source*: Robert Spaulding, Jr, *Imperial Japan's Higher Civil Service Examinations* (Princeton, NJ: Princeton University Press, 1967), 301.

Period	Number passing	Percentage of all passing candidates		Percentage of top ten candidates each year	
		Samurai	Commoner	Samurai	Commoner
1894–1901	319	45	55	46	54
1902–1909	588	37	63	36	64
1910–1917	1145	31	69	18	82

The foregoing statistics all point to the effects of education as an agent of mobility in the early Meiji. Yet, this is not to suggest an even and equal access to schooling, power and status. Keeping in mind that the samurai only accounted for 5.6 per cent of the total population (JMOE, 1963), we realize with sobriety that the former warrior class still was over-represented in the élite in the prewar period. While the system of entrance exams did serve as an agent of mobility, its role was conditioned by the larger social context.

TAIWAN AND KOREA IN JAPANESE COLONIAL EDUCATION

Toward the end of the nineteenth century, forces of nationalism, evangelism and capitalism started the age of intensified expansion. Much of this took place in Africa, but new colonies were formed also in Southeast Asia. Northeast Asia also came under imperialist pressure.

In Japan, education had been immediately perceived as one key to modern nationhood; it took the Meiji leaders only slightly longer to develop an appetite for colonial power. By the 1880s, some of Japan's new leaders were beginning to wonder if colonial conquest was not an essential part of achieving parity with those Western nations that were dividing up China's commercial cities. Would having a capacity for colonial expansion not exempt Japan from the humiliations of unequal treaties, extra-territoriality and being lectured to by the Western powers? Foreign Minister Inoue Kaoru expressed this increasingly popular line of thought in 1887: 'We have to establish a new, European-style empire on the edge of Asia.' Thus, Japan's phenomenally rapid modernization had another face: it turned barbaric, at the time it was seeking what it labelled modern, enlightened ways (Wray and Conroy, 1983). Imperialism in Japan assumed the subterfuge of Pan-Asianism. By the Treaty of Shimonoseki of 1895, China relinquished all its claims to a special role in Korea and ceded Taiwan and Pescadores to Japan. As the first colony acquired, Taiwan brought Japan into the coveted position of the only non-Western colonial power.

Then, the conflicting imperialist ambitions of Russia and Japan led to the Russo-Japanese War of 1904–5. For both sides the cost was heavy, but the victories went to Japan. With US mediation, the two sides reached the 1905 Treaty of Portsmouth, whereby Japan gained recognition of its supremacy in Korea (Eckert *et al.*, 1990; Myers and Peattie, 1984). Meiji Japan's victory demonstrated that Japan had by that time turned from a victim into a peer in the new imperialism (Schirokauer, 1989; Duus, in Wray and Conroy, 1983). Taiwan and Korea thus became the formal colonies of Japan until the end of World War II. Japan created public schools as one pillar of control and development in both colonies. The other key pillar was a strong police force.

Japanese colonial education: Historical context and contrast

Two years after the Japanese took over Taiwan in 1895, while Japanese troops still battled Taiwanese resistance, Japan opened tuition-free Japanese language schools to which they invited islanders of all classes, ages and both sexes. Izawa Shuji, an educator who believed all education should be financed by the state, was responsible for the start of public education. He hoped to duplicate in Taiwan all the functions of education with which the home islands were then familiar (Tsurumi, 1977, 1984).

Japanese education in Taiwan was basically intended as an instrument of colonial development and was initially developed at the level of basic compulsory schooling. It was designed to educate the masses in literacy, economic usefulness and political obedience, and the first Japanese public elementary or common schools consequently focused on the Japanese language and arithmetic. In addition, one of the major tactics was to lift Confucian morality from its historical context and to apply it selectively to the Japanese-oriented system, namely by stressing those elements of the classical tradition which urged loyalty and obedience to one's superiors, and ignoring those which encouraged identification with China (Tsurumi, 1984).

In 1898, 76 common schools were established. Eight years later 180 government elementary schools catered to approximately 32,000 pupils. Only about 5 per cent of Taiwanese children were enrolled in the elementary schools and the average daily attendance rate amounted to less than 66 per cent of those enrolled. In the period 1906–18, the common school system was expanded and upgraded. Even as late as 1937, when the policy of assimilation designed to bring the civil rights of the Taiwanese into line with those of the Japanese was first introduced, educational inequality and school segregation between the ruling Japanese and the ruled Taiwanese still remained. To what extent the assimilation programme advocated by the Japanese government in Taiwan was successful is still a controversial issue, which will be discussed later in this chapter. There is no doubt, however, that linguistic assimilation was an important indicator of the impact of Japanese education (Tsurumi, 1984). According to data based on the five censuses carried out by the Japanese government in Taiwan, 27 per cent of the Taiwanese could either read, write or speak Japanese by the end of Japanese rule (Tsai and Chiu, in Shavit and Blossfeld, 1993). Given the role played by education in the colony and its traditional function throughout much of China's history, it is not surprising that the Taiwanese perceived Japanese higher education as a means of improving their position in life (Tsurumi, 1977). Japanese education in Taiwan was essentially a colonial education which was used as a means of assimilating and transforming a segment of traditional China into a part of the Japanese empire.

Korea was not occupied until 1910, but Japanese educational policies began to be enforced in the country at least from the start of the protectorate.

In Korea, Japanese educational objectives, approaches and structures were similar to those in Taiwan. Koreans were to be changed into loyal Japanese subjects capable of modern life and work. In Korea too, the Japanese were interested in slow but steady expansion of basic elementary education. They discouraged demands for 'unnecessary' higher education. But as in Taiwan, they ended up becoming reluctant architects of a policy that reproduced the full Japanese educational system in Korea. In Korea, as in Taiwan, the education system was revamped in 1922 by a Rescript proclaiming integration and assimilation. In fact, from pre-protectorate days, the Japanese in Korea looked to Taiwan for educational models for Korea. Nevertheless, it became rapidly apparent that education in Korea was not going to be quite like education in Taiwan in several ways.

To start with, Japanese rule over Taiwan, while vigorous and firm, was not as harsh as that over Korea. The major reason for this difference was the difference in historical background. When Japan assumed control over Taiwan, it encountered only sporadic resistance. Taiwan had no tradition of local cultural and political independence. Korea, by contrast, boasted a culture older than that of Japan and a tradition of truculent independence.

The situation that existed in Korea before the protectorate was also far more complex in Korea than in Taiwan. The Japanese colonial education system in Taiwan was carefully planned and controlled from the beginning. Great pains were taken to train local teachers. Teaching was a very honourable calling which the Japanese treated with great respect. In contrast, Japan was not as free to plan in Korea. What they considered to be 'the wrong sort of teacher' colonial officials treated very badly. Material conditions were worse for Koreans under Japanese rule than for Taiwanese. In Taiwan, land policies and agricultural technology brought a good deal of prosperity to the rural élite and some segments of the agrarian population. In Korea, farmers suffered from the land registration policies. Agricultural and industrial policies brought more hardships to Koreans than to Taiwanese. Historically, the gentry of Taiwan thought rule by a foreign invader was nothing new or particularly shameful. Korea, on the other hand, had its own proud traditions and ancient civilization. Japan annexed Korea just after the seeds of a modern nationalist movement had begun to sprout (Tsurumi, 1984).

These dissimilarities notwithstanding, Japan governed all its colonies for the benefit of the homeland. Thus, in both Taiwan and Korea, Japan's policies were designed to control the local population and to exploit local resources through selective modernization. Japanese rule over Taiwan and Korea, accordingly, shared certain characteristics: in both cases the police were prominent, and dissent was repressed; transportation and communications networks were developed; agricultural production was encouraged and increased, turning Taiwan and Korea into 'agricultural appendages'. Until the 1930s, industries were actively discouraged. In both colonies, public health was improved, leading to population growth. Basic education was fostered, emphasizing knowledge about Japanese culture and the use of the Japanese language in a policy of partial assimilation (Schirokauer, 1989).

The socio-political situation in colonial Taiwan and Korea, drawn in a broad brush above, provides us with a background for examining the educational development there. In doing so, I will start with the organizational structure of colonial education. Due to their constant expanding, reshaping, revamping and renaming, I will keep to the key configuration of the school system.

The educational structure: Some preliminaries

Neither Taiwanese nor Koreans had demanded a Japanese education, but rather it was imposed upon them as part of colonial rule. This enforcement of a new educational system on the colonies created a dual structure composed of the Japanese system and the local system. While the existing local schools were private and in the main traditional, the Japanese ones were mandatory, public and modern, as shown in Figure 2.1.

The local system here refers to the existing schools when Japan came to the colonies. The local school was almost a synonym of traditional schools at the beginning of colonial rule, especially for Taiwan. But this also includes a certain number of modern schools set up by missionaries (see Figure 2.2). In Taiwan, missionary schools, few in number, were immediately squelched by the strict Japanese control. An early Westerner recalled:

> The missionaries, who were the pioneers of western education in Formosa, suffered a grievous blow when the growth of public education enabled the Japanese to order the closure of the elementary department in missionary schools. (In H. W. Lee, 1964: 33)

In Korea, by the turn of the century before the Japanese annexed it, elementary schools/secondary schools and even colleges had been erected by missionaries (Tsurumi, 1984). However, while the Korean authorities showed no earnest interest in their development, much of the public funding for their development was embezzled by officials. In consequence, even the schools opened for privileged children, like 'Yugyon-konwon College', dwindled in time (O, 1979).

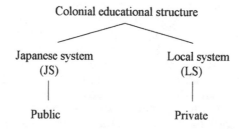

Figure 2.1 The Japanese educational structure in the colonial countries.

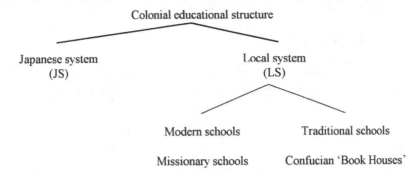

Figure 2.2 The Japanese colonial educational structure: the local system.

Japanese rule, for better or worse, undermined the *ancien régime* in Taiwan and Korea. In education, the impact was perhaps most felt by the traditional private schools that disseminated Confucian canons. This refers particularly to the private academies, called 'Book Houses' (c. *shufang*; j. *shobô*; k. *sôdang* or *keulpang*).[11] They were parallels of Japanese *shijuku* (private schools) found during the Tokugawa period and early Meiji.[12]

Book Houses were the main school system before colonization, and remained essential rivals to the Japanese institutions of education long after annexation. The Japanese tried to contain and control Book Houses in Taiwan, *shufang*, by reforming their curricula, 'stealing' their students away to Japanese schools, or simply closing them if they were suspected of preaching anti-Japanese thoughts. In Korea, because Christian schools were more formidable, Book Houses were treated with relatively more favour. The Japanese even founded a New Confucian academy to promote the study of the classics. Regulations governing Book Houses in Korea became compulsory only in 1929. Overall, Book Houses received more toleration in Korea than in Taiwan. Nevertheless, the Japanese took them only as makeshift substitutes (Tsurumi, 1984). The Japanese rulers in Korea, however, cautioned themselves that 'any radical measures should not be taken, as these institutions have existed for a long time, drastic reform or abolition would not be popular'.[13] As a result, Book Houses in Korea even increased in number for a period of time. But in both Taiwan and Korea they diminished in the long run, as clearly indicated in Table 2.5.

---

[11] Because of some differences in their names, and because of their common nature and for the purpose of clarity and convenience, in the ensuing text I refer to this category as 'Book Houses', a literal translation from the Chinese characters.

[12] A detailed treatment of Japanese *shijuku* is given in Rubinger (1982).

[13] See 'Instructions Concerning the Enforcement of the Chôsen Educational Ordinance' issued by the Government General of Chôsen, in CSNG (1926).

Table 2.5 The change in the total number of 'Book Houses' in Taiwan, 1899–1939, and Korea, 1912–35. *Source*: Munemitsu Abe *et al.*, *Kankoku to Taiwan no Kyôiku Kaihatsu* (The educational development in Korea and Taiwan), (Tokyo: Ajia Keizai Kenkyûjo, 1972), 56, 259.

Year	Number of Book Houses in Taiwan	Year	Number of Book Houses in Korea
1899	1421	1912	16,540
1909	655	1920	24,030
1919	301	1925	18,510
1929	160	1930	14,957
1939	17	1935	6209

As Zhi-ting Wang (1959) records, by 1943 there were only two Book Houses left in Taipei. A time-honoured system of schools that had been maintained for centuries, and which had taken on a new role of literacy and education in the transitional period, finally gave way to the dynamic, new schooling of imperial Japan.

Japan-built education

The Japan-built modern school system can be broadly grouped into two main types, academic and vocational, as shown in Figure 2.3. Vocational education, such as medical science and agriculture, has been an important part of education in Japanese colonies. Given the main theme of my study, however, I confine myself to academic schooling and its selection system.

Academic schooling in colonies was the replica of that in Japan in many ways: the implemented ideology of a universal and compulsory education; the clear distinction and articulation of elementary, secondary and tertiary levels corresponding to school ages; the modern teaching subjects and curriculum, precisely calculated by hours required and scheduled in the time frame; and the standard rules regulating students in terms of discipline, code of conduct, academic progression and completion, etc.

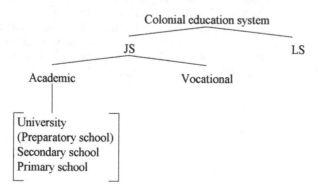

Figure 2.3 The Japanese colonial educational structure: the Japan-built system.

In the prewar period, the ascending steps of academic schooling in Japan, Taiwan and Korea were Primary school → Middle school → Preparatory school for university → University. Unlike the modern system, there was no high school. The preparatory schools or 'higher schools (*kôtô-gakkô*)' looked like the current high schools, though their graduates would automatically enter the universities (see Figure 2.3).

One important feature of colonial education is the ethnically divided two-track system, which emerged definitely in 1906 (Tsurumi, 1977: 40). It is a prominent characteristic which we ought to address now.

Segregation in primary schools

The Japanese army and officials brought with them into the colonies a growing number of children. To cater to their need for education, government primary schools were built up. In Taiwan, the first primary school for Japanese children was established in 1897.[14] The primary schools for Japanese pupils were called '*shô-gakkô*' in Taiwan and Korea, which was a standard term already used in Japan. At the beginning, *shô-gakkô* in Taiwan admitted only Japanese pupils and the primary schools opened to local children were called 'common schools (*kô-gakkô*)' in Taiwan and 'ordinary schools (*futsu-gakkô*)' in Korea. As the ordinary school was very much patterned after Taiwan's common school, the two were very similar. The ethnic ratio over time in Taiwan is indicated in Table 2.6.

Primary schooling is the start of formal learning, the cornerstone of education. At the time when modern education had just begun, its importance was apparently more obvious. It was at this main stage of education that Japanese and Taiwanese/Korean children were separated.

By 1944, only 10 per cent of Taiwanese children got into *shô-gakkô* that catered for Japanese students. On the other hand, very few Japanese children attended *kô-gakkô*. As Taiwanese scholars complain, the *shô-gakkô* differed from the *kô-gakkô* in that the *shô-gakkô* had (1) a better teaching faculty and school facility, (2) higher-quality textbooks imported from Japan (textbooks in *kô-gakkô* were compiled by the local government), and (3) a better admission rate in middle schools (Z. T. Wang, 1959: 47–8). To get into post-primary education, entrance exams were required, which were based on the Japan-imported standard textbooks rather than local ones. This posed a major barrier to the Taiwanese students (Y. H. Li, 1970: 1153–7). These charges were at least evidenced in the comparison of how much was spent on Japanese and Taiwanese students, presented in Table 2.7.

As is shown in Table 2.7, per capita expenditures for Japanese had been about twice as much as that for Taiwanese. As a result, Taiwanese families generally wished to send their children to *kô-gakkô*. Understandably, that was very hard, if not impossible.

---

[14] Zhi-ting Wang (1959) dates the founding of the first primary school for Japanese as 1903. Here I follow the date given by Tsurumi (1977) and Abe *et al.* (1972). Wang's data might be erroneous, as in 1898, similar schools were already found established in Taihoku (Taipei), Keelung, Shinchiku and Tainan (Tsurumi, 1977: 263n).

Table 2.6 The Japanese–Taiwanese ratio in primary schools: *Shô-gakkô* (School for Japanese) and *Kô-gakkô* (School for Taiwanese). *Source*: Munemitsu Abe *et al.*, *Kankoku to Taiwan no Kyôiku Kaihatsu* (The educational development in Korea and Taiwan), (Tokyo: Ajia Keizai Kenkyûjo, 1972), 257.

Year	Shô-gakkô			Kô-gakkô		
	Japanese J	Taiwanese T	T/J	Japanese J	Taiwanese T	J/T
1904	2552	–	–	–	23,178	–
1914	11,600	–	–	–	62,961	–
1924	22,852	930	4.1%	11	220,501	0.005%
1934	38,136	2456	6.4%	39	333,901	0.001%
1944	50,599	5044	10.0%	19	872,507	0.002%

Table 2.7 Per capita expenditures on Japanese and Taiwanese students in Taiwan (in yen). *Source*: *Taiwan Jijô*, 1931, 1935, 1940, quoted from E. Patricia Tsurumi, *Japanese Colonial Education in Taiwan, 1895–1945* (Cambridge, Mass.: Harvard University Press, 1977), 239–40.

Year	Japanese students	Taiwanese students
1931	¥55.2	¥29.4
1935	¥49.3	¥26.5
1940	¥50.0	¥26.9

During 1920–1, Taiwanese children began to have permission to enter Japanese *shô-gakkô*. The new Education Rescript of 1922 declared all schools equally accessible to Taiwanese and Japanese. In the same year, Korea duplicated Taiwan's reform of integration (Tsurumi, 1977, 1984).

What was achieved by that effort? Let us examine the integration ratio given in Table 2.8. The pattern appears to be very close to that of Taiwan. By the end of the War, the Koreans in *shô-gakkô* increased from approximately 300 in 1922 to more than 5000 in 1943. However, they accounted for no more than 8 per cent, suggesting an even less successful integration than Taiwan. In both Taiwan and Korea, few Japanese were in schools opened for the local population.

The 1922 Education Rescript officially aimed at abolishing 'discrimination in education' (Tsurumi, 1977: 99), but ethnic segregation in primary education, as noted, largely remained a stark reality throughout colonial rule, being most notable and intransigent at the primary level of education:

> Japanese administrators claimed that aspirants from both ethnic groups were judged equitably in open competition and that the coveted places went to the most proficient. They explained the less successful performances of Taiwanese applicants in terms of language handicaps and lower academic achievements. In specific cases this may have been true, but it was an open secret that the Japanese who controlled admissions did not discard their long-standing practice of protecting the interests of the rapidly growing Japanese community. (Tsurumi, 1977: 103)

Table 2.8 The Japanese–Korean ratio in primary schools: *Shô-gakkô* (School for Japanese) and *Futsu-gakkô* (School for Koreans). *Sources*: For 1922 data, CSNG, *Chôsen ni okeru Kyôiku no Gaikyô* (The overview of Korean education), (Seoul: CSNG, 1941), 12; for 1936 data, Munemitsu Abe *et al.*, *Kankoku to Taiwan no Kyôiku Kaihatsu* (The educational development in Korea and Taiwan), (Tokyo: Ajia Keizai Kenkyûsho, 1972), 68; for 1940 and 1943 data, CSNG, *Nihon Shokuminchi Kyôiku Seisaku Shiryô Shûsei* (A collection of historical documents on the Japanese colonial policy in Korea), (Seoul: CSNG, 1926), No. 62, pp. 1–2; No. 61, pp.1–2.

	Shô-gakkô *(School for Japanese)*			Futsu-gakkô *(School for Koreans)*		
Year	Japanese J	Koreans K	K/J	Japanese J	Koreans K	J/K
1922	51,588	328	0.64%	140	236,032	0.06%
1936	84,714	2061	2.43%	617	798,224	0.08%
1940	92,554	4609	4.98%	896	1,380,769	0.06%
1943	96,548	5557	5.76%	993	1,927,789	0.05%

Post-primary education

Integration policy in post-primary education accomplished much more. In Taiwan after 1922 a Rescript was issued, and the distinction between Taiwanese and Japanese disappeared in form. The ratio of Taiwanese students in secondary education greatly increased, as plotted in Figure 2.4.

The improvement was more notable if we look at the data of middle schools given in Table 2.9. In 1921, the Taiwanese accounted for only one quarter of the total number of middle school students. By 1940, compared to 1921, while the number of Japanese students quadrupled, Taiwanese increased seventeen-fold. This shows that, once the Taiwanese overcame the obstacles in language and culture, they could perform remarkably well. It also suggests that the situation did improve in favour of the Taiwanese as Japan achieved mass expansion and improved integration in the colonies.

Having said that, we also need to realize that racial segregation and discrimination in education did not disappear; it was a stigma of colonialism. First of all, as given in Table 2.10, the acceptance ratio in middle schools differed significantly for Japanese and Taiwanese.

As clearly shown, the likelihood of a Japanese applicant entering middle school is about twice that of a Taiwanese applicant. According to Yuanhui Li (1970), in due course, Taiwanese became more and more interested in education, which caused the rapid increase in the number of applicants. But no more than 20 per cent of them were accepted.

Furthermore, after the 1922 Integration Rescript, Taiwan's middle schools were still divided into two groups, one for Japanese students and the other for Taiwanese. The two-track segregation was still there, although the names of schools did not show it (see Table 2.11). The data in Table 2.11 show first that Japanese and Taiwanese students had never really integrated. They were placed in two different sub-systems, and they received very different treatment.

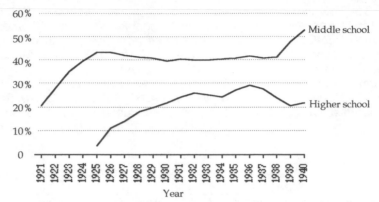

Figure 2.4 The ratio of Taiwanese students in middle schools and higher schools in Taiwan, 1921–40. *Source*: Based on Yuanhui Li, *Nihon Tôchika ni okeru Taiwan Shotô Kyôiku no Kenkyû* (A study of Taiwan's primary education under Japanese rule), (Taizhong: Taizhong Normal School, 1970), 1173, 1154.

Table 2.9 The number and ratio of Japanese and Taiwanese students in middle schools in Taiwan, 1921–40. *Source*: Yuanhui Li, *Nihon Tôchika ni okeru Taiwan Shotô Kyôiku no Kenkyû* (A study of Taiwan's primary education under the Japanese rule), (Taizhong: Taizhong Normal School, 1970), 1153–4.

Year	Japanese	Taiwanese
1921	1230 (79.51%)	317 (20.49%)
1925	1963 (56.49%)	1510 (43.45%)
1930	2917 (60.36%)	1910 (39.52%)
1935	3404 (59.07%)	2357 (40.90%)
1940	5186 (47.03%)	5832 (52.88%)

Note: The figures in parentheses indicate the percentage of the total number of middle school students in Taiwan.

By the end of the War, the number of Taiwanese middle school students approached that of Japanese, but when we look at the population they served on Taiwan, the ethnic difference and contrast stand out (see Table 2.12).

The inequity of secondary education between the locals and the Japanese becomes obvious when we put the statistics about the number of middle school students in a demographic context. In Korea, the situation is very similar for middle schools (see Table 2.13). During the period under review, 1935–9, the number of Korean applicants for middle schools doubled from 15,000 to 29,000. Meanwhile, their acceptance declined from 21.48 per cent to 15.85 per cent. This suggests that Koreans rapidly became interested in modern education, but under Japanese rule their chances of getting it, however, shrank. It appears that these shrinking chances were comparatively narrower than those which the Taiwanese were given, as we reviewed earlier.

A general picture of Japanese-initiated colonial education is now taking shape. Under Japanese rule, a modern education emerged, grew up, and spread out on an unprecedented scale. This expansion was gradual, but epochal. It was led by colonialism in search of land, resources, and sphere of influence.

And yet, as the education system in Japan was reproduced in the colonies and Japanese faculties moved to the new 'frontier', the meritocratic principle embedded in Japanese education was also carried over. In consequence, the assimilation and integration issue ran into its own dilemma. The Japanese already perceived the technical predicament of that policy. Shibata, Director of the Educational Bureau in Korea in 1922, professed in a statement:

> For my part I believe, in so far as the ideal is concerned, in the advantage of co-education [i.e. integrated education of Japanese and Korean] being adopted in accordance with the fundamental principles of impartiality, non-discrimination, and cultivation of fraternal friendship. The two peoples, however, differ from each other in their knowledge of the national language as well as in thought and habits of life, and from the practical view-point there are circumstances that perforce make the adoption of separate education more or less unavoidable. (Cited from the English version in CSNG, 1926 (16): 11)

Behind the sensational propaganda, there is nonetheless something realistic in the difficulty in the assessment of integration. Even if the Japanese were earnest, the highly exclusive homogeneity of Japanese culture had to make the task even more daunting. What was fundamental, though, was the near incompatibility between the colonial interest and the educational meritocracy in the entire enterprise. The contradiction was that the colonizer and colonized were destined not to be equal. Ideals and fantasies flaunted in the declared policy serve, more often than not, the basic role of ideology: to maintain an imagined or concealed relationship, to forge a false consciousness (Mannheim, 1936; Lukacs, 1971). In that perspective, integration is, in the final analysis, a 'vehicle for social control' (Myers and Peattie, 1984: 41).

Table 2.10 The acceptance ratios of Japanese and Taiwanese in middle schools in Taiwan, 1922–37. *Source*: Yuanhui Li, *Nihon Tôchika ni okeru Taiwan Shotô Kyôiku no Kenkyû* (A study of Taiwan's primary education under Japanese rule), (Taizhong: Taizhong Normal School, 1970), 1155–6.

	Number of applicants		Number accepted	
	Japanese	*Taiwanese*	*Japanese*	*Taiwanese*
1922	1124	1611	539 (47.95%)	331 (20.55%)
1925	1084	2741	490 (45.20%)	409 (14.92%)
1930	1389	2542	677 (48.81%)	433 (28.27%)
1935	1799	3329	850 (47.25%)	617 (18.53%)
1937	2216	4954	1136 (51.26%)	635 (12.82%)

Note: The figures in parentheses indicate the percentage number of applicants.

Table 2.11 Percentages of applicants accepted in major 'Japanese' and 'Taiwanese' middle schools, 1941–3. *Source*: E. Patricia Tsurumi, *Japanese Colonial Education in Taiwan, 1895–1945* (Cambridge, Mass.: Harvard University Press, 1977), 118–19.

Boys' schools

Year	Japanese				Taiwanese			
	Taihoku 1	Taihoku 3	Taichû 2	Tainan 1	Taihoku 2	Taichû 1	Tainan 2	Tamsui Private
1941	53.6	35.1	64.8	70.5	15.2	16.0	16.7	27.2
1942	80.1	40.8	77.8	71.2	29.2	16.3	21.9	22.6
1943	69.6	70.6	74.7	80.8	21.9	26.5	24.3	26.7

Girls' schools

Year	Japanese				Taiwanese			
	Taihoku 1	Taihoku 2	Taichû 1	Tainan 1	Taihoku 3	Taichû 2	Tainan 2	Tamsui Private
1941	55.9	35.0	49.3	81.5	23.8	18.9	27.7	48.8
1942	61.7	30.3	81.3	68.8	21.3	24.7	25.7	44.7
1943	68.9	56.2	79.7	71.9	19.7	33.0	22.7	38.9

Table 2.12 A comparison: Taiwanese and Japanese students in Taiwan's middle schools against ethnic population, 1943–4. *Sources*: Zhi-ting Wang, *Taiwan Jiaoyü Shi* (History of education in Taiwan), (Taipei: Taiwan Shudian, 1959), 58–9; Yuanhui Li, *Nihon Tôchika ni okeru Taiwan Shotô Kyôiku no Kenkyû* (A study of Taiwan's primary education under Japanese rule), (Taizhong: Taizhong Normal School, 1970), 1121.

	Taiwanese	Japanese
Number of middle school students in Taiwan (1944)	(Boys) 7230 (Girls) 4855	(Boys) 7888 (Girls) 8396
Total number of ethnic population in Taiwan (1943)	61,338,670	397,090

Table 2.13 Acceptance ratios of Japanese and Korean students in middle schools in Korea, 1935–9. *Source*: CSNG, *Chôsen ni okeru Kyôiku no Gaikyô* (An overview of Korean education), (Seoul: CSNG, 1941), 17–18.

	Japanese			Korean		
	Applicants	Accepted		Applicants	Accepted	
1935	3049	1441	(47.26%)	15,020	3227	(21.48%)
1936	3422	1688	(49.33%)	19,542	3381	(17.30%)
1937	3549	1925	(54.24%)	20,338	3609	(17.75%)
1938	3620	1892	(52.27%)	26,564	4137	(15.57%)
1939	3732	2125	(56.94%)	29,071	4608	(15.85%)

As a result, in the discriminatory environment of Japanese colonialism, Japanese and Taiwanese/Koreans were not evaluated equally. The exams were used as the arbiter, but they were conditioned by colonial interest as the grand premise. In her comment on entrance exams for middle schools, Patricia Tsurumi (1977) writes:

> Japanese who did not do well enough in entrance examinations to gain admission to schools that had formerly been all-Japanese institutions were often accepted into what had formerly been a Taiwanese middle school or higher girls' school – even though their academic performance fell short of Taiwanese classmates in the same institution. (116)

The fusion of colonialism and modern education caused Japanese policies in Taiwan and Korea to be ambivalent and inconsistent. In Taiwan, Japanese spared no effort to push Japanese literacy and basic education; the Japanese administration organized education committees composed of, among others, local dignitaries. These dignitaries were asked not only to organize public education, but also to finance it. Japanese principals and teachers constantly visited parents and earnestly talked to them about the importance of sending their children to school (Tsurumi, 1977). Japanese local policemen also visited Taiwanese families from door to door, trying their best to persuade the local people to learn Japanese or to send kids to school (Z. T. Wang, 1959).

In the same vein, Japanese authorities resorted to extreme measures in Korea to get the young into ordinary schools. It was commonplace for Japanese colonial schools to entice pupils by providing them with textbooks, school supplies and free lunches, or to send the district chief and the police to pressure families to send their children to school. Sometimes pupil-hungry officials went so far as to hold parents in detention and release them only on the condition that their children attend school. As a result, by 1918, there were 464 ordinary schools with nearly 88,000 pupils in Korea. At the same time, there were 26 private ordinary schools serving 2830 pupils (Tsurumi, 1977).

For post-elementary education, however, the Japanese showed great reluctance and reservations in how open the door should be for the Taiwanese and Koreans. After the Education Rescript on integration and equal treatment was issued in 1922, all secondary and higher schools (in Taiwan and Japan) became equally open to Japanese and Taiwanese alike. In Korea, the Taiwan reform was also duplicated. However, as Patricia Tsurumi (1984) contends, in *actual practice*, officials were far from blind to the ethnic origins of applicants to the most prestigious schools. Zhi-ting Wang (1959) reveals how that was so. He listed four factors that offset the 'fairness' of the entrance exam system for secondary schools:

1. The students who could enter the secondary level were largely from élite elementary schools that Taiwanese or Korean children generally could not enter in the first place.

2. The oral test in the Japanese language was considered very important. For Taiwanese or Korean children, this posed a great obstacle, especially during the early years of annexation.
3. The selection of entrants was supervised by an 'admissions committee', in which the chair and most of the committee members were Japanese. Wang (1959) is convinced that the ethnic composition of the committee was definitely disadvantageous to the natives.
4. It was claimed that there was an unofficial quota or ratio between Japanese and Taiwanese children. According to that quota, in a school for Japanese students, the Taiwanese ratio could not exceed 20 per cent. There was, however, no limit on the number of Japanese in any kind of school (Z. T. Wang, 1959: 92).

As a result, while the format of and questions in the entrance exams were similar in the ruling country and its colonies, the entrance system was distorted in the colonies in the interests of the Japanese. While Taiwanese or Koreans struggled against cultural odds in the exams, certain factors extraneous to exams also made it hard for them to compete on impartial terms.

For more illustration of that point, we may go a step further to the higher schools, which issued a sure ticket to universities. Based on the data we have, let us compare the 1936 entrance requirement in the top higher schools in Japan and in Taiwan. As noted earlier in this chapter, the élite higher schools in Japan were the 'number schools', within which the First Higher School was the best, because it was the ladder to Tokyo University. In Taiwan, the Taihoku Higher School was the equivalent of this First Higher School, as it was the ladder to Taihoku Imperial University, the No. 1 in Taiwan. Entrance to the First Higher School was essentially decided by written exams only, clear and simple. This was the same for all the 'number schools' in Japan. For the Taihoku Higher School, however, there were two channels of admission: one was through exams (*yûshi*) and the other was a non-exam (*mushi*) channel.[15] The ratio of students that entered Taihoku Higher School through the two channels was half-and-half (Z. T. Wang, 1959). The exam channel was no different from the First Higher in Tokyo. The non-exam channel had, however, the following description in the entrance requirement:

> [The candidate] needs to have good health, academic excellence, upright behavior, and a recommendation letter from his school principal.[16]

Unlike the exam channel, this recommendatory channel was of course much under the sway of subjective judgement. According to Wang (1959), this

---

[15] See 'Showa 11-nen Jôkyû Gakkô Seito Bôshû Yôkô' (1936 information on the admission into the higher-level schools), in NSMS (Tokyo: Obunsha, 1936), Appendix, pp. 1–16.

[16] See 'Showa 11-nen Jôkyû Gakkô Seito Bôshû Yôkô', *op. cit.*, pp. 2–3, 16.

was where racial discrimination was at its worst. Qualification based on ethic behaviour was a murky criterion, and recommendations were hard to compare.

In Japanese 'number schools', physical health and moral behaviour were not neglected. As Donald Roden (1980) notes, for the First Higher School, its prospective students were expected to show 'acceptable manners, health, and demeanor', as defined by the administration. Even the 'brightest candidate' might be denied admission for reasons of physical handicap or unsound behaviour. Nevertheless, when the exams were the primary cut-off criterion, those precautions were most likely used only for exceptional cases. In Taiwan's Taihoku Higher School, however, in the non-exam channel, subjective evaluation gave Japanese administrators far more control. The difference is expressed in Figure 2.5.

As shown in Figure 2.5, in Japan, a small number of positions in non-élite higher schools admitted students without exams. In Taiwan, even in the élite track, half of the students entered through a non-exam channel. This was apparently more convenient for the Japanese administration.

Japanese historians like Furuno Naoya (1994) may have different views about what was really going on during that period. Naoya concedes that, in the Taiwanese Higher Schools, there were a lot more Japanese than Taiwanese. But, instead of referring to it as discrimination, he contends that, as a matter of fact, Taiwan's Higher Schools were founded for the Taiwanese. Japanese applicants for the school were those with no hope of getting into the élite 'number schools' in Japan. He argues that the reasons for admitting fewer Taiwanese was that the academic level of Taiwanese students was not high. They lost out in fair competition. Furthermore, if these Taiwanese students applied for Japanese schools instead, their future would be much brighter (Furuno, 1994: 237–8).

What we have here seems to be two different pictures of the role of entrance exams in Japan's colonies, one negative, the other more positive. They are hard to verify, because, when admission involves more than an exam, we can never know what actually went on behind the office doors of the Japanese admissions committee. What is clear from the above analysis, though, is the stark reality that Taiwanese and Koreans were consistently disadvantaged in colonial education throughout Japanese rule.

Nonetheless, the above analysis does not imply that the merit system was a smokescreen, or a hypocritical ideology that was used to conceal the real motive and reality. It only shows that, when education and colonialism came together, the latter debilitated the meritocratic principle of education.

Being critical leads easily to being cynical and blind, which should be warded off by any means. It is beyond doubt that we must give the Japanese due credit for creating an education system in Taiwan and Korea. The most outstanding achievement of Japanese education in the colonies was the grand project of primary education which reached all segments of the rural and urban populations. The high rate of attendance of school-aged children was unheard of before. By 1942, about 40 per cent of school-aged children had primary education in Korea (Table 2.14).

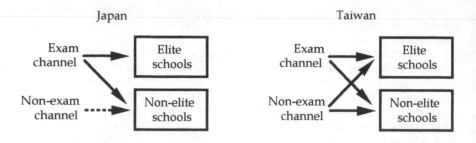

Figure 2.5 A comparison: the entrance exam and non-exam channels for higher schools in Japan and Taiwan during the colonial period.

The rate of school attendance was even more impressive in colonial Taiwan, as presented in Table 2.15. By the end of WWII, less than three quarters of school-aged children in Taiwan enrolled in elementary school. The local education initiative embraced numerous far-flung villages and smaller units of settlement, which may be called hamlets. Native children received formal Japanese schooling in the small education centres (*kyôiku sho*) which grew out of the early efforts of policemen to teach the Japanese language and arithmetic to the children of chieftains. Children would be collected together and given rudimentary instruction in exchange for the medicines police officers handed out to their parents as rewards (Wang, 1959; Xu, 1993). As Patricia Tsurumi (1977) concludes:

> In comparison with the educational opportunities other colonial rulers offered the people they dominated, the Japanese in Taiwan were far from niggardly. With the exception of the Americans in the Philippines, no other colonial power in Asia or elsewhere approached native education with anything like the seriousness of purpose of Japanese educators in Taiwan. The care that went into formulating and executing educational plans was outstanding. The Philippines excepted, no colonial education system under a Western flag received such a generous input of funds and skilled personnel. (224)

She went on to say that the Japanese probably expended educational funds more effectively than Americans in the Philippines, judging from the achievements. As late as 1946, only 58 per cent of elementary school children continued in school after the second grade in the Philippines (ibid., 226–7).

In assessing the implication of the growth of schooling in the Japanese empire, Cater Eckert *et al.* (1990) comment thus:

> The growth of elementary and secondary schools during the colonial period and the participation of millions of Koreans in the pre-1945 industrialization of Korea, Japan, and Manchuria left the peninsula with an impressive pool of literate and experienced workers by 1945. Since then this pool has been continually enlarged in conjunction with the proliferation of new schools and the reconstruction and expansion of the manufacturing industry. Very few countries

have been as blessed as South Korea with such a well-educated and adept working class in their early stages of development. (402)

In the next section, we will move from the bottom of the educational structure to its top, the university, where the élite core class was produced.

Table 2.14 Percentage of Korean school-aged children enrolled in elementary school, 1910–42. *Source*: Wonmo Dong, 'Assimilation and social mobilization in Korea', in Andrew C. Nahm, *Korea Under Japanese Colonial Rule: Studies of the Policy and Techniques of Japanese Colonialism* (Western Michigan University: The Center for Korea Studies, 1973), 146–82.

Year	Number of students	Rate of attendance
1910	20,562	–
1915	67,556	–
1919	89,288	4.6
1925	385,415	9.9
1930	492,604	12.2
1935	720,757	17.6
1940	1,385,944	32.4
1942	1,779,661	39.4

Note: School-aged children refer to the 7–14-year-old age cohort in the population.

Table 2.15 Percentage of Taiwanese school-aged children enrolled in olomontary school, 1907–44. *Source*: E. Patricia Tsurumi, *Japanese Colonial Education in Taiwan, 1895–1945* (Cambridge, Mass.: Harvard University Press, 1977), 148.

Year	Boys	Girls	Total
1910	–	–	5.76
1915	–	–	9.63
1920	39.11	9.36	25.11
1925	44.26	13.25	29.51
1930	48.86	16.57	33.11
1935	56.83	25.13	41.47
1940	70.56	43.64	57.56
1944	80.86	60.94	71.31

Note: School-aged children refer to the 6–14-year-old age cohort in the population.

IMPERIAL UNIVERSITY: THE ULTIMATE GOAL OF SCHOOLING

We live in a world where the nation-state has become the dominant force in human governance, and also where the worldwide advancement of learning has become the single most influential factor affecting the human condition; and the relations between them are an increasingly important aspect of society.
– *Clark Kerr*, Higher Education Cannot Escape History, *1994*

The university crowns the enterprise of modern learning. In Japan, the link between higher education and the nation-state is one of the closest links possible. The Meiji regime nationalized the purpose of learning as soon as it set up the first institution of higher learning, Tokyo Imperial University. This became the model for all the imperial universities both in Japan and in the colonies. The fact that the Japan-built Taipei (Taihoku) Imperial University (1928) and Seoul (Keijô) Imperial University (1926) have been the very apex of university ranking in Taiwan and Korea gives an idea of the Japanese influence on élitist education in the two territories.

In the eyes of a student, a university is, first and foremost, a gate. To analyse how it worked in the prewar era, we first review the test questions. I have chosen World History for human science, and Mathematics for natural science, because both have been very 'normative' and stable subjects, and both have been better kept as subjects of exams. Let us first look at the World History exams in Japan and its colonies.

Prewar exams on World History

In the days of yore, Peter the Great resided in the palace in Moscow. Yonder, he learned mathematics from the Dutch. He also took the wind of the world powers and academic advancement in the West. This whetted the ambition in his heart. He craved to travel there, and to make Russia powerful. Hence, in the year 1690, escorted by Russian aristocrats, he sailed to the four corners of Europe. In *Amsterdam* he became a shipyard worker, learning the craft of vessel building. He also grappled with the gist (*yôshi*) of the geography, politics and other disciplines. Then, he cruised to *Germany*, *England* and other places again. In due course, he returned home with an expertise in literature and a hundred and one other skills (*hyakugei*). He reformed the system, opened up academic research, and built the new capital '*Petersburg*'. He encouraged manufacturing and trade, and, shortly afterwards, with a strong navy and an army, he laid a firm foundation of national wealth and strength. Russia extolled his flourishing achievement, and honoured him as the Great Emperor (*daitei*). [italics were originally given as underlining][17]

---

[17] This is a translated excerpt from *Mankoku Shiryaku* (A concise history of ten thousand nations), edited by Japan's Normal School, and published by Monbushô, the Japanese Ministry of Education, in 1875. The book has two slim volumes, thread bound in the Chinese classic method. It was used as the history textbook for the

The above passage is an excerpt selected from an antique history textbook for Japanese elementary schools, dated 'Meiji 7', or 1875. It represents one of the earliest samples that typified the way in which the Ministry of Education presented world history to the Japanese. What ran through the rest of that textbook is a simple chain of revolutions and wars, plus a series of central figures who led them and rode the tide of history, just like Peter the Great.

Before World War II, global history in Japan was called *gaigokushi* (history of foreign nations), where the world was split into two major geographical halves. One is the so-called *Shiyôshi*, or history of the 'Western Ocean': Europe, America and Australia. The other is *Tôyôshi*, or history of the 'Eastern Ocean', centred in Chinese civilization. In *Shiyôshi*, stories like that of Peter the Great abound, opening the window on the West. They were a tangible manifestation of the Japanese Charter Oath that 'wisdom and knowledge shall be sought throughout the world for the purpose of promoting the welfare of the empire'. *Tôyôshi*, on the other hand, reflects a great ambivalence on the part of the Japanese toward Asia. While the glory of the Oriental past was almost unrivalled at the early Meiji, it grew dim and the giant empire was incompetent in the face of Western intrusion. *Mankoku Shiryaku* (JMOE, 1875), the global history cited at the beginning, is a nascent Japanese account of that historical contrast.

After the Pacific War erupted, education in world history took up a very nationalist role. Apart from its didactic purposes, education in history also aimed to reveal the 'ulterior truth of Western aggression in Eastern Europe', and the significance of the 'Great East Asia Co-prosperity' (Shinohara, 1989). In addition, there was a need to draw lessons from the world powers in how they handled their colonial enterprises. All these were candidly reflected in the entrance exams that led to colleges. Some examples are given below. The 'hint' (*hintto*) is given in the original text which outlines the main points of the correct answer:[18]

Example I
Question: Describe the activities of the world powers in Africa.
[*Hint for the correct answer*: Describe separately the activities of the UK, France, Belgium, Germany and Italy, especially the conflict between Italy and Egypt.]
– 1936 entrance exam question for Shinto Royal Academy (*Shingô Kôgakukan*) (Obunsha: NSMS, 1936: 34).[19]

---

elementary school. It might well be the first version of elementary school books for history, as the Fundamental Code of Education (*Gakusei*) was promulgated only one year before. For further information on the teaching of history in the Meiji, refer to Shinohara (1989).

[18] Examples given below are taken from Obunsha, ed., NSMS (Tokyo: Obunsha).

[19] 'NSMS' is an acronym for *Nyûgaku Shiken Mondai Shôkai* (Entrance examination questions and answers), a journal published by Obunsha, Japan.

Example II
Question: Describe the United Kingdom's activities in India.
[*Hint for the correct answer*: First write about the start of the East India Co., and the establishment of its bases at Bombay, Calcutta, etc., and the military conquest of local resistance and domination by the East India Co. of all of India. ...]
–   1939 entrance exam question for Seoul Imperial University (Obunsha: NSMS, 1939: 85).

A large number of prewar history exams also revolved around East Asia. One main theme in the exams concerned the rivalry of world powers in the region, which posed a growing challenge to, and conflict with, Japanese expansionism. Knowledge of the history of Western intrusion into the Asian region became more and more necessary. Before 1936, there was no history exam for the élite number schools. After 1937, exams concerning East Asian history (*Tôyôshi*) and geography appeared for the First Higher School:

Example
Question: Write about the history of the relationship between Japan and Manchuria after the Meiji Restoration.
[*Hint for the correct answer*: (1) After the Sino-Japanese War, the Japanese Imperial Army obtained the Liaodong Peninsula. However, due to the Tripartite (Russia, Germany and France) Intervention, Japan withdrew from the land to preserve the *status quo ante bellum*. (2) Russia occupied Manchuria and advanced toward Korea, which led to the Russo-Japanese War. (3) The Imperial Army occupied the railroad east of Changchun City. ... (6) Japan recognized the independence of Manchuria. (7) Japan withdrew from the League of Nations. (8) Friendship between Japan and Manchuria.]
– 1937 entrance exam question for Japan's First Higher School (Obunsha: NSMS, 1937: 33).

A similar question was given in 1938, which exacted a good understanding of the origin of Sino-Russian conflict:

Example
Question: Write about the negotiation between Qing China and Russia on the territory of Siberia.
[*Hint for the right answer*: The question requires a discussion of Russian aggression in Siberia prior to the Sino-Japanese War, and a series of unequal treaties that Russia enforced upon the Qing court that led to the takeover of Siberia from China.]
– 1938 entrance exam question for Seoul Imperial University (Obunsha: NSMS, 1938: 38).

History exams also propelled students to learn the 'laws of civilization' in their historical perspective. Again, the disintegration of imperial China served as a didactic lesson:

Example
Question: Why did China undergo frequent dynastic rises and falls?
[*Hint for the correct answer*: In China, an emperor was empowered by Heaven, and the premise was love toward his subjects. When he lacked that, he would lose his legitimacy, and hence revolution might occur. The Chinese system thus differed essentially from the everlasting imperial lineage (*mansei ikkei*) in Japan, which was the foundation of our nation.]
– 1939 entrance exam question for Seoul Imperial University (Obunsha: NSMS, 1939: 85).

During the War, history exams appeared to be quite closely related to the interests and needs of the Japanese empire. Still, they were not always confined to a short-sighted utilitarianism. Some questions were apparently designed just to measure the depth of knowledge:

Example
Question: Explain the following figures:
(a) Charles Martel (b) John Calvin
[*Hint for the correct answer*: (a) Charles Martel (690–741): Ruler of the Franks (714–741), grandfather of Charlemagne. In the battle of Tours the Muslims, having crossed into France, were decisively defeated by Charles Martel and the Franks. (b) John Calvin (1509–64): French Protestant theologian of the Reformation. He was persecuted and hunted for his cause, and was banished in 1538.]
– 1936 entrance exam question for Shinto Royal Academy (Obunsha: NSMS, 1936: 34).

The above questions concerned only figures in remote history, not really immediately 'useful' or pragmatic. They simply measured the candidates' competitiveness. In this respect, *Tôyôshi* is also a vast area that challenged one's memory and mastery of history:

Example
Question: Explain the following terms:
(1) Ming-taizu (2) Xuan-zhuang (3) Hong Kong
[*Hint for the correct answer*: (1) Ming-taizu: Yuan-zhang Zhu, the first emperor of Ming dynasty (1368–1644). He restored the feudal system, shook up bureaucracy, and enhanced national defence. (2) Xuan-zhuang (596–664): famous Buddhist monk during the Tang (618–907) dynasty. (3) Hong Kong: A small island at Guangdong Gulf, occupied by the UK in 1897 after the Opium War; a major commerce centre in East Asia.]
– 1938 entrance exam question for Seoul Imperial University (Obunsha: NSMS, 1938: 38).

The foregoing examples give us some idea of what kind of historical knowledge the students were supposed to have before they could enter university. They were selected from exams given in Japan as well as in its colonial territories. Were there any differences between the test questions for Japanese universities and universities in Korea and Taiwan? If so, what were they? To answer them, let us compare questions in exam papers in totality. The History Exam usually consisted of two to four big questions, and students needed to answer them in the form of a short essay. As cited, Japanese élite number schools started to test students in history in 1937. Look at a sample of the exam paper for the First Higher School in 1937:

The History Exam for the First Higher School
Duration: two and half hours. Total scores: 90 points.
Question 1. Write about the two great Ise Shinto Shrines.
Question 2. Describe the features of the Momoyama culture.
Question 3. Write about the relationship between Japan and Manchuria after the Meiji Restoration.
– The 1937 entrance exam questions of history for Japan's First Higher School (Obunsha: NSMS, 1937: 33).

As the three questions suggest, the élite school required a prospective applicant to be more versed in Japanese culture and the intra-regional issues of East Asia (*Tôyôshi*) than in those of Europe. To compare, the following is a test paper for Seoul Imperial University:

History Exam for Seoul Imperial University
Duration: n.a. Total score: 100 points.
Question 1. Why did China undergo frequent dynastic rises and falls?
Question 2. Describe the history of the Liao (907–1125) dynasty.
Question 3. Describe the activities of the UK in India.
Question 4. Explain the following terms: (a) Jiankang (b) Sun Wen
– 1939 entrance exam questions of history for Seoul Imperial University (Obunsha: NSMS, 1939: 85).

Compared to the First Higher School, Seoul University appeared to ask more from the candidates, covering both Western and Eastern history. While the exam paper of the former gave more weight to Japanese culture, the latter examined Europe and China. It seems that the two papers were looking for different types of people: one was inward-looking, conversant with Japanese politics and arts, while the other was more competent in international affairs. The second type might be more appropriate for the future élite in Korea. Now, let us have a look at the exam questions in the paper for Taipei Imperial University:

History Exam for Taipei Imperial University
Duration (for both History and Japanese exams): 3 hours.
Total score: 100 points.
Question 1. What are the positive contributions and negative impacts of foreign (Western) culture?
Question 2. Describe the origin of samurai politics and its influence upon the later age.
– 1942 entrance exam question for Taipei Imperial University (Obunsha: NSMS, 1942: 27).

Question 1 calls for a fairly good understanding of Western culture before one might talk about its merits or demerits. For both Seoul and Taipei Imperial Universities, examiners seemed to be more interested in the applicants' understanding of Western culture. What was under scrutiny might be both adequate knowledge of the West and a regime-sanctioned 'correct attitude' toward it.

In the prewar period, world history was taught in both elementary and middle schools. In middle schools, the number of class hours spent on world history was greater than those for Japanese history (*kokushi*). To apply to a Japanese university or its preparatory schools, an applicant had to sit an exam that placed more stress on Japanese history or *Tôyôshi* than on European history (Shinohara, 1989), for reasons yet to be adequately determined. It might well be 'Nipponcentric' nationalism, especially as the West became more and more an irreconcilable enemy. Furthermore, during wartime, for a prospective student, his ideological purity and nationalistic consciousness needed to be examined first. While our data are scant, one documentary evidence for this political psychology is found in the 'General Rules of Instruction for Primary Schools' (*Shô-Gakkô Kyôsoku Kôryô*), drafted by Egi Kazuyuki and published as early as 4 May 1881. Article 15 of the 'General Rules', relating to the classes of history, 'shifted the emphasis drastically from world history to virtually exclusive concern with Japanese history, and pronounced it particularly important to cultivate a spirit of reverence for the emperor and love for one's country (*Sonnô aikoku*)' (Hall, 1973: 351–2). It is reasonable to add that this shift of emphasis was pushed further in the wake of WWII.

Prewar exams on mathematics

In an effort to 'seek knowledge from throughout the world', the tenet of Westernization written in the 1868 Meiji Charter Oath, mathematics was made rudimentary. Meiji leaders like Mori Arinori (1847–89), the first Education Minister of the Meiji regime, emphasized mathematics as one of the three most important academic studies, together with the English language and the legal system (Hall, 1973: 88).

In the early years, mathematics seemed in some way more situational. The following is an example taken from the 1939 university entrance exam held at the national level by the KMT Nationalists in Mainland China. In the five-problem maths exam, four were pure maths, but the fifth is linked to the situation then:

Example
On the bank of the river there is a cannon post, which is 30 feet above the river surface. There are now two military ships in the river. Seen from the cannon post, the depression angles of the ships are $30°$ and $45°$ respectively. The angle between the two lines linking the ships with the base of the post is $60°$. What is the distance between the two ships?
– 1939 China's national-level university entrance exam (TBX, 1983: 39)

This problem was not only 'realistic', but also historical. In the middle of World War II, the ships mentioned probably referred to the Japanese invasion force in particular. A parallel of such questions was found in the entrance exam for a university preparatory school in 1936 in Japan. In the maths entrance exam for the First Higher School, later Tokyo University, for example, two questions involved real-life situations, one of which is a war topic: it asked how many hours were needed for 'transporting cannon shells' (Obunsha, 1936: 168). Other war-theme questions included, for instance, the calculation of 'the height of an aircraft above the lake', or what speed a military troop needed to maintain in order to reach its military base on time as commanded (ibid., 1936, 1939).

Unlike the volatile subject of history, the test format of Japan's exams has been marked with a degree of stability. First of all, maths had always been used for screening in prewar Japanese schools. The test hours, number of problems, and the composition of problems all show a constancy and tradition for different schools. As it is hard to discuss each school, I discuss the First Higher School, admission into which guaranteed a ticket to Tokyo University. The reason for choosing it is that the school was earmarked by Japan's Ministry of Education as the model institution whose policies would be emulated by other academies in matters of curriculum, student regulations, etc. (DIKG, 1939; Roden, 1980).

The entrance exams for this top élite school in Japan apparently worked well, and no change was discernible in them. For the exams of each year, the same instructions for answering the questions were reproduced in almost identical detail, such as 'use upper-quality Western style paper (yôshi) as the answer sheet', 'Write the answers in a horizontal manner underneath each question', etc. (Obunsha, 1936–9). The simple pattern may be seen in Table 2.16. Due to the limitations of archival availability, only the information for four consecutive years is collected here, but it may still give some idea of prewar maths exams in Japan. First, the academic level of competition for university was the end of middle school, since to get from preparatory school into university was all but automatic. There might be some trigonometric function or logarithm questions for some papers, but the general questions are plane geometry and second-degree equations. There seemed to be no questions relating to differentiation/integration, probability or vectors. In other words, meritocratic screening in maths was done at the end of middle school, rather than at high school as it is now. The typical maths problems are represented in the following:

Example I

Algebra question. x, y, z are real numbers. If $x + y + z = 5$, $x^2 + y^2 + z^2 = 9$, then x, y, z are not smaller than 1 and not larger than $2\frac{1}{3}$.

Example II

Geometry question. AB is the diameter of the circle given. From endpoint A draw a line that cuts the circle at Q. Take point B on the extension line of BQ, and then draw a vertical line PR from P to the tangential line to the circle at B. If PQ is equal to PR, prove that P is on the circumference of a certain circle.
– 1937 entrance exams on maths for Japan's First Higher School (Obunsha: NSMS, 1937: 42–3).

Example I required mathematical operations using factoring and equation plus inequality rules. Example II assessed the mastery of the triangle axiom of congruence, which belonged to plane Euclidean geometry. Both belong to the middle school level. This does not imply that they were easy and simple.

The question in Example II did not supply the graph, which is produced opposite. Therefore, the task of drawing it correctly to visualize the structure spatially is crucial:

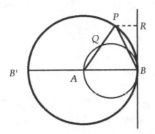

Without this graph, it is really hard, if not impossible, to figure out the intricate relationship between lines, angles and triangles. To understand that relationship, despite the possible imprecision in a scribbled graph, one requires composure and geometric vision.

Now, let us look at the maths problems in the exams for Taipei and Seoul Imperial Universities:

Examples of algebra questions

Taipei Imperial University

If $x^2 = y^2 + z^2 + 2ayz$,

$y^2 = z^2 + x^2 + 2bzx$,

$z^2 = x^2 + y^2 + 2cyz$,

prove:

$$\frac{x^2}{1-a^2} = \frac{y^2}{1-b^2} = \frac{z^2}{1-c^2}$$

– 1942 entrance exam questions on maths for Taipei Imperial University (Obunsha: NSMS, 1942: 55).

Seoul Imperial University

If $x = \sqrt{px+q}$,

and p, q are real numbers,

$p \neq 0$,

$q \neq 0$,

Calculate: the value of x.

– 1938 entrance exam questions on maths for Seoul Imperial University (Obunsha: NSMS, 1938: 61).

If we compare the two examples with that for Japan's First Higher School, we may find a nuance of difference in terms of how difficult they were. Korean questions may appear more straightforward than Taiwanese and Japanese problems. Otherwise, they were similar because all involved two-degree equations, a major area of middle school algebra. That kind of commonality was also found in the geometry:

Table 2.16 The pattern of entrance exams of Japan's First Higher School, 1936–9. *Source*: Obunsha, NSMS (Tokyo: Obunsha, 1936), 39.

Year	1936	1937	1938	1939
Duration of test (by hour)	3	3	3	3
Score (by points)	180	180	180	180
Number of questions	6	6	6	6
Situational questions	2	1	1	1
Plane geometry (by number)	3	3	3	3
Algebra (by number)	3	3	3	3

Examples of algebra questions

Taipei Imperial University
G is the gravity centre point of ABC, an inscribed triangle of circle O.
Calculate the value of $BC^2 + CA^2 + AB^2$.

Seoul Imperial University
The diagonals AC and BD of ABCD, an inscribed quadrilateral, cross each other at O at right angles. The line linking the midpoint of AB and O crosses DC at H. Calculate $\angle MHC$.

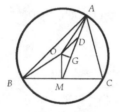

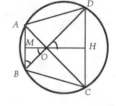

– 1942 entrance exam question on maths for Taipei Imperial University (Obunsha: NSMS, 1942: 56).

– 1938 entrance exam question on maths for Seoul Imperial University (Obunsha: NSMS, 1938: 61).

The maths exams used for universities in Taiwan and Korea shared a couple of points with those used in Japan: the chance of entering university was determined in the middle school, where the harsh acceptance ratio was as low as one in ten. The types of questions included:

- Plane geometry
- Second-degree equations
- Some trigonometric functions
- Some logarithm questions

There seemed to be no questions relating to differentiation/integration, probability or vectors. In other words, unlike maths exams today, university screening back then did not assess high school maths.

Due to the great competition for the First Higher School, as well as the two imperial universities, I would say the examples given here represent some of the toughest 'brain teasers' in the prewar era, although they were far easier than the entrance exams of today. For one thing, screening for university today has not only been raised to the high school level, but, as we will see in the ensuing chapter, widened to an almost all-embracing scope.

Was the colonial exam system a gate of mobility for Koreans and Taiwanese?

The racial division between Japanese and colonial children was unambiguous at each level of education. Segregation between Japanese and local schools was a fact of life at the elementary level. In the middle schools, segregation persisted, but a quota of 15 per cent was reserved for the local children in the schools for Japanese (Z. T. Wang, 1959). The same phenomenon seemed applicable to tertiary education, which will be the focus of study in this section. Figure 2.6 shows the limited ratio of local students during a considerable period of colonial rule.

From the above, we can see that the imperial universities of Japan in the colonies mainly served Japanese from the late 1920s to the end of the War. This seemed to provide stark counter-evidence to the claim made by Japanese colonists in 1922 that they were not like other empire builders because they had stopped making 'the education of the children of their colonial nationals a first consideration'. The Education Rescript of 1922, they proclaimed, had abolished discrimination in education. Government general officials continually asserted this throughout the 23 years of Japanese rule that followed 1922. Later, the situation changed slightly for the better if we examine the ethnic ratio across the years (see Figure 2.6). During that period, on average only one fifth of the Taihoku (Taipei) university students were Taiwanese, and about a little more than one third of the students of the imperial university in Korea were Korean, with the exception of 1943 (Table 2.17).

All told, there is no unequivocal evidence showing that discrimination was an official policy. I concur with Tsurumi (1977) that 'the problem for Taiwanese applicants to Taihoku was that Japanese were favored – *not officially of course* – in entrance selections, and since the number of places was small to begin with, only a few could ever hope to get in [italic added]'. Due to the absence of documentary or even verbal evidence of the racial preference for Japanese, conclusions relating to this issue often sound unreliable. Wonmo Dong (1973), for example, contends that:

> In my examination of the educational data that was compiled by the Government-General of Korea, I *have found reason to conclude* that the Japanese colonial regime had set a definite ethnic quota in the prestigious Keijô (Seoul) Imperial University and that in other government-operated special (professional) schools, *a strict quota was also applied* on an ethnic basis. (1973: 161)

He further asserts that the percentage of Korean students 'fluctuated between 31.4 in 1925 and 37.7 in 1942 and that at no time it showed a sharp increase or decrease in terms of absolute numbers and percentages' (ibid.: 161).[20] Dong's conclusion on the 'strict quota' without any direct archival evidence is scholarly unsound, although it matched the empirical statistics.

My own scepticism of any official discrimination stems first from the actual aim in opening imperial universities in colonies. The cardinal purpose for both Taihoku and Keijô was to attract, control and contain the local élite. One grave concern was their outflow to Japan or Mainland China, where radical ideologies were pernicious and subversive to Japanese rule (Matsumoto, 1960; Z. T. Wang, 1959; Y. H. Li, 1970).

This concern seemed to take precedence over the schooling of Japanese children or the urgency of academic research in the colonies. The acceptance ratio may substantiate that policy direction. Table 2.18 shows that the acceptance ratio for Taiwanese and Koreans was not the same. For Koreans, the acceptance ratio was very low. For Taiwanese, however, it was twice as high as the Japanese, which pointed to a moderately meritocratic factor. Further evidence of the meritocratic factor of the examination system was shown by comparison between departments. In the medical science department of Taihoku Imperial, Taiwanese often had a larger, or dominant share until the close of World War II. Few Taiwanese majored in agriculture, contrary to the over-represented Japanese in that field.

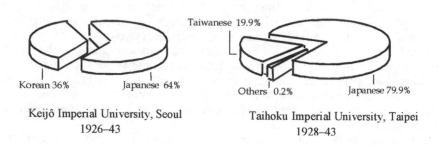

Taiwanese 19.9%

Korean 36%   Japanese 64%   Others 0.2%   Japanese 79.9%

Keijô Imperial University, Seoul   Taihoku Imperial University, Taipei
1926–43   1928–43

Figure 2.6 The average ethnic ratios in Keijô Imperial University (1926–43), Korea, and Taihoku Imperial University (1928–43), Taiwan. *Sources*: Based on data from Jae-Chol Chung, *Iljeui Dae Hankook Sikminji Kyoyuk Chongchaeksa* (History of educational policies of Imperial Japan in colonial Korea), (Seoul: Iljisa, 1985); Yuanhui Li, *Nihon Tôchika ni okeru Taiwan Shotô Kyôiku no Kenkyû* (A study of Taiwan's primary education under Japanese rule), (Taizhong: Taizhong Normal School, 1970).
Note: Average ratio is the sum total of the ethnic ratios each year divided by the number of years.

---

[20] In fact, the percentage of Korean students in Seoul Imperial University did rise well past the range of 31.4–37.7 per cent. The data show that it reached up to 45.98 per cent in 1943. Refer to the previous discussion on ethnic ratios in imperial universities for some more details.

Table 2.17 Ethnic ratios of students in Keijô (Seoul) and Taihoku (Taipei) Imperial Universities, by percentage. *Sources*: Zhi-ting Wang, *Taiwan Jiaoyü Shi* (History of education in Taiwan), (Taipei: Taiwan Shudian, 1959), 152–5; Jae-Chol Chung, *Iljeui Dae Hankook Sikminji Kyoyuk Chongchaeksa* (History of educational policies of Imperial Japan in colonial Korea), (Seoul: Iljisa, 1985), 397.

Year	Keijô Imperial University[a]		Taihoku Imperial University	
	Korean	Japanese	Taiwanese	Japanese
1930	35.33	64.67	11.11	88.89
1935[b]	31.80	68.20	21.93	78.07
1940[b]	39.01	60.45	26.40	72.98
1943 or 1944[c]	45.98	54.02	23.81	75.07

Notes: a. Data for Keijô Imperial University included the students of Law and Literature Departments and Medical Science Department. b. A small percentage of students of Taiwan's Taihoku Imperial University came from other areas. c. 1943 for Keijô Imperial University, and 1944 for Taihoku Imperial University.

Table 2.18 The numbers and rate of acceptance for Japanese and Taiwanese applicants to Taihoku Imperial University, 1943. *Source*: Yuanhui Li, *Nihon Tôchika ni okeru Taiwan Shotô Kyôiku no Kenkyû* (A study of Taiwan's primary education under Japanese rule), (Taizhong: Taizhong Normal School, 1970), 2355.

Ethnicity	Number of applicants A	Number accepted B	Accepted to applicants ratio B/A
Japanese	411	159	38.69%
Taiwanese	34	27	79.94%
Korean	8	1	12.50%
Total	453	187	41.28%

Note: Only data for 1943 are available.

We may also notice in Table 2.18 that there were many more Japanese applicants than Taiwanese applicants for Taihoku Imperial University. This may demonstrate a reluctance of the Taiwanese higher school students to apply for it. In 1942, for example, there were 143 higher school graduates in Taiwan (108 Japanese and 35 Taiwanese). In the same year, 293 Japanese applied to Taihoku Imperial University, whereas only 14 Taiwanese applied (Y. H. Li, 1970). I ascribe this to two factors. First, the entrance requirements and examinations were not attuned to the ethnic particularity of the local students. To compete with native Japanese in answering questions in Japanese was a losing battle at the outset. Furthermore, for applicants to human science, questions were hopelessly related to complex Japanese history, culture and politics, a blatant case of cultural bias. There was no evidence, however, that the Japanese established a battery of exam questions with an overt intent of discrimination. They were just as 'Japanese' as other exams, and that already created enough obstacles for local students.

Second, there was a constant exodus of local students from Taiwan to Japan, as indicated in Table 2.19, because of:

1. The attraction of metropolitan life and mobility. A number of Taiwanese students passed Japan's civil exams and worked in the Japanese government, such as Courts, Finance Ministry, Railroad Ministry, etc. In 1922, the year when the Taiwan Educational Rescript was issued, a rapidly growing number of children were sent to Japan, some of whom barely reached school age.
2. More intellectual and political freedoms, which were ideal for student activities and overseas patriotic ferment. Patriotic students from the colonies organized themselves into revolutionary or nationalist groups not only in Tokyo, but in some big cities of China.
3. Non-discriminative admission to Japanese schools (Matsumoto, 1960; Furuno, 1994; Lan, 1993). Of course, the higher ranking prestige and better academic conditions of schools in Japan also swayed students' decisions.

Education in the Japanese empire, as we saw it, thus stood in contrast to the colonial West. European schools, as Altbach and Kelly (1978) note, were generally not accessible to the colonized. Segregationist selective admissions and high cost were the main barriers. While cost was also a problem for families in Japanese colonies, selection seemed to be a lesser one. The Japanese government was very tolerant of this influx, and schools in Japan were open to them (ibid.).

Table 2.19 Number of Taiwanese overseas students in Japan, 1938–42. *Source*: Naoya Furuno, *Taiwan Jindaihua Mishi* (The secret history of modernization in Taiwan), translated by K'o Kek-tuun from Japanese into Chinese (Taipei: Diyi Chubanshe, 1994), 239.

Year	1938	1939	1940	1941	1942
Middle school	1298	1783	1699	1823	1793
Vocation school	352	478	544	634	694
Other school	765	1078	1436	1675	2077
Higher school	145	177	201	249	258
Specialized school	1250	1553	1798	1992	1939
University	322	377	310	303	330
Total	4132	5446	5988	6676	7091

THE PREWAR TYPOLOGY OF TUTORING ACADEMIES: *JUKU, BUXIBAN* AND *HAKWON*

Tutoring academies, in a broad sense, refer to privately run supplementary educational establishments operating outside regular school hours. They are divided into two types: academic – such as language, maths, science – and non-academic – such as piano or martial arts. In a specific sense used here, the tutoring academy is academically oriented to the 'ultimate goal of helping their clients' children do better in entrance exams' (Rohlen, 1980: 209–10). In the following pages, the term 'tutoring academies' is rendered into local languages: *juku* or *yobiko*[21] in Japan, *buxiban* in Taiwan, and *hakwon* in Korea.

In Japan, *juku* had its genesis in the Tokugawa era (1618–1868). During the Tokugawa period, officially sponsored *juku* or temple schools were expanded with the approval of local governments but without financial support to provide basic education to all interested commoners. These early *juku*-type schools were called *'terakoya'* which literally meant temple school. However, during the Tokugawa period the distinctions between 'public' and 'private' schools were not clearly defined. The Tokugawa era saw the development of various types of *juku* schools with vastly different philosophies, curricula and teaching styles. The academic *juku* founded during this period helped to establish the foundation of Japanese learning based upon meritocratic and egalitarian principles.

Although enrolment in these types of early *juku* were dominated by the samurai or warrior class, children from the merchant and commoner classes could enter and compete equally based on their knowledge and ability with children of a higher social class. However, these schools were considered élitist in the sense that their graduates usually received retainers as government officials. In some respects, this tradition of élitist meritocratic selection tradition was continued by the original 'imperial universities' founded in the early Meiji years.

The equivalents of *juku* in Taiwan and Korea were called *shufang* and *sôdang* respectively. *Shufang* was a version of Chinese *sishu* (j. *shijuku*) in Taiwan. Its important position was attested by the fact that at the time of annexation there were as many as 1707 *shufang* with an enrolment totalling 29,941 (H. W. Lee, 1964; Z. T. Wang, 1957). In ancient Korea, *sôdang* were private schools that were found in every large village, supported either by individual families or by the entire village. They were more similar to *terakoya* in Japan, as both were at the primary level. *Sôdang* could be found everywhere before and during Japanese annexation.

During the Meiji era, Japan formally ended its feudal period of isolation and began to import Western ideals and technology. The new government leaders realized that if Japan was going to maintain its sovereignty it must use education as a tool for expediting the modernization and national development process. Therefore, one of the first actions taken by the Meiji

---

[21] *Yobiko* refers to the *juku* which caters particularly for the exam preparation of *rônin* students.

leaders was an all-out effort to establish free public primary schools throughout the nation during the 1870s and 1880s. This strong emphasis on public education reduced the relative importance of the '*terakoya*' type academic *juku* in Japan. However, the teaching of the traditional Japanese arts in skill-oriented *juku* continued to flourish during this period. The non-academic subjects that were taught by *juku* at this time, like the abacus and calligraphy, were primarily for the purpose of basic general education or job training rather than for supplementary education for the purpose of advancement up the educational hierarchy.

The new-type tutoring academies in Japan: *Nyûgaku-nan* and its consequence

By the turn of the 1900s, there was every sign that Chinese classic education had come to a crushing end. Tutoring academies dwindled and slid into a lost world of extinction. Institutionally, however, they revived in the new order. Let us first look at prewar Japan.

The modern schooling of Meiji Japan created both an educational miracle and a dilemma. One such dilemma was '*nyûgaku-nan*', or the difficulty of entering university, as indicated in Table 2.20. The acceptance rate for imperial universities may look deceptively high: about one out of two could enter. But to get into public higher schools, the chance was only one in ten, quite slim indeed. Because of the narrow gateway to higher schools, each year a large number of middle school graduates turned into *rônin*, waiting to try again (see Table 2.21).

In Table 2.21, we can see quite clearly the school acceptance rates over the years and the consequential pattern of the students' behavioural pattern in prewar Japan. Each year, as entering the higher schools became prohibitively more difficult, one third of the middle school graduates became *rônin*. Out of this group, the increasing majority decided to prepare for the entrance exams the following year. They were the predecessors of the *rônin* army today.

Table 2.20 The acceptance rate of prewar Japanese schools, by percentage, 1923–37. *Source*: Yoshiro Shimizu, *Shiken* (Examinations), (Tokyo: Iwanami Shoten, 1957), 9.

Year	Middle School	Public Higher School	First Higher School	Imperial universities
1923	44.9	15.9	10.8	74.4
1927	54.3	9.5	6.5	66.7
1930	69.5	16.7	11.2	62.4
1935	58.4	13.7	10.2	60.0
1938	n.a.	12.1	11.3	65.7

Note: Acceptance rate = (number of entrants ÷ number of applicants) × 100%.

Table 2.21 Middle school graduates and *rônin* who decided to repeat the entrance exams in Japan, 1923–35. *Source*: Yoshiro Shimizu, *Shiken* (Examinations), (Tokyo: Iwanami Shoten, 1957), 9.

Year	Total number of middle school graduates	Total number of rônin	
		Studied at home	No information
1923	28,856	–	7703 (26.7%)
1924	32,856	–	9084 (27.7%)
1925	37,560	–	10,883 (29.0%)
1926	45,097	–	13,884 (30.8%)
1927	50,146	9088 (18.2%)	6716 (13.3%)
1928	54,042	10,990 (20.3%)	5015 (9.7%)
1929	58,384	15,386 (26.5%)	3323 (5.7%)
1930	56,083	13,343 (23.8%)	4502 (8.0%)
1931	59,595	15,346 (25.8%)	3279 (5.6%)
1932	60,401	16,229 (26.9%)	2828 (4.7%)
1933	59,375	16,379 (27.6%)	2835 (4.8%)
1934	56,479	15,918 (28.2%)	2585 (4.6%)
1935	54,447	15,778 (29.0%)	2295 (4.2%)
1936	56,560	14,052 (24.9%)	2485 (4.4%)
1937	55,621	14,327 (25.7%)	2364 (4.2%)
1938	61,234	10,869 (17.8%)	4478 (7.3%)

Note: The figures in parentheses indicate the percentage of the total number of graduates.

According to Shimizu Yoshiro, a classic authority on Japan's exam system, due to the chronic bottleneck in entering university and the growing number of *rônin*, *juku* business began to prosper. From the end of the Taisho (1912–26) to the beginning of the Showa Era (1926–89), Japan's *yobiko* were established one after another in Japan to cater to growing demand (Shimizu, 1957: 42).

Shimizu (1957) observes that most of the *juku* and *yobiko* evolved from three sources: (1) traditional private schools (*shijuku*); (2) tutoring classes attached to middle schools; and (3) universities or vocational schools that set up schools for exam preparation. This should have been a protracted, slow process starting from the early prewar period. During the initial phase when the academic *juku* were being formed, it was more likely that *juku* or *yobiko* were converted from the formal *shijuku* with a Confucian tradition. Due to the informal nature of *juku*, however, we know very little about their number and size, and have very little detailed information on how they were run. A conservative estimation may put the number of these *juku* in the region of 700.[22] It is reasonable to imagine that one of these *juku* would not be very different from what Rohlen (1980) observed in Fukuoka in 1968:

[22] One reason for the lack of statistics about the total number of *juku* in Japan is that many of them were not officially accredited (Ogura, 1987). Some approximate

[The *juku*] was conducted by my landlady, a former schoolteacher. The twelve or so students that showed up each day belonged largely to nearby shopkeepers' families who were too busy to help their children with their homework. There was something of a daycare center quality about the operation. The neighborhood provided precious few things to do or places for elementary school children to play. My landlady instructed the children using their school textbooks and focused on the regular assignments their teachers had given them for the next day. Seated at makeshift benches placed on *tatami*, they solved problems, wrote characters, and recited facts together. It was not a well-planned or crisply run program and often it seemed to be more and more confused than the teacher (not to mention her tenant) could handle. Most *juku*, large or small, trace their roots to such simple beginnings. (215)

This observation may well be an ethnographic sketch of a Japanese *juku* class in the prewar period as well.

The history of *yobiko* in Japan can be traced as early as 1894 (Tsukada, 1991). According to Ikuo Amano (1990: 77–9), the gap between middle school and university was the primary reason for the advent of the *yobiko* schools. Noteworthy is the language discrepancy: the early institutions of higher education all conducted their classes in foreign languages, whereas Japanese was used in middle schools. The ambitious young people who aspired to university usually dropped out of the prefectural middle schools after a few years to take up study in one of the private schools where English was emphasized. It was only in those schools that they could obtain the qualifications required for passing the college exams. Until the end of the 1870s, most of these private schools were categorized as middle schools. However, as Amano argues, they were the forerunners of today's preparatory schools. The Japanese examination industry thus came into the foreground together with the establishment of the modern school system, and has 'enjoyed a history of over one hundred years' (Amano, 1990: 78–80).

However, it was, as cited earlier, somewhere between 1925 and the 1930s that *yobiko* began to crop up notably (Shimizu, 1957). Of the three largest *juku*-cum-*yobiko* corporations, two were founded before WWII: Sundai Yobiko was built as early as 1919, and Kawaijuku in 1933. While we do not have historical data available to describe this expansion, by the middle of the 1930s the highly developed, large *yobiko* had already been established. In this regard, one rare source of information was the special magazines for exam-taking students. *The Examination Journal (Juken Junhô)*, issued by the Obunsha Publishing Company, is one major publication in this field. Apart from the latest news on college admission, exam trends, and keys to tricky problems, the Journal also carried a rich pop literature that reflected the 'test culture' and student life. The centrefold cartoon picture (*manga*) in the 1936 issue (Vol. 6, No. 25) presented a

---

estimation is however possible. In JMOE (1977) it is indicated that, by 1977, 3.4 per cent of the *juku* in Japan were built before 1946. If we presume the total number of *juku* in 1977 was 22,000 (Rohlen, 1980: 213), then we may estimate that, by the end of WWII, there were at least more than 700 *juku* (= 22,000 × 3.4%).

bird's-eye view of a crowded, bustling *yobiko*. Its campus resembles in every way a fully developed middle school in Japan:

> The entrance to this *yobiko* school was an iron gate hinged on two concrete gateposts. In the school, students wearing clothes of all sorts, kimonos, middle school uniforms or jackets kept piling in. At the entrance, the honourable principal in a stiff, dark pin-striped suit bowed to the incoming students, chanting: 'Welcome! Welcome!' There was a lawn in the campus. On both sides of the walkway were two-storey buildings, the type found in middle schools. In the big classrooms, students were taking their mock tests (*moshi*). Each classroom accommodated about 40–50 students. One student in the picture had to take his test outside, because the room was fully packed.[23]

The high institutionalization of the *yobiko* school, its building, its class arrangement, and its popularity were quite close to those of the 1990s. The picture enables us to recreate the prewar *yobiko* with ethnographic data in historical mode. Meanwhile, its genre was comic, and the terse narratives printed in the 'balloons' satirize the exam system:

> In the testroom, one student jumped from his chair, crying: 'I have done all the questions!' This shocked his neighbour so much that he forgot all his answers. One student was sharpening his pencil with a huge samurai sword, which was an auspicious legacy from his ancestors. At the corner, a vibrating alarm clock was ringing: 'You have 30 minutes left!' A 'balloon' beside a bespectacled student with a long beard read: 'I have been a *rônin* 43 times!' In a distant window, a student was watching a black crow on the roof, sighing: 'How I wish to be you! A bird does not have to take exams!'

This picture, half-descriptive and half-comical, is valuable and useful here as it reflects the life, thoughts and tension of the students facing exams. It also helps to reconstruct an overall picture of the cram business in Japan prior to 1945: a large number of small-sized, family-run *juku* dotted Japan, reminiscent of the ancient village schools; modern tutoring academies also burgeoned, growing in size and number after the late 1920s. In the *Examination Journal*, similar pictures, large or small, appeared frequently. They depicted minute facets of the hectic life style of young students (especially *rônin*): how they travelled by train from one school to the next for exams, how they crammed at their dorms, and how they tried one-hundred-and-one ways to improve the efficiency of their learning. This pop art presentation pieced together a mosaic of the vigorous life stimulated by exams.

---

[23] This and the following narrative passages are my description based on the picture in Obunsha, *Juken Junhô* (The examination journal), (Tokyo: Obunsha), 6(25): 88–9.

History of tutoring schools in Taiwan

Modern education in Taiwan was started by the Japanese, and so were the tutoring academies. The word for 'tutoring academy' is *buxiban*, meaning 'the class of supplementary education'. During Japanese rule, schools set up for supplementary education mainly included Japanese language schools, youth training institutes, and workshops that taught a variety of vocational skills.

Japanese Language Tutoring Schools (*riyü chuanxisuo*) established by the Government-General in 1895 were acknowledged as the first tutoring academies in Taiwan (Leng, 1977). By 1896, the Schools had campuses at fourteen places, including Taipei. Later on, Chinese and some courses on common knowledge of modern life were also included in the curriculum. In 1899, by the Rescript on Common Schools (*kô-gakkô*), most of the schools were closed down, and their facilities were transferred to the primary schools. As a result, private *buxiban* teaching the Japanese language sprouted up everywhere to fill the vacuum that Japanese tutoring schools had left. These *buxiban* were warmly encouraged and supported by the Japanese. In 1930, the Government-General transformed the privately run *buxiban* into a public management system. The curricula of *buxiban* also became generalized: while Japanese remained the main teaching content, it gradually became a tool for people to learn sports, music, arithmetic, and knowledge used in everyday life (Leng, 1977).

Another early type of *buxiban* was the Youth Training Institutes (*Qingnian Xünlian Suo*). In 1925, the Youth Institutes were only open to Japanese youth, and their role was social education focused on moral values and patriotism. In 1932 Taiwanese-oriented Institutes were set up. Their courses included a wide range of subjects, such as moral training (*shûshin*), Japanese language, history, geography, physics, chemistry, maths and music, as well as trade business, industrial skills, etc. Compared to the Language Schools, Training Institutes were much more normalized and played multiple roles in adult supplementary education.

In addition, there were a host of other types of supplementary education attuned to people's different needs and working schedules. These included night schools, housewives' seminars and academic lectures. They taught mechanics, electricity, commerce, accounting, sewing, tailoring, and even the Taiwanese vernacular. After World War II, all Japanese schools were shut down. But the effect of Japanese supplementary schooling should not be underestimated. As non-formal education, it had tremendously raised the level of literacy, basic vocational skill and knowledge of modern life. Its influence on postwar supplementary education was equally tremendous. The new Nationalist regime in Taiwan soon realized the demand for supplementary education. They started with Mandarin Chinese Language Schools, followed by vocational education, education for the uneducated (*shixüe minzhong*), correspondence, and tertiary-level supplementary education.

The genesis of *hakwon*, a Korean version

It is interesting to note that, given strong political and ideological disapproval and control, self-justification or legitimacy has been the lifeline of the *hakwon* in Korea. This is demonstrated in the way the history of academic *hakwon* is presented by the Hankook Hakwon Chong Yunhaphwe (HHCY) or the 'Unified Association of *Hakwon* of Korea'. The genesis of early *hakwon* was traced to the first Danish-style Farming-Movement School set up by the YMCA in 1929. Schools of similar nature – defined as *hakwon* by HHCY – were later opened in eighteen cities across Korea. They taught not only farming and agriculture, but foreign languages, ethics and nationalism. During 1920–34, a period of Japanese colonial rule, these *hakwon* held altogether 60 ten-day training sessions, and 40,000 people participated. They widened the international perspective of local people and they became the cradle of many national leaders. Admittedly, however, a yawning difference exists between those missionary-type training schools and today's exam-oriented academic *hakwon*. What appears evident is a conscientious search by *hakwon* owners for a decent ancestral lineage that would earn them respect and esteem.

It should be noted that the tutoring academies specifically established for the entrance exams were not found in prewar Taiwan and Korea. This was first because the tutoring academies established in the two colonies were harshly supervised and controlled by the colonizers. They strictly followed the stipulations made by Japanese rescripts. Even in Japan the government frowned upon the *rônin* phenomenon and *yobiko* life, although they could not do much about them. In the colonies, however, they were not likely to issue permission for this kind of 'waste of time and energy'. Secondly, as cited, for a Taiwanese or Korean to enter middle school or university in the colonies was not merely an academic matter. It hinged heavily on ethnic origin and political status. For that reason, there was not much impetus for students to cram for exams. Thirdly, for Taiwanese and Koreans, the standard of living was generally a lot lower than for Japanese. Average families therefore could not afford expensive extracurricular schooling and one or two years of *rônin* life. The rich Taiwanese/Korean families would simply send their children to Japan if they wanted them to get a good education. With that alternative in their minds, it did not seem worthwhile to be a *rônin* in the under-developed colonies.

A DISCUSSION

In early Meiji Japan, the imperial exam system, as Rohlen (1983) emphasizes, is a grand solution to a dilemma between modernity and national culture. As a group-oriented society, Japan can 'choke on its own narrow particularism if it does not have well-entrenched mechanisms that counterbalance its powerful tendencies to allocate rewards and favors on the basis of personal affiliation' (ibid.). That 'solution' was an important upshot of Westernization, accomplished through constitutionalization and legalization. This was part of a process of Eurocentric globalization, the sweeping tendency to isomorphism that has 'ritualized' many aspects of education worldwide (Ramirez and Boli, 1987; DiMaggio and Powell, 1983). The vigour and fidelity of this systemic emulation was in blossom as early as in the 1872 Fundamental Code of Education (*Gakusei*), as discussed at the beginning of this chapter (see Table 2.22).

Table 2.22 Elements of the new school system drawn from Western systems. *Source*: Donald H. Shively, *Tradition and Modernization in Japanese Culture* (Princeton University Press, 1971), 48.

Country	Provisions included in the new school system	Percentage
France	64	43.5
Germany	39	26.5
Netherlands	17	11.6
England	11	7.5
America	9	6.1
Russia	1	0.7
Other	6	4.1
Total	147	100

The data in Table 2.22 show that the modernization of Japanese education is heavily imbued with Westernization, which was selective and country-based. In that sense, isomorphism necessarily encompasses a variety of scenarios and models in Europe, which could not be summarized into a uniform pattern. In the case of the imperial exam system the model is Prussian in particular. And yet, we cannot call it 'Germanization' instead of Westernization, because that would obscure the universal attributes of those models, such as constitutionalism, rationality and capitalism.

Modern systems of exams were not severed from the Oriental past. The Qing imperial exams were officially abolished in 1905, but exams of a similar nature were, however, held in the same year to identify qualified officials (Chang, 1932; Sheng, 1958). The old Korean and Japanese systems also long predated the European experience, although their accessibility was much more limited than in China. By at least the early eighth century, both countries already had an exam system modelled on the *keju* system (Amano, 1990; Ji, 1992). The 'Chinese Plan' to establish a *keju*-style system, ratified before the 'Prussian Plan' by the Japanese body politic, serves as a modern testimony to the need for that tradition. That tradition is a lion's den of heritage, which I circumscribe as a 'Cultural Sphere of East Asia' (Fairbank, 1968; Nishito, 1973; Gao, 1984; Vandermeersch, 1987). In my argument, it constitutes not only Confucianism, but also a vestige of Oriental administrative and legal laws (*lüling*), Chinese sciences, Mahayana Buddhism, a Chinese version of the religion, and to cap it all, the Chinese language. The legacy of the past, significantly revived during the colonial rule of the Japanese empire, can now no longer be seen as no more than a liability, as Max Weber hypothesized.

Given the important nature of the convergence of Western models and Eastern continuity, we need a hypothetical label for it to do justice to both contributors to East Asia today. I thus use the term 'dimorphism', which affirms that modernization is a process of fusion, when world culture and local culture together shape the modernity. Dimorphism is not a substitute for the institutionalistic 'isomorphism'; it only serves as its important and indispensable modification.

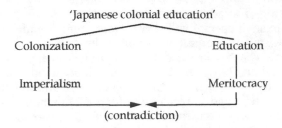

Figure 2.7 The deep structure of 'Japanese colonial education'.

The histories of education in East Asian societies have been intertwined. The apogee of this relationship was the Japanese colonial empire where Japan forced its influence on Taiwan and Korea. Meyers and Peattie (1984) describe these colonial structures as an 'anomaly', as the cultural heritage that Japan shared with its subject peoples was unique among the imperialist powers. Hence, the Japanese assimilation policy betrayed an inherent self-contradiction. In principle, the entrance exams for colonial schools were surprisingly 'meritocratic' and 'egalitarian'; Japanese and Taiwanese or Koreans were segregated only by Japanese language proficiency. Yet, in reality, the system had two ethnic tracks. Though some Taiwanese performed better than Japanese in the entrance exams, decisive favour was given to Japanese applicants. This resulted in the paradox of Japanese students going to imperial universities in Taipei and Seoul, while students from the colonies went to Japan where their ethnic origin was less of a barrier to getting into colleges.

What confuses our reasoning is not the reality itself. Rather, it is our classification and our language. 'Japanese colonial education', either as a research topic or as a historical reality, has semantically two analytical dimensions at the deep structure, as schematized in Figure 2.7.

There is no doubt that during colonial rule education was highly instrumental. It aimed to subdue patriotism, to justify colonial domination, and to produce a loyal workforce in the Japanese empire. All these were the logical pursuit of an imperialist power. However, education in Taiwan and Korea was a necessary extension of modern education in Japan, which was built upon the fundamental principles of meritocracy and egalitarianism. When colonialism took over education, the latter then was distorted to serve the interest of colonizers. In this perspective, we may see better why colonial students might get less discriminatory treatment in Japan: because education there was not dominated by the unrelenting laws of colonialism.

The analytical framework also helps us to compare the prewar exam systems of Japan, Korea and Taiwan in search of their commonalities and differences. Education in the colonies was a carbon copy of the Japanese system; the signs of duplication were visible everywhere, including the selection system. Our analysis of entrance policy and requirements has found no major discrepancy among the three systems. Each year, information on applications and entrance exams for schools in Japan and in Taiwan, Korea or occupied China was publicized together. The uniformity of the information gives one an impression that all were Japanese schools, without exception. The admission ticket was pure and simple: exam scores. Our study of exam papers for Tokyo, Taipei and Seoul Universities also shows a high degree of similarity and standardization.

The selection systems in the colonies betrayed a major difference from the Japanese system, however. Both documentary evidence and scholarly literature point to a major non-exam channel. Apparently, that might well give a convenient leverage to Japanese in favour of themselves.

That suspicion was confirmed by Taiwanese historians. There was a yawning divide between Japanese and local people in Taiwan and Korea, which was quite different from the situation of Koreans and Taiwanese in Japan. Despite improvement in later years, children were segregated throughout colonial rule. The merit system was severely twisted by an unofficial, but firmly implemented, quota system in favour of the Japanese.

As time passed, the operation of the system did undergo changes for the better. The exam system paved the pathway to advanced education for a small number of Taiwanese and Koreans. The colonial rulers had to reform sooner or later, because the principles of meritocracy and egalitarianism were the legitimate basis on which Japanese education rested.

As expressed in Figure 2.8, the 1922 Educational Rescript marked the start of a slow-paced progress towards integration and growth. That resulted in Taiwanese/Koreans gaining a greater chance of post-elementary schooling. The reform grudgingly reduced some of the colonial impact in the field of education, but it was still far from satisfactory in the eye of the local population. The Japanese achieved great things in colonial education, but that alone could not pacify the relentless struggle to overthrow colonial domination.

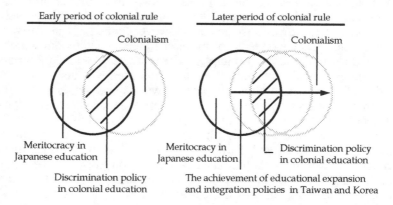

Figure 2.8 The effect of colonialism on the educational systems in East Asia (Korea and Taiwan) during Japanese colonial rule.

It needs to be clarified here that what Taiwanese and Koreans detested was not Japanese education *per se*. It was the colonialism and imperialist drive which jeopardized the application and credibility of meritocracy. The anti-Japanese sentiment sprang from that dimension. On the educational dimension, ideals embodied in Japanese education have not been buried along with colonialism. They have been, I would argue, more appealing to the Taiwanese and Koreans than ever before.

The legacy of Japanese education in Taiwan and Korea is twofold. It is, first of all, physical and institutional: today's leading schools and universities are all inherited from the colonial age, the lasting effect of their administration; admission and management are also to a certain extent passed down. The legacy is also conceptual. The Japanized Confucian values of merit, revived during the Meiji era, have been the guiding concepts in teaching and learning. Japanese education planted the seed of meritocratic expectation, idealism, and hope of mobility. Once emancipated from colonialism, Taiwanese and Koreans aspired not only to fulfil the ideals that Japanese education had left behind, but also to outperform the Japanese.

The Japanese legacy has helped to shape the exam system on several accounts. Paramount is the status of the gatekeeper – achievement exams. A candidate's written response to a battery of problems is the sole criterion. Other means of measurement, such as interviews, recommendations or middle school grades, have been insignificant, if ever used. Next, as in the prewar period, there is a close credentialistic link between schools and élite positions, for which exams were the nodal points. Exam scores rank schools in order. The former Japanese imperial universities still sit at the top of this educational pyramid. Secondary schools are also ranked accordingly, depending on how efficiently they can have their students recruited by universities. In the final analysis, the Japanese-created public education in Taiwan and Korea took the exam system as its centrepiece. Today, exams are an epitome of knowledge, justice, impartiality and, moreover, social mobility.

For a further scrutiny, I moved from the macro-level of the system to the micro-level of the exam questions in World History and Mathematics. These were two areas where the Japanese wished to benefit from the West. For mathematics, the test design was kept unchanged throughout Japanese colonial rule. The problems were essentially abstract, hard and highly competitive. It should be noted, however, that prospective students were identified at the middle school level, which is in marked contrast to the maths exams for university today, as everything before senior high school may appear in the test paper.

World history was an important tool for exploring Western civilization. After the Pacific War erupted, however, education in history took up a definitely new role: propaganda. It helped to reveal the 'ulterior truth' of Western imperialism, and the significance of the Nipponcentric 'Great East Asia Co-prosperity'. Meanwhile, evidence also points to a need to draw lessons from the world powers about how they managed their colonies, although this was more discernible in the exam content for imperial universities in the colonies. This seems to suggest a different emphasis in selecting the élite, depending on whether the prospective student would be working in Japan's homeland or overseas.

The high rate of competition and elimination generated by exams has two inevitable by-products in Japan, Taiwan and Korea: the exam-repeater (*rônin*) and the tutoring academy. This was also the case for prewar Japan. Data show that, because of the austere competition rate, one third of the middle school graduates became *rônin* each year. It is estimated that by the close of WWII there were already hundreds of academic *juku* schools. *Yobiko* began to crop up in the mid-1930s.

The genesis of supplementary education in Korea and Taiwan is also traced back to colonial times. Unlike in Japan, however, there is no evidence to indicate the organization of the tutoring academy for exams in prewar Taiwan and Korea. This absence, I would hypothesize, was mainly historical. First, the tutoring academies established in the two colonies were harshly confined and controlled by the colonizers. The Japanese rulers would not support and tolerate cram schools which they perceived as a waste of time and energy. Secondly, for a Taiwanese or Korean, to enter middle school or university was not simply an academic matter – it was predicated on ethnic origin and political status. Therefore, there was no great impetus for students to cram hard. Thirdly, as the standard of living of Taiwanese/Koreans was lower than Japanese, tutoring would be too expensive to afford. Hence, there must have been very little demand for the cram enterprise.

CHAPTER 3

A comparative history of university entrance examinations: from 1945 to now

The American way of life cannot survive unless other peoples who want to adopt that pattern throughout the world can do so without fear and in the hope of success.
– *Harry S. Truman, cited from Frank Gibney,* The Pacific Century: America and Asia in a Changing World

Student: Teacher, this question in the history exam has a problem.
Teacher: How come? Let me see – it says 'the Imperial Civil Exams were abolished in Guangxü 31 [1905 AD].' What is wrong with that?
Student: It is not true, ...
Teacher: Why not?
Student: They have not been abolished at all!

– *Kuling,* Spending one's entire life in exams, *1994*

The year 1945 was a year of rejuvenation. It testified how alterable the course of history could be. The Japanese colonial empire crumbled, which was, remark Eckert *et al.* (1990), 'unimaginable only a few years earlier'. Nations, though war-torn, were finally set free, colonizers and colonized alike. The War, and the end of it, affected the economic, political and educational structures in unprecedented rapidity and scale.

Life did not turn easier immediately after 1945. In China, the clouds of civil war were quickly gathering, as people celebrated the victory of the Anti-Japanese War. The Korean War between Communist and non-Communist forces lasted from 1950 to 1953. Japan was still in ruins, cities largely destroyed, the economy wrecked. In Japan, the devastation extended to the psyche of the population, unprepared for defeat, and never having been occupied by a foreign victor (Schirokauer, 1989). Nevertheless, an entirely new chapter of independence, peace and prosperity gradually began.

In the postwar era, universal education, a steady population increase, gradual economic growth, a rise in living standards, and a credentialistic interest and investment in children's education, all exerted a mounting pressure on the entrance exam system for the universities, where places for students were relatively stable. It should be noted in particular that, even at the time when, especially in the private sector, universities underwent rapid expansion, competition was not miraculously alleviated. The underlying reason was that, in the society of credentialism, the universities have a twofold function: (1) the advancement of education – to learn and know more; and (2) the social redistribution of the valuable 'commodities' – power, money and status. Within a population, only a very small minority was spurred on in life by pure intellectual curiosity and pursuit. The vast majority sought education with some particular secular interest and anticipation in mind.

In society, the 'commodities' are limited in amount. When the universities grow in number, the chances of higher education increase. But, those 'commodities', I would argue, generally do not increase in the same proportion. An inevitable consequence was the 'depreciation' of the value of higher education. It followed that 'university' did not mean much for a prospective candidate, unless it promised its graduates 'commodities'. Hence, the aspiration to enter *any* university turned into one for *some* high-ranking university. In a meritocratic world, to reduce competitiveness through a proliferation of opportunities for higher education is all but an illusion.

In this chapter, I continue my search for the commonalities and differences among the exam systems of Japan, Korea and Taiwan, similarly to what has been done for the prewar period. In addition, I attempt to tackle a major issue commonly framed and posed in the discourse: why, through numerous reforms in peace and war, did the exam systems in East Asia remain largely intact and 'intractable'? Given the complexity of the postwar exam system and its effects, this chapter focuses only on the history of exams, leaving the other issues to the succeeding chapters.

The postwar Occupation, reconstruction, and economic take-off were changing landscapes of socio-political cultures, against which I describe the remoulding of the exam systems, their trends and patterns. Then I move the histories of the three systems into an intra-regional, comparative framework in search of any parallel or non-parallel, and convergence or divergence. I next discuss how the university entrance exam, as an integral part of higher education, has an impact on the hierarchical structure of the university system. Finally, I summarize my preliminary findings with reference to the entrance exams as history.

THE BEGINNING OF NEW EXAMS IN EAST ASIA

The historical influence of modern Western education on East Asia cannot be overemphasized. The wonder at and admiration for the new Western civilization swept over Japan ever since early Meiji. Johann Pestalozzi, Friedrich Froebel and John Dewey were not simply names of note to

Asians.[1] They symbolized genuine education in a new era. And yet, it is fair to state that no impact was comparable to that of the postwar period, highly condensed in the form of education reform, especially for Japan and Korea. The school systems were restructured, the Chinese character-based written language was subjected to some fundamental revamping, and new ideas were injected into the existing systems of thought. Exam systems were no exception. In fact, they bore the very brunt of the reform thrust. A detailed review of this period would generate us some useful insight.

World War II destroyed the Japanese empire and removed Japanese influence from the region for the next twenty years. Taiwan and Korea were liberated from the shackles of Japanese colonialism. The atomic bomb and the steel skeleton of the Memorial Cenotaph in Hiroshima came to symbolize the superiority of the US in almost every field. Western system democracy, epitomized by American idealism, left an enduring impact on popular thought and on most institutions of public life.

Before moving into this new era, let us begin with the baseline portrait of the new exam systems immediately after 1945. In Japan, the very first postwar entrance exams were given in March 1946; these were not yet subjected to American overhaul and censorship, since the US Educational Mission had just arrived in Japan in the same month. These school-held achievement exams were so similar to the prewar ones that, for a while, it looked as if the old system would resume its work as before. However, it proved to be short-lived. In March 1946, the US Education Mission of more than a score of American educators came to Japan for a 30-day visit. They were all prominent educators, but their ideas of Japanese education were largely dependent upon a slim 91-page brochure, a stopgap publication issued by the Headquarters. One of its purposes was to cram the Mission members with the history of Japanese education from the earliest time to the Occupation (Trainor, 1983). Based on this limited intramural information, the Mission submitted its working report in less than a month. In criticizing the Japanese-style exams, it proposed that 'knowledge must be acquired that is broader than available in a single prescribed textbook or manual, and deeper than can be tested by stereotyped examinations'.[2] As a result, the Headquarters articulated its grave concern for the old Japanese exam system. In consequence, less than one year after the mission arrived, a new system was planned and implemented which heralded a drastic change in the entire structure of examinations (Masuda *et al.*, 1961). In 1947, the entrance exams

---

[1] Johann Pestalozzi (1746–1827), Swiss educational reformer. His theories laid the foundation of modern elementary education. He believed that choice of pedagogical method should be based on the individual's development and concrete experience. Friedrich Froebel (1782–1852), German educator and founder of the Kindergarten system. He stressed pleasant surroundings, self-activity, and physical training for children. John Dewey (1859–1952), American philosopher and educator. He rejected authoritarian teaching methods, regarding education in a democracy as a tool to enable the citizen to integrate his or her culture and vacation usefully.

[2] See 'Report of the [First] US Education Mission: Digest, March 1946', in Beauchamp and Vardaman (1994).

for higher schools included both an achievement test and a newly added IQ test. Unlike the achievement test which was designed to measure students' mastery of school-taught knowledge, the new test tried to predict one's academic prospects. Two years after the Occupation was over, the IQ test was abolished.

In Taiwan, the Chinese Nationalist government took over the island from the Japanese in 1945. Two years later, the postwar entrance exam method (*zhaosheng banfa*) was issued in 1947, which was similar in structure to the formal system during Japanese rule. The written entrance exams were the only substantive gauge for selecting students, and they were given by individual schools. The Ministry of Education, however, stipulated the required subjects for university entrance exams. For humanities, they are: Chinese, English, Maths, Civics, History, Geography and Physics/Chemistry (TMOE, 1987: 1419–20). No oral interview, recommendation or school grades were needed.

In Korea, from 1945 to 1953, the entrance exams were administered and supervised by individual universities. The subjects in the exams included Korean, English, Maths, Social Studies, and at least one optional vocational course (KMOE, 1992b). In the early stage the admission quotas were not filled and as an encouragement, the suspension of military service was offered to students. The privilege of exemption later gave rise to unqualified admissions and illegal arrangements involving many university administrations. The latter cost the universities their credibility and legitimacy in giving the entrance exams autonomy (KMOE, 1992b; Lee, 1993).

Among the three new postwar examination systems, the Japanese one was perhaps most Americanized, simply because the structural overhaul of the system was designed and enforced by Americans during the Occupation. If the Japanese had been left alone to rebuild their education, the exam system would have had a lot in common with the Korean and Taiwanese ones: the achievement test working as the exclusive gatekeeper for university admission, the basic knowledge (language, maths and social science) used for quality control, and individual universities being responsible for the administration of the selection exams. That likelihood of similarity was evidenced by the 1946 exams held in Japan. In the new era, as we will see next, the commonalities among the three countries became salient.

JAPAN: THE MISSION OF AMERICAN PSYCHO-METRICIANS

In August 1945, when Japan surrendered, the majority of students were still hidden away in the rural and suburban areas because of air raids. The deserted schools were reopened in September 1945. With all the chaotic aftermath and devastation, by March the next year students were ready to sit for the higher-school entrance exams. As the first exams administered after the War, the unusual event drew much attention from the public and press. This was what an on-site correspondent saw at the First Higher School when the 1946 entrance exams began:

> At the Komada campus, trees had turned green and fragrant cherry flowers were in smiling blossom, quivering in the breeze coming from the South Pacific. Before long, a huge crowd of exam candidates gathered in front of the School.

The overwhelming majority of them were soldier-turned *rônin* in faded army uniforms. Among them, some still looked young, like kids ... Their average age, I learned, was 21. The faces of these *rônin* glowed with aspiration to raise Japan up again by science. I could see they were very serious and that made them promising and trustworthy. (Obunsha: *Keisetsu Jidai*, March 1946: 18)

That year, for 400 positions at the First Higher School, a total of over 3500 people applied which forced the pass rate down to one in ten. For the 32 official higher schools, there were more than 55,000 applicants in 1946 (Obunsha, NSMS, 1946). Many had served in the Imperial Army, Navy or Air Force. Considering the grand-scale damage of the War, one is easily astonished at the resilience, speed of recovery, and obsession with exams.

The Occupation reform: The American IQ test, et cetera (1945–63)

The Americans assigned to reconstruct Japan were a naively confident group that neither questioned the superiority of their own approach nor understood much about Japan (Rohlen, 1983). American educators criticized the wartime Japanese system in the following words:

The system was based on a nineteenth-century pattern which was highly centralized, providing one type of education for the masses and another for the privileged few. It held that at each level of instruction there is a fixed quantum of knowledge to be absorbed, and tended to disregard differences in the ability and interests of pupils. Through prescription, textbooks, examinations and inspection, the system lessened the opportunities of teachers to exercise professional freedom. The measure of efficiency was the degree to which standardization and uniformity were secured.
– 'Report of the US Education Mission to Japan', 1946, cited from Rohlen (1983), 64.

Recently published documents of Occupation policy, most of which used to be top secret, help us to reconstruct the first chapter of the new democratic Japan. The resolution of the Allies to remould Japan into a democratic society relied heavily on a large dose of American educational thinking. This was an intriguing historical chapter in that in essence it was an almost unprecedented experiment in the application of great ideas. Its cardinal goals were the 'democratization, demilitarization and decentralization' of Japan (Beauchamp and Vardaman, 1994). Not only did American educators dictate the way Japanese education should be reshaped, but as a result, intense pressure was exercised on many key aspects of Japanese culture (Hall and Beardsley, 1965). Or, as Rohlen (1983) notes, 'wherever the prewar system differed from the American ideal, it was undemocratic and unprogressive'.

The reform of the entrance exam system was under the jurisdiction of the Civil Information and Education Section (CIES), one of the special staff sections attached to the General Headquarters located in Tokyo.[3]

---

[3] The following discussion on the exam reform during the Occupation draws largely on Masuda *et al.* (1961).

Set up on 22 September 1945, CIES dealt with the Ministry of Education. According to the diagnosis made by the Americans, Japan's system of student selection and promotion lacked an understanding of psychometric theory. Under pressure from CIES, Japan's Ministry of Education established in 1947 the Committee for Formulating Intelligence Quotient (IQ) Examination Questions. Its cardinal goal was to 'couple democratic principles with modern psychology and with American selection methods'.[4] In 1947, an IQ exam (*Chinô Kensa*, or *Interichento Tesuto*) was given for the first time in Japan. In the same year, its name was altered to the 'Scholastic Adaptability Test' (*Shingaku Tekisei Kensa*).[5] This was a lengthy test paper, composed of three categories: general, human science and natural science. Both its design and formulation adhered closely to the Americans' guidance and recommendations (*shidô to jogen*) expressed by Vivian Edmiston.[6] In addition to the achievement exams, it became a mandatory basis for all selection to the tertiary level of education. All national universities, and later all universities, including local, public and private ones, used these test scores for selecting entrants (Tadashi, 1988; Masuda *et al.*, 1961).

Now, due to the salience of the psychometrics in the American-led reform, we need to pause here for a moment, looking at some basic concepts about exams. 'Test' or 'exam' is a measuring instrument for assessing and documenting student learning. Industry and government alike have been prodigious users of tests for selecting workers. Research workers often rely on tests to translate theoretical concepts (e.g., intelligence) into experimentally useful measures. The commonly used tests in the educational field are the achievement test, aptitude test and IQ test. All three tests are single-occasion, one-dimensional, timed exercises. Otherwise, their difference is comprehensive.

The **achievement test** is a device used to evaluate the individual's present academic or vocational skill. It is used to measure students' 'school taught' learning in such areas as reading, writing, maths and science.

When intended to predict relatively distant future behaviour (e.g., success in school), it is called an **aptitude test** (Wick, 1973; Hart, 1994). The aptitude test is the examination that attempts to determine and measure those characteristics of a person that are regarded as indices of his or her capability to acquire, through future training, some specific set of responses (intellectual, motor, and so on). The test assumes that people differ in their special abilities and that these differences are related in a predictable manner to their later achievements.

---

[4] Vivian Edmiston, 'The selection measures used for the applicants to the higher level schools', see the 'Annexed Documents', pp. 294–8 in Masuda *et al.* (1961).

[5] *Shingaku Tekisei Kensa* is commonly translated as the 'Scholastic Aptitude Test'. See, for example, Tadashi Hidano, 'Admission to higher education in Japan', pp. 9–25 in Heyneman and Fägerlind (1988).

[6] The form and content of *Shingaku Tekisei Kensa* is discussed in Chapter 4, 'What kind of exams? Questions of world history and mathematics in the three countries'.

Both achievement and aptitude tests may be put under the rubric of the 'maximum performance test'. Their major distinction lies in 'time': the achievement test measures what the student *has* learned up to the moment of testing; the aptitude test measures the student's *ability* to learn in the future. However, in the eyes of the psychometrician, their distinction might just be murky. 'This similarity should not be too surprising', rationalizes John Wick (1973): 'for how could anyone possibly predict what a student can do or learn without measuring what he has done or learned? You must measure current achievement level to predict future performance level' (pp. 152–3).

The **IQ test,** or **intelligence test**, is designed to measure the capacity to make abstractions, to learn, and to deal with novel situations. The most widely used intelligence tests include the Stanford–Binet Intelligence Scale and the Wechsler scales. The Stanford–Binet Scale is the American adaptation of the original French Binet–Simon intelligence test; it was first introduced in 1916 by Lewis Terman, a psychologist at Stanford University. The individually administered test, revised in 1937, 1960 and 1972, evaluates persons two years of age and older and is designed for use primarily with children. It consists of an age-graded series of problems whose solution involves arithmetic, memory and vocabulary skills. The test is scored in terms of intelligence quotient, or IQ, a concept first suggested by German psychologist William Stern and adopted by Lewis Terman in the Stanford–Binet Scale.

The IQ was originally computed as the ratio of a person's mental age to his chronological (physical) age, multiplied by 100. Thus, if a child of 10 had a mental age of 12 (that is, performed on the test at the level of an average 12-year-old), then the child was assigned an IQ of $(12/10) \times 100$, or 120. A score of 100, for which the mental age equalled the chronological age, was average; scores above 100 were above average, scores below 100 were below average. The concept of mental age has fallen into disrepute, however, and few tests now involve the computation of mental ages. Yet many tests still yield an IQ; this figure is now computed on the basis of the statistical percentage of people who are expected to have a certain IQ.

Intelligence test scores follow an approximately 'normal' distribution, with most people scoring near the middle of the distribution curve and scores dropping off fairly rapidly in frequency away from the curve's centre. For example, on the IQ scale about two out of three scores fall between 85 and 115 and about nineteen out of twenty scores fall between 70 and 130. A score of about 130 or above is considered gifted, while a score below about 70 is considered mentally deficient or retarded. Intelligence tests have provoked a great deal of controversy about what kinds of mental abilities constitute intelligence and whether the IQ adequately represents these abilities, with debate centring on cultural bias in test construction and standardization procedures (Hanson, 1993; Herrnstein and Murray, 1994).

Given the enormous literature on and critique of educational measurement, the above account is cursory and over-simple. Still, it may be adequately helpful, when we analyse the substance of the American reform in Japan. The American-initiated SAT test in Japan, as cited, is an interesting phenomenon. Its name changed from 'IQ Test' to 'adaptability or aptitude test', but there was no substantive change in its IQ-type content.[7] It in fact remained largely an IQ test that aimed at measuring students' intelligence which was not associated with special achievement, and which was impossible to prepare. This vital principle, however, was later found questionable and unfulfilled in the test administered in Japan.

To administer the new system, the SAT supervising committees were set up at both the prefecture and county levels, with the president of the national universities acting as directors. After each exam, the sample questions and answers and information on overall scores were publicized and published in major newspapers. Students and parents naturally showed a keen interest in the new tests. Their new format, to which Japanese students were so unaccustomed, led to the postwar rise of cram schools (*yobiko*) and mock tests (*mogi shiken*), since university applicants needed to prepare themselves for the new competitive measure (Masuda *et al.*, 1961).

The SAT was used for about seven years. In 1955, at the end of the Occupation, it was entirely abolished. While the Americans were present, it was endowed with uncontested legitimacy and firm institutional support. In this sense, the SAT had every structural advantage to succeed. There also appeared to have been a close cooperation on both sides in educational circles. The Japanese embraced the Occupation-sponsored reforms and democracy. The American educational advisers were also flushed with a sense of mission and warmed by the realization that their views were being respected (Hall and Beardsley, 1965).

Why did it fail then? In my opinion, it was due to the deeply embedded factor of cultural and educational tradition. The erosion of the legitimacy of the American approach began early. Public criticism grew, until in 1952 people started to talk about its abolition. Harsh castigations appeared in newspapers and mass media. As a result, an *ad hoc* committee was organized, consisting of people in the fields of secondary and tertiary education, psychometrics and academia. Their deliberations led to the ultimate abolition of the SAT. Apart from budgetary problems, the main reasons and criticisms given by the Japanese were in the following areas:

1. *Validity.* The SAT failed to fulfil its goals as a psychometric measurement of innate ability. Innate ability was not supposed to be divisible into disciplines like human science, as was done in the SAT. Next, statistics showed that SAT scores could be significantly improved with preparation, which was contrary to the meaning of innate ability. Also, the SAT had an 'extremely low correlation' with higher school GPAs as well as the scores attained in the entrance achievement exams for university.
2. *Extra workload.* The SAT, together with achievement exams, turned out to be a double burden too heavy for students to bear in terms of psychological and physical stress and travel expenses.
3. *Lack of support.* The national and public universities, together with the higher schools, as the essential stakeholders, all exerted pressure and called for the abolition of the SAT (Masuda *et al.*, 1961).

---

[7] For a detailed discussion of the SAT test, refer to Chapter 4.

To verify statistically the criticism of the aptitude test is beyond the scope of this book, and to me it is only secondary in importance. What was essentially expressed behind all of the detailed criticisms was a deepening distrust of the American Occupational reforms by the Japanese. In retrospect, the fact that the guiding hand of postwar reforms belonged to the US Occupation authorities, and not the independent will of the Japanese people, later also gave the Japanese government an excuse to blunt the momentum of the reform and regain control over national education (Nakauchi et al., 1986).

The scepticism of the SAT was focused at the very core of its theoretical basis. The aptitude test or IQ test does not sample some important traits: performance on manual tasks, manual dexterity, vocational skills, creativity, motivation, personal characteristics (such as honesty, neatness, integrity, perseverance, promptness or orderliness), or anything about the person's social skills. The intelligence or aptitude test measures none of them. Each of the above is important for success in life (Wick, 1973). While the neglect or dismissal of these personal traits might be tolerated in the US (since the IQ test had been popular for a long period of time), in East Asian societies, some of these factors, especially motivation, perseverance, neatness, orderliness, etc., are highly appreciated and directly associated with that form of intelligence. For that reason, the intelligence test would be critically considered not only as a 'mismeasure of man', to cite the title of a bestseller book criticizing the IQ test, but as a mismatch for Japanese culture.

Eight years later in 1963, a non-profit institution called the Talent Development Institute was established. It offered three kinds of test: a scholastic aptitude, a vocational aptitude, and an achievement test. Though many upper-secondary schools used these scores for vocational guidance, only a few universities used the tests to select entrants. Universities would give their own entrance exams of achievement in a fashion not very different from the prewar situation. In this, Edwin Reischauer, ambassador to Japan in the Kennedy administration, notes that although the occupation focused its efforts on reforming education in Japan, it seems to have produced nothing but temporary confusion. He goes on to say:

> This astounding change [increase in the number of students in high schools and universities], which has been a determining factor in altering Japanese society, is a clear outgrowth of prewar trends toward developing a meritocracy of education and has been made possible primarily by Japan's postwar affluence. (Reischauer, in Wray and Conroy, 1983: 340)

The gate of two stages (1979–89)

In February 1971, the National University Association (NUA, *Kokudaikyô*) organized a special committee to investigate improvements in the selection system and the feasibility of the Joint First-Stage Achievement Test (JFSAT, *Kyôtsu ichiji shiken*) for national universities. It aimed to assess the overall scholastic attainment, to create and provide data about applicants for college, to relieve colleges from the ever-increasing workload creating and grading their own entrance examinations, and moreover, to simplify and rationalize the selection system (YTH, 1989; Schoppa, 1991). The NUA proposal for the reform was greatly encouraged by the Ministry of Education. At a conference held by the Ministry of Education, a plan was presented for

improving the college entrance examination system, including the introduction of a jointly administered achievement test (JMOE, 1992).

In November 1974, the NUA conducted its pilot test for the Joint Test
with approximately 3000 upper secondary school third-year students to
assess the results of the research. The ideological justification for a nationwide norm-referenced system of examination is reflected in the '1975
Proposals for the Reorganization of High Schools' drafted by the Education
and Culture Committee of the ruling Liberal Democratic Party. The
Proposals strongly advocated the reorganization of education according to
the government's ideology of ability (nôryoku shugi): 'The principle of
competition is the principle of human existence. In its absence progress is
inconceivable. Societies that fail to adopt constructions of ability in accord
with these truths are doomed to stagnate and perish' (Horio, 1988).

In May 1976 the Preliminary Institution for Research and Improvement
of the National University Entrance Examination was established at Tokyo
University with the objective of carrying out further research on the JFSAT.
In May 1977, the National Center for University Entrance Examinations was
established, and Mutsuo Kato, former president of Tohoku University, took
office as president of the Center. In December 1977, the Center and 120
national and local public universities collaborated on a simulation JFSAT for
upper secondary school third-year students; 63,609 applied for the test
(JMOE, 1992).

The JFSAT for national universities was finally administered for the first
time in 1979. The new examination required all applicants to be examined in
seven subjects from five subject areas (mathematics, science, Japanese
philology, social studies and a foreign language). Therefore, to prepare for
it, the students had to fill virtually all of the 90-odd units of their upper
secondary courses with the same broad selection of courses they had studied
(Schoppa, 1991). The second stage of examinations was individually developed, administered and graded by the faculties of the universities to which
students applied.

The JFSAT was designed to eliminate excessively difficult test-questions,
and to eradicate the 'examination hell' (shiken jigoku). Since its inception,
however, the test was criticized for differentiation of students based on
hensachi,[8] growing hierarchical ranking of colleges, and the overheating of
the 'examination war' (YTH, 1989).

The New National Center Test (1989–Now)

In this highly critical atmosphere, Japanese Prime Minister Nakasone made
examination reform one of his education reform promises in the 1983
elections and spoke of 'abolishing' the Joint Test exam on repeated
occasions after that date. Yet, he never actually spelled out what would
follow the abolition of the Joint Test. In 1984, the Ad Hoc Council on

---

[8] Hensachi, or 'deviation value' in English, is a Japanese norm-referenced grading
system initially based on the 1922 US IQ test. Through mock lists, it helps students
to monitor their probability of getting into schools of their choice. Since 1960,
hensachi has been widely used and referred to for education and employment
purposes in Japan. For the formula, see note 17.

Education (AHCE, *Rinkyôshin*), an advisory council, was set up under Nakasone's office. Paying close attention to the opinions of such concerned parties as the National University Association and the Private Universities Association, the Fourth Subcommittee of the AHCE led by Iijima Soichi quickly arrived at a strategy for reform. The plan was to reform the Joint Test system, which used to be limited to national and a few local public universities, so that all universities (including private) would be able to participate in a flexible manner. The new test was to be called the '*Kyôtsu Tesuto*' (Educational test). However, Nakasone's primary concern was the examination's role in limiting the creativity and diversity of Japanese students. He objected to the way in which examinations played such a large role in determining an individual's future. JFSAT, he believed, was the root of the standardization of Japanese education. Thus, he wanted the outright abolition of the standard university entrance examination. With each university thereby forced to develop its own test, the standardizing influence of the exam system would be mitigated.

Iijima could not accept Nakasone's proposal for several reasons. First, as a university official he represented an academic community which prized the ideal of a student trained in a broad range of school subjects encouraged by the existing Joint Test. He could see the need for some flexibility, but was not willing to abandon the ideal altogether. Second, he argued that neither students nor universities could deal with the workload required by a totally unstructured system of examinations. Students would not know what to study for, and university officials would have to go through the time-consuming process of drafting their own examinations. Most importantly, however, he represented the view that university officials ought to be able to determine their admission procedures themselves. His own plan had been worked out in detail with various university organizations and was purposely vague in order to leave the universities with some latitude to deal with the issue on their own (Schoppa, 1991).

In June 1985, the National Council on Educational Reform recommended the introduction of a new national examination to replace the Joint First-Stage Test. In February 1988, the University Entrance Examination Improvement Conference published the annual report on 'Improvement of University Entrance Examinations'. In April 1988 Mikio Arie, former president of Hokkaido University, took office as president of the National Center for University Entrance Examinations. Under his leadership, the Center began to prepare a new test for university entrance and to provide relevant information on individual universities. After intensive work for over a year, the first National Center Test for University Entrance Examinations (NCT, *Daigaku nyûshi senta shiken*) was given in January 1990 to replace the JFSAT (JMOE, 1992).

In the NCT, question-items are designed by the Expert Committee on Setting Test-Questions composed of 380 members – teachers from national, local public and private universities throughout Japan. The committee is divided into working groups according to each subject, and each working group holds a number of meetings over the year to set the final questions. The NCT is carried out at about 350 examination halls jointly held by the Center and colleges, each of which is linked to the Center by means of a communication system consisting of facsimile and telephone lines (JMOE, 1992).

EXAMS IN KOREA: ATTRITION WAR OF REFORMS

In contrast to Japan, where universities made a 'U-turn' from American-sponsored IQ tests to their own achievement test for entrance screening, in Korea university-based achievement exams were very much left undisturbed after 1945. That contrast was mainly caused by the policy difference that American occupation headquarters adopted towards Korea versus Japan. American policy orientation can be found in some confidential documents of the Occupation Headquarters, opened to the public only recently:

> ... Military Government has been purposely slow to change the system it found in Korea, for the policy has been to let the Koreans decide the educational system they want. Another important point is that the Koreans, having lived under Japanese rule for forty years and having been educated largely in Japanese schools either in Japan or Korea, are familiar with the Japanese system; in other words, the Korean view of the Japanese educational system is different from the American view. Indeed, one may accurately say that, aside from such changes as replacing the Japanese language with the Korean language and Japanese nationalism with Korean nationalism and Japanese teachers with Korean teachers, the Koreans have made no radical changes in the educational system they have lived with since 1905.[9]

These words suggest Americans' tolerance of and non-interference in Korean education, although they did not appreciate the system at all. They also indicate that, in the eyes of Americans, Japanese remnants were largely kept intact in the new Korean education. At any rate, Koreans were given a free rein, while in Japan, the exam system was a main target for the unflinchingly coercive reform carried out by the Allies.

Non-interference did not imply that new education was immune from the impact of Western educational thought. In fact, as is abundantly shown below, the reforms that the new Korean exam system underwent seem far more radical and bold than those in Japan and Taiwan. Since 1945, more than ten reforms on exams have been instituted in Korea, and most of them were drastic. Given their complexity, before I go into detail, a chronicle of the reforms in university entrance exams will be helpful:

1945–53	College-based Entrance Test (CET)
1954	National Unified Test (NUT) plus CET
1955–61	CETs or no testing
1962–3	National Entrance Test (NET)
1964–8	CET
1969–80	National Preliminary Test (NPT) plus CET
1981	NPT plus High School Scores (HSS)
1982–5	National Scholastic Achievement Test (NSAT) plus HSS
1986–7	NSAT plus HSS plus Essay Test (ET)
1988–93	NSAT plus HSS

---

[9] US Army Military Government in Korea (USAMGIK), 'History of Bureau of Education from 11 September 1945 to 28 February 1946', pp. 37–145 in Tae-Su Chung (1992).

The main events in this history, one may observe, have been the power shifts back and forth between the university and the government. To understand this untiring war of attrition for authority, let us start from 1945.[10]

Independent exams by individual universities (1945–53)

After the War was over, the US Army Military Government in Korea (USAMGIK) tried to use the American higher education system and policies as a model, and Korean universities started with a high degree of openness and autonomy. From the end of WWII to the Korean War (1950–3), new colleges were created, and the number of college students suddenly increased. After the Korean War, regional national universities in each province were built up to provide an opportunity for higher education to local students (J. S. Lee, 1993).

During that period, the official goal of Korean educational policy was first to set up an educational system appropriate to a free and democratic system and to eliminate the illiteracy of the majority of the people. This meant a focus on compulsory schooling. The college entrance system was a matter of comparatively little concern. Furthermore, since the impact of the Korean War overwhelmed all else soon after the establishment of the new government, naturally the problem of the college entrance system was pushed to the back of the queue. From 1945 to 1953, the entrance exams continued to be administered and supervised by individual universities. This College Entrance Test (CET) included physical examinations and interviews along with a written exam. The main sorter for admissions, a written exam, tested as many subjects as possible to normalize the high schools. Usually a CET required Korean, English, Maths and Social Studies with at least one optional vocational course being tested. The CET, based on an open and autonomous higher education policy, continued without much change through three years of US military rule and right up to the end of the Korean War (J. S. Lee, 1993).

In the early days of the new government, every college was frequently below quota because of the lack of admissible people, and a few years later, the autonomy granted to universities was being abused by recruitment beyond set quotas. The greatest problem during the CET period was the prevalent admission of the unqualified, and improper admission for military exemption during the Korean War. This generated grave scepticism concerning university autonomy. Public opinion criticized entrance tests that fell short of impartiality and equitable access. Therefore, in 1954, the National Unified Test (NUT) accompanied the CET. However, NUT was cancelled one year later. Except for 1962–3, the CET continued to be used until 1968 (J. S. Lee, 1993). From the above review, one can hardly detect any remarkable alteration in exam structure, except that the Japanese language was replaced with the Korean language. This echoes American comment in the confidential report cited earlier, that, after 1945, 'the Koreans made no radical changes in the educational system they have lived with since 1905'.

---

[10] For the Korean literature, my primary thanks go to Carl Porter for his generous and comprehensive help, with specific references to his highly faithful rendition of J. S. Lee's article cited subsequently.

Joint exam system: National Unified Test (NUT) plus CET (1954)

In the early days of the new government, colleges did not have enough students because of the lack of admissible people. A few years later, however, the autonomy granted to universities was being abused by excessive enrolment. The greatest problems were a prevalent admission of the unqualified and an improper admission for military exemption during the Korean War. As a result, serious doubt arose concerning university auto-nomy. Public criticism came from every sector of society, charging that CET entrance exams did not have a spirit of fairness or equal opportunity. Therefore, in 1954 the National Entrance Test (NET) was introduced. It was given prior to the university administered CET. The NET was a written test; passing was determined by a student's total scores in the tested subjects (J. S. Lee, 1993; KMOE, 1992b).

However, NET was soon criticized also for several reasons. It was set up without adequate prior consultation with the university authorities. The universities were thus not happy, taking NET as an infringement of univer-sity autonomy (J. S. Lee, 1993). It was also criticized for giving students an extra burden given the dual system of exams. Also, 'a considerable number of students from rich and high class families failed in the examination system' (KMOE, 1992b: 12). As a result, the NET was abolished very soon after it was set up, and the universities continued to give their own CET until 1968 (J. S. Lee, 1993).

A return to independent exams by universities (1955–61)

The failure of the joint exam system brought back independent exams by universities during 1955–61. After 1958, however, some of the national and public universities introduced a method of selecting students without exams. The high school grades and students' personalities constituted the criteria of evaluation (KMOE, 1992b).

In 1962, Park Chung Hee, a major general, came to power in a relatively quiet coup, and he became the key figure in a new configuration of power (Eckert et al., 1990). As part of the educational renewal policy of the new government, the CET was abolished and replaced by the National Entrance Test (NET), the reason for which will be discussed next.

The National Entrance Test System (1962–3)

In the early 1960s, the Park Chung Hee Military Government initiated massive recruitment of civil bureaucrats through highly competitive national examinations. By the late 1970s, his system served to 'eliminate those bureaucrats who were recruited in the 1950s through a very corrupted spoils system' (Kim and Jung, 1993: 95). The stress in these civil service exams was on a solid, merit-based system. This had an inevitable impact on educational selection. In 1962, as a part of the National Reconstruction Movement of the Park government, exams by individual universities were replaced by a single state exam system, the National Entrance Test (NET), for university admission. It was an effort to enrol more intelligent students from low-income families, and to improve the quality of college education by preventing unqualified students from getting into colleges (McGinn et al., 1980). In 1963, the NET was used as the first-round exam, one that qualified successful applicants for the exams given by each university. However, universities were disgruntled, criticizing the NET as a grave infringement of their autonomy. In the years that followed, a dogged seesaw battle continued between the universities and the government over control of the exams. It was only after 1969 that the government asserted full control over the national exam system.

A return to the independent exam system again (1964–8)

While political power was won by the civil government over matters of standard content, universities retained their autonomy in administering the entrance exam. The required subjects corresponded to the time allotment for subjects in the high school curriculum. It was perhaps students who suffered most from the ceaseless alterations in the exam system. When a required subject was suddenly dropped for the next year, students had to readjust their preparation accordingly.

In the independent exam system, students who had special skills in art, music, physical education and science were selected within the admission quota according to the special criterion set by the president of the individual universities. Within a single area, privilege was given to vocational school students, art and music students, and physical education students.

During this period, mismanagement of the entrance exams and admission of an excessive number of students degraded the quality of university education. 'Improprieties and absurdities related to the entrance exams' frequently occurred in a considerable number of universities (J. S. Lee, 1993). The gap in academic level between different universities widened, and a large number of college graduates were unemployed (KMOE, 1992b).

The eventual national control over university entrance exams (1969–93)

The continuous improper conduct of admissions within the university administration of entrance exams caused society to mistrust universities. As a result, in 1969 the Ministry of Education promulgated the Ordinance for the National Preliminary Test (NPT) as the qualifying exams for university entrance. By the Ordinance, the government assumed total control of the system. The tested subjects were Korean, Social Studies, Maths, Science, English, and Vocational Education (or Home Economics). Korean History was added in 1972.

This was the time when competition for university became fiercer. The dual exam system, national and university, also generated the double burden of preparation and overheated out-of-class tutoring (J. S. Lee, 1993). People from different sectors of society appealed for the abolition of university-held exams. In 1980, another reform abolished the exam system administered by individual universities. Only the NPT and high school scores were used to assess students' application for university.

In the years that followed, the national entrance exams changed their forms and titles from NPT to National Scholastic Achievement Test (NSAT) (1982–5). Given the growing importance of the university entrance system, in August 1985, by a Presidential decree, the National Institute of Educational Evaluation was established to take charge of the exam administrative work. This marked a major step further towards the centralization and externalization of the exam system.

In 1994, NSAT was further replaced by the National Ability Test (NAT) (1994–present). In the meantime, consideration has been given to high school scores. In 1982–5, for example, NSAT accounted for over 50 per cent in the total scores, and high school scores 30 per cent or more. But high school grades had some inherent weakness. Because the high school scores for each student were above the baseline level, their deviation was small. In reality, even in 1994, when the weight of high school grades reached 40 per cent of the total score for entrance assessment, its real weight was less than 10 per cent (TMOE, 1992: 13). According to the estimation made by Jong Seung Lee (1993), the actual weight of high school scores was even lower, no more than 4.9 per cent. As this has been a main thrust in Korean reform of recent years, I will come back to the topic later.

To sum up, the Korean system of university entrance exams underwent many reforms, with the drastic ones often related to political factors, such as the turbulent transition of state power. In actuality, although these twists and turns appeared dramatic, their end result could not transcend history, as political culture did not break out of the boundaries of the larger cultural context. A typical example is shown in the process of meritocratization, as centralization, standardization and the growing role of an achievement exam all point to the fact that the actual status of the exam-based evaluation-selection system has been enhanced rather than weakened. A major focus of the reformers' exhausting efforts concerns who controls the system, but the character has only intensified.

In retrospect, universities lost their authority because: (1) some used inappropriate or low quality test questions; (2) their administration of exams was unprofessional; (3) there were occasional corruptions in the exam process; and (4) there was a lack of overall coherence in the selection of test subjects and the design of test questions. The national-controlled entrance exams were introduced, because (1) they serve to make for a greater uniformity and fairness; (2) they professionalize the design and evaluation of questions; and (3) they administer the entrance exams in a more systematic and coherent manner. Its weaknesses are seen as (1) forcing uniformity on assessment standards; (2) not enough attention given to the unique characteristics of individual universities; (3) an infringement of the academic authority of universities (KMOE, 1992b).

TAIWAN: INHERITOR OF THE DRAGON GATE

If the Dragon Gate has been revamped repeatedly in Korea, in Taiwan it was cautiously kept intact through the prewar period. One reason for this contrast is that the political situation in Taiwan was not as turbulent as in Korea – a contrast equally notable under Japanese rule, too. The political transition to a stable democracy has been peaceful, unlike the recurrent succession crises in Korea. The people of Taiwan also have remained relatively patient and docile under the rule of the monolithic Nationalist government. Strikes were almost unknown. Due to the pattern of industry in Taiwan – a patchwork of thousands of small family-owned firms – the growth of a labour movement lagged far behind that of South Korea (Gibney, 1992: 354). Moreover, one may argue, as the inheritor of both the *keju* system and the Japanese exam system, the Taiwan Chinese accepted the exam-centred system more willingly than others.[11]

In 1949, as the Chinese Communists took power on the mainland, the Nationalist regime of Chiang Kai-shek and the remnants of his army escaped to Taiwan. Initially, the US government refused to provide military protection, but two days after the outbreak of the Korean War on 27 June 1950, President Truman ordered the Seventh Fleet to safeguard Taiwan from Communist attack. Unlike in Korea, the US presence as a military posture was not accompanied by administrative authority, and Taiwan was never put under Allied occupation. Thus, Taiwan's exam system was much less influenced by the US than was the case for Japan and Korea. Through the havoc wrought by Japanese militarism (1937–45), the Nationalist–Communist civil war (1945–9), and other socio-political crises, Taiwan's exam systems for both the university and the civil service were to an amazing extent uninterrupted. As a matter of fact, these systems have been so stable and almost shock-free that we need to understand the reasons. The historical formations in the Chinese *keju* system seem to be the basis of this stability – especially as the beliefs corresponded well with the Japanese imperial system of achievement-based entrance exams. That continuity was made possible through a collective memory stored in a myriad of individual mentalities, the 'atoms' of social culture. In that sense, the anxious obsession with exams, and the narrow avenue of credentialism, both found in Taiwan, suggest that the modern system of evaluation is very similar culturally to the age-old imperial system of exams.

University-based exams (1945–53)

Two years after the Nationalists took over Taiwan in 1945, its government issued the new entrance exam method (*zhaosheng banfa*). Apart from substituting the Mandarin vernacular for Japanese, it was very similar in structure to the system during the Japanese colonial era. The written entrance exams were the only substantive gauge for selecting students, and they were given by individual schools. However, the Ministry of Education provided for the required subjects in university entrance exams. For humanities, they are: Chinese, English, Maths, Civics, History, Geography, Physics and Chemistry (TMOE, 1987: 1419–20). No oral interview, recommendation or school grades were needed.

During the eight years of its implementation, the method encountered some problems that finally led to its reform. First of all, travelling from school to school for the university-held exams was very exhausting for students. Second, without coordination among universities, a student could be unnecessarily accepted by two or more schools to which he/she applied. Third, some less prestigious schools might be unable to get enough students.

---

[11] In a telephone survey conducted in 1991 sponsored by the Taiwan Administrative Department (*Xingzheng yuan*), of 1067 people interviewed, 70.5 per cent supported the current national entrance exam system, and only 15.6 per cent wanted to abolish it. See TMOE, *Daixüe Duoyuan Ruxüe Fang'an* (Multiple university entrance programme), (Taiwan: Taiwan University Entrance Exam Center, 1992), note 35, p. 68.

Also, the administration of exams was expensive, and its workload was increasingly heavy.

The unified exams: From four universities to all (1954–5)

In search of a better solution, four schools, the National Taiwan University (the Japanese-founded Imperial University), the Teachers' College, the Taizhong Agriculture College and the Tainan Industry College, joined together in 1954 to give a unified entrance exam (*Lianzhao*) among themselves. A 'Unified Admissions Committee' was set up to coordinate the organizational work. The *Lianzhao* was so successful that the Ministry of Education decided to adopted a similar system for all schools. In 1956, the Ministry of Education issued the 'Unified Entrance Exam Method' which nationalized the entrance exams for both the public and private universities under a single system. The required subjects were the 'Three Principlisms' (the official ideology), Chinese, Chinese History/Geography and English. The subjects for the special areas include: Maths, World History/Geography, Physics, Chemistry, Biology, etc. The total scores of exams were the only criterion for the decision. There was no limit on the number of universities to which one could apply.

About 40 years have elapsed since the unified exams were first instituted, and their principle and structure have not changed. The entrance exams and the assignment of students to universities have been administered at the national level, under the supervision of the Taiwan Ministry of Education. Ever since the '1956 Entrance Exam Method' went into effect, no individual university, be it national or private, has given its own entrance exam.

To know why the system had such 'longevity', we need to learn the initial causes of its being set up. They included: (1) reduction of labour and financial expense; (2) reduction of the cost, preparation burden and anxiety on the part of students; (3) alleviation of the problems of under-admission in some universities or departments; (4) the increase in the students' chances of admission; (5) the strengthening of impartiality by externalizing the exam administration (TMOE, 1979). Many of these causes are also applicable in explaining the emergence of the national entrance exam systems in Japan and Korea.

Ministry of Education: Tightening the screws (1976–Now)

The unified exam system (*Liankao*) was initially a rotation system. Each year, one university would be selected as the chief sponsor for administering the exam. One problem with this arrangement was that there was no continuity or 'technical transfer'. As it rotated to a new university, that school had to learn the job from the beginning. To tackle that problem and ease the transition, in 1976 Taiwan's Ministry of Education established the 'University Entrance Examination Committee'. Its members consisted of university presidents, educators, and specialists in the field. The committee was put under the direct auspices of the Ministry, and the Education Minister acted personally as its chair.

Since then, *Liankao* has undergone some technical changes, such as computerization, the participation or withdrawal of the military academy, the weight of different subjects in the total scores, or the combination or separation of exams for university and vocational schools. However, there has been no structural or substantive reform. The national entrance exams have become so legitimate in these characteristics that universities seemed much less interested in changing the *status quo* than the Koreans were. This does not mean that no alternative has ever been considered. Scholars have no difficulty in turning out blueprints of new, exciting reforms. The common thrusts of these plans have been (1) to enrich assessment methods and expand the scope of choices (departments); (2) to preserve the existing fairness by maintaining the unification of exams; (3) to emphasize both basic and specialized knowledge; (4) to improve the quality of test questions, and so on. However, these reform plans seldom left the drawing board. This was because, first of all, the notion of using exams as the main gauge of selection has been accepted by the populace. It is attuned to the Chinese valuation system concerning such essential questions as: what is fair and just? It fits Chinese meritocracy in determining an élite, and it rewards behaviour and the kinds of skills Chinese admire. Second and perhaps most important, the existing system has simply worked well, in spite of the intellectual criticism.

The attitudes of Da-you Wu, a renowned Taiwanese scholar highly critical of exams, may give us an idea of the ambivalence that reformers have toward entrance exams. In 1975, Wu proposed to use only high school grades and abolish the entrance exams. In 1988, he proposed to replace exams with the US model of evaluation. In 1990, however, Wu asserted that 'I think the most feasible method is to keep the *Liankao* exams as the primary criterion for university screening, and in the meantime, to reduce the competition by increasing the acceptance ratio.' Rick Chu, a senior news-paper journalist, explains why the system has survived: 'Despite all the negative effects of the entrance exam system, it has been, admittedly, the "cleanest" system that we have ever had in our society. It has been unpollutable by privilege, graft, or corruption.'

THE HISTORICAL TRENDS OF EXAM SYSTEMS IN EAST ASIA: COMMONALITIES AND DISSIMILAR-ITIES

In the foregoing pages, we traced the modern exam systems to their origin, about one hundred years back in history. These hundred years have been eventful. Japanese colonialism reproduced a public education system in Taiwan and Korea, and they did so using the exam-centred system. After WWII, the experiences that Japan, Taiwan and Korea went through were significantly different from each other. The aftermath of WWII brought each a war-torn land, but the ways they reconstructed it differed greatly. As shown in our review, the same can be said about their new education.

Due to the US Occupation, the postwar development of the exam system was heavily influenced by Western educational concepts, especially Amer-ican ones, both in theory and in practice. Nevertheless, not very long after the Occupation, certain major trends found in the exam systems of Japan, Korea and Taiwan went diagonally opposite to what American educators would appreciate. Moreover, despite their early disparity, by the end of the 1960s, the modes of the three systems came to a point when they began to bear some significant resemblances.

Commonalities and differences

The modern entrance exam systems of Japan, Korea and Taiwan have covered a period of around one hundred years. Within these hundred years, if we compare the patterns of how the three systems have changed, we can discern commonalities and differences. In other words, we can see parallels and non-parallels. Do their features, however, become more similar to or more distinct from each other over time, do they show convergence or divergence? Based on the historical review and discussion we have just covered, I schematize this historical process in Figure 3.1.

Now, some explanatory notes are in order. During colonial times, because of the duplication of Japanese education and exam systems in Korea and Taiwan, a single arrow is used to show uniformity. During the Occupation, the Japanese exam system had been basically American, which diverged from the other two. The postwar reconstruction brought the three exam systems closer to each other in terms of their form and content, and their importance as a pathway of mobility. During this period, the Japanese managed to remodel their system in a more Japanese fashion. As the performance in achievement became once again the critical differentiator, the Japanese approach returned to the East Asian norm in assessment. Meanwhile, the wavy line for Korea expresses a troubled authority relationship between the state and universities, unsettled for quite a long period of time.

After economic take-off, the three systems demonstrated a convergence pattern on a number of accounts. First, in all three countries, written exams were the essential differentiator for university students. The other forms of evaluation, such as oral exams, interview or recommendation, have in general not been taken seriously or given a central role. Second, the achievement scores were taken as the main and largely exclusive criteria for university admission.

The other cognitive measurements, such as the IQ test, which were intensively experimented with for quite a long period of time during the Occupation in Japan, have been proven largely unacceptable as a key criterion for scoring and sorting candidates. Third, some fundamental knowledge, such as of mathematics, English, native language and social studies, became the officially authorized subjects for assessment. Fourth, a very close meritocratic and/or credentialistic nexus connected schools with élite positions, for which examinations were the nodal points.[12] Fifth, the exam system is a key element in the formation of a clearly configured, hierarchical and unimodal ranking of universities, confirmed by and corresponding to the link between school and the workplace.

---

[12] 'Meritocratic' here is used to refer particularly to selection depending directly on the exams. Exams for different professions are typical examples. 'Credentialistic' refers to selection that takes into significant consideration the credentials that the applicants hold. In the latter case, the screening entrusts its technical responsibility to the authority of schools.

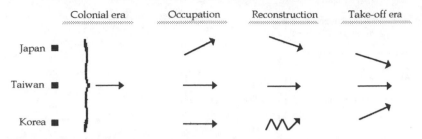

Figure 3.1 The convergence process in the historical development of the entrance exam systems, Japan, Korea and Taiwan.

In this process, most salient perhaps was the centralization of university entrance exams, and the growing importance attached to the state in shaping and conducting exams.

While this often is largely a matter of authority between university and government, the process meanwhile serves to further perpetuate the exam system as a legitimate path of social mobility through official patronage. In his critique of the exam system, Karl Marx writes:

> The examination is nothing but the bureaucratic baptism of knowledge, the official recognition of the transubstantiation of profane knowledge into sacred knowledge.[13]

In these words, while it is arguable whether all the tested knowledge is 'profane' in nature, his penetrating observation about the inherent link between the exam system and authority is thought-provoking. In this sense, centralization or nationalization of the three exam systems have brought that 'baptism', or 'official recognition', to its highest form. However, as I need to add later in this section, this 'baptism' in East Asia has much to do with the legacy of tradition. Figure 3.2 shows in detail how the different developments in the exam system in the three countries eventually came to the convergence point of centralization.

Centralization implies a growing interest or concern on the part of the state in the selection process, and the augmenting power it has achieved in the control of the process. It also implies the externalization and standardization of the university entrance system. While this was an important phenomenon in past decades, it is not the core of the matter.

Centralization warrants our special interest only because it has irretrievably reinforced the cardinal principle underpinning the East Asian exam system. That principle is meritocracy as measured by achievement criteria, and it is predicated upon equitable accessibility to schooling and impartial objectivity in the exam process. It is equally predicated upon a closed articulation between education and workplace. All five common features mentioned earlier are the facets of that principle.

---

[13] Karl Marx: *Critique of Hegel's Doctrine of the State*, cited from Bourdieu and Passeron (1994).

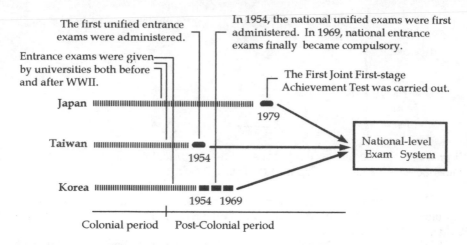

Figure 3.2 The centralization of the university entrance exam system in Japan, Korea and Taiwan.

In the East Asian type of exam system, the importance of the principle of fair play cannot be over-emphasized. In terms of grading, anonymity is needed on the part of the exam-takers. Then, whenever possible, the exam questions are designed in an impersonal format of multiple choice, computerized, adaptive and readable.

Another side of de-emphasizing personal and subjective factors is shown in the assessment criteria: recommendations and interviews are not used or are kept to a minimum. The dismissal of high school grades in considering admissions is also an effort to keep at bay any possible favouritism or connection, with the exception of the Korean case, which I will discuss shortly.

Yet, the exam systems are not identical for the three countries. Taiwan's system has shown all five common features for the longest time. Korea has headed in the same direction, but uncertainty over control has prevailed for quite a period of time. Nevertheless, Korea has been sharing the basic features of the model for a long time. In Japan, the Occupation seemed to lead Japan toward a very different future. But it did not. As early as 1952, when the Treaty of Peace came into effect, Japanese education began to depart from the original course of the American plan. However, the transformation back into a Japanese-style system took years, and Japan was thus late in terms of convergence with other East Asian countries.

The three systems are not only different in the timing of their centralization. Dissimilarities also exist, for example, in the frequency of reforms, and their results, as perceptible in our historical review. How does one explain that in the big picture we have just drawn?

In explaining the historicist approach to the convergence and difference of cultural patterns, C. J. Erasumus uses the example of 'canoe paddle' found in certain societies:

If the purpose was to develop a hand-held instrument for propelling a craft through water where sails or long poles could not be used, there was a fairly narrow range of variation in the physical properties the instrument could have. It could not be too long or it would be unwieldy. It could not be too short or it would lose the propelling power of a man's two arms. It had to have a blade-like surface, *although the shape of the blade could be leaflike, round, rectangular, or of some intermediate form* [italic added]. (Bee, 1974: 75)

Erasumus points out that 'convergence' was the result of a combination of similar logical, natural or cultural limitations or conditions (in Bee, 1974). By the 'paddle' metaphor, he wants to say that common features allow for certain non-essential differences. Accordingly, in our discussion, we need to find both the differences among the three systems, and their 'meaning' or significance in the convergence process.

As noted, the major dissimilarities were often attributable to an 'idiosyncratic' experience the country had. For instance, the Japanese system differed a lot from the Korean and the Taiwanese ones in the 1950s, because of the US-initiated overhaul of the exam system. In Korea, the turbulent political situation generated drastic changes. Because of the importance of Presidents in the national decision-making process, such factors as presidential personality, the length of tenure, and the power transition are proven to have repercussions on the university screening system. Keeping these historical differences in mind, let us now focus on the major dissimilarities among the current three exam systems, as listed in Table 3.1. One dissimilarity is that the Japanese centralization pattern of the entrance system differs from the Taiwanese and Korean ones. In Japan, the national-level First-Stage Achievement Test (JFSAT) was instituted in 1979, which was almost two decades later than in the other countries. Furthermore, the JFSAT or its later version, the Center Test, was limited in its role. It was (1) only used for first-round cut-off elimination for national/public university entrance; and (2) the final decision was made by individual universities, not the Ministry of Education (see Figure 3.3).

After the JFSAT was put into use, the national universities still gave their own. Most of the private universities preferred not to use the system at all, unlike in Korea and Taiwan, and they were allowed not to do so. What I need to add, however, is that the centralization of entrance exams is still an ongoing process, which has been more successful recently than before. Pessimistic researchers underestimate the Japanese adaptability and the vitality of the culturally anchored exam system. In his stress on systemic inertia, Peter Frost (1992) asserts that the Japanese government 'has not succeeded in getting private universities to join in' the JFSAT or the Center Test (29). Yet, his generalization does not account for the empirical data. At the time of his writing, the private universities had already joined in the national exam system at an unusual rate. An update is given in Table 3.2.

There is no doubt that national sponsored exams have been voluntarily accepted by a rapidly growing number of private universities. However, unlike in Taiwan and Korea, neither the JFSAT nor the Center Test was designed to grab autonomous power from the universities. It only served as another check-point of quality control. The final decision remains with each university and department. This dual exam structure doubles the burden of preparation, although its relentless objectivity apparently gives the entire assessment process more credence than otherwise. In Taiwan and Korea, the entrance exams have absolute objectivity, as the scores of the national entrance exams are very much the sole criterion.

Table 3.1 Key differences among the current entrance exam systems of Japan, Korea and Taiwan. *Source*: My compilation.

	Does the state decide who gets into a university?	Does the university give entrance exams?	Are high school grades used as criterion?	Are interviews used as criterion?
Japan	No	Yes	No	No.
Korea	Yes	No	Yes. 40% of total scores (but only 4.9– 10% in reality)	Yes, but insignificant
Taiwan	Yes	No	No	No

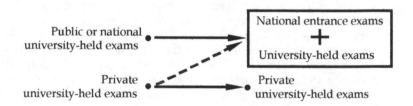

Figure 3.3 The status of the university-held exam system after the national entrance exam system was established in Japan.

Table 3.2 The number of Japan's private universities joining the National Center Test, 1990–6. *Source*: Data for 1990–4: Jiji Tsûshinsha, *Kyôiku Deta Randdo* (A databook of educational statistics), (Tokyo: Jiji Tsûshinsha), 1993: 40, 1994: 41; data for 1996: JMOE: *Juken Annai* (Information on entrance exams), (Tokyo: Daigaku Nyûshi Sentâ, 1996), 58–63.

Year	Number of universities	Number of departments
1990	16	19
1991	21	24
1992	32	46
1993	57	85
1994	73	123
1996	122	231

Another major dissimilarity concerns the value of high school grades. Unlike Japan and Taiwan, Korean reformers have been pushing especially hard for the incorporation of high school grades in the total evaluation. Although this issue was touched upon in the historical review of the Korean case, we should give it some more attention.

In 1993, high school grades were weighted at 30 per cent, and the exam score at 70 per cent. In reality, however, that could be superficial. To find out why, let us look at the composition of the total scores combining exams with high school scores. The maximum scores for entrance exams was 340 (70 per cent), for high school it was 145.7 (30 per cent), and for the total score it was 485.7 (100 per cent):

	Total score =	Exam score +	high school score
Max. scores	485.7	340	145.7
Percentage	100%	70%	30%

Of the 145.7 points (the maximum high school score), 131.1 points are curriculum scores, and 14.6 points are the attendance scores. Curriculum grades are divided into ten levels, while the lowest, bottom level 10 is 113.1 points. The difference in points does not exceed 18. In addition, attendance grades are divided into five levels with 1.5 points separating each level, so the highest score is 14.6 points, and the lowest 8.6 points. Therefore, high school scores range from the highest scores of 145.7 points (= 131.1 + 14.6) to the lowest of 121.7 points (= 113.1 + 8.6). **When combined with the total NSAT score of 340, high school scores contribute only about 4.9 per cent** (= 24 ÷ 485.7) (J. S. Lee, 1993), as shown in Figure 3.4.

Because a student could get at least 121.7 points as a high school score in the worst scenario, he or she did not really have to worry about the 24 point (5 per cent) difference. Therefore, as Jong Seung Lee (1993) reveals, to include the high school scores was no more than a superficial emphasis in the hope that this could 'normalize' the high school curriculum.

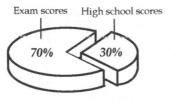

Exam scores   High school scores

70%   30%

The ratio of exam scores and high
school scores to the total scores

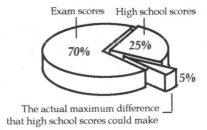

Exam scores   High school scores

70%   25%

5%

The actual maximum difference
that high school scores could make

Figure 3.4 The difference that high school scores can make in Korea's university entrance assessments. *Source*: Based on Jong Seung Lee, 'Guageo Haegyeolnoryeogeui Yeogsa' (The history of past solution efforts), in Bum Mo Chung *et al.*, eds, *Gyoyugeui Bonyeoneul Chajaseo-ibsiwa Ibsigyoyeogeui Gaehyeog* (Restoring Korean education from the bondage of entrance examination education), (Seoul: Nanam, 1993), 127–54.

To sum up, after WWII ended, the entrance exams of Japan, Korea and Taiwan experienced a series of changes, some large and some small. These changes developed in each nation independently. This independence reflected a different historical experience of American occupation and different political contexts. Despite this diversity, however, a common direction is perceivable. This refers especially to, among many others, the central importance of meritocracy, impartiality, and an epistemology that stresses the link between knowledge and effort.

An important phenomenon in the history of exams was the growing control of the state which perpetuated them as the officially legitimate system. Our further scrutiny of the exam systems in Japan, Korea and Taiwan illustrates that dissimilarities did exist among them, but over time a general convergent trend is also observable.

REASONS FOR THE SIMILARITIES: ECONOMIC GROWTH, DEMOGRAPHIC FACTORS AND CULTURAL LEGACIES

The modern features of exam systems are greatly affected by the larger, social context. The factors include, first of all, the economic achievement and the gradual prosperity of the people. The United Nations defined the 1960s as the 'Decade of Development', which was particularly true for East Asia. In the mid-1960s, shortly after the makers of Japan's 'economic miracle' had set their course for the future, a similar set of transformations was taking place in other East Asian economies as well. This slowly caught the attention of the West by a growing volume of exports from the East to the US and Europe. Since 1963 the annual GNP growth rate of Korea, for instance, averaged close to 10 per cent, holding just under that figure into the 1990s. As a result, Korea's per capita GNP increased from a meagre $87 in 1962 to $6700 in 1992, all at current prices.

Taiwan's growth rates were similarly spectacular, with corresponding structural changes in industry and exports. The national GNP in 1982 was twelve times that of 1952. By 1990, Taiwan's hard-currency reserves approached $70 billion (Gibney, 1992; KOIS, 1993; Wade, 1990).

With perhaps the fastest GNP growth in the Third World, Korea and Taiwan also had an income inequality lower than most of the developing economies, a challenge to the conventional wisdom that early stages of economic development require a higher level of income inequality (Borthwick, 1992: 288; World Bank, 1991: 137), as plotted in Figure 3.5.

In Taiwan, particularly, growth accompanied unusually equal income distribution, more so than in Japan, Korea or the US, and much more equal than in the typical developing countries. Taiwan had by far the most equal income distribution in a sixteen-country comparison based on data from the late 1960s and early 1970s and using total disposable household income net of taxes (Wade, 1990: 38; Fei, Ranis and Kuo, 1979). One major equalizing agent is the common access to higher education and thus the opportunities to climb the social ladder. In a World Bank sponsored study about how Taiwan achieved rapid economic growth with equity between the 1950s and the 1970s, John Fei, Gustav Ranis and Shirley Kuo (1979) conclude, *inter alia*:

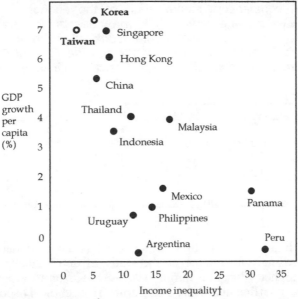

Figure 3.5 Income inequality† and the growth of GDP in selected countries 1965–89. *Source*: Based on World Bank data, cited in World Bank, *World Development Report 1991: The Challenge of Development* (Oxford: Oxford University Press, 1991), 137.
Note: † The ratio of the income shares of the richest 20 per cent and poorest 20 per cent of the population. Data on income distribution are from surveys conducted mainly in the late 1960s and early 1970s.

For Taiwan this finding [i.e. high growth with low inequality] is not particularly surprising. The imperial examination system, institutionalized long ago in traditional China, continues to hold sway. *Rigorous and impartial entrance examinations are annually held at all levels of formal education. Because wealthy families do not have the marked special advantages frequently encountered elsewhere, access to educational opportunities is thus relatively equal for all* [italic added]. (321)

Another important fact in East Asian economic growth is the high savings rates of Japan, Korea and Taiwan. Japan has a high savings rate mainly because of the low level of assets and high cost of housing. In 1991, in the total financial household assets, the savings accounts amounted to 52.0 per cent in Japan, as compared to 18.4 per cent in the US, and 42.2 per cent in Germany (FPC, 1993:69). In Korea, private savings also reached an historic high, and by 1987 Korea had passed a point where domestic savings exceeded domestic investment (Amsden, 1989). Compared to Japan and Korea, the savings rate was even higher in Taiwan. By 1975, Taiwan's ratio of net savings to net national product had exceeded that of Japan (25.3 per cent against 22.7 per cent). Since then, the Taiwanese have had about the highest savings ratio in the world (Wade, 1990: 61) (see Table 3.3). In societies obsessed with credentialistic status, the high savings naturally boosted expectation and investment in education, especially for the next generation.

Table 3.3 A comparison: monetization of the economy, expressed by M2†/GNP, by percentage. *Source*: IMF: *International Financial Statistics*; for Taiwan data: *Taiwan Statistical Data Book*, cited from Robert Wade, *Governing the Market: Economic Theory and the Role of Government in East Asian Industrialization* (Princeton: Princeton University Press, 1990), 64.

Country	1955	1965	1975	1980	1985
Taiwan	13	30	57	65	109
Japan	60	79	68	86	97
Korea	10	12	30	34	46
Philippines	19	19	25	17	21

Note: † M2 refers to savings consisting of currency plus bank deposits [original note].

As a result, higher education, which used to be a modern luxury, has become increasingly affordable. In the study of determinants of attendance in Japanese higher education during 1965–84, Kazuhiro Arai (1990) finds the regression coefficients of the Per Capita Household Disposable Income and Average Wage are highly significant, which implies that availability of investment funds is very important in the decision to invest in higher education (in Lee and Yamazawa, 1990). An imaginable corollary is, of course, the intensifying pressure and attention riveted on the Dragon Gate of the university entrance exam.

The widening of educational opportunities in the wake of the steady population growth in peace time is another factor exerting crushing pressure on the entrance system. In Japan, at the end of WWII, secondary education enrolled 61 per cent of the relevant age cohort, and colleges only 5.8 per cent. In 1990, these figures had risen to 96.1 per cent and 33.2 per cent respectively. These figures could be higher if we add special vocational schools and *rônin*. In Taiwan, enrolment rates by school-aged groups are 65.7 per cent for secondary education, and 10.0 per cent for higher education in 1976. In 1990, they rose to 95.3 per cent for secondary, and 45.0 per cent for higher. In Korea, from 1966 to 1990, the enrolment rates rose from 41.4 per cent to 97.8 per cent for the middle school level, and 26.4 per cent to 87.6 per cent for the high school level. The rate for higher education increased from 8.8 per cent in 1970 to 38.1 per cent in 1990 (JMOE, 1994; TMOE, 1994; KEDI, 1993). Obviously, as secondary school enrolments approached a universal level and application to higher education involved more than half of all high school graduates, the importance of university entrance exams came to dominate the educational landscape and the attention of parents and students. The computerization of the exam format and the grading system is one inevitable consequence of this change. Just as necessary, however, was public acceptance of the exam system's legitimacy and fairness. Through such measures as reinforcing impartiality, transparency, common accessibility, and so on, officials in all three countries continued to try to strengthen public confidence in much the same manner.

All told, however, the exam systems as found in East Asia are not necessarily an automatic consequence of either economic development or demographic pressure. In a broad comparative perspective, the economic level, for instance, may not correlate well with one or another selection system. Among the advanced countries, we find many screening methods (IQ tests, aptitude tests and achievement tests). In the same vein, the idiosyncrasies of the East Asian approach, such as the proliferation of cram schools, the vast army of exam repeaters (*rônin* in Japan, *Jai su saeng* in Korea, and *Chonkao sheng* in Taiwan), the emphasis on achievement measures, the close meritocratic nexus between school and governmental or corporate positions, the very long hours of knowledge absorption, etc., are a combination hardly found elsewhere.

In that regard, what is evidenced through our detailed review is the importance of a cultural legacy. Culture is the repository of a tradition's ideals and basic institutional solution to problems, deeply rooted in a fixed historical past. Our reconstruction of the Meiji and the Japanese colonial era demonstrates with clarity that, soon after the tide of foreign influence inundated East Asia, there was also a revival of interest in the tradition of examinations to select for merit. It was manifest in the step-by-step official resurrection of Confucian values in Meiji Japan. Diligence in learning and the equation of scholastic achievement with overall human merit (or virtue) survived and were actually strengthened by the Japanese colonial experience and by Westernization.

What is the role that tradition plays? To pursue this, let us consider the 'canoe paddle' metaphor again. People make the paddle not by first thinking hard about its best length or shape. They simply learn how to make it from their father, or their grandfather, or their master. Or they can make it simply by following the example of an existing paddle. In other words, the craft of paddle-making largely comes from the transmission of a cultural legacy. As I will discuss next, the East Asian systems of entrance exams have been crafted much like such a 'canoe paddle'.

In 165 BC a civil service system based on recommendations and examinations, both emphasizing moral excellence, was instituted in China. Thereafter both oral and written exams were occasionally used. After 622 AD an essentially open competitive exam was given regularly (Têng, in Bishop, 1968). The civil service examination of ancient China, *keju*, has been generally recognized as the original source of examination systems found subsequently in the civilizations of Europe, Egypt, Babylonia-Assyria and Persia. As the *Encyclopaedia Britannica* (11th and 14th edn) reads:

> The oldest known system of examinations in history is that used in China for the selection of officers for the public services (c. 1115 BC) and the periodic tests which they undergo after entry (c. 2200 BC).[14]

On the merits of the Chinese imperial exam system, Bertrand Russell (1922) spells out laconically: 'A widely-diffused respect for learning; the possibility of doing without a hereditary aristocracy; the selection of

---

[14] For the difference in the date of the earliest exams in China, Ssu-yü Têng (1968) explains: 'Apparently the statement of the Encyclopaedia is based on the Chinese classics, which, though they purport to describe the examination system of ancient kings, were actually written about 400 or 300 BC.'

preservation of Chinese civilization in spite of barbarian conquest' (46–7). This summary made by a contemporary modern philosopher may well reflect what inspirations early Westerners might have found in the ancient wisdom. He goes on, stating: 'But, like so much else in traditional China, it has had to be swept away to meet modern needs. I hope nothing of greater value will have to perish in the struggle to repel the foreign exploiters and the fierce and cruel system which they miscall civilization.'

Nevertheless, contemporary evidence has shown without doubt that the Chinese system of imperial exams had a direct influence on the modern adoption of the civil service examination systems in England, India, France, the United States and Japan (Williams, 1848; Monroe, 1931; Têng, 1968; Miyazaki, 1976; Huang, 1992; Eckstein and Noah, 1993).

In Meiji Japan, as cited, the earliest endeavour to copy Chinese imperial civil exams is the 1869 'Kanda Plan'. Its landslide victory in the Japanese Parliament revealed the need for both the modern bureaucracy and cultural proclivity, though the Plan was too premature to take effect. In the same way, the development and transformation of the modern exam systems in Japan, Korea and Taiwan, as we have reviewed and analysed, exhibit certain features that run parallel to the Chinese imperial civil service exams (*keju*).

First, like the court-controlled recruiting machinery of *keju*, in the three nations, countless college-level authorities for screening university entrants merged into a central authority supervised by the government, which put students into a pecking order all across the nation. Its institutional climax was marked by the centralization of key elements of the entrance exams by the governments.

Second, like *keju*, which exacted an alignment to Confucian canons and their textual exegesis as the state orthodoxy, in the modern systems of Japan, Korea and Taiwan, mathematics, English, native language and social studies, etc., were core knowledge categorically defined by the state.

Third, both the *keju* and modern exams for university entrance depended heavily on written responses to a whole battery of questions. The distrust of the *viva voce* (oral test) as the means of measuring achievement is obvious for both the imperial *keju* and the East Asian screening systems. Other forms of assessment, such as interview, recommendation, GPA, etc., even if used, are insignificant.

Fourth, *keju* was an externally imposed exam with great uniformity in its format and content. In the past years, entrance exams in Japan, Taiwan and Korea also demonstrate a growing tendency towards externalization and unification, although in Japan, university-held exams are still used. Assessment of students is independent from their schooling.

Fifth, a unique feature of the modern university entrance system is the large army of repeaters in the three countries. In a way, it is a ritual that rewards unyielding character and hard-earned achievement instead of facile success. This had its notorious coordinate in the *keju* era, when it was not uncommon for a scholar to have failed a dozen or more times in higher-level examinations. In the late-Qing Dynasty, these examinations were usually held at three-year intervals. The whole lives of such luckless scholars were thus devoted to their studies and examination halls (Ho, 1964).

Sixth, a very close meritocratic and/or credentialistic nexus bound schools with élite positions for which examinations were the nodal points.[15] This is a modern application of the cardinal principle embodied in *keju*, i.e., *'Xüe er you ze shi'*, or 'those who excel in their study should become officials' (*Analects*: 19.13).

These commonalities shared by modern and ancient systems are unique as compared to the number of alternative examination systems in the rest of the world. *Keju* stood alone as the preferred route to success. Government service was the most honourable and the most worthwhile occupation. And the examinations played a large part in determining the composition of the élite, by modelling as well as selecting the men who operated the political system (Schirokauer, in Miyazaki, 1976). Those words are fairly appropriate for modern systems of university entrance exams as well.

To define this phenomenal process in which parallels between the modern systems and imperial exams converged, I use a term, 'Kejurization'. By that coinage, I am not suggesting an incident of atavism. It would also be an exaggeration to say that *keju* was the chrysalis of the present exam systems in East Asia. Rather, I use it to describe a major development, which, while highly institutional in its structure, manifests certain reutilization of traditional ideas and cultural dispositions. Accordingly, to explain why 'Kejurization' occurred at all, I first need to discuss Asian 'regionalism', to borrow the term from Rozman, to show how that region differs from others.

All justifications for a regional focus on East Asia have rested primarily on the assertion of a common cultural heritage (Rozman, 1991). Asianists often use terms such as 'cultural sphere' (c. *Dongya wenhuaquan*; j. *Ajia bunkaken*), 'to underscore the long cultural interaction between China and its neighbours: the forming of East Asia as a Sinic-centred world order' (Fairbanks, 1968). A critical element of this cultural order was the widening use of Chinese in its written form (*tongwen*), and the use of Chinese characters adapted to and integrated with vernacular Japanese and Korean (Nishito, 1973; Joe, 1981; Gao, 1984; Vandermeersch, 1987). As the first writing system in East Asia, they carried the Chinese language, Confucianism, Chinese civil laws (*luling*), Chinese sciences, and the Chinese version of Buddhism, the Mahayana school.[16] Through local adaptation and resistance, these became five common denominators for the cultural sphere of East Asia approximately during the Sui–Tang Dynasties (581–906 AD). In *The Problem of China* (1922), Bertrand Russell comes to the conclusion that the Chinese use of ideograms is one of the major features that gives Sinica

---

[15] See note 12, p. 92 above.

[16] The word 'Mahayana' literally means 'greater vehicle', reflecting the claims of its followers to more inclusive and powerful teaching than those of their predecessors in the Hinayana, or 'lesser vehicle', a term generally resented by Theravada Buddhists. Mahayana Buddhism has as a central concept the potential buddhahood innate in all beings. Buddhism entered China, where it encountered resistance from Confucianism and Taoism, and from there spread to Korea (fourth cent. AD) and to Japan (sixth cent. AD).

its distinctive character. Russell and others consider written Chinese as one of the main qualities that makes Chinese society and the educative process so unique with a profound effect on Eastern civilization (Smith, 1991). Russell quotes a Chinese scholar, Chi Li, as follows:

> Language has been traditionally treated by European scientists as a collection of sounds instead of an expression of something inner and deeper than the vocal apparatus as it should be. The accumulative effect of language-symbols upon one's mental formulation is still an unexploited field. Dividing the world culture of the living races on this basis, one perceives a fundamental difference of its types between the alphabetical users and the hieroglyphic users, each of which has its own virtues and vices. ... The Chinese language is by all means the counterpart of the alphabetic stock. It lacks most of the virtues that are found in truth, it is invulnerable to storm and stress. It has already protected the Chinese civilization for more than forty centuries. It is solid, square, and beautiful, exactly as the spirit it represents. Whether it is the spirit that has produced this language or whether this language has in turn accentuated the spirit remains to be determined. (Russell's quote, in Smith, 191: 16)

While language and Confucianism are more important, and perhaps more pertinent to our discussion of 'Kejurization', there were interdependence and reciprocity among those five elements (Gao, 1984). Together, they define and describe a large part of mentalities, meritocracy, work ethics, family structure and state legitimacy in East Asia. The Cultural Sphere was over-shadowed by Western intrusion and modernization. But its deep structure survived, and like a zillion-terabyte database, the inner dimension of the Cultural Sphere is still at work.

It is worth noting that what jump-started this disintegrating culture was Japanese colonialism, paradoxically the darkest in modern East Asia. It all began with the revival of Confucianism in imperial Meiji, as noted early in the previous chapter. Though once forsaken, this ideology was revitalized in Meiji as the core of a modern educational system, one we could label as 'Japanized, Modernized Confucianism'. The Japanese influence and the impact of re-Confucianization in the Japanese colonies should not be underestimated.

In their discussion of foreign influence on Korean education, Sungho Lee and Sung-Hwa Lee point out: 'It is important to keep in mind that whatever form of education Korea has had, whether it is system or thought, the greatest influence was brought from Japan' (S. Lee, 1989: 96). Japanese education in Korea has left the Koreans with a centralized system of university governance, including 'the entrance exam system, the unchallenged authority of professors, and the academic subject-matter-centered curriculum' (S. Lee, 1989: 95). In Taiwan, due to the even longer colonial rule, the impact of Japanese education could be even stronger than in Korea, though this might be overshadowed by the arrival of the Nationalist government from Mainland China. The fact of the matter is that Taiwan's universities built during Japanese colonial times have been the foundation of higher education in the later years (Wu, Chen and Wu, 1989).

The vestige of the East Asian Cultural Sphere defines many characteristics of the modern system of selection, such as the meritocratic principle, folk belief in the Dragon Gate, veneration for learning, respect for authority, and so forth. This whole set of linguistic, epistemic and socio-political components pave the way for Kejurization.

But, of course, we should not forget some more direct impacts that the old exam systems left on the new. As noted, the system in Taiwan shows considerable continuity of the imperial civil exams. In Korea, the civil exam system was administered for 900 years (958–1894) with a view to promoting Confucianism and consolidating a central authority of a unified Korea (Ji, 1992). After national unification, increasing bureaucratization and the need to offset the dominance of aristocrats once made the state-held civil exams a prime avenue of mobility. In Japan, civil service exams were first tried in the early eighth century, modelled after the *keju* system. However, Japan's system differed from imperial *keju* in a couple of ways. First and foremost was perhaps the link between exams and employment. While in China those who succeeded in the exams always got a high-ranking civil service position, in Japan the main route to the élite positions was hereditary privilege. As a result, while in China the system reduced the power of aristocracy, in Korea and Japan, it reinforced rather than altered the ascriptive status (Amano, 1990; Deuchler, 1992; Robinson, 1991).

The systems of civil service exams were abruptly terminated in China, Japan and Korea. However, Confucianism was rejuvenated by colonial education and a hybrid of the meritocratic exam system and an ethnic segregation policy that was implemented in Korea and Taiwan. They provided a catalyst for the re-emergence of an Asian version of the exam systems in the modern era.

All the features of Kejurization converged on one unique phenomenon: a national pecking order of universities based on a national pecking order of students. It enables the central authority to dictate what the élite should be, what they should know, and select them accordingly.

HOW DID THE UNIVERSITY ENTRANCE SYSTEM AFFECT THE UNIVERSITY SYSTEM *PER SE*? A STUDY OF HIERARCHICAL ORDER

One remnant of the past within the contemporary Japanese education system is *Kanson minpi*: 'reverence for the official institution and contempt of the private' (Amano, 1986; Enzan, 1992). '*Kan*' or 'official' stands for '*kan gaku*', schools established by the government, which is a synonym of today's *kokuritsu* (national). The phrase *Kanson minpi* is originally Chinese, and it is even more obviously embodied in the education systems of Taiwan and Korea. In 1886, Japan's Imperial University Order was promulgated, transforming the University of Tokyo into the first Imperial University.

The pattern was duplicated by the Japanese colonial administration establishing imperial universities in each colony – which duplicated this structure of putting a public university at the top of the system. The Order clearly set forth two principles in the new system of education: (1) universities should serve the need of the state; (2) the state-run universities were the primary training ground for the bureaucratic élite (Cummings *et al.*, 1979; NSDR, 1987). In the postwar era, *Kanson minpi* was exemplified in the continuing pre-eminence of the former imperial universities. The result is a state-controlled hierarchism (Amano, 1986; Enzan, 1992). This is also manifested in the extensive differences between the national and private universities in each country. This pecking order of university ranking enables the government to create with efficiency a meritorious class of élite and a new generation. That pecking order is in fact a reflection of the pecking order of students, and the sole arbiter for making that order is the entrance exams – a system almost 'Procrustean' in its high but rigid standards.

Pecking order, or ranking, is often thought of as a matter of vanity. In Japan, Korea and Taiwan, however, the hierarchical order of fame is valued very substantively. It is immediately associated with the career prospects of students, family investment in education, and the employment pattern of the government and corporate world (Rohlen, 1983; Inui, 1993). For a university itself, the prime concern for ranking is how it reflects and affects the viability of the university. Japanese universities have been subjected to different rankings through an array of variables. This is in part because higher education is associated with the growing interests of different stakeholders, who need to evaluate and rank universities in a way meaningful and informative to them. A study of how universities are ranked by each of these interest groups could be very revealing. In theory, there could be an infinite number of ways to organize universities in ranking order. For instance, universities might be ranked by students' evaluation of them, by the number of popular professors, by the dissertations published, by library acquisitions, or by the satisfaction scale of teaching, service, cuisine or facilities. Here, I would choose variables that I consider as essentials underpinning the generally adopted view of how universities are ranked. They include the total scores of entrance exams in the three countries (in Japan, a more informative value for them is the *hensachi*, to be discussed later), high-level positions in government and companies, the amount of funding for university research projects, and the number of research papers completed jointly by the university and companies. These criteria relate the role of university to society and national development in such fields as industry, science and technology, as well as the élite core for leadership or workforce.

The pecking order of ranking arranged by all the variables mentioned above splits along the divide between national and private universities. This 'binary pair', to borrow a structuralist term, marks each university, codifying it in a number of ways. It codifies its financial source, the very lifeline of the institution. While national universities are fully funded by the government, the private universities receive very insignificant, if any, support from the government. It also codifies the distinction of selectivity. For the national universities, James and Benjamin (1988) observe:

> The Ministry supports the system as being the best way to allocate scarce student places and jobs. It is perceived as meritocratic; no matter what a student's connections, there is no way to get past the barrier except to succeed on the examinations. There are no admittance quotas of any other sort and places cannot be bought, especially at national universities.

Private universities, on the other hand, are more likely to base some of their admissions on letters of recommendation (James and Benjamin, 1988). Fifty per cent of private universities do so for students who do not have sufficiently high test scores (JMOE, 1975). In the wake of the more recent declining application ratio for private universities, 90 per cent of private universities are enthusiastic in using recommendations or other easy measures to attract more students (Kuroki, 1994). The data for 1992 are given in Table 3.4. For private universities, the acceptance ratio is 37.2 per cent for the entrance exam system, but 99.8–99.9 per cent for recommended students from affiliated or designated high schools, which is virtually a rubber-stamp process (NSDR, 1993). Partially as a result of their market-oriented 'behaviour', the private universities are in general not viewed as élitist, except for one or two. The majority serve as 'shock absorbers', responding rapidly to the ups and downs of demographic changes. At the same time the national universities maintain their status and high quality by maintaining the number of schools (James and Benjamin, 1988).

Take Japan. As Figure 3.6 shows, private universities increased rapidly after WWII, but their expansion does not weaken the status of national ones, not only because national universities are well funded by the state, but also because they retain their élite position by a strict gate-keeping entrance exam system. The university 'gate' is often seen as vital because it provides an express to socio-academic mobility. Japanese measure how difficult it is to enter by the competition ratio (*kyôsô ritsu*) and deviation scores (*hensachi*).[17] The competition ratio is = examinees ÷ those who succeeded.

Table 3.4 The number of students admitted into universities through recommendations, by national and private universities, 1992. *Source*: NSDR, *Nyûshi Seido to Shiritsu Daigaku: Shiridai Nyûshi no Kenjô to Kadai* (Entrance examination system and the private university: the status and issues of the entrance exams for private universities), (Tokyo: Nihon Shiritsu Daigaku Renmei, 1993), 15.

Category	Total number of admitted students	Number of students admitted through recommendations	Percentage of students admitted through recommendations
	A	B	B/A
National	104,893	6918	6.6%
Public	15,290	1487	9.7%
Private	421,259	147,735	35.1%
Total	541,442	156,140	28.8%

---

[17] The formula for *hensachi* is: $Hensachi = \left(\dfrac{score - average}{S.D.} \times 10 \right) + 50$

(S.D. = Standard Deviation). For example, if in a maths test, student A = 76, B = 55, C = 58, D =100, E = 65, F = 60, G = 50, H = 0, then,
average (for all the students) = (76 + 55 + 58 + 100 + 65 + 60 + 50 + 0) ÷ 8 = 58,
and S.D.= $\sqrt{\left\{ (76-58)^2 + (55-58)^2 + (58-58)^2 ...+(0-58)^2 \right\} \div 8}$ = 26.41.

So, student A's *hensachi* = $\left(\dfrac{76-58}{26.41} \times 10 \right) + 50 = 56.8$.

Likewise, student D = 65.9, and student H = 28.

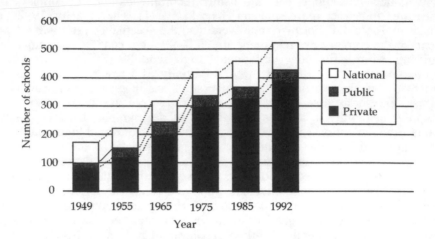

Figure 3.6 The postwar increase of national, public, and private universities in Japan, 1949–92. *Source*: Based on Jiji Tsûshinsha, *Kyôiku Deta Randdo* (A databook of educational statistics), (Tokyo: Jiji Tsûshinsha, 1994), 32.

This indicator could occasionally be misleading, however. A university could attract a lot of students to apply not because it was better, but because usually they found it easy to enter. In this sense, *hensachi* is more reliable. It is a norm-referenced scoring system indicating how well one student performed in the mock tests of entrance exams as compared to the whole group. By studying the average *hensachi* of those who entered a university, one can have a pretty accurate idea of how difficult it is to succeed. *Hensachi* can indicate the academic achievement of a student as compared to other students, or the difficulty level of a university as compared to other universities. The data on rankings are published periodically by Obunsha, a Japanese commercial firm which supplies information eagerly purchased by prospective students, and they tend to be stable across fields and time. Obunsha bases its estimates on mock exams it gives which simulate actual examinations. The following tables are created on the basis of Obunsha data. The range of difficulty scale by *hensachi* is given for the top ten national and private universities. By comparing the élite schools in these two categories, these tables try to find out if there was a fixed pattern of how their difficulty scales relate to each other, and how this pattern, if any, changed over the past years (see Table 3.5).

In Table 3.5, the *hensachi* for liberal arts of the top ten national and private universities are given side by side. For example, in 1975, the best university in this discipline was Tokyo University, with a *hensachi* score of 69.2. The tenth of the national universities was Tohoku University, and its *hensachi* was 61.9. Thus, we have a range of 69.2–61.9 for the top ten national universities. In the same way, the *hensachi* for the top ten private universities was 65.5–60.6. The difference between them was 3.7–1.3, as the number 1 national is 3.7 higher than the number 1 private, and the number 10 national is 1.3 higher than the number 10 private. The *hensachi* for physics are given in Table 3.6.

Table 3.5 *Hensachi* ranges of liberal arts for the top ten Japanese universities, by national and private universities, 1975–94. *Source*: My calculations, which are based on Obunsha, *Daigaku Nyûgaku Nan'i Rankingu* (The ranking of difficulty scale for entering universities), (Tokyo: Obunsha, 1975, 1980, 1992, 1994); and Kôzo Futatsugi, *Kyûteikokudai no Hôkai* (The fall of former imperial universities), (Tokyo: WAVE, 1993), 54.

Year	National universities	Private universities	NU–PU difference
1975	69.2–61.9	65.5–60.6	3.7–1.3
1980	68.1–62.3	66.0–61.7	2.1–0.6
1985	74.8–64.5	70.6–64.0	4.2–0.5
1992	71.7–64.6	68.7–64.2	3.0–0.4
1994	75.4–68.2	71.0–66.4	4.4–1.8

Table 3.6 *Hensachi* ranges of physics for the top ten Japanese universities, by national and private universities, 1975–94. *Source*: My calculations, which are based on Obunsha, *Daigaku Nyûgaku Nan'i Rankingu* (The ranking of difficulty scale for entering universities), (Tokyo: Obunsha, 1975, 1980, 1992, 1994); and Kôzo Futatsugi, *Kyûteikokudai no Hôkai* (The fall of former imperial universities), (Tokyo: WAVE, 1993), 54.

Year	National universities	Private universities	NU–PU difference
1975	65.3–57.1	63.0–53.4	2.3–3.7
1980	67.2–58.7	64.7–56.6	2.5–2.1
1985	72.4–62.4	68.7–59.5	3.7–2.9
1992	71.2–62.5	67.3–62.1	3.9–0.3
1994	73.3–65.2	69.3–62.4	4.0–2.8

If we look at minimum scores needed for entrance into public and private universities by a wider scope of departments, Tokyo and Kyoto, the two old Imperial universities, are on top; almost all public universities rank above the median in most subjects. A minority of private universities are also above the median, Waseda and Keio leading the list. Table 3.7 illustrates that ranking division in August 1983.

In Table 3.7, the number of public universities is relatively constant across fields whereas private universities are concentrated in low-cost areas such as economics and literature, which they consequently dominate. Although private universities constitute 70 per cent of the total, the percentage of private universities above the median is always less than 50 per cent (usually more than 30 per cent), and the percentage of public universities above the median is always above 50 per cent (usually more than 70 per cent). In the two areas where most private universities are found, many of them new, small and specialized institutions, the disparity between the two sectors is, paradoxically, the greatest. Tokyo and Waseda consistently head the list for their respective sectors (James and Benjamin, 1988).

Table 3.7 Minimum entrance examination scores for public and private universities, by fields, 1983. *Source*: Estelle James and Gail Benjamin, *Public Policy and Private Education in Japan* (London: Macmillan Press, 1988), 85.

	Econ. and Business	Lit. and Educ.	Law	Science	Engineer.	Medical Science
Number of public universities	42	46	25	37	57	49
Number of private universities	100	117	28	25	55	28
Total	142	163	53	62	112	77
Number and percentage of public universities above median	42 (100%)	45 (98%)	14 (56%)	21 (57%)	41 (72%)	35 (71%)
Number and percentage of private universities above median	30 (30%)	36 (31%)	12 (43%)	10 (40%)	15 (27%)	3 (11%)
Public range of scores	77–52	75–55	76–53	71–47	71–44	77–58
Private range of scores	72–38	69–38	73–38	68–38	65–39	72–46
Top public universities and scores	Tokyo (77)	Kyoto (75)	Tokyo (76)	Tokyo (71)	Tokyo (71)	Tokyo (77)
Top private universities and scores	Waseda (72)	Waseda (69)	Waseda (72)	Waseda (68)	Waseda (65)	Waseda (72)

In Taiwan, the concept of *Kanson minpi* (reverence for the official institution and contempt of the private) is more pronounced.[18] The public–

---

[18] The Japanese '*Kanson minpi*' is a word-for-word translation of the Chinese phrase: '*Guanzün minbei*'.

private division of higher education is more clear-cut, and less complex than in Japan.

First of all, the nationally administered entrance exams in Taiwan, *Daixüe Liankao*, are the only arbiter for entering universities, regardless of being national, public or private. Individual schools do not give their own exams for admission. Second, the leading private universities in Taiwan are far less prestigious than Waseda and Keio in Japan. The pecking order of these higher institutions for 1994 is given in Table 3.8.

Fujen and Dongwu, the two best private universities in Taiwan, are ranked as low as the twelfth and thirteenth places. This is very close to the popular concept that almost any national university is more prestigious than the private universities. Similar to Taiwan, in Korea national entrance exams are the only sorter for universities. However, unlike Taiwan, top private universities enjoy better ranking in Korea similarly to Waseda and Keio.

To summarize the foregoing analysis, we can see that the scores for the best national universities remain higher than the private ones across the years. This suggests that it is generally harder to get into a national university than a private one, although at the lower level of ranking, this difference may be smaller, as one can perceive in Tables 3.5 and 3.6 for Japan.

Table 3.8 The rankings of the top fifteen universities by the minimal scores of *Daixüe Liankao*, Taiwan, 1994. *Source*: My calculation, which is based on Longmen, *Lishi Shiti Xiangjie* (History exams: questions and answers with annotated answers), (Taipei: Longmen, 1994a), unpaginated appendix.

Rank	Category	Name of university	Minimal scores of entrance exams
1	National	Taiwan Normal College	444.18
2	National	Taiwan University	440.10
3	National	Politics University	428.94
4	National	Gaoxing Normal College	416.43
5	National	Zhanghua Normal College	408.33
6	National	Taibei Normal College	402.92
7	Metropolitan	Taipei City Normal College	399.38
8	National	Jiayi Normal College	396.80
9	National	Zhongxing University	396.65
10	National	Qinghua University	393.33
11	National	Taidong Normal College	392.57
12	• Private	Fujen Catholic University	390.15
13	• Private	Dongwu University	388.47
14	National	Pingdong Normal College	386.60
15	National	Jiaoda University	386.38

Notes: The 'minimal scores' is the average of all minimal requirement scores for different departments of the university.
• refers to the private universities.

Still, even for Japan, by measuring the *hensachi* of the top ten, the difficulty ranking of the national universities has always been higher than that of the private universities in the past 20 years or so. Thus viewed, the alleged 'reverence for the official institution and contempt of the private' (j. *Kanson minpi*; c. *Guanzün minbei*) survives today as a reality.

Hensachi, the normalized value of entrance exams, is a facile and handy index to rank Japanese universities. Yet, it does not answer the question of why they are so ranked. Ranking shown through *hensachi* is composed of and conditioned by academic, economic and career factors, all deeply grounded in the Japanese social as well as economic structure. To explain that point, I will use the metaphor of the 'Gate'. More often than not, scholars focus on the entry point of Asian universities. In observing their screening role, Shinil Kim (1992), for instance, likens a Japanese university to a movie theatre, as, for both university and the theatre, an admission ticket is the most important requirement. A more accurate metaphor, however, needs also to include the 'interior' and the 'exit' (Arimoto, in Asahi, 1994). By that I refer to a university as an academy in its own realm, and as an enterprise that provides the outside world with human resources, both of which are fundamentally important. Let us start with the 'exit'.

A university can be ranked by its 'exit', the school–workplace inter-relationship in terms of career mobility. The important function of the university 'exit' has drawn overarching concern from people, as it puts to an end the academic life of students and leads them to social mobility. One way of assessing this 'exit' is to rank universities by counting their graduates who become presidents in Japanese companies (*Shachô*), as shown in Table 3.9.

In Table 3.9, for all Japanese companies, domination by graduates from the private universities is obvious. This is perhaps even more so for small companies. But the executive positions of the large Japanese companies, as shown in the rightmost column of Table 3.9, have been largely taken by national university graduates. Furthermore, as is demonstrated in Asahi (1994), in a Japanese company planning- and strategy-related responsibilities usually go to graduates of those universities with top *hensachi* levels, which means Todai-led national universities, especially former imperial ones, plus Keio and Waseda.[19]

In contrast, employees from private universities are assigned to the implemention level. Different credentials bring graduates into basically two different worlds of a Japanese company: 'administrative level = menial labour = private universities' and 'planning/strategic level = mental labour = top *hensachi* universities' (Akaike, 1994), although it is equally true that some 'local' national universities, such as Chiba, Hiroshima, Okayama, Yamaguchi, etc., also join the majority of private universities in producing manpower for dealing with daily routine work. This division of labour is schematized in Figure 3.7. As expressed here, at the decision-making level, a large proportion came from national universities, while the daily business level was largely composed of graduates from private universities.

---

[19] The former imperial universities refer to, in the hierarchical order of ranking, Tokyo University, Kyoto University, Tohoku University, Kyushu University, Hokkaido University, Osaka University and Nagoya University.

Table 3.9 University ranking by the number of presidents (*Shachô*) of Japanese companies who graduated from different universities. *Source*: Teikoku Deitâbankusha, *Cosmos 2*, in Asahi Shinbunsha, ed., *Daigaku Rankingu: 561 Daigaku Daigakkô Sôlan* (University ranking: an overview of 561 colleges and universities), (Tokyo: Asahi Shinbunsha, 1994a), 72–5.

Rank	Type of company		
	General[a]	Small	Large[b]
1	Tokyo Univ.	• Keio Univ.	Tokyo Univ.
2	• Keio Univ.	Tokyo Univ.	• Keio Univ.
3	• Waseda Univ.	• Waseda Univ.	• Waseda Univ.
4	Kyoto Univ.	Kyoto Univ.	Kyoto Univ.
5	• Japan Univ.	• Nihon Univ.	Hitotsubashi Univ.
6	• Chûo Univ.	• Chûo Univ.	Tohoku Univ.
7	• Meiji Univ.	• Meiji Univ.	Osaka Univ.
8	Touhoku Univ.	• Doushisha Univ.	• Nihon Univ.
9	Hitotsubashi Univ.	Tohoku Univ.	Kobe Univ.
10	• Doushisha Univ.	• Rikkyo Univ.	• Chûo Univ.

Notes: • The dot means private universities.
a. Companies of more than 300 employees. b. Large companies with publicized registration.

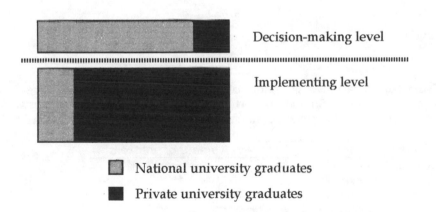

Decision-making level

Implementing level

▨ National university graduates

■ Private university graduates

Figure 3.7 A schema of *Shachôs'* responsibilities in Japanese companies by national or private university graduates.

The picture of the university–job market interrelationship would be far from complete without including the career situation in government and public offices. The primacy of the élite university graduates in that vast bureaucracy has been illustrated by Rohlen (1983). Most of the top-echelon bureaucrats came from former national universities. A typical example may be the premiership, as displayed in Table 3.10.

This preponderance of national graduates in the body politic will be easier to understand if we bear in mind that the chief purpose of the imperial university was to meet the needs of the state apparatus, which was expressly defined in the '1886 Imperial Decree of Imperial University'. One of these needs was to supply the government with élite bureaucrats. While this may not be found in the written goals and objectives of the national universities now, there seems to exist a tacit compact of employment between the government agencies and the élite national universities (see Table 3.11).

In Table 3.11, the élite national universities claimed the lion's share of the high-level civil service. The students produced by these former imperial universities have been entrusted with the major positions in Japan in government and business. Together, they came to form the socio-economic core to support and sustain an advanced nation as early as the early Meiji era. Given the eventful, tumultuous transformation of contemporary Japan, it is amazing that this pattern has not altered much.

Another necessary component for being a top-ranking university lies in its academic accomplishment. Using the earlier metaphor, this factor can then be compared to the activities carried out in the university 'interior'. To some, this may be considered as an even more important factor than the previous one, since the primary task of higher education is scholastic pursuit. One important index for this is how many research projects have been completed with support from external funding sources.

In Japan, there are approximately 400 funding companies (*josei zaidan*), out of which about 65 were directly involved in academic research. Table 3.12 is related to the number and amount of completed research projects funded by these 65 major funding sources.

Table 3.10 The university origin of Japanese Premiers for both pre- and post-war periods. *Source*: Based on Kôzo Futatsugi, *Kyûteikokudai no Hôkai* (The fall of former imperial universities), (Tokyo: WAVE, 1993), 76–9.

Name of university	Number of premiers
National university	31
Tokyo University	15
Kyoto University	2
Kobei Commerce University	1
Tokyo Commerce University	1
Army Academy	6
Navy Academy	6
Private university	5
Waseda University	3
Meiji University	1
Keio University	1
Others	3
Total	39

Table 3.11 Universities ranked by the number of successful students for the higher-level national civil service examination, 1922, 1973, 1993. *Sources*: Asahi Shinbunsha, ed., *Daigaku Rankingu: 561 Daigaku Daigakkô Sôlan* (University ranking: an overview of 561 colleges and universities), (Tokyo: Asahi Shinbunsha, 1994a), 165; and Kôzo Futatsugi, *Kyûteikokudai no Hôkai* (The fall of former imperial universities), (Tokyo: WAVE, 1993), 71–2.

Rank	1922		1973		1993	
	University	Students	University	Students	University	Students
1	Tokyo	496	Tokyo	449	Tokyo	508
2	Kyoto	200	Kyoto	204	Kyoto	197
3	• Waseda	127	Tokyo Engineer.	67	Tokyo Engineer.	101
4	Tokyo Engineer.	108	Hokkaido	58	• Waseda	95
5	Tohoku	106	Tohoku	55	Tohoku	88
6	• Tokyo Science	84	Nagoya	45	Hokkaido	69
7	Hiroshima	64	• Waseda	42	Nagoya	69
8	Osaka	56	Osaka	39	Tokyo Engineer.	58
9	Tsukuba	50	Kyushu	37	Kyushu	56
10	• Keio	46	• Nagoya Engineer.	26	• Keio	51

Note: • The dot means private universities.

In terms of research competence as judged by the funding organizations, there is no question that the national universities as a whole are overwhelmingly superior to the private ones. Even Waseda and Keio were ranked very low. The decision to offer projects is based on the importance of topics and the recommendation of reputable professors or associations (Asahi Shinbunsha, 1994a). Even when we included research institutions of Japanese companies such as NTT, Nissan or Toshiba, national universities still had the vast majority of research paper publications (Futatsugi, 1993).

The review of those three reference points, the 'gate', the 'exit' and the 'interior', brings out a ranking configuration, wherein the élite national universities and the private universities contrast markedly. In the past couple of years, the gap between national and private, which seemed to be closing for a while, has widened again. This resulted from problems on both sides, especially the problems of the private universities. First is the 'bubble-economy' recession. In Japan, while huge sums of money were made on paper, the ultimate basis for much of the lavish spending was likely as not the hopelessly distended values attached to relatively small chunks of earth, glass and concrete in down-town Tokyo. In 1992, the Nikkei Index Tokyo Stock Exchange was 60 per cent down from 1989, and real estate plunged 50 per cent: 'everything in the country was suddenly worth half of what it had been two years earlier' (Gibney, 1992; Greenfeld, 1994). The budgetary stringency for education, plus the impact of the student population decrease, generated a bleak picture, a winter for higher education, or, in the Japanese term, an era of 'university elimination' (Arimoto, in Asahi, 1994a; Kuroki, in Asahi, 1994a).

Next is the demographic factor. According to Arimoto Akira (in Asahi, 1994a), Director of the Higher Education Research Center, Hiroshima University, as a result of the population decrease of 18-year-olds, to keep the existing number of universities running alone requires an increase of the enrolment ratio from the current 28 per cent to 40 per cent.

To cap it all, from 1993, the 18-year-old population started to decrease, which plagued the private sector most, since they were subject to free-market regulation, and the economy scale was their lifeline. The decline of their enrolled freshmen was the major part of their plight.

First, the awesome burden of high examination fees, tuition, etc. in the private universities drove students from private universities located in big cities to more affordable local national/public universities. The relaxation of the First-stage Entrance Exams in its requirement also made those who initially aimed at private universities think it easier to try the national or public ones. The outcome of these three factors is shown in Table 3.13.

Nine major private universities, including Waseda and Keio, suffered from over a 10 per cent decrease in applicants. Anti-climatic to this dismal situation, new schools and/or departments have cropped up on an unprecedented scale ever since the end of the first 'Baby Boom' in 1968 (Kuroki, 1994).

Table 3.12 Universities ranked by completed research projects supported by the external funding organizations, Japan, 1993. *Source*: Josei Zaidan Shiryô Sentâ (The information center of funding institutions), quoted from Asahi Shinbunsha, ed., *Daigaku Rankingu: 561 Daigaku Daigakkô Sôlan* (University ranking: an overview of 561 colleges and universities), (Tokyo: Asahi Shinbunsha, 1994a), 90–1.

Rank	Name of university	Number of projects	Funding (in ¥1000)
1	Tokyo University	353	934,602
2	Kyoto University	192	389,540
3	Osaka University	182	363,600
4	Tohoku University	151	331,700
5	Kyushu University	143	294,385
6	Tokyo Engineer. University	95	227,117
7	Hokkaido University	133	218,130
8	Nagoya University	111	207,868
9	Hiroshima University	94	168,420
10	• Keio University	72	124,049
11	Tsukuba University	67	121,895
12	Chiba University	58	105,908
13	Kumamoto University	34	83,280
14	• Waseda University	47	81,360

Note • The dot means private universities.

One of its causes was the relaxation of the government's Regulation Policy of Private Universities (*kisei seisaku*) in the late 1980s. In the 1960s, the Japanese government played an unimportant role in the market economy, and the private universities had to resort to expansion to keep managerial performance from falling by the law of 'economy of scale'. But from 1976 onward, the state provided subsidies for the private universities, and, as a trade-off, the private universities yielded their control of student enrolment quotas to the government. As a result, while the government subsidy did not generate fundamental changes to the features of the market economy, government control of the student quota did give rise to two consequences:

1. it imposed a 'coercive cartel' on the private universities and contained their economic size and relative differentiation;
2. as the quota system in a way 'froze' their scale economy, private universities had to raise the tuition for each student to sustain the schooling and maintain their profit (Yonezawa, 1992).

After 1986, the government resumed its non-interference attitude towards the private universities and this unleashed a new surge of expansion. To characterize the current predicament of private universities simply as a demographic event, as some Japanese scholars did, would cursorily dismiss such important factors as government policy, market economics, the prolonged recession and, above all, the after-effect of the entrance exam policies.

Table 3.13 The change in the number of applicants for Japan's major private universities in 1994 over 1993. *Source*: Based on Hiroshi Kuroki, *Kenshô Daigaku Kaikaku* (Examine university reform), (Tokyo: Ronsôsha, 1994), 28.

Name of university	Reduction (–) or increase (+) of students	
	Number	Percentage
Aoyama Gakuin University	+ 697	+ (1.5)
Jôchi University	– 1259	– (4.3)
Chûo University	– 16,079	– (19.3)*
Doshisha University	– 4917	– (11.4)*
Fukuoka University	– 1882	– (3.8)
Hosei University	– 8562	– (12.2)*
Japan Women's College	– 2498	– (20.1)*
Kansai University	+ 8588	+ (10.3)*
Kansai Gakuin University	– 6562	– (16.3)*
Keio University	– 6564	– (11.1)*
Meiji University	–11,539	– (13.9)*
Rikkyo University	–1251	– (3.1)
Tohoku Gakuin University	– 1882	– (8.7)
Tokai University	– 402	– (0.8)
Vocational College	– 498	– (1.3)
Waseda University	– 14,435	– (10.9)*

Note: * marks a decrease or increase of over 10%.

A DISCUSSION

After World War II, the Western impact, especially through the American presence, was notable in East Asia. Due to this, there was a rapid expansion of enrolments, the implantation of democratization, and some decentralization of education in the three countries. This change can be described as part of a process of Eurocentric globalization, the sweeping tendency to isomorphism that has comparatively ritualized many aspects of formal education worldwide (Ramirez and Meyer, 1981; DiMaggio and Powell, 1983; Ramirez and Boli, 1987). Before long, however, in East Asia the national examination systems, very much contradictory to this new direction, re-emerged, justified by a broadly felt need to regulate quality, weed out corruption and give more chance to bright, low-income students (McGinn *et al.*, 1980). In a word, meritocracy was valued despite Westernizing trends and this was embodied in exam systems. This re-emergence occasioned two forces, which I define as a 'pulling force' and a 'pushing force'. By 'pulling force', I refer to the expanding governmental control of the system surrounding the entrance exams since the 1950s. The institutional climax of this was marked by the nationalization of key elements of entrance exams by the governments: 1954 in Taiwan, 1969 in Korea and 1979 in Japan. My term 'pushing force' refers to the '*juku* phenomenon', a growing proportion of students sent by parents to cram schools in an educational 'arms race' (Rohlen, 1980). In Tokyo, 94 per cent of the students attending *juku* came from public schools, demonstrating the limited capability of public schools to prepare them for tertiary education (Kouichi, 1990). In all of East Asia, while the exam systems are subjected to growing centralization, the sources of knowledge dissemination have become decentralized and privatized, manifested in the proliferation of *juku* in Japan, *buxiban* in Taiwan, and, to a lesser extent, *hakwons* in Korea.

In comparing and contrasting, we find a convergence pattern among the exam systems of Japan, Korea and Taiwan in the postwar era. This pattern bears the following coordinates with the ancient imperial exams:

1. a hierarchical pecking order of students across the nation;
2. state authority in ratifying and empowering core knowledge;
3. a heavy dependence on written forms of questions and answers;
4. a strict uniformity and standardization of test form and content;
5. the 'phenomenon of repeaters (j. *rônin*; k. *Jai su saeng*; c. *Chonkao sheng*)'; and
6. the close meritocratic nexus forging schools with power and status.

This combination was hardly found elsewhere. To accentuate its cultural basis and context, I coined the term 'Kejurization'. While we may state that ideals of the remote past were the conceptual origin of Kejurization, it is however the meritocratic principle, policy and *praxis* institutionalized during the Meiji era that jump-started this modern process.

Exams, as a new merit system, completed the transition of society from particularism to universalism. The coupling between achieved status and social status was a legalization process embodied in a series of major laws of education and recruitment. The meritocratic system of exams did not and perhaps could not serve as an equalizer of different social strata, because inequality is attributed to a much larger contextual structure. But it may still work towards efficiency and excellence through mobility, often achieving a balance between excellence and equality. The hierarchical status of national and private universities is a typical case in point. The competitive entrance exam system supplies the élite national universities with high-standard students, who have contributed to the leadership and economic growth in East Asia. In the three countries, the merit system has also helped to maintain social equilibrium, justice and impartiality, and legitimacy of authority, and it has produced an intensely motivated, highly achieving and hard-working élite as well as manpower.

CHAPTER 4

What kind of exams? Questions of world history and mathematics in the three countries

I know the kings of England, and I quote the fights historical,
From Marathon to Waterloo, in order categorical ...
I'm very well acquainted too with matters mathematical,
I understand equations, both simple and quadratical,
About binomial theorem I'm teeming with a lot o' news –
With many cheerful facts about the square on the hypotenuse.

– *Major-General Stanley, in W. S. Gilbert*, The Pirates of Penzance, *Act 1*

'What knowledge has been tested in exams?' To me, in search of the rationale of university entrance exams, that is the question of questions. Before everything else, one basic fact, albeit a truism to many, needs to be clarified. It is taken for granted that, in Japan, Taiwan and Korea, exam questions should be posed and answered in black and white. *Viva voce* (oral test) and other oral forms of exams or assessments, such as interviews, have in general not been taken with genuine seriousness and sincerity. That clarification legitimizes us to focus on the written form of exams.

An exam paper is subject to immediate depreciation as soon as the exams are over. However, these previously taken exams may tell us a great deal about the students' frame of mind and the intellectual profile of the would-be core class. They may also be used diagnostically, like a cardiogram, to show the strengths and weaknesses of the students. To literally untie those archival packages, brush away the dust, and peruse them made me feel like I was reading personal files. It also furnishes a valuable telltale of education in different historical periods.

This chapter attempts to learn what the exams required the students to know. I have chosen World History for human science, and Mathematics for natural science, because both have been very 'normative' and stable subjects, and both have been better kept as subjects of exams through history. Comparatively, other subjects are inconstant and less available as historical records. In an exploratory approach, I try to find out what kind of questions were asked in exams. What kind of intellectual ability was needed to answer them? How have the entrance exams changed over time? What kinds of efforts were made to change them? And, how did the same subject differ in how it was examined in the different countries? In each of the sections, 'Never Forget World History' and 'Mathematics: The Basics of Western Knowledge', my study follows the chronological order of the postwar period. The form and content of typical sample questions is scrutinized before a generalization is made about their overall pattern and their trend.

NEVER FORGET WORLD HISTORY

> When pressed to answer the query 'Why history?' historians have fallen back on the long-standing defenses of history as a teacher of moral or practical lessons, an object of nostalgia, a justification for either old or new regimes, a gratification of human curiosity, a witness to God's power, and, of course, a science.
> – *Ernst Breisach*, Historiography, *1983*

History, as part of education, was suspended in December 1945 by the Headquarters of the Allied Occupation, because the 'Japanese Government has used education to inculcate militaristic and ultranationalistic ideologies which have been inextricably interwoven in certain textbooks imposed upon students' (Beauchamp and Vardaman, 1994). When the history course was reopened the very next year, its function was supposed to be a world of difference from the old one. From 1946 to 1948, entrance exams were given by different universities. There were two test papers under the general categories of *bunka* (human science) and *rikka* (natural science) with a mixture of disciplines in each. *Bunka* might include English, Japanese, ancient Chinese and some history. *Rikka* generally consisted of maths, chemistry and physics. The exam questions show a continuity of the prewar style. The two main questions related to world history are listed below:

Questions:
- Describe the circumstances before and after the 1898 Hundred Days reform in China.
- In which year of the Western Calendar (*seireki*) did the Meiji Reform take place? What was the domestic situation in the US and all the European countries?
- 1946 exam questions, First Higher School (Obunsha, NSMS, 1946: 3)[1]

The above questions demanded a historical rethinking of the reform movements in the East with a comparative reference to the world powers. It seemed to be an effort to reflect all over again on the history of Eastern modernization from the outset, given the miserable defeat of Japan in World War II. Furthermore, the exam engaged the young élite with the past of both the East and the West in a more rudimentary, more holistic manner. This included histories of not only statecraft, but also politics, science and comparative culture:

---

[1] The First Higher School later became part of Tokyo University.

Example I
Question: What were the three main political trends in Europe in the nineteenth century?
– 1947 Exam question, First Higher School (Obunsha, NSMS, 1947: 1)

Example II
Question: Explain the development of Western science at the early years of the modern age.
– 1948 Exam question, Second Higher School (Obunsha, NSMS, 1948: 2)[2]

Example III
Instruction: Answer the following questions on the Renaissance Movement:
Questions: (1) When and where did it begin? (2) Write three similarities between Renaissance culture and Greek culture. (3) Write two aspects of influence that geographical discovery had upon Europe.
– 1948 exam questions, Sixth Higher School (Obunsha, NSMS, 1948: 64)[3]

While the themes of these exam questions were visibly altered, the format of the new exams did not change, however.

The educators from the US were not happy with this 'new *sake* in the old bottle'. In one of the reports of the US Education Mission, American scholars strongly advised the Japanese to use an IQ examination (*Chinô Kensa*) to supersede the achievement test (Masuda *et al.*, 1961). Under their repeated exhortation in the name of the Occupation Headquarters, an IQ Examination for the University Design Committee was formed under the auspices of the Ministry of Education. Its cardinal goal was to 'couple democratic principle with modern psychology and educational concepts in sorting methods'. The work of the Committee was significantly swayed by Dr Vivian Edmiston, an American specialist working for the Civil Information and Education Section (CIE) in the Occupation Headquarters. Edmiston spelled out in minute detail what the exam should look like in at least two documents.[4] This IQ exam for university in Japan should have only a small number of categories. But each category should encompass many question-items to guarantee its validity. These items should be arranged in an easy-to-difficult continuum, and the 'test time should be three hours' (Edmiston, in Masuda, 1961: 294). Her ideas turned out to be the guidelines

---

[2] The Second Higher School later became Sendai University.

[3] The Sixth Higher School became Okayama University in 1949.

[4] The Japanese version of the documents, 'Recommendations by Dr. V. Edmiston' and 'The selection measures of the applicants for higher level school admission', are included in the 'Annexed Documents' in Masuda *et al.* (1961).

for establishing perhaps the first IQ exam for university in Japan. It was later renamed the 'Scholastic Adaptability Test (SAT, *Shingaku Tekisei Kensa)*'.[5]

From 1948 to 1954, to apply for university, one needed to sit two major sets of exams: one was the SAT, or IQ assessment exam, and the other was the achievement exam. The tenet of this bifurcation came from the psycho-epistemological conviction that our brains have two major functions. One belongs to a lower order function, memory and the accumulation of pieces of knowledge. The other is a more important function, innate ability, composed of the analytical, synthetical, comparative and other traits to think and solve problems.

The IQ exam did not last very long. It lost its major university patrons in the late 1940s, and was finally abolished in 1954, the causality of which was addressed in detail in Chapter 3. What warrants mentioning is that, while the content of the IQ exam was forsaken, its technical part, the multiple choice, assumes an incredible life of its own. From 1950 onwards, the use of multiple choice proliferated like mushrooms after a downpour. The reform of format greatly affected or altered what exam-takers needed to do. The contrast between the two exam formats may be shown in Table 4.1, which attempts to analyse the merits and demerits of essay-writing and multiple-choice questions. The epistemic comparison may, admittedly, need to be more sophisticated. What I intend to demonstrate is that the difference in emphases is a major factor that accounts for the discrepancy between the two.

From 1949 to 1952, the high school graduation rate rose steadily, but the university acceptance ratio rose much faster, as shown in Figure 4.1. From 1948 to 1950, the number of high school graduates grew by 61 per cent. The number of university students expanded from 11,978 to 224,923, a tenfold increase within two years. We can assume that the number of applicants for university increased at a similar pace. This exerted an enormous pressure on the role of exams to sort, screen and differentiate. As a result, entrance exams suddenly increased their number of questions and scale of difficulty. This is also found in world history:

Example
Instruction. Fill in the blank with the proper words.

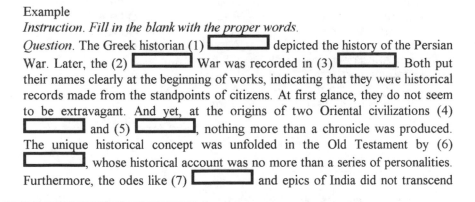

Question. The Greek historian (1) [＿＿] depicted the history of the Persian War. Later, the (2) [＿＿] War was recorded in (3) [＿＿]. Both put their names clearly at the beginning of works, indicating that they were historical records made from the standpoints of citizens. At first glance, they do not seem to be extravagant. And yet, at the origins of two Oriental civilizations (4) [＿＿] and (5) [＿＿], nothing more than a chronicle was produced. The unique historical concept was unfolded in the Old Testament by (6) [＿＿], whose historical account was no more than a series of personalities. Furthermore, the odes like (7) [＿＿] and epics of India did not transcend

---

[5] *Shingaku Tekisei Kensa* is commonly translated as the 'Scholastic Aptitude Test'. See, for example, Tadashi Hidano, 'Admission to higher education in Japan', pp. 9–25 in Heyneman and Fägerlind (1988).

the limit of written history. In China, either *The Historical Record (Shiji)* written by the excellent Chinese historian of the Han Dynasty, (8) ________, or (9) ________, the work of Ban Gu, treated the deeds of the rulers as the backbone of history. Japan's six-country-histories books, starting from (10) ________, were also official accounts of history. In comparison, the uniqueness of Greek historians becomes self-evident.

Answer: (1) Herodotus (2) Peloponnesus (3) Thucydides (4) Egypt (5) Mesopotamia (6) Hebrews (7) Veda (8) Sima Qian (9) *Hanshu* (10) *Nihon-shoki*.[6]

– 1951 entrance exam questions for Tokyo University (Obunsha, NSMS, 1951:11-2).

The above test question text warrants an analysis as it had some traits that I would term as 'prototypical' of the later exams. First, unlike earlier essay-writing types of exams, this question, like many other multiple-choice questions, provided the main body of the information, with the essential parts left blank.

Table 4.1 A comparison of the essay-writing test and multiple-choice test. *Source*: My compilation.

	Essay writing	*Multiple choice*
Reading	Little	A lot
Processing new, given data	None	A lot
Recalling memorized information	A lot	A lot
Conceptualizing	A lot	Little
Organizing data	A lot	Little
Expressing	A lot	None
Analysing	A lot	A lot
Comparing new, given data	Little	A lot
Differentiating data	Little	A lot
Making judgement	A lot	A lot
Choosing from alternatives	None	A lot
Writing	A lot	Little or none

6 Herodotus (c. 484–425 BC), ancient Greek historian. Thucydides (c. 460–400 BC), ancient Greek historian. Peloponnesus, formerly Morea, peninsula in southern Greece. Veda, oldest scriptures of Hinduism. Sima Qian (145–? BC), a noted Chinese historian. *Hanshu*, an official history of the Han Dynasty. *Nihon-shoki*, the oldest history of Japan.

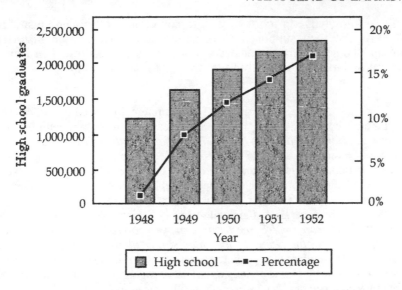

Figure 4.1 Percentage of university students in high school graduates, 1948–52. *Source*: Based on JMOE, *Mombu Tôkei Yôran* (Tokyo: JMOE, 1994d), 24–7.

A student was asked to fill them up with key words. To do so, he or she needed to get acquainted with a very wide scope of historical events, figures and dates. This is, however, easier said than done. The example given here is only a randomly selected, very small part of the encyclopedic knowledge required. To achieve this 'encyclopedia quality', excessive amounts of information were needed (Rohlen, 1983: 98). Second, while preparation for the exam involved almost all-encompassing knowledge, it was kept within very 'narrow realms of learning', as the exam paper required accurate data (ibid.). Third, compared to the earlier exams, the example given during the late 1950s seemed to be further and further away from a pragmatic purpose. It seems more a demand for proof of 'pure' intellectual achievement. Still, world history exams motivate students to embrace a world of brilliant minds, landmark events, reconfiguration of historical maps, and an evolving process ever since the Stone Age. While it aims at differentiation by esoteric knowledge, a mandate of 'never forget our past' is also evident.

The three points noted above exhibit some features that have been kept intact in the world history exams. Soon after the suspension of history courses was over, every student had to prepare for the world history section of the university entrance exams. Due to this institutionalization, the exams have since followed a pretty stable pattern, because, as Rohlen (1983) points out, 'each announcement of an intention to change the exams significantly is met with near panic by parents, teachers, and students'. They fear that a disadvantage will thus be created. One consequence of that stability is that, when it is possible to establish the continuity of the exams, it also becomes easier for us to find some pattern and compare it with other systems, such as that in Taiwan. What interests me are such questions as: What kind of historical knowledge are the Japanese élite expected to possess? What is the focus of that knowledge in terms of geographic concentration, and historical period? How are they supposed to organize and retrieve such historical information? To search for the answers, I start with a question taken from a recent exam of Japan's University Entrance Examinations Center:

Example
Text. Originally in China, the word '*tei*' [c. *di*, emperor] referred to the 'celestial god'. Later, a combined word '*kô-tei*'[7] was created to mean god with beaming brilliance. (1) *It was used as the title of the monarch that ruled the 'world under the heaven'.* Ever since then, the politics of emperorship lasted for a long time in China's traditional political system. In Europe, the concept of 'emperor' started from ancient Rome. Words such as 'emperor' in English and 'Kaiser' in German are translated into Japanese as '*kô-tei*'. Their origin can be traced back to endowed titles for generals or the family names of the rulers in Rome. (2) *After the fall of the Roman empire, the term 'emperor' carried with it an important meaning, indicating the status of the ruler sitting above the kings of various places.* In the contemporary and modern histories, (3) *even the word 'imperialism', a term that expresses the trend of the world powers after the end of the nineteenth century,* can be etymologically traced to Rome.

Question 1. Referring to the italic part of (1), from the following items (a)–(d) about the origin of the title '*kô-tei*', choose one correct answer.
(a) The monarch of the Yin Dynasty, who held strong power through divine politics, called himself '*kô-tei*'.
(b) When the Zhou Dynasty established a feudal system, the title 'emperor' started to get used.
(c) The King of Qin, who unified China, initiated the title of '*kô-tei*'.
(d) During the Han Dynasty, when neighbouring countries started to pay tribute to China, the title of '*kô-tei*' started to get used.

Question 2. Referring to the italic part of (2), from the following items (a)–(d), choose the one wrong answer:
(a) Karl the Great was honoured with the Crown of Roman Emperor by Leo Pope III.
(b) Ivan IV, while putting the aristocratic force under control, carried out totalitarian politics, and formally used the title of Czar for himself.
(c) Wilhelm I, after coming to the position of German Emperor through a national plebiscite, adopted an active foreign policy embodied in the invasion of Mexico.
(d) Queen Victoria had the title of Indian Empress at the time of being the Queen of England.

Question 3. Referring to the italic part of (3), from the following items (a)–(d), choose the one that is appropriate for the characteristic phenomenon of the imperialist age during World War I.

---

[7] This word only exists in Chinese and it is read as '*di*' as compared to '*kô-tei*' in Japanese. The word is never used for Japanese royalty.

(a) In industrialized European nations, monopolized capital was formed, and overseas export of capital began to prevail.
(b) As the result of the second Industrial Revolution, the United Kingdom possessed, as the 'world factory', overwhelming economic power.
(c) The opposition between the imperialist camp and the anti-imperialist camp of republic countries deepened.
(d) In those countries of world powers, while the military force and some particular parties promoted totalitarianism, parliamentary politics dwindled.
Answer: (1) c; (2) c; (3) a.
– The 1994 exam questions of Japan's Center Test (Kyôgakusha, 1994), 5–6.

In this example, we can also take note of the blend of historical interests, especially of the West and the East. The East here refers especially to China.[8] The format of this example has been used at least for the past ten years in Japan. The question is composed of two main parts. The first part is the main body of one paragraph, containing 5–10 lines. It resembles a short essay, with one central theme, and several sentences to support the theme. These sentences are conceptual in nature. This text is complete, and its role is to furnish some kind of introduction or background information. Three or four of the sentences in the text have numbers attached, and questions are given based on these numbered sentences. In each question, a group of four factual statements are provided, and the student is asked to pick the right or wrong one out of the four. The schema presented in Figure 4.2 may help us to understand the pattern.

In a typical history question, the main-body statement may appear plain, but its actual depth generally transcends the level of students. In fact, most of the texts in this part were based on simplified versions of original publications, atlases, or works of history (Kyôgakusha, 1994). It is pertinent to and potentially based on some facts given in the second part of the question. These facts are available in the textbook.

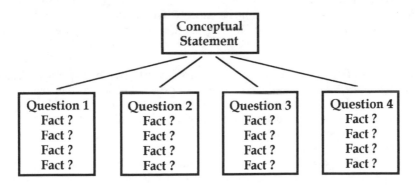

Figure 4.2 The typical structure of world history exams given by Japan's University Entrance Exams Center.

---

[8] That the East refers especially to China is indicated by the analysis in Kyôgakusha (1994), 1.

The main task for the student is to search through his or her knowledge, and verify whether they are right or wrong. The conceptual part may always be new to the student, because the specialization, such as the etymology discussion in the above example, or their sophisticated comparative dimension, could not be found in an official textbook. They thus constitute a part of the exam which is unfamiliar and unpredictable, and which may cause test anxiety. And yet, a close look shows that the backdrop they supply does not really matter that much. In actuality, one may give the answers to all questions without bothering with the main text.

Overall, the Japanese world history exam is quite 'normal' in its design, if we take SAT, GRE or TOFEL as 'normative'. This is demonstrated in these aspects: (1) the main format is multiple choice; (2) for each question, there is only one key randomly mixed up with three or four wrong choices; (3) there is no punitive deduction of scores even if the answer is wrong. This conformity is more obvious if we look at the Taiwanese national university entrance exams (*Liankao*). In Taiwan, world history does not have a separate exam. It is included in the general history exams. An exam is divided into three parts that are different in their formats. Part 1 is quite similar to Japanese exams, as the following example may show:

Example
Question. As his main contribution, this Greek philosopher laid the foundation for logical reasoning, thus enabling inference to achieve optimal effects. As an encyclopedist thinker, he contributed to, among other things, the progress of empirical science. His name is:
(a) Thales (b) Socrates (c) Plato (d) Aristotle
Answer: (d).
– 1992 exam question of Taiwan's *Liankao* (Longmen, 1994a: 81-2)

This is a very typical multiple-choice question: based on a given statement, the student is expected to identify the correct answers for that statement. This type of question probably serves as the minimum requirement in the exam, although the content might be more difficult despite the format. The questions in Part 2, which are of 'multiple answer' type, are quite different:

Example
Instruction. Each of the following questions is worth two points. Each question has five answers. At least one of them is correct, but more than one correct answer is possible. If you choose one correct answer, you get one fifth of a point; a wrong answer causes a deduction of one fifth of a point. If you do not answer a question, your score for that question is zero, and there is no score deduction for it. Mark your answers on the answer sheet provided.
Question. Compare the socio-cultural status of Buddhism during the North–South Dynasty (420–589 AD) with that of Christianity in Medieval Europe. Which of the following statement(s) is/are correct?
(a) Buddhism and Christianity were the only religions for the population, and there were no competing religions.
(b) Buddhism and Christianity were the essential source of ethics of daily life during those periods.
(c) Both Buddhism and Christianity were facing the problem of conflict with secular authority.

(d) Christian priests are the main conveyors of knowledge and culture, but Buddhist monks were not the only stratum of intelligentsia.

(e) The church is the centre of life in Medieval Europe, and the temple is the centre of life for the populace in the North–South Dynasty.

Answers: (c) (d)

– 1992 exam question of Taiwan's *Liankao* (Longmen, 1994a: 81–8)

This question is one of the extreme cases that could fail students easily. First of all, the 'North–South Era' is a dynastic period that one may hear of, but because of its anarchical and transient nature, it is less known than the other dynasties. The question is formidable both because of its narrowly selected historical periods, and because of the need for a sophisticated cultural comparison. The difficulty stems not only from its content but also from its perplexing format. Within the five answer-stems, there could be two, three or four correct ones, depending on the particular question. So it was not good enough to know only what was right and what was wrong. One had to know *all* the right answer-stems to get the credit. The examinees therefore had to weigh and compare answer-stems carefully in making a judgement. This was more time-consuming than the one-correct-answer question. For the latter, if you were certain of a right answer, you did not need to look at the rest. Therefore, in this multiple-correct-answer part, you can easily get substantial punitive deductions of scores.

Some other questions may not be that tough, but because they test conceptual rather than factual knowledge, they fall into the grey area between black and white choices. The following question in Part 2 is a case in point:

Example

Question. Japan was fatally defeated in World War II. And yet, in the 1980s, it became one of the major powerful nations in the world. What are the reasons for this national growth and re-emergence?

(a) With the help of the United States, Japan promulgated the new Constitution, and established democratic-partisan politics.

(b) With the help of the United States, Japan built new factories, and proceeded fast with the reconstruction work.

(c) The rate of population growth is constantly high, and thus there is no shortage of labour.

(d) Defence accounts for only a percentage in the total national budget, and the country spent a lot on economic growth.

(e) Japan went all out with industry and trade, while giving little attention to other fields; therefore, although it is strong economically, its academic and cultural aspects lag behind the US.

Answer: (a) (b) (d)

– 1992 question of Taiwan's *Liankao* exams (Longmen, 1994a: 81–6)

This question is a useful pursuit of the causes of Japan's postwar growth. All the correct answers could be very cogent and valid. Yet, to attribute Japan's success to US assistance, the new Constitution and democratic governance, the reconstruction, and the small defence budget can be an oversimplification, to say the least. Without a new Constitution or a democracy, is it incontestable that national growth would have been slow? Answer (e) is not just indisputably false, either. Here lies the dilemma of constructing a valid multiple-choice question for non-factual issues: on the one hand, the wrong answers should look as good as the right one(s). On the other hand, they should be wholly untrue. This is the challenge that only a factual statement can easily meet. This is also why the Japanese exams are essentially made up of factual choices, as seen in the foregoing pages. In a way, an examination of facts is a stratagem to eschew any effort to impose 'correct' answers on controversial questions. 'My favorite authority on this subject is', claims Diane Ravitch (1995) while discussing the history standard in the US, 'the 19th-century English philosopher John Stuart Mill. In "On Liberty", Mill recommends national examinations but insists that questions on disputed topics should not turn on the truth or falsehood of opinions, but on the matter of fact that such and such an opinion is held, on such grounds, by such authors, or schools, or churches.' This is apparently an effort to achieve objectivity.

The third part of Taiwan's exams consists of 'non-choice' questions. They ask students to write concise answers to such questions as:

Example
Question. In 1898, at the end of the Spanish–American War, the then US President William McKinley (1843–1901) was hesitant about the takeover of the Philippines.
(a) If he had determined to rule the islands, what kind of tradition in American foreign policies would he violate? One year later, the United States became more actively involved in the Far East [sic].
(b) What important foreign policy was adopted and advocated by the United States?
[*Answer hint*: (a) Isolationism in the Monroe Doctrine. In 1823, the fifth US President James Monroe (1758–1831) enunciated a keynote statement, claiming that the American continents were no longer open for colonization by European powers and that the US would view with displeasure any European intervention in the Americas. Although the Doctrine was not an international law, it was invoked successfully and became important in US foreign policy. (b) Open Door policy. In the nineteenth century, China was divided into separate spheres of influence by the major world powers. The US, as a lesser power, feared that an actual partition of China would damage American trade and sought to preserve equal privileges. US Secretary of State John Hay advanced the Open Door policy in two major notes in 1899 and 1900. Ever since then, the Open Door was affirmed as the US traditional policy toward China.]
– 1992 question of Taiwan's *Liankao* exams (Longmen, 1994a: 81–10)

This part of the question is almost like essay writing. It has six points, equal to three multiple-choice questions. While this has been a very conventional and reliable way of knowledge checking, it is admittedly hard to grade given the huge number of test papers. On the other end of the extremes of both the regular multiple-choice and short essay answers, there is some very refreshing modification of machine-readable questions in the Taiwan paper:

Example
Question. A fleet of Slavic commercial ships, loaded with furs and honey, was travelling downstream from the city of Kiev. They finally cast anchor at a sea

port. This was the political and commercial centre in the ninth century, inhabited by several hundred thousand people. The Slavic merchants paid the custom tariff, and then sold their merchandise to businessmen in the city. With the gold coins they earned, they purchased large amounts of handicrafts and prepared to ship them back to Kiev. This sea port is:

(a) Constantinople (b) Alexandria (c) Athens (d) Venice

Answer: (a)

– 1993 exam question of Taiwan's *Liankao* (Longmen, 1994a: 82–3)

The distinct genre of this question is apparent. It can never be mistaken as a question from the Japanese exams, which have been academically sober for over ten years. Taiwan's exam questions, as shown above, give some buoyant, tale-like information, before the question is actually raised. This recent trend in the exams may include anecdotes, witty quotations, historic dialogues, or a light-hearted record from a traveller's journal. The three parts of Taiwan's exam, with different styles and emphases, form a hodge-podge. It has something like a miniature thesis, something like the TV game 'Jeopardy', and something like the kids' show 'Where in the World is Carmen Sandiego?' However, this is not to say that the Japanese exam-makers are just content with the *status quo* and make no attempt to change. While the test content was stable, Japanese world history exams became, in a sense, more 'colourful' than Taiwan's. This is shown in the increased number of illustrations attached to the test questions. These may be maps, photos, sketches or graphs, as indicated in Figure 4.3.

Figure 4.3 compares Taiwanese and Japanese exams. The Japanese exams, as may be indicated above, were provided with more and more illustrations over time. To me, this was an effort to balance out the bookish texts. As a result, the Japanese exams have more illustrative pictures attached, while their difficulty scale, content and format remain as pallid and evenly standardized as before. The Taiwanese exams, on the other hand, are marked with stylish changes of format, and they are very tough in terms of both their design and their grading method. The diversified and occasionally very difficult nature of Taiwan's exams stems from its horrendous task. Japanese exams have a 'division of labour'. The national exams screen the national university applicants for the preliminary cut-off. The national schools then hold their own second-round screening exams. Each private university gives its own as well. The contrast with Taiwan is obvious. *Liankao* are the only exams for screening university applicants throughout Taiwan.

The foregoing study gives us some concrete ideas about what the world history exams look like. However, it is not sufficient for us to generalize about things like the weight in the different content or the trend of any change. We may see that the exams touch upon both Western history and Eastern history. But we do not know if the histories of different areas maintain a certain ratio in the exams. We do not know if the Japanese are more interested in the history of industrialized countries or the developing world. We also want to know how the multiple-choice questions are compared with essay writing or other test formats. The answers to these questions may help us to understand better the future generation of Japanese in terms of their historiographic outlook.

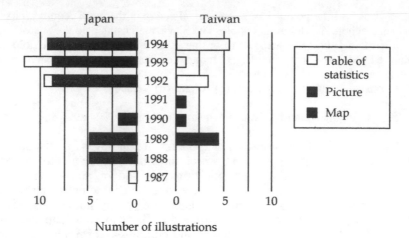

Number of illustrations

Figure 4.3 A comparison of the number of illustrations used in the world history exams of Japan and Taiwan, 1987–94. *Sources*: Based on Kyôgakusha, *Daigaku Nyûshi Sentâ Shiken Mondai Kenkyû: Sekaishi* (Questions and annotated answers of the exams given by the National Center for University Entrance Exams: World History), (Tokyo: Kyôgakusha, 1994), passim; Longmen, *Lishi Shiti Xiangjie* (History exams: questions and answers with annotated answers), (Taipei: Longmen, 1994a), passim.
Note: The pictures include maps, photos, drawings and sketches.

Which parts of the globe are seen as more important by the Japanese in their exams? To answer this query, the test content is categorized into geographical areas of (1) West (America–Europe), (2) West Asia + Central Asia + Africa, (3) South Asia + Southeast Asia (4) East/North Asia, and (5) international. A study of the national-level Center Test and 68 universities (Obunsha, 1994) shows the global distribution of the test items, as plotted in Figure 4.4.

In Figure 4.4, the West's share amounts to 47.2 per cent, the highest of all areas. The second largest share is East and North Asia, which, as the study explains, refers specifically to China (ibid.). This pie-chart indicates clearly that the Japanese rivet their main attention on Western history. Meanwhile, keeping in mind that the West actually consists of quite a number of countries, including the US, France, Britain, Germany, Russia, Australia, etc., we would note that, in the exams of most universities, China is given an amazing amount of attention.

This may well result from the fact that China is the cradle of Eastern civilization, and that the Japanese are so much moulded or affected by its influence. It seems that a lot less attention is given to other parts of the world. This may be surprising, not only because these vast areas have been as important and eventful, but also because they boast an equally glorious past, such as found in India or Egypt. A chronological examination of this global distribution shows that the situation has not changed much in the past ten years (see Figure 4.5).

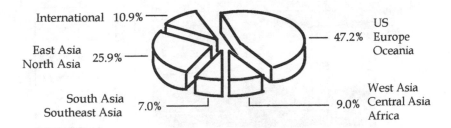

Figure 4.4 Geographical shares of different areas in world history exams for Japan's Center Test and 68 universities, 1994. *Source*: Based on Obunsha, NSMS: 'Sekaishi' (World History), (Tokyo: Obunsha, 1994), 1.

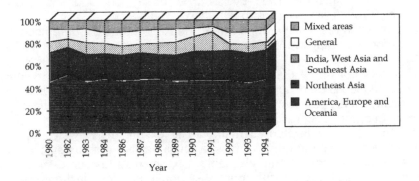

Figure 4.5 Geographical shares of different areas in Japan's national-level exams of world history, 1980–94. *Source*: Based on Obunsha, NSMS: 'Sekaishi' (World History), (Tokyo: Obunsha, 1980–94).

Now, after a study of the geographical dimension of world history, I turn to its temporal dimension: which periods in world history are more important? This question concerns the purpose of learning history. We may consider it as a means of transmitting culture, of relaying our tradition forward. Figure 4.6 may provide us with some clue.

Figure 4.6 shows a fairly even proportion of all periods in history in Japan's world history exams, although the share of the late contemporary period (from the US Civil War to WWI) was slightly larger. That might indicate a particular interest on the part of the Japanese in the recent past in human history, when the modern world began to take shape, and East–West interaction grew intensive. Overall, however, the balanced periodization is best explained by a faithful adherence to the official textbook and fair, predictable distribution.

To sum up, our study of world history exams shows a couple of coordinates in the comparative study of exams of world histories between Taiwan and Japan. Both utilize multiple choice as their format to achieve grading efficiency and impartiality. Both are hinged securely on official textbooks for their source of test content. Both focus primarily on Western history, with secondary priority given to China-centred Eastern history.

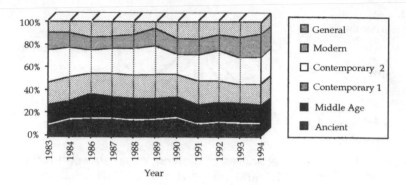

Figure 4.6 The proportion of different periods in Japan's national-level exams of world history, 1983–94. *Source:* Based on Obunsha, NSMS: 'Sekaishi' (World History), (Tokyo: Obunsha, 1983–94).
Note: Contemporary 1 – the period after the Renaissance. Contemporary 2 – the period after the Civil War in the US. Modern – the period after WWI.

This does not imply that the exams of Japan and Taiwan are identical, however. In fact, great differences are found in their format, design and scale of difficulty. In the past ten years or so, Japan's exams have maintained their uniform question design, their dependence upon factual knowledge, and their standardization in item-difficulty. The exams of Taiwan show, in contrast, more diversified test-formats; a much harsher grading system; and an assortment of conventionally reliable assessments plus some success in making questions more gleeful, more easy-going, and less anchored in rote memorization. Our study does not clarify why the future élite need to be judged by how much they know about Hellenic culture or Tang Buddhism. What is clear, though, is a prerequisite for them: a 'spirit travel' back to the previous millennium, an extension of personal experience through the flow of time.

MATHEMATICS: THE BASICS OF WESTERN KNOWLEDGE

Whatever exists at all exists in some amount. To know it thoroughly involves knowing its quantity as well as its quality.
– *E. L. Thorndike, 1918*

Number, according to the Pythagoreans, is the key to the cosmos, exemplified by the musical scale and the distances between the planets. A. Comte (1798–1857) treats maths as the basis of basics in sciences. H. Gardner (1983) lists the links between maths and memory, language, science and art, such as the 'rationality of music'. Meanwhile, maths is almost unsurpassed in its abstraction and 'independence'. Aristotle contrasts it with physics and metaphysics, for it is not based on being or existence. Gardner argues that the mathematician's world is one of invented objects and concepts with no direct parallel in everyday reality. Hence, maths is the most culture-free subject; yet, it 'is not devoid of cultural bias' (Valverde, 1984). That duality stems from the fact that maths is a numerical form of inner logic not only for nature, but also for the human world.

The issue of this 'duality' is relevant to the discussion here for two reasons. First, it is directly related to the concern of optimizing maths education, either by teaching or by examination. Second, a salient difference in regard to that issue is notable between maths exams in Japan and Taiwan. What I want to know in this section is how the abstract versus the concrete antithesis in maths is reflected in the entrance exams. Following that direction, I will see, as a result, how difficult these exams are in terms of their breadth and depth of knowledge, how they compare with each other, and how this obsession with maths exams affects the maths proficiency of the population.

In the university entrance exams for maths, an effort to make it free from 'non-maths' bias is apparent. Two examples given below, one from a 1993 Japanese exam paper, the other from a 1994 Taiwanese paper, show the norm of maths problems: purity, narrative parsimony and impeccable logic. The Japanese paper was a 60-minute exam, and the problem in this example would take approximately 20 minutes. The example from Taiwan is one of the fifteen problems in the exam paper.

The commonalities of the two problems are: both use a multiple-choice format; both are purely abstract, no real situation is involved; both check only the correct answers, the operation procedure is not testable. Although the Japanese problem requires a series of answers, they are actually answers to different, and quite discrete, problems linked up superficially. They are not the 'semi-products' in the middle of the calculating process towards the final outcome. Finally, both of them need to apply maths knowledge at different levels. The Japanese problem calls for the nature of numbers, factoring, second-degree equation and cubic equation, and the Taiwanese problem calls for number, factoring, and trigonometric function.

The similarity discussed above does not mean the 'duality' issue is solved. As a matter of fact, it remains a recurrent dilemma for educators or test-makers alike: to give a real-life question and test application ability? or to give a pure maths question to test high-order thinking such as mathematical logic? After World War II, 'pure maths' has been the mainstay of the discipline, despite an appeal to put maths back into the real world as 'a tool for life' (*seikatsu tame no yôgu*) (Ogura, 1978). Keen criticism of neglecting maths' link to reality can be traced back to 1949, and long esoteric debate continued later on the merit of abstract versus applied maths.[9]

---

[9] See for example, JMOE (1949).

Examples
Taiwan

Japan

Instruction. Each of the following problems counts for 5 points. Each problem is given 5 answer stems. Please choose the correct one and mark its number on the answer sheet. A wrong answer would cause a deduction of 1/4 of the scorepoints for the question. If no answer is given, there is no score or deduction.
Question.

The value of $\dfrac{1+i\tan\dfrac{\pi}{8}}{1-i\tan\dfrac{\pi}{8}}$ is equal to

Instruction. The following question counts for 24 points.
Question. a, b, p, q are real numbers, $a > 0$. If for the equation $X^2 + ax - 2a - 4 = 0$, the two answers are (a) and $-a -$ (b), which are also the two answers of the cubic equation

$$X^3 + pX + qX - 4a - 8 = 0,$$

another answer to this cubic equation is (c d), and

$$p = a + (e), \quad q = (fg)$$

Also, if the two answers for $X^2 + bX - a^2 = 0$ are answers for the cubic equation, then, when $a = b$,
$a = b = (h) + \sqrt{(i)}$
if $a \neq b$, $a = (j)$, $b = (k)$.

(a) $\dfrac{1}{2}+\dfrac{\sqrt{2}}{2}i$ (b) $\dfrac{1}{2}+\dfrac{\sqrt{3}}{2}i$

(c) $\dfrac{\sqrt{2}}{2}+\dfrac{1}{2}i$

(d) $\dfrac{\sqrt{2}}{2}+\dfrac{1}{2}i$

(e) $\dfrac{\sqrt{2}}{2}+\dfrac{\sqrt{2}}{2}i$

Answer. (e).

– 1994 maths question of Taiwan's *Liankao* (Longmen, 1994b), 83–1.

Answer.
(a) = 2, (b) = 2, (cd) = –2, (e) = 2,
(fg) = –4, (h) = 1, (i) = 5, (j) = 2,
(k) = 0.

– 1993 maths question of Japan's New Center Test (Kyôgakusha, 1994a), 2–3.

Still, a highly conceptual form of maths has been dominant in advanced maths and entrance exams. This, I would argue, is not only the result of the uniqueness of maths. It might also reflect the traditional value of *wasû* (Japanese mathematics). In Japanese maths, lasting memorization of formulas, brief and correct answers, swift but accurate computation are held as essentials (Kito, 1989). While it is hard to verify this cultural trait in maths,

Japanese exams in the past several years did show a grudging link to concrete problems, which contrasted somewhat with a more applied inclination in the Taiwanese exams. The situational problems in Taiwan's exams seemed more 'lively' and diverse than the Japanese ones (Figure 4.7).

Caution is needed here as the comparison is confined to university entrance exams in particular. Japanese textbooks at the elementary level, for instance, were full of life. A look at the table of contents of the Grade 6 textbook would prove this: 'Survey of the Area of the School Campus', 'Summer Vacation', 'Height of Tree', 'Growth of the Plant', 'Temperature', and so on.[10] Why, then, was Japan's maths test for college so lifeless? Purity of maths as a discipline aside, I think there were three reasons: (1) it was hard to design a practical question in advanced maths; (2) confusion or factors irrelevant to maths in a real-world question might complicate the test and affect its reliability and objectivity; (3) practical questions with lengthy narration needed a lot more time to complete and this would reduce the number of items to be tested. Relatively more attention was accorded by the Taiwanese to coupling maths with 'reality'.

How then would one evaluate this discrepancy of maths' link to the real world? Without a reliable study of the effects of 'abstract maths' versus 'living maths', it is preferable to treat them as two systems with different focuses, rather than searching for a norm-minded interpretation. Perspective on a learning situation may vary from culture to culture, but, as Cole and Bruner (1971) and Bacon and Carter (1991) claim, each approach to maths education may be equally valid.

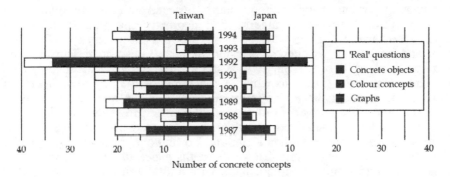

Number of concrete concepts

Figure 4.7 A comparison of numbers of concrete concepts used in university maths entrance exams in Taiwan and Japan, 1987–94. *Sources*: Longmen, *Shuxūe Shiti Xiangjie* (Maths exams: questions and answers with annotated answers), (Taipei: Longmen, 1994b); Kyôgakusha, *Daigaku Nyûshi Sentâ Shiken: Sûgaku* (Questions and annotated answers of the exams given by the National Center for University Entrance Exams: Mathematics), (Tokyo: Kyôgakusha, 1993b).
Note: 'Concrete' refers to the number of concrete objects, colour concepts or graphs used to make the question more tangible. Examples include cards, coloured balls, dice, farmland, savings account, etc.

---

[10] For more information in this respect, see Kaigo (1964).

There is little doubt in the minds of teachers in Japan and Taiwan that maths is structured with an incremental degree of complexity and difficulty. In other words, to understand a concept or area, one has to understand those that form its base. Within this hierarchical science, each level is composed of its basics and its higher, more complex field. The ascending stepping stones to the top can be put in approximately the following order:

Nature of numerals → mathematical array → linear equation → two-degree equation → polynomials → index and logarithm → trigonometry → two- and three-dimensional vectors → linear-equation group → circle and globe → conic curves (hyperbola, parabola, etc.) → differentiation and integration → probability

The above is only an attempt to show the general order instead of the exact locus of each step. A study of Taiwan's *Liankao* maths exam shows it investigates almost everything in that 'pyramid' (see Figure 4.8). What made the maths exam of Japan conspicuously different from that of Taiwan, as may be seen in Figure 4.9, is primarily differentiation and integration. Japanese students need to be competent in basic differentiation/integration before getting into college, whereas in Taiwan this area is left unchecked. While this suggests that Taiwan's maths in high school might give more attention to a better mastery of the basics, it may also imply that Japan's maths courses were faster, as shown in Figure 4.9.

Figures 4.8 and 4.9 prepare us for a comparison of what was used recently to test students' maths intelligence. An outstanding commonality between the two exams is their broad scope. Neither is limited to the terminating portion of high school maths. Instead, both require students to have a thorough review of algebra and geometry spanning from G7 to G12.[11] However, the globe is tested in Taiwan but not in Japan; differentiation and integration, as cited, are tested in Japan, but not in Taiwan. The marked contrast between the two systems lies in technical specifics of content. First is the degree to which a machine could grade test papers. In both exams, students have to supply an answer to the question instead of choosing the right answer from the wrong ones. However, the Japanese paper is totally computerized and thus machine-readable, whereas half of Taiwan's exam papers need hand-grading. To find out how they differ, let us first look at the Taiwan paper. Taiwan's maths paper, like the one for world history, is divided into two major parts with a totally different design. 'Part One' consists of machine-readable multiple choice:

Example I
If $\sin \theta$ is one answer to $4x^2 + 4x - 3 = 0$, then the value of $\cos 2\theta$ is:

(a) 1 (b) $\dfrac{\sqrt{3}}{2}$ (c) $\dfrac{\sqrt{2}}{2}$ (d) 0.

Answer: (d).
– 1994 exam question of Taiwan's *Liankao* (Longmen, 1994b: 83-1)

---

[11] The maths categorization may differ somewhat between Japan and Taiwan, but they refer to basically similar areas.

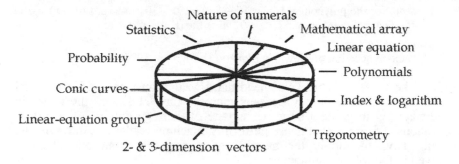

Figure 4.8 Score proportions for different areas of maths in Taiwan's *Liankao* maths exam, 1994. *Source*: Based on Longmen, *Shuxue Shiti Xiangjie* (Maths exams: questions and answers with annotated answers), (Taipei: Longmen, 1994b).

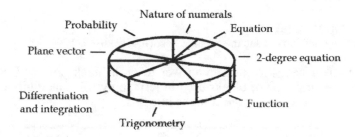

Figure 4.9 Score proportions for different areas of maths in Japan's New Center Test maths exam, 1993. *Source*: Based on Kyôgakusha, *Daigaku Nyûshi Sentâ Shiken: Sûgaku* (Questions and annotated answers of the exams given by the National Center for University Entrance Exams: Mathematics), (Tokyo: Kyôgakusha, 1993b).

'Part Two' is further divided into two types of test formats. One needs the fill-in-the-blank short answer; the other needs to produce the whole calculation procedure:

Example II
Instruction. Each of the following questions counts for 6 points. On the non-multiple choice answer sheet, please mark down the question number, and then give the answer.
Question. In a boxing tournament, each player must have one match with all the others. There are altogether 78 matches. The total number of players is (c).
Answer: (c) = 13.
1994 exam question of Taiwan's *Liankao* (Longmen, 1994b: 83-2)

Example III
Instruction. Each of the following questions counts for 10 points. On the non-multiple choice answer sheet, please mark the question number and then write the calculating process.

Question. For the polynomial $f(x) = x^4 - 5x^3 + 19x - 30$, one root of $f(x) = 0$ is $2 + i$. If a is a real number, and $f(a) < 0$, give the range of a.

Answer: $-2 < a < 3$
– 1994 exam question of Taiwan's *Liankao* (Longmen, 1994b: 83-3)

Both of the types in 'Part Two' need hand-written answers, and both need hand-grading, too. This may perhaps increase the validity of the exam in some way, but to grade a large percentage of that age cohort – the task is horrendous. Japanese exams are uniformly machine-readable. And still, the students have to supply the answer rather than choosing one. This is achieved in the following manner:

Example
Four points $O(0, 0)$, $A(3, 0)$, $P(\sqrt{5}p, p)$, $Q(\sqrt{5}q, -q)$ are on the *xy*-plane. $P > 0$, $q > 0$. If $\xrightarrow{\text{OP}}$ and $\xrightarrow{\text{AP}}$ are vertical to each other, then $p = \dfrac{\sqrt{(a)}}{(b)}$.

Answer: (a) = 5, (b) = 2
– 1993 exam questions of Japan's Center Test (Kyôgakusha, 1994: 6)

An exam-taker needs to give an answer to each blank box, and each box, unlike the general type of blanks used in tests, only fills one digit or symbol, such as + or –. The answer sheet looks like this:[12]

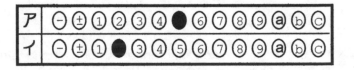

A common format similar to that of a personal information form is then used for collecting responses from examinees. That is only to show that trivial technicality has some potential for tackling the inherit weaknesses of computerized test papers. The fact that this design has been used for all problems in the maths exam in the past ten years or so indicates that it is well accepted. This can also be said for Taiwan's maths exams. This kind of stable *status quo* suggests their workability as a screening device. It may also reflect a take-it-as-given kind of attitude on the part of people.

This acceptance is manifested in the tolerance of the wide coverage of maths content in exams. In Japan's case, the weight of the content in maths exams shows a certain shift, which is a kind of irregular factor that can throw students off. This is especially so for the period after 1990 (see Figure 4.10). Figure 4.10 shows that some test areas, such as statistics and integration/differentiation, were quite stable in proportion. Other areas like index, logarithm, set collection, etc., were used in some years, but not in other years.

---

[12] The two symbols in the left column are letters of the Japanese alphabet, *katakana*, which is used as the answer number in exams of maths, accounting, etc.

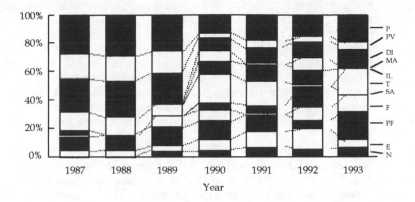

Figure 4.10 The proportion of different areas of maths by the number of questions in Japan's national-level maths exams, 1987–93. *Source*: Based on Kyôgakusha, *Daigaku Nyûshi Sentâ Shiken: Sûgaku* (Questions and annotated answers of the exams given by the National Center for University Entrance Exams: Mathematics), (Tokyo: Kyôgakusha, 1993b), 9.
Note: The categories of exam questions for each column include, from bottom to top: N = Number, E = Equation, PF = Plane figure, F = Function, SA = Set algebra, T = Trigonometry, IL = Index and Logarithm, MA = Mathematical array, DI = Differentiation/Integration, PV = Plane vector, and P = Probability. Note also that some categories are not tested in certain years.

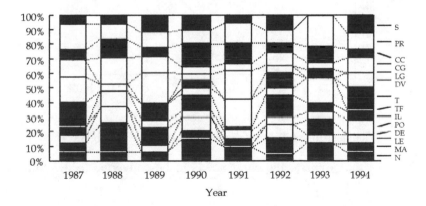

Figure 4.11 The proportion for different areas of maths by scores in the maths exams of Taiwan's *Liankao*, 1987–94. *Source*: Based on Longmen, *Shuxüe Shiti Xiangjie* (Maths exams: questions and answers with annotated answers), (Taipei: Longmen, 1994b).
Note: The categories of exam questions for each column include, from bottom to top: N = Number, MA = Mathematical array, LE = Linear equation, DE = 2-degree equation, PO = polynomials, IL = Index and Logarithm, TF = Trigonometric function, T = Trigonometry, DV = 2/3-dimension vectors, LG = Linear-equation group, CG = Circle and globe, CC = Conic curves, PR = Probability, and S = Statistics.

The waxing and waning, disappearance and re-emergence of areas might be an intentional design to make the exams less predictable, and thus more reliable in assessment. The historical change of maths content in Taiwan's entrance exams runs parallel to Japan's (see Figure 4.11).

What can we learn from that changing pattern of content indicated in Figures 4.10 and 4.11? First of all, college-bound students must prepare themselves systematically with a comprehensive scope in maths, and that is basically the same for Japanese and Taiwanese students. The exams are therefore very challenging, just considering the tremendous workload involved in review.

But we still do not know how difficult it is for each area or problem. For that purpose, let us take statistics, one of the most difficult areas in high school maths. From each of the most recent Japanese and Taiwanese maths papers, I choose one major statistics problem. The following is from Taiwan's 1994 paper:

Example
Question. There are 100 students in Grade 6 of Zhongshan Elementary School. After taking a maths exam, the distribution of scores is shown in the chart. The frequency is given in parentheses. If the frequency of each group is evenly distributed within that group, then the average is (a).

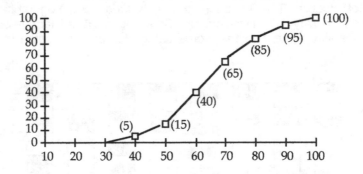

– *Answer:* a = 64.5.
– 1994 exam question of Taiwan's *Liankao* (Longmen, 1994b: 83-3)

To solve the problem, the chart needs to be converted to the following data:

Data	f_i	median X_i	$d_i = \dfrac{X_i - 65}{10}$	$d_i f_i$
30–40	5	35	−3	−15
40–50	10	45	−2	−20
50–60	25	55	−1	−25
60–70	25	65	0	0
70–80	20	75	1	20
80–90	10	85	2	20
90–100	5	95	3	15
	100			−5

Based on the data in that table, $\bar{d} = \dfrac{\Sigma d_i f_i}{100} = -0.05$, and because $d_i = \dfrac{X_i - 65}{10}$, $X_i = 10 d_i + 65$, and then, $\bar{x} = 10\bar{d} + 65 = 64.5$, which is the answer to the question.

The above problem is not complicated. It requires an average application of the essential concepts of statistics, the frequency distribution in particular, and the ability to tabulate the data based on the graph presentation given. And yet, without repeated exercises, without a good command of the basics, problems may arise from: (1) being unable to tabulate data in the chart; (2) choosing the wrong statistical equation, or (3) forgetting the equation $\bar{d} = \dfrac{\Sigma d_i f_i}{100}$. Both (1) and (2) may be the result of a poor understanding of the subject or a lack of practice, and (3) may result from a lack of review. Now, let us examine a similar question in the 1993 Japanese exam, the closest counterpart to the above example of Taiwan's exam:

Example

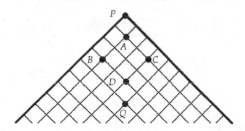

Question. From Point P to Point Q, there are altogether (ab) shortest routes. In these routes, there are (cd) routes passing though point C, (ef) routes passing through point D, and (gh) routes passing through points C plus D.
Answer: (ab) = 70, (cd) = 16, (ef) = 40, (gh) = 48.
– 1993 exam question of New Center Test, Japan (Kyôgakusha, 1994)

The question requires an application of the factorial axiom of partition $\dfrac{n!}{p!q!r!\cdots}(p+q+r+\cdots=n)$. For the answer of (ab), the axiom

$$\frac{n!}{p!q!r!\cdots} = \frac{8!}{4!4!} = \frac{8\times7\times6\times5}{4\times3\times2\times1} = 70.$$

(The solution of the other questions is omitted here.) This question is somewhat more difficult than the last one: because the unknown variables here are two-dimensional (plane), while the one in Taiwan's paper is only one-dimensional. However, caution is needed here in generalizing beyond this single pair of questions.

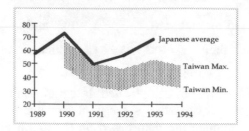

Figure 4.12 The average scores of all applicants to university in the national-level maths exams in Japan and Taiwan, 1990–4. *Sources*: Based on Longmen, *Shuxüe Shiti Xiangjie* (Maths exams: questions and answers with annotated answers), (Taipei: Longmen, 1994b), 83-20; Kyôgakusha, *Daigaku Nyûshi Sentâ Shiken: Sûgaku* (Questions and annotated answers of the exams given by the National Center for University Entrance Exams: Mathematics), (Tokyo: Kyôgakusha, 1993b), 7–8.
Note: The full scores are 100 for both Japan and Taiwan.

Table 4.2 The average scores of all applicants to university/college in the national-level maths exams in Japan and Taiwan, 1990–4. *Source*: Ibid.

		1989	1990	1991	1992	1993	1994
Taiwan	(Min.)	n.a.	49	34	31	37	33
	(Max.)	n.a.	70	52	48	55	50
Japan	(Average)	58.7	73.4	50.7	56.9	69.1	n.a.

The entrance exams' scale of difficulty is closely watched and measured annually by specialists in both Japan and Taiwan. This information can help students to decide whether to concentrate on the basics or on the difficult questions. But for us, the scale of difficulty is hard to assess, because it all depends on its criteria and the average examinee level. The same problem could be hard for some but not for others. According to some professional assessments (Longmen, 1994b), the trend in Taiwan is for maths exams to become easier, focusing more on basics and their application. Nonetheless, the average scores have fallen, as shown in Figure 4.12 as well as Table 4.2.

The scale of difficulty of Japan's exams did not show a clear trend, although the average scores of the Japanese were higher than those of the Taiwanese. It may be that the Japanese exams were easier. Or, if the papers were similar to each other, it may also mean that Japanese students achieved higher scores. However, both hypotheses are no more than guesswork.

The foregoing discussion of maths exams referred particularly to the human science major. If we acknowledge that the maths requirement for the natural sciences is a lot tougher, we can say that college-bound students as a whole should be somewhat more competent. What percentage of the population is relevant to our discussion then? If we look at 1990, Japanese students of higher education amount to 32.1 per cent of the age group, and in the past couple of years, it seemed to have become easier. The data show that the applicant ratio in the age group was more than 48 per cent (JMOE, 1994; Shimizu, 1994). Thus nearly half of the 15–18-year-olds in Japan had to take maths very seriously and prepared for it. More than one-third of that age-cohort – those who passed the exams – did pretty well, otherwise they could hardly be accepted. According to the statistics, the average achievement for 1990 university applicants (passed plus failed) was 73.4 points out of 100, which implies, on average, about half of all 15–18-year-old Japanese answered correctly two-thirds of the advanced maths problems. In Taiwan, students in university and college amounted to 34.13 per cent of the 18–21 age cohort in the population (TMOE, 1993a); their competition ratio is 37.37 per cent, about 3:1 to 4:1 (TMOE, 1992). The achievements of exam-takers are 49–70 out of 100 points (Longmen, 1994b), suggesting they could complete about half to two-thirds of the exam correctly.

The content of achievement exams in the two countries has been criticized as representing the low order in the cognitive world.[13] The effort to downgrade, shake up, change or even abolish them has never ceased. The best time to accomplish it was often at a transitional period in history. The Allied Occupation of Japan is a typical case in point. After the Occupation, the IQ examination (*Chinô Kensa*), later renamed Scholastic Adaptability Test (SAT, *Shingaku Tekisei Kensa*), was designed for college admission. It was a radical effort to replace the achievement test with an aptitude test. The new SAT was a lengthy paper of 2.5 test hours, used for all applicants to national schools (*kanritsu*). It tried to test knowledge using a screening process 'uncontaminated' by achievement. The test was answered by blackening the ovals on the answer sheet, which was perhaps the first machine-readable paper ever seen in Japan. At its inception, it already had a highly developed form, including, for example, highly Complex Multiple-Choice (CMC) questions and Context-Dependent Item Set (CDIS) questions to test reading ability and rationality.[14] The test consisted of three major parts. The first, the general exam, counted for 50 per cent, the second, humanity, 25 per cent; and the third, natural science, also 25 per cent. It was used for both natural- and social-science majors, though grading weight differed. One major novelty is composed of building blocks. A test-taker was asked to draw out one block from a stack of blocks of the same shape and size. The question was how many blocks one needed to remove from above it so that the stack would not collapse (see Figure 4.13).

The block question aimed to gauge intelligence which was not associated with special achievement and which was impossible or hard to train. However, it was quite likely that a student with a geometry bent would have a better chance in the test. The dizzy, eye-straining layers, dimensions and missing segments of blocks could make a 'gifted' but untrained mind sink. And yet, what was tested could hardly be psychometrically defined as innate intelligence. It basically required some kind of essential geometry, plus some knowledge of optical perspective.

---

[13] The classification system for various levels of human intelligence separates the cognitive area into six hierarchical levels, including (1) Knowledge, (2) Comprehension, (3) Application, (4) Analysis, (5) Synthesis, (6) Evaluation. A classic work in this field is Bloom (1956).

[14] For details of these test item designs, refer to Case and Downing (1989); Shahabi and Yang (1990).

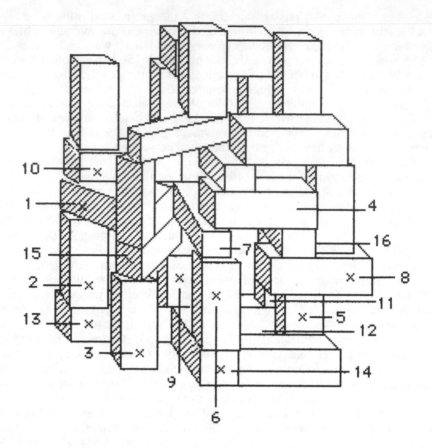

Instruction: In this picture, a number of rectangular blocks of the same size and shape are piled up on one another in a structure as demonstrated. Each block has a part unperceivable in the graph, and each has a number attached. Now, to take out one numbered block, one has to move some other blocks so that the structure will not collapse.
Questions: How many blocks need to be moved, if you take out the following blocks:

(1) Block 5:	(a) fewer than 7;	(b) 8;	(c) 9;	(d) 10
(2) Block 6:	(a) 8;	(b) 9;	(c) 10;	(d) 11
(3) Block 7:	(a) 14;	(b) 13;	(c) 12;	(d) fewer than 11
(4) Blocks 8, 10:	(a) 14;	(b) 13;	(c) 12;	(d) fewer than 11
(5) Blocks 2, 9, 11:	(a) 17;	(b) 18;	(c) 19;	(d) Others

Figure 4.13 A typical question in the American-sponsored IQ-type aptitude exams for university entrance in Japan, 1948. *Source*: Obunsha, NSMS (Tokyo: Obunsha, 1948), 3.

Optical perspective is not an innate visual concept. In the West, it was invented and formulated in the fifteenth century during the late Renaissance. Perspective is a special method employed to codify our three-dimensional space so that it may be put on a flat surface in a 'scientific' way. Its presumption is arbitrary: objects are foreshortened as they recede into the distance, with lines converging to a vanishing point. In reality, there is no such vanishing point. In China, for instance, perspective was never invented or used until it was introduced from abroad, which would be a negation of the inborn nature of 'perspective', though a simplified one. Without a learned knowledge of perspective or some basic idea of geometric shape, one would have a hard, if not impossible, time trying to fulfil the task. According to the official document, the purpose of the blocks was to check IQ in a 'spatial relationship' (Masuda *et al.*, 1961). In fact, it was all but a geometrical game with its disciplinary boundary hidden. This may partly explain why the aptitude test was not taken seriously in Japan: the ability assessed by it often borders on the knowledge the person has achieved.[15]

In the American-initiated SAT, 25 per cent of the questions were devoted to the vaguely termed 'humanity'. It blended language, vocabulary and common-sense ideology. The test-taker's task was to pick out the right answer, and put it in the blanks of a text. Topics like this one might be related to world affairs:[16]

Example
Instruction. The following text is incomplete, with its missing parts indicated by blank boxes. Each box has a number attached. For each box, there is a corresponding group with the same number. Choose the correct stem in the group that matches the blank box:

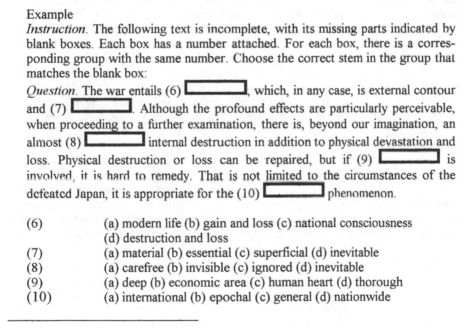

Question. The war entails (6) [_____], which, in any case, is external contour and (7) [_____]. Although the profound effects are particularly perceivable, when proceeding to a further examination, there is, beyond our imagination, an almost (8) [_____] internal destruction in addition to physical devastation and loss. Physical destruction or loss can be repaired, but if (9) [_____] is involved, it is hard to remedy. That is not limited to the circumstances of the defeated Japan, it is appropriate for the (10) [_____] phenomenon.

(6)	(a) modern life (b) gain and loss (c) national consciousness (d) destruction and loss
(7)	(a) material (b) essential (c) superficial (d) inevitable
(8)	(a) carefree (b) invisible (c) ignored (d) inevitable
(9)	(a) deep (b) economic area (c) human heart (d) thorough
(10)	(a) international (b) epochal (c) general (d) nationwide

---

[15] For a discussion of the achievement test, aptitude test, and IQ test, see Chapter 3, 'A comparative history of university entrance examinations: from 1945 to now'. For the commonalities between aptitude and achievement tests, refer to, for example, Wick (1973).

[16] The following are taken from Obunsha, NSMS (Tokyo: Obunsha).

Some features of the SAT as shown in our two examples, spatial and textual abilities, warrant comments here. First, it embodied a concept about basic intelligence which could be free from any achievement. Second, in these aptitude tests, knowledge seemed to be composed of detachable, basic units, like pieces of brick that formed an edifice. To understand the inter-relationship between words or objects, to take out, put in, and arrange the key components in the right order and right place, seemed to be regarded as significant in our brains. It was certain, as cited previously, that American scholarship influenced the initiation of the IQ-oriented, multiple-choice type of examinations. While IQ measurement was treated with misgivings, in the wake of rapid mass education, the multiple-choice type questions seemed to come in at the right time: it fulfilled the daunting task of sorting a credential-minded populace. In fact, it obtained an irreplaceable status in the system of examinations for both the Ministry of Education and many universities.

A DISCUSSION

The vast span of time we have covered in our study might make it difficult to recapture what we have reviewed. However, two important common denominators in the East Asian exam systems make the task less formidable. These are an emphasis in the exams on achievement and the constant reliance on written rather than oral answers. Our comparison is made on two dimensions: one is temporal, that is, comparing the present with the past to see how things changed with time; the other is cross-national. In the following discussion, caution may be needed when I switch gears between the two.

A reconstruction of prewar exam papers from occasionally skimpy data provides clues to a number of contrasts with postwar exams. The prewar ones involved fewer topics of the disciplines and asked fewer questions. They were easier. That generalization is applicable to Japan, Korea and Taiwan, because, in the Japanese colonial empire, higher education was virtually a unified system.

The prewar world history exams presupposed a didactic, utilitarian purpose in studying history. As nationalism had sway in Japan, world history was less examined relative to Japan's national history. When world history was addressed, stress was laid on such current concerns as world rivalry and colonies. Referring to the maths exams, they always formed the basic entrance requirement. Again, the problems were generally easier than now, with problems concentrating largely on the middle school level.

The Allied Occupation after the War brought with it a flood of new educational concepts and methods. Due to postwar growth, new techniques, such as machine-readable multiple-choice formats, were accepted willingly and instantly by Japan, Korea and Taiwan. The new psychometric theory was not adopted, however. Achievement eventually became the major criterion in entrance consideration, despite academic castigation and a series of trials of its alternatives.

Today, the primary commonality among exams in Japan, Korea and Taiwan is that, by encompassing and compressing the full scope of text-books into a highly condensed form of questions, entrance exams become a test of competency rather than qualification. In that sense, as compared to the prewar period, utilitarian purpose seems to be blurred. But this results in higher quality of achievement. In exams, the *idiot savant* may score higher. However, rote effort, although important, is merely the prerequisite, or the bottom line. It would be simplistic to state that the more one stored in one's brain the larger the chance of success. In maths, problem solving requires 'learning by exercising'. Judging ability is vital for multiple-choice questions. Like other forms of assessment, high-calibre ability in application, analysis and comparison was needed by high achievers.

While achievement was depended upon in both the pre- and post-war periods, the method of measuring it underwent great alteration, which is similar among the three countries. Today, unlike in the past, the ability to organize, articulate or present reasoning seems secondary to the brief but correct answers in the exams. This may result from the inherent weakness of the multiple-choice format. It may also derive from the fact that too many papers need to be graded. That change brought with it a neglect of the inference process.

Similarities aside, the exams of Japan and Taiwan are not identical, however. In the past ten years or so, Japan's exams have maintained a pallid uniformity, standardization and evenly spread scale of difficulty. The world history exams taxed disinterested factual knowledge. The exams of Taiwan show more diversity in comparison. The scale of difficulty varies greatly in one paper because its grading system is harsher. Taiwan's exams include a blend of conventional questions and some experimental ones, which aim to make questions more gleeful, more easy-going, and less anchored in rote memorization.

How valid are these exams as a stimulant to learning and as a selection device? To answer this question, we have to look at the 'genuine ingredients' of mathematics and history, and then check the exam papers accordingly. Maths likes quantity, pattern, symmetry, abstraction and deduction. It prepares people to find precise statements about a fuzzy, indeterminate universe. Davis and Hersh (1986) summarize intellectual components of mathematization in a progressive order:

1. Ability to symbolize, abstract, and generalize the primary experiences of counting and spatial movement A sharpened sense of quantity, space and time.
2. Ability to dichotomize sharply: yes, no; true, false; 0,1.
3. Ability to discern primitive causal chains: If A, then B. Ability to concatenate and reason about such chains.
4. Ability and willingness to extract out of the real an abstract surrogate; and the willingness to accept formal manipulations of the abstract surrogate as an adequate representation of the behaviour of the real.
5. Ability and desire to manipulate and play with symbols even in the absence of concrete referents, thus creating an imaginary world which transcends the concrete.

The type of questions asked in the maths exams in Japan, Korea and Taiwan seems to fulfil all these components. Multiple choice, by the way, especially suits the dichotomy of true and false in item (2). At the lower and 'primitive' level, however, the exams are less functional. For instance, students are not supposed to extract out of the real an abstract surrogate: they do not have to translate a 'real' problem into maths. But they need to do a lot of formal manipulation of equations. The logic seems to be that if they can do the higher order, they will be able to do the lower. It also shows that eliminating the incompetent has become a more salient role of exams.

Maths education and maths exams equip students with an intelligence. They do not prepare students with a craft instead. In Table 4.3, maths achievement is associated with the orientation of future career.

The meaning of maths lies in shaping a mind appropriate in a modernized world. In his *Analytical Philosophy of Technology* (1981), F. Rapp identifies eight requirements of mind:

1. Valuation of work
2. Efficient management
3. Impulse for technological creativity
4. Rational thought
5. Objectification of nature
6. Mechanistic view of nature
7. Experimental investigations
8. Creation of mathematical models

What maths exams asked from the students relates to item (4) rational thought; (5) objectification of nature; (6) mechanistic view of nature; and (8) creation of maths models. In that sense, maths and its exams have a more fundamental role to play, rather than merely job-bound numeracy.

Why is a social science subject like world history needed then? To answer this question, let me first cite Eckstein and Noah (1993) in their discussion of history exams: 'history is an instrument for instilling in students a sense of national and personal identity, a view of their nation's place in the world, past and present. Historical facts and their interpretation vary from country to country, and from time to time. A nation's history curriculum is subject to reinterpretation as a result of new research, but changes, as well as controversial or sensitive topics and approaches, are often slow to become incorporated into the examination syllabus. However, the content of history examinations is often quickly affected by swings in "official" political ideology, especially when governments sponsor efforts to revise the content of a school's history programme.' This observation is cogent and valid in highlighting the ideological function. The early Japanese version of world history underpinned Meiji oligarchic ideology of 'Civilization and Enlightenment' (*Bunmei Kaika*), an article of faith in 'mimesis', to use a historian's term (Toynbee, 1947), or a phenomenon of 'global isomorphism' of education, to borrow from the institutionalists (Ramirez and Boli, 1987; DiMaggio and Powell, 1983). The historical themes of colonial expansionism in prewar Japan and democracy in the postwar period also related to the dominant ideology. Nevertheless, world history is not only a tool of ideology for many reasons.

First, unlike other topics in political ideology, such as the 'Three Principlisms' in Nationalist Taiwan, world history is based on a large number of facts, some of which, such as historical dates, actors and events, though adorned with thick ideology, speak for themselves. Therefore, unlike a 'pure' ideology class, world history is only partially confined by orthodoxy.

Table 4.3 Students' career orientation and maths achievement. *Source*: Toshiaki Inoue, *Gakureki no Shinsô Shinri* (The deep-structural mentality of credentialism), (Kyoto: Sekai Shisôsha, 1980), 153.

Career plan	Percentage in the high maths scores group	Percentage in the low maths scores group
Presidents of a company *(Shachô)*	37.5	11.5
University professors	27.6	4.2
Elementary school teachers	27.6	11.3
Congressmen	22.7	6.2
Professional sportsmen	20.3	26.0
Painters	19.5	24.7
Singers	7.0	16.7
Farmers	6.0	17.3
Workers	3.1	11.6

Second, as amply discussed earlier, an important role of world history is simply to justify elimination by holding a 'Jeopardy'-like test of how much one can know. In the wake of increasing competition for access to higher education, exams had less chance to weed out those who did not know. In consequence, they became a partition device that cut off those who knew less. World history had an excellent potential for that.

Third, to learn to know is not only to burden people with a greater load of knowledge. To learn world history is to gain access to a major source of information. As the world becomes more and more interdependent, one nation can no longer ignore the existence of others. In that sense, world history might tell us a lot about the strengths and weaknesses of different countries. For the late developers, that source often referred to the West, as shown in the preponderating weight given to Western civilization. Despite their great achievement, Japan, Korea and Taiwan have never ceased emulating the West in a wide range of fields, from fashion to government structure. Like world history, the priority accorded to English and English exams is another good example of how important the continued Eurocentric globalization still is. To catch up has become second nature there.

The fourth role of world history and its exams is cultural transmission. The world we live in has witnessed a process in which meaning, customs and thoughts are getting lost or are receding from us. A simplified case in the East is the naked fact that the young know fewer and fewer ancient concepts and Chinese characters. Certain portions of the value-belief system have already been pulverized by time and turned to dust before our eyes. People often deplore it, and strive to carry on the traditional virtues and experiences. World history exams, I would argue, are part of that effort. One message they send to the younger generation is just that 'there was a past' (Russell, 1922).

CHAPTER 5

The cram world: why so large in East Asia?

No matter how high the rugged mountain,
A trekker will always find a path to tread;
No matter how rough and deep the water,
There is always a ferry for you to board.

– A couplet found in a G12 classroom, Affiliated High School of Normal College, Taipei

Every day is a Decisive Battle!
– Motto of Yoyogizemi, a big juku *in Japan*

In East Asia, the most salient manifestation of the effects of the university entrance exam system is perhaps the advent and expansion of cram schooling.[1] The fact that the exams need preparation is not unique to East Asia. In Victorian (1819–1901) England, for instance, *juku*-like cram schools for the entrance exams for high school or university grew rapidly, and cramming became a 'staple of student life' (MacLeod, 1982: 178, 224). What is unrivalled, however, is the scale of the mobilizing effect of the exams in Japan, Korea and Taiwan. The cram industry has been a billion-dollar business in Japan, as well as in the other East Asian countries.[2] Yet, it

---

[1] The 'cram school' refers to *juku* or *yobiko* in Japan, *hakwon* in Korea, and *buxiban* in Taiwan. While there are different types of cram schools, in this book, unless specified otherwise, these proper terms refer particularly to those schools used for cramming subjects taught in school with an ultimate goal to get both at-school students and exam-repeaters into universities.

[2] The income of Taiwan's academic *buxiban* for 1992 was equal to US$212 million, with a net profit of (annual income – annual expenditure) over US$13 million

has not been very much documented or updated. Heavily hinged on officially defined knowledge, it does not even have a niche in the official education structure. In a word, cram schools exist in limbo, a place with no identity. Because of a lack of scholarship, we are very much kept in the dark in terms of what has been really going on in that ever-expanding world. We do not know, for instance, what the cram enterprises look like. What exactly has been going on inside them? How has their business changed? Who attended them? What effects does the cram experience have on children? In this regard, in the epilogue of 'The *juku* phenomenon: an exploratory essay', Rohlen remarks:

> I doubt that it is coincidental that cram schools similar to *juku* are regularly found today in Korea, Taiwan, and Hong Kong, three more societies with a Confucian past that are growing industrially at notably high rates. The behavior and attitudes associated with *juku* strike me as being related to the particular character of economic and social development in East Asia today. Nor does this insight serve to reduce my personal uneasiness. Perhaps I have to learn to better balance *tatemae* and *honne*? (Rohlen, 1980: 242)

Bearing a similar purpose and query in my mind, I explored the cram world in Japan, Korea and Taiwan. In the following pages, I first portray the *juku* in Japan, the *buxiban* in Taiwan, and the *hakwon* in Korea, followed by an analysis of their business competition within each country. My study is then divided into three main levels of analysis. The first level is the physical plant of cram schools, with its architecture and school culture. At the second level, the students, I work out the students' attendance ratio, and depict their life as related to the 'exam war' in three case studies. At the third level, I examine what kind of knowledge was taught at these tutoring academies, and how it was taught.

A PORTRAIT OF THE CRAM WORLD

The cram school industry is a combination of industry and education. It is governed by assorted principles relating to the cognitive process, assessment, competition, cost-benefit, cost-efficiency, etc. As a result, the cram industry differs from both industry and schools in a fashion that can hardly be articulated without some detailed description. Let me portray *buxiban* first.

The avenues of knowledge: Taipei, Taiwan

At the heart of Taipei, the Shinko Mitsukoshi Building, a Japanese-funded department store, looms high, like a tall, slim rectangular cube of sapphire. Lofty above the lower skyline, the whir and rush of congested traffic, and a multitude on diverse errands, this ultra-modern landmark serves as a symbolic reminder of what Taiwan has achieved in the past decades. Many Taiwanese are still amazed at their recent past, a time of undisturbed growth, swift modernization, individual and familial prosperity, economic take-off,

---

(TMOE, 1993b: 29–33). In Japan, the total market size of the academic *juku* was US$6.1 billion in 1985, and US$11.7 billion in 1991 (YKK, 1994: 80).

and a swelling middle-class to which most think they belong.[3] The neighbouring Hilton Hotel, with its elegant gilded glass, pivoting doors, dimly-lit parlour and the classic air of its exterior, seems blurred away in this metropolitan scene.

It is a little past 5:00 p.m. on Saturday. Just at the foot of the Mitsukoshi Building, the fluorescent neon-lit signboards begin to blink, shine, and fantasize their colours and patterns. The thicket of signboards overlap and interface with one another, vying with each other like trees reaching out for space. In a different metropolis, such as Bangkok, Hong Kong or Tokyo, they might well be mistaken for cocktail lounges or electronic shops, or a demi-mondaine world. This is, however, a district densely dotted with *buxiban*, private academies that prepare people for different sorts of important tests, and pave the way to a better education or a better job.[4] For the Chinese, this is often subconsciously thought of as *Deng longmen*, or 'ascending the Dragon Gate', a dream from which many Chinese have not yet awakened after several thousand years.

Most *buxiban* are concentrated along two streets – the Nanyang and Xüchang Avenues – which intersect one another like a crucifix writ large in the hub of the city. This is the area famous for their 'Cram Avenues (*Buxi-jie*)'. In this vicinity, what catch your eye are the large-sized commercial billboards advertising competing *buxiban*. Almost omnipresent, they dot the skyline, side by side with the dazzling trademarks of Sony TVs, Toshiba refrigerators or Marlboro cigarettes.

As evening falls, hundreds of classroom windows are lit up. Swarms of students begin to stream in. Most of them wear dark-blue and baggy school uniforms. They are middle or high school students who finished school around 5:00 p.m. and rushed here for the tutoring course at 7 or 7:30. In the teeming crowd, some are *Chongkao sheng*, those who failed the entrance exams for college but are determined to try again for the second, third or even fourth time. If they were in Japan, they would be respected for their tenacity and unyielding will. Here in Taiwan, however, they are sometimes referred to sarcastically as '*Jiadun sheng*', i.e. losers who have no place to go but to squat at home.

---

[3] Statistics show that, in 1994, on average approximately 1.58 families possess a private automobile in Taiwan. The GNP per capita of Taiwan reaches as high as $10,215. Its foreign reserve is $7.2 billion, one of the highest in the world. See '*Yazhou Zhoukan* Jingji Minsheng Toushi' (*Asia Journal* data on economy and living standard), (*Yazhou Zhoukan* (Asia Journal), 2 January 1994), 35; also Wade (1990).

[4] *Buxiban* include academic schools, natural science schools, sports schools, information schools, home economy schools, arts schools, and business schools, etc. According to the statistics of TMOE (1993b), there were altogether 3356 *buxiban* in Taiwan in 1992, within which 1522 are academically-oriented (*wenli buxiban*). Due to the focus of the research, I will subsequently only discuss *wenli buxiban* that prepare students for getting into regular schools as an ultimate goal. This is applicable for Japanese and Korean cram schools as well.

Students generally travel here by bus, the easiest and most economic means of transport. On the bus, if they are lucky enough to get a seat, they utilize their time reviewing class notes. But, as the bus runs very fast and everything inside is violently jerking and rolling, some students would rather listen to their Walkman music instead. Students might also listen to an English tape, trying to familiarize themselves with the normal speech flow or challenging themselves with the vocabulary. They might also make tapes of their own, so that they could listen to a class lecture again, or grasp the recorded pieces of knowledge that they try to ingurgitate. A few come by scooter, a very popular means of transport in Taipei because of their speed, parking convenience, and ability to bypass the traffic jam. But scooters generally belong to university students.

In the area, the reception offices of *buxiban* companies are lined up on both sides, conspicuous for the smiling faces of immaculately dressed secretaries behind the desk, glossy commercial posters and exquisite interior design. Big spotless windows, broadly open entrances, and cool air-con breezes are all inviting to the anxiety-ridden students who are in desperate need of help. Competition is heated and severe, and *buxiban* administrators need to brag about their strengths so that they can win trust. The foremost factor in commercial promotion is the 'rate of success'. Posted high on the windows of many offices is a long list of their students from the previous year who just squeezed into good colleges. The names of the top students are writ large on separate sheets of decorated papers, like a row of red-label-Christmas-sale posters in a mall:

> Facilitation! (red)
> Mr. so and so:
> The Law Deptment
> Taipei University
> Scores: 492 (red)

Advertisements like this would easily strike a chord in the trembling hearts of those boys and girls whose parents have been harbouring dreamy expectations for them. Some *buxiban* also give out free publications of detailed information about successful students, their names, phone numbers, high schools and the names of their universities. The rate of success is a primary concern for students and their parents in selecting a *buxiban*. Taiwanese are sophisticated clients who think a lot before making their choice. The list of successes is the most persuasive weapon, in both Taiwan and Japan, to win trust and reliance from patrons.

A unique example of this psychological warfare is given by the 'Gongjian', a multi-purpose *buxiban*.[5] At the portal to its large lobby, a Sharp TV monitor plays at fast-forward speed an award ceremony for successful clients that entered élite colleges. From morning till night, the screen indoctrinates the passer-by with the jerky motions of award certificate

---

[5] Pseudonyms are used for students and tutoring schools whenever deemed necessary.

delivery, hand-shaking, and the successful candidates beaming with flying colours. The subtitles describe each student: 'Mr so-and-so, winner of first place for Business Management at Fu Jen University'. This endless spectacle of honour and accomplishment aims at overcoming the disarray and distrust of their potential clients.

Now, it is dinner time. Children in uniform with satchels are seen all over the place. Some are waiting in semi-circles for their turn around a flood-lit Chinese snack stall, some are devouring noodles at the open-air eaters' table, some are wandering and shopping briefly in bookstores, boutiques, bakeries or game rooms. Before long, they will file into a vast classroom hall illuminated as brightly as broad daylight. For most of them, the real challenge of the day is yet to begin.

The academic *buxiban* came to the fore in Taiwan in the 1960s. Those were the 'good old days' for the people in the business because their numbers were few, and they lived in peace with each other. The two 'grandfathers' in the business, Jianguo and Zhicheng *buxiban*, attracted students to their campus without even the help of information brochures. The successful story of these two gave rise to the growth of *buxiban* as a burgeoning enterprise. In due course, both their management and their pedagogy underwent professionalization. Meanwhile, a number of middle school teachers joined together and founded the 'Xue-er' *buxiban*. Students were trained here like soldiers. Their heads were shaved, and they were subjected to caning, if necessary, as disciplinary punishment. The Spartan and tough cramming style, however, did work miracles in the university acceptance ratios. Their hard-earned success became notoriously well known (Zheng in ZR, 11 August 1993; Ge in ZR, 10 August 1993).

In the ensuing years, as more and more Western educational concepts were imported and the economy of Taiwan began to take off, corporal discipline became less acceptable, and the small-sized tutoring class was considered outmoded. Entrepreneurs vied to upgrade their classrooms and offices in an effort to make them look grand, amenable and superficially luxurious. The new-generation entrepreneurs in the cram business started to expand classes for younger students, and opened the so-called 'Baby Class' (*Wawa ban*). In an extreme example, a *buxiban* rented all the classrooms of an elementary school during the summer and transported the kids of the first-year middle school there for tutoring classes. The demand was so high that they had to 'erect chalkboards in the hallway to give lectures' as there were not enough classrooms (ibid.). This frenzy led later to the tightening of supervision and regulation of cram classes for school students, as explained in the '1985 Rules for Establishing and Administrating the Short-Term *Buxiban*'. Academic *buxiban* are not allowed to enrol elementary students, and also, the middle school students are not allowed to have tutoring classes from Monday morning to Saturday noontime. Yet, these rules were hardly observed at all (TMOE, 1989, 1993b).

In the wake of the economic take-off of the past ten years, 'enterprisation' in business management occurred everywhere in Taiwan, which breathed new life into the cram industry. Well-printed brochures of information and application multiplied, commercial media were put into full play to gain momentum, promotion work reached inside the school to solicit applicants. This stimulated market demand and the cram population reached its record high.

The 'City of *Juku*' and beyond: Tokyo, Japan

Yoyogi, a convenient subway station on the Yamanote Line, is well known as the 'City of *Juku*', as the *juku* industry flourished there like ultramodern electronics in Akihabara. Yoyogizemi, a big *juku* company, dominates the valuable ground area, the traffic, the commercial skyline, and also the air by its satellite TV transmission. Young men and women constantly come and go for the 90-minute course. At the congested intersection, white-collar 'responsible staff' (*kakariin*) wearing the armband of 'Yoyogizemi' stand in line maintaining traffic order. They look no different from bank clerks: young men in their twenties, neat and clean, wearing neckties, white shirts and blue pants. Apart from traffic control, they are also responsible for parking and safeguarding cars, checking attendance and student ID passes, supervising classes, cleaning blackboards, picking up trash from the podium, and making sure audio facilities etc. are intact during the short recesses.

It was a surprise to me in 1994, when I visited Japan for the second time, that Yoyogizemi appeared to have become far more dynamic than they were one year earlier. As before, colourful advertisements hung from their big buildings. And also as before, young *kakariin* were placed in the street. But, there were more of them, almost overstaffed by Japanese standards. There were also more senior security guards in greyish blue uniforms watching the key positions on the campus. The bank-clerk-type staff were playing a wonderful charade right in the centre of the street. As the traffic lights changed, they rushed back and forth at the major intersections, directing the congested flow of traffic and pedestrians, most of whom were, of course, their clients. Their *kaishain* appearance, efficiency and dexterity attracted much attention from onlookers. For both students and their parents, their activities could be an excellent commercial, and I suspect that this was just one of the reasons for keeping them in the street. The students attending Yoyogizemi dressed plainly and looked very serious, which contrasted sharply with the gaudy and carefree boys and girls in Hibiya.

Juku schooling is ultramodernized. Private satellite transmission makes sure that the very best teaching is beamed to the four corners of the country. Volume of sound, speed of instruction, efficiency of teaching and students' reaction are closely watched through a monitor system by the control centre, and adjusted or manipulated accordingly. In a way, *juku* resembles manufacturing industry. First, there is a clear-cut division of labour with clear-cut duties and objectives for everyone. As a result, everything runs smoothly, and every minute is counted. Teachers, officials, receptionists and *kakariin* all have their well-defined tasks, and optimal efficiency is thus made possible. Second, the economy of scale is the fundamental rule for benefit maximization. While the quality of teachers is superior since many of them are employed from élite universities, their audience is kept to the full capacity of the classroom. Third, thanks to 'scientific' administration, every detail is taken care of to ensure the final quality of this mass production – students thus gain a solid and competitive command of what they ought to know. Fourth, economy of scale enables Kawaijuku and other companies to achieve the best quality for everything in school: best teachers, best audio-video facility, best information network, and best service. Even the eraser is the best: it is king-sized, twice the length of an ordinary one, always new and soft, and can clean the blackboard in a smooth, sweeping, effortless fashion.

Table 5.1 The estimated total number of *rônin* in Japan, 1965–70. *Source*: Tsuyoshi Makino, *Yobiko ni au: Seishun no Kyôiku* (Meet in the *yobiko*: education of the young), (Nagoya: Fûbaisha, 1986).

Year	Number
1965	100,000
1966	120,000
1967	150,000
1968	170,000
1969	200,000
1970	190,000

The first *yobiko*, a special cram school for *rônin*, can be traced back to as early as 1894 (Tsukada, 1991). But according to Tsuyoshi Makino (1986), it was after 1965 that the *juku* business started to undergo some phenomenal changes. In the world arena, Japan had just finished hosting the Olympiad, and had normalized its foreign relationship with South Korea. At home, people began to have their own '3Cs', i.e. car, colour TV and 'cooler', a loan word for air-conditioning. The first baby-boomers entered secondary schools. The accumulated wealth and demographic factors caused the number of *rônin* to mount steadily after 1965, as seen in Table 5.1.

While the economic surplus of Japanese families boosted the enrolment ratio of *juku* schools, the villainous image of *juku* was also somewhat improved. The administrators of Yoyogizemi, a large *juku* company, succeeded in using the *juku* industry to hook up the Japanese desire for education to consumers' behaviour, and project a popular and bright image for the *juku*. What is also noteworthy is the changes in the institutional patterns of the *juku* in Japan. Before, *juku* were locally based, and they aimed at local universities. From 1965 on, however, partly because of the administration of the nationwide 'First-Stage College Entrance Exams', *juku* were nationalized. Thus, as I will address in detail later in this chapter, the 'one-county-one-college-one-*juku*' pattern was almost brought to an end (Makino, 1986).

The schools once forbidden: Seoul, Korea

In Korea, for a whole decade, cramming in order to get into college was a crime. It was only after 1989 that prohibition of cram practices was alleviated. Today, however, for an untrained observer to find the telltale mark that prohibition has left is not that easy. In Seoul, academic tutoring companies, or *hakwon*, generally have their own educational buildings. These multi-storey learning centres can be as impressive and tall as that of Yoyogizemi in Japan, but they are, in comparison, sparsely scattered. They also keep a moderate profile. Big *hakwon* posters are visible in the subway trains and buses, which provide parents with a convenient sketch map of their branch campuses. Unlike in Japan, however, outdoor commercials for *hakwon* are short on detail, and information is only obtainable at the *hakwon* office. While Taiwan's *buxiban* spare no effort to blow up their own image as providers of efficient ladders to university, Korean *hakwon* are cautious in projecting their profile in the market. The prohibition policy still mirrors a justified ideology, and its alleviation has been a grudging concession on the part of the regime.

In each of the three countries, there is one particular area in which the cram businesses are found. In Seoul, this is in Shinsôl-dong, where all sorts of *hakwon* buildings stand tall along both sides of its thoroughfare. Academic *hakwon* are less impressive and distinguishable in this cohabitation as very few of their signs show their speciality. In contrast to the flamboyant signboards decorated with incredible promises in Taiwan, the signboards found here have only a phone number in large type, and advertisements are minimal. At the entrance to the *hakwon*, one or two senior male desk clerks relentlessly mount guard over the narrow passage in the lobby as students pile through. Cram schools generally look stately outside, but their interior seems dilapidated and badly needs a new coat of paint or some repairs. Power conservation makes many classrooms dim-lit and almost eerie. All this makes the atmosphere in Korea appear more dismal than in Taiwan or Japan.

It is interesting to note that, given the strong political and ideological censure and control, self-justification or legitimacy has been the lifeline of the *hakwon* in Korea. This is demonstrated in the way the history of academic *hakwon* is presented by the Korea Unified Association of *Hakwon* (Hankook Hakwon Chong Yunhaphwe (HHCY)). The genesis of early *hakwon* was traced to the first Danish-style Farming-Movement School set up by the YMCA in 1929. Schools of a similar nature – defined as *hakwon* by HHCY – were later opened in eighteen cities across Korea. They taught not only farming and agriculture, but foreign languages, ethics and nationalism. During 1920–34, a period of Japanese colonial rule, these *hakwon* held altogether 60 ten-day training sessions, and 40,000 people participated. They widened the international perspective of local people, and they became the cradle of many national leaders. There is no doubt, by the way, that a yawning difference exists between those missionary-type training schools and today's exam-oriented academic *hakwon*. What appears evident is a conscientious search by *hakwon* owners for a decent ancestral lineage that would earn them respect and esteem.

After the Japanese colonial rule was over, the YMCA changed its name to YMCI, and the 'old *hakwon*' experienced major changes in their objectives and functions. Korean, Japanese, English and maths were taught there, which were geared to the entrance exams, and *hakwon* grew in number. Occasionally, subjects expanded to cover whole school subjects. During the Korean War of the 1950s, universities in Korea moved to Pusan. Even in those chaotic days, English, Korean and maths, the three basics, were still taught in temporary *hakwon* shelters in Pusan. After 1953, those *hakwon* in exile came back to Seoul and regained their previous popularity. In 1957, the Korea Unified Association of *Hakwon* was set up, and its president was the director of an academic *hakwon*. The next year, a '*hakwon* boom' started as a result of the institution of national exams for civil servants.

From 1960 onwards, the basis of *hakwon* was solidly strengthened. Their costs soared as competition for both high school and college intensified. There were also *hakwon* for repeaters (*gaesoo saeng*), a parallel to Japanese *yobiko*. During that period, *hakwon* changed their status from educational non-profit institutions to profitable ones, and it thus became obligatory for them to pay taxes. The business of *hakwon* became manifold. They not only provided information, published journals and magazines, and awarded scholarships, but also carried out literary campaigns and some community services.

In 1973, as part of the decentralization policy, the government closed down *hakwon* in the north of Seoul, and moved the rest from the city centre to less populated areas. In 1987, *hakwon* were prohibited as a major measure to 'normalize' schooling. After a long decade, prohibition was alleviated, and yet, the *hakwon* as an institutionalized extracurricular education has yet to step out of the dark shadow of illegitimacy.

Korean education has been subjected to a sequence of radical, disconcerted changes, which, more often than not, came about because of the political tremors of power. Many think that these changes, instead of alleviating the problem, complicated it. The high-handed interference of authority was critiqued by Korean scholars as hastily implemented stop-gap measures.[6] But, there is one 'Achilles' heel' even in many 'salvationist' scholarships or reform plans. While focusing on the utopian world of 'liberal education' and 'higher education for all', reformers tend to forget the meritocratic role of the entrance exams, as the workplace and society in Korea, or East Asia at large, always need a meritocratic order to allocate the educated to suitable positions. In this sense, the three countries bear a cultural resemblance to one another. As Rohlen (1980) puts it, reality begins with the assumption that 'everyone is facing the same severe social realities with essentially the same desires. The facts of life are that competition decides success and that all Japanese want educational success because it leads to better employment, higher status and more power. Society is seen as "naturally" hierarchical, but the top is open to those who through special effort struggle upward.' This in-depth revelation throws light on what most of the reforms failed to incorporate. As a result of the equalization policy and the abolition of high school entrance exams, even in the élite high schools, teaching has become a daunting task. There are too many students in each class, and their diversity is too wide to handle. In consequence, teachers have complained that they can't and don't correct and grade homework any more. This seems to make academic *hakwon* inevitable.

RIVALRY IN THE CRAM WORLD

It is a truism that competition always exists in the business world. What is the mode of competition in cram schools, a world dominated by scholarship and intellectuals? And, how does the situation differ in Japan, Korea and Taiwan? To begin our pursuit, let us first look at the case of Japan.[7]

---

[6] See for instance Young-hwa Kim (1993).

[7] The inter-*juku* competition has not been adequately documented even in Japanese literature. A major source for my study here is Makino (1986).

Japan's 'SKY War'

Competition among cram schools did not intensify much in Japan until the mid-1960s, when the *juku* industry had to adapt to the newly instituted national system of college entrance exams. All of a sudden, these enterprises found that, whether they were big or small, they were having to play the game by the same rules. The initial phase of nationwide competition was competition in institutional restructuring and reorientation to centralized exams, which only the largest companies could possibly afford. Among them are the three giants (*ôtejuku*), 'Sundai', 'Kawaijuku' and 'Yoyo-gizemi'. Their rivalry is jocularly termed as the 'SKY War', an acronym taken from the initials of the names of the three largest companies (Daisan Shokan, 1993: 248–9). Yoyogizemi worked hard on its own new image, which has pretty much metamorphozed from a 'necessary evil' to a people's academy with a soft, bright profile. Founded in 1957, Yoyogizemi now boasts 31 schools in Japan, with 369,000 students, 1250 teaching faculty and 2105 office staff members. The best illustration of the restructuring endeavour, however, is found in Kawaijuku.

Established in 1933, Kawaijuku claims itself to be a non-profit educational foundation, headquartered in Nagoya. Today, the company has 44 school campuses in 23 major cities of Japan, and its offices are set up in Sendai, Niikata, Nakano, Shizuoka, Kanazawa, Okayama and Kagoshima, as well as Taipei, London and New Jersey. Fifteen hundred administrative personnel are responsible for a total of 140,000 students. It is a large educational system that provides: (1) assistance in college entrance exam preparation; (2) an information network for examinations; (3) language courses for both foreign and Japanese students; (4) pre-school education; (5) general education, such as language, information technology, management and design; (6) art and other types of cultural education; (7) publication of journals and references; (8) educational research; and (9) correspondence courses.

Kawaijuku used to be a small-sized, ordinary *juku* in Nagoya, the fourth largest city in Japan. But, it was two people at the department-chief level (*buchô*) that made some real changes. Both of them entered the *juku* world from elsewhere. One of them used to work at a Japanese company branch in Seattle, and the other came from a stock exchange company. They considered it naïve to run a *juku* as an 'educational industry'. Rather, a *juku* should be before anything else an 'information industry'. In their mind, a tutoring class was a process of retailing knowledge and information directly geared to the exams, and the knack of *juku* success lay in the needs of the majority of customers – students and their parents. They envisioned that a *juku* should be an information exchange network across Japan. Pieces of information would be collected from the student/parent customers at different local campuses, and then analysed and synthesized at headquarters. Important findings would not only serve as the basis for decision making, but would also be commoditized and sold back to customers at the local level. As the first step in this restructuring, the Kawaijuku National Entrance Exam Information Center, the first of its kind, was set up. Kawaijuku offices were computerized, and *hensachi*, a score system convenient for comparing achievement, was adopted.[8] This novel concept or 'Conquer Japan Strategy (*zenkoku seiharosen*)' was emulated by other *juku* only ten years later. What was triggered by this Kawaijuku expansion was a keen rivalry in the business.

The effect of reform in Yoyogizemi and Kawaijuku was bitterly felt by the rest. One of them is the other largest *juku* in Japan, 'Sundai *Yobiko*', established as early as in 1919. As a result of competition, the company retreated to Kyoto and Osaka. The other small businesses either became affiliated or were absorbed into the system of the big *juku*. One typical example was Kawaijuku's purchase of the entire Kyushu Heiwa Cram School: a takeover of all of its school buildings, land, staff and students. A group of those independent, small companies formed a large, loosely knit *Daishinkan* (College Entrance Research Society). As a result, the competition changed not only the management policy and *juku* schools, but also their entire pattern. Four large systems came into configuration, as schematized in Figure 5.1.

The nationwide 'Conquer Japan' war unfolded in 1978. Kawaijuku built up its campus in Tokyo. Its so-called 'Green Courses' sent a large number of students into Tokyo University. This was a thunderbolt to other *juku* companies. Sundai decided to retaliate through land purchases at Kawai's headquarters, Nagoya. But the move was forestalled by Kawaijuku: it had already bought up or rented all the unused land around the train stations, and Kawaijuku promotion boards could be seen everywhere.

The 'Conquer Japan' rivalry shook the business. In 1985 alone, more than 30 *juku* companies went bankrupt. In consequence, the three *juku* giants made a *de facto* 'conquest' of some major cities in Japan. For example, in Tokyo, the main rivals were Yoyogi and Sundai, and Kawaijuku was an uneasy third. In Yokohama, it was Kawaijuku versus Yoyogi, with Sundai somewhat in fourth place, although the third one, JPS Academy, incidentally, only teaches English. In Nagoya, it was Kawaijuku versus Yoyogi; in Hiroshima, Kawaijuku versus YMCA.

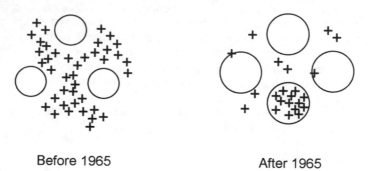

Before 1965   After 1965

Figure 5.1 A schema of the structural change of Japan's *juku* organization before and after 1965.
Notes: O stands for the big *juku*, including Yoyogi, Kawaijuku, Sundai, and, after 1965, the *Daishinkan* (College Entrance Research Society).
+ are the small *juku*.

---

[8] For the formula for *hensachi* see Chapter 3, note 17.

Taiwan: Wild competition among *buxiban*

A study of competition among *juku* reveals a gulf of difference between *honne* and *tatemae*, or 'appearance' and 'reality'. As a foreigner studying *juku* in Japan, I was unable to detect a trace of their competition by myself. It is hidden behind a thick *tatemae*, as perfect as Japanese wrappings. If this *tatemae* has a parallel in Taiwan, it is very thin. The *buxiban* take their competition very personally. People work hard to improve their own image, and they work equally hard to debase their rivals. This is not to suggest that competition in Taiwan is tougher than in Japan, which is untrue by any standards. The fact of the matter is, in Taiwan business competition is imbued with emotion. In Japan, the clash and feud are devastating, but noiseless. In Taiwan they are full of sound and fury, scoff and sarcasm, sometimes with a tinge of black humour. This is a paragraph I quote from a *buxiban*'s hard-covered, glossy brochure. It denounces certain *buxiban* outside of the Nanyang Cram Avenue:

> Some *buxiban* fail to improve their students' score achievement, but they refuse to learn from the good teaching methods of our Cram Street. Their administration is sluggish, but they are not willing to adopt our rules, either. Their campus is surrounded by small motels, game galleries, dark public houses, and they conceal their places from the parents' eyes. What right do they have to criticize our Cram Street? It only serves their ulterior interest of enrolling more students. ...
>
> My colleagues, please don't play tricks and reverse right and wrong any more, that could only make the image of our *buxiban* even more tarnished.

In a slim publication from a different *buxiban*, there is an essay criticizing categorically its neighbouring *buxiban*'s 'ugly' activities, which included (1) pretending to be a student and writing impostor letters to criticize other *buxiban*; (2) pretending to be the administrator of a *buxiban* and calling parents for immediate payment for the tuition; (3) inducing students of one *buxiban* to transfer to theirs; (4) spreading rumours about the other *buxiban*'s viability to smirch their image and scare students away; (5) trying to attract more students into their schools by the attractive appearance of boys and girls already enrolled in the *buxiban*. In Cram Street, it is not at all difficult for me to get a pamphlet containing that kind of denunciation. They show both the rhetoric and reality in this competitive world.

All told, however, the main thrust of the rivalry lies in the success rate in getting into universities. As described earlier, publicizing the list of winners was the most important weapon in this exam war. An impressive example is given by the 'Gongjian', a multi-purpose *buxiban*.[9]

Beating competition in the *buxiban* market means that fulfilling a few key factors is needed. One such factor can be termed educational 'ecology'. A typical example is given by the 'New Dragon' (*shinlong*) *buxiban*, which brags in minute detail about their 'Ten Big Privileges'. They are printed on the first pages of every textbook or information brochure the company

---

[9] See above, pp. 155–6 and note 5.

publishes. I list the gist of those 'privileges' below. They typify how a *buxiban* in Taiwan creates its own image and presents it to the public:

Ten Privileges of the 'New Dragon'

1. *Ideal location.* Close to the Street of Bookshops, 'New Dragon' is enveloped in the literati milieu, only 50 metres away from the train station.
2. *Clean environment. Sanitary staff work in shifts 24 hours a day* to clean the floor, classroom, drinking-water fountain and lavatories.
3. *Excellent faculty.* The nation's best teachers are invited here for every course. Foreign teachers are available to revise students' compositions.
4. *Perfect facilities and guaranteed safety.* 'New Dragon' has been wholly remodelled. Four new elevators and a fire exit are newly built. Students have the privilege of free access to our self-study centre, *the biggest in Taiwan.* Classrooms are spacious and well designed for lectures. All classrooms are equipped with *microphone amplifiers used by television stations. The magnetic blackboards are made in Japan, and chalks that generate no powder residue are produced in France.*
5. *Considerate service.* The teaching assistants stay with the class the whole day to lend help to students, and there are consultants around who are specialized in life guidance to help solve diverse problems for students.
6. *Enthusiastic administration.* The administration offices and classrooms are located on the same floor to facilitate administrative work. Advisers are *as kind as baby-sitters.* Attendance records, curfews and leave systems are strictly carried out. Students who smoke are absolutely forbidden from registration so as to ensure the quality of the student group.
7. *Efficient system.* The mock tests are formulated entirely after that of *Daxue liankao* (National University Entrance Exams). The resulting scores will be reported to students at the fastest speed. Test papers are scanned and graded by computer, which not only provides students with detailed explanation, but also an analysis of their mistakes.
8. *Welfare and benefits.* 'New Dragon' will pay its students' life insurance in full. Low tuition is our set policy. Registered students will be given a series of publications related to university entrance exams. 100% student loans are available. Payment will be made only after attending class.
9. *Free computer service.* Students can use our computer system for university applications. All students can come back to us for a part-time job.
10. *Complete and useful publications.* Our textbooks are printed with superb quality and are highly helpful in enhancing your strength. We supply the latest news on the *Daxue liankao*, and publish mock tests with answers from across Taiwan soon after they come out. Our students can make full use of our publications free of charge.

The text given above is replete with amusing exaggerations. The superlative degree is unsparingly used. Words like 'Japan-made magnetic blackboards', 'chalks imported from France', etc., are no more than marketing phraseology. Behind the commercial embellishment, however, is a reflection of some educational presumptions held by the Taiwanese majority that the *buxiban* need to satisfy. The 'Ten Privileges' paint an ideal ecology, and it is necessarily based on the Taiwanese ideals of education. This ecology includes modern facilities, a team of trustworthy teachers, efficient mock tests plus computer information services, and good administration. Last but not least is a relentless extraction by the *buxiban* of students' time on academic work.

Rivalry among the cram businesses exists everywhere in these three countries. In Taiwan, however, it struck me as far more above board. At the information desk, the secretary is willing to slash tuition fees so as to get a competitive edge. When a parent inquired about tuition for his son, the young secretary gave him a whole pile of brochures and offered him without a blink a 5.4 per cent discount on the six-month tuition, 46,500 new Taiwan dollars (about $1788), which meant a 100-dollar discount. To beat the competition from the neighbours, the discount can sound unbelievable. At a *buxiban* that orients specifically to National Taipei University, tuition is offered for 38 per cent less. The tricky part here is that, unlike the Japanese *juku*, *buxiban* generally do not print tuition prices in their information. So the original prices are somewhat hard to determine. This would make the bargain as meaningless as one struck in a flea market: no matter how much you gain, you always lose.

Other kinds of awards are also used to attract students. In the above-mentioned 'New Dragon', for instance, tantalizing prizes are offered to the top scorers. In a 200-person class, the first 20 students can get awards within the range of 40–800 US dollars. Some *buxiban* send other gifts, such as Chinese–English dictionaries or reference books. However, the most important competitive edge is billboard and newspaper advertisements, as reflected in Table 5.2.

If we compare the commercial advertisements of Taiwanese *buxiban* with those of Japanese *juku*, some differences are perceivable. In Table 5.2 and Figure 5.2, we see that billboards were the most common method of attracting students in Taiwan. No parallel was found in Japan. Taiwanese also used newspapers a lot (40 per cent), while Japanese used them much less (2.2–8.7 per cent). Commercials for academic *juku* were not much found on TV in either country. The reason might be that TV is too expensive for *juku*, or it is too easy to provoke ideological criticism. It appears that, overall, Taiwanese cram enterprises were more open to the public in competition as compared to the Japanese *juku*.

While the competition among cram schools was similarly fierce in Japan and Taiwan, their institutional patterns differed. This is shown in the comparative data on Japan's *yobiko* and its equivalent in Taiwan, *shengxüe buxiban*, as summarized in Table 5.3.

Although the dates of the statistics for Japan and Taiwan were different in Table 5.3, the proportional pattern of the sizes of cram schools are notable and valid. Schools with fewer than 200 students accounted for 50 per cent in Taiwan as compared to 38.2 per cent in Japan. For schools with more than 1000 students, the figure was 27.8 per cent for Japan, and only 8.0 per cent for Taiwan. On average, Taiwan's *shengxüe buxiban* were smaller than Japan's *yobiko*. In Japan, the giant *juku*-cum-*yobiko* companies dominated the market; in Taiwan, the market was segmented into small 'turfs'.

Table 5.2 The methods of commercial promotion used by *buxiban* in Taiwan, by percentage, 1992. *Source*: TMOE, *Taiwan Diqü Gelei Duanqi Buxiban Gaikuang Tongji Diaocha Baogao* (Report of statistic survey on short-term *buxiban*), (Taipei: Taiwan Ministry of Education Statistics Office, 1993b), 100-1.

Methods	Newspaper	TV	Radio	Billboard	Others
Percentage	40.26	8.71	4.53	90.18	52.20

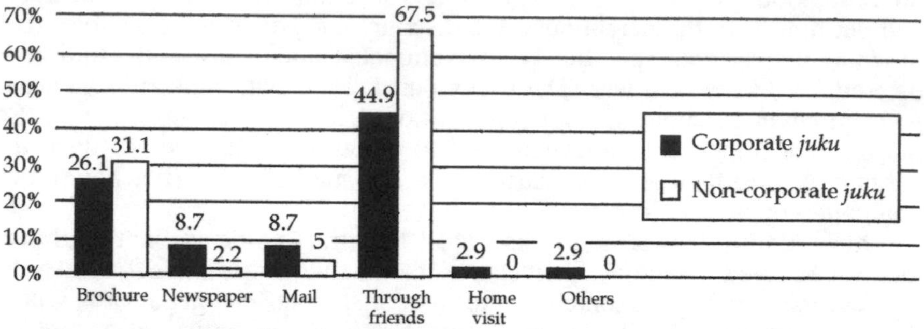

Figure 5.2 The methods of commercial promotion used by *juku* in Japan, by percentage, 1986. *Source*: JMOE, 'Kyôiku Sangyô ni kansuru Chôsa: Gakushûjuku Sangyô o Chûshin ni', pp. 293–314 in *Kyôiku* (Tokyo: Ministry of Education, 1987), 310.

Table 5.3 A comparison of cram school sizes: Japan's *yobiko* and Taiwan's *shengxüe buxiban*. *Sources*: Shigeru Akanuma *et al.*, *Za*Yobiko. Omoshirokunatta Yobiko o Kaibô* (A dissection of the fascinating *yobiko*), (Tokyo: Daisan Shokan, 1986), 284–319; TMOE, *Taiwan Diqü Gelei Duanqi Buxiban Gaikuang Tongji Diaocha Baogao* (Report of statistical survey on short-term *buxiban*), (Taipei: Taiwan Ministry of Education Statistics Office, 1993b), 78–80.

	School size by number of students				
	<200	200–499	500–999	>1000	Total
Taiwan	270	160	63	43	537
	(50.3%)	(29.8%)	(11.7%)	(8.0%)	(100%)
Japan	76	46	24	60	216
	(38.2%)	(21.3%)	(11.1%)	(27.8%)	(100%)

Note: Both *yobiko* and *shengxüe buxiban* are cram schools for full-time repeaters. The data for Japan are from 1986; the data for Taiwan's *buxiban* are from 1992.

Data also indicate a trend of combinations of independent *juku* enterprises in the past years, while *juku* companies grew larger. From 1976 to 1985, syndicated chain companies increased from 5.9 per cent to 27 per cent in total. Ownership also had changed its pattern: privately owned companies decreased from 88.3 per cent to 74.5 per cent, whereas corporate companies increased from 11.7 per cent to 25.5 per cent. This was a clear sign of syndication, described by the Japanese as the 'chain transformation' (*keiretsuka*) (JMOE, 1985; YKK, 1994).

In Taiwan, the lack of syndication can be imputed to the government policy of regulations (Zheng, in ZR, 11 August 1993). However, it may be better understood if we keep in mind the larger perspective of industrial structure. Enterprise groups in Japan, Korea and Taiwan display distinctive organizational patterns of ownership, management, finance and production. Measures of country-specific isomorphism confirm the uniformity of firm characters within each country, and the differences among them. The ownership pattern of business groups in Japan is different from that in Taiwan. Japanese business groups embrace the largest number of individual firms, with an average of over 112 firms for each of six intermarket groups. Taiwanese business groups are smaller than Japanese and Korean ones, typically having fewer than eight affiliated firms each (Orrù, Biggart and Hamilton, 1961: 367–8).

THE CRAM WORLD: ARCHITECTURE AND CULTURE

A school provides a special space where education is undertaken. This space is shaped by its architecture, capacity, colour, illumination, heating and ventilation, as well as by equipment such as blackboards, desks, chairs and decoration. All these need to be designed to fit the educational uses and physical capabilities of human beings in school. How do cram school conditions meet their educational purposes? And, how do they reflect the essential role and features of cramming as an industry? These are questions the following pages try to answer.

Buildings: The role and spirit of the space

In Japan's big cram schools, educational buildings are generally divided into two large types. One is bluntly utilitarian: cement buildings that resemble big boxes and are composed of numerous small boxes – the classrooms. Basic facilities for lectures include nothing but a dark green glass chalkboard, chalk and felt eraser, and rows of long desks and chairs that serve four or five persons each. The interior is whitewashed with lime and water. Graffiti are never or seldom seen. Elevators are small and slow, but always work. These buildings look greyish and weather-beaten, giving an impression that might parallel the cloisters of the mediaeval age. They match the image of the exam: the gruelling, macho rite of passage. These buildings are witness to the early years of the cram industry.

The other type is newly built, voguish and attractive. They are the new additions to the original campus, obviously an outcome of the financial surplus. They serve as a showcase, an overstated presentation of the efficiency and success that the cram corporation has achieved. The new buildings are very often used as the information and registration offices or the headquarters, especially for big companies.

The Kawaijuku headquarters at Nagoya is a modern building with an elegant profile resembling a major bank. Its nonconformist shape is composed of vertical rectangles adjoined by triangles, and the overall surface is shielded in dark mirrored glass. It is connected by an overpass ramp structure to its adjacent cluster of lecture buildings. In Tokyo, Sundai *Yobiko* School buildings are located in the downtown area. These two-storeyed low-rises have an exterior facade that might be mistaken for a chic shopping mall or a coffee-house. The architecture of the Yoyogi headquarters seems boxy, nonfigural and commonplace in design. However, on its rooftop, the huge antenna disc for satellite transmission courses is a 'decoration' as powerful as the functionalist design.

Unlike the old, the new design hides the harsh side of cramming life by its cool conditioned air, refined surface contour, subtle, concealed lighting, and amiable multi-colours. It is a persuasive, appealing *tatemae*. The former type of building is a more accurate reflection of the dismal reality of life. It seems to be a stoic language insisting that, to succeed, one has to suffer. The three cram giants, Kawaijuku, Yoyogi and Sundai, all have these two distinct building groups, almost half and half in their number.

Today, Kawaijuku and the other *juku* are not only designed in a modern fashion, they are also so equipped. Computerized matrices and statistical graphs are available for students to input, retrieve and compare their achievement scores. Services are provided for students' *sinro shidô*, or 'guidance for their future course'. Upon entering a *juku* after a visit to an ordinary middle school, or even university, you cannot help contrasting shining and clean lavatories, classrooms and corridors in the *juku* with the dilapidated ones in traditional schools. These buildings are brand new or remodelled, both of which are very costly, and only a company with a large-scale economy can afford that commercial-minded vanity.

To explore the '*honne*' or the inner world of the *juku*, let us start with the entrance lobby of Sundai *Yobiko*, a puissant competitor of Kawaijuku and Yoyogi. In Tokyo, the eight major campuses of Sundai are clustered in Ochanomitsu, in the neighbourhood of the Meiji University. Like most *juku*, the Sundai parlour is divided into two main utilitarian areas, separated by a counter. Inside the counter is the administrative area for receptionists, cashiers and secretaries. Their desks are closely laid out and piled with documents. On one side of the counter is the entry lobby, which gives access to the classrooms upstairs. The elevator is quite spacious, and the staircase is modestly wide. There are no janitors or security personnel guarding the entrance. The lobby is also a place that provides information such as class schedules, application forms, and other basic information.

In the lobby, what catches a visitor's eye first is a large print-out of the assigned seat numbers (*shiteiseki*) for *juku* students. The seating is hierarchically arranged from the front row to the back, based on the result of the preceding mock tests. Only student numbers were given, but the names of the top 15–20 high achievers were publicized elsewhere as a rewarding message. I noticed that students often flocked around this conspicuous list, scrutinizing those names of honour in deep thought. Occasionally, I could overhear comments like: '*xxx san sugoi deshita ne* (Mr/Miss xxx was really great)!'. This hierarchical seating which I observed in the Sundai school is generally not found in Yoyogi and Kawaijuku (Komiyama, 1993), although I saw them in Kawai's main campus in Nagoya. To my knowledge, both Kawaijuku and Yoyogi in Tokyo adopted 'free seating (*jiyû seki*)' instead. It is observed that in extreme cases, the names of the worst three or ten scorers were posted in public for punitive purposes (ibid.). However, I have never observed this situation for myself.[10]

In Korea, the *hakwon* generally had their own buildings consisting of both the office and the classrooms, like the Japanese *juku*. These buildings were multi-floored and huge, also like the Japanese ones. But, the difference was apparent upon entering the building. Let me describe the *hakwon* in Seoul that I visited. Like *juku*, there was an administrative area at the entrance, where information pamphlets were on display for free distribution. Yet, unlike *juku*, which had a free flow in and out, this *hakwon* was like a secured 'fortress'. Access to the classrooms inside was made narrow by a desk or a turnpike, and was guarded by one or two watchmen. They were generally senior males, stern-faced and vigilant. Their pretentious air and impatience suggested that their chief duty was to safeguard against and scare away the unwanted, although they were also supposed to give information. The attitude of the loyal 'gendarmes' reflected a cautious self-consciousness of the cram business in Korea. In all three countries, the cram business has been very cautious about its public image because of its vulnerable legitimacy. This was especially notable in Korea as a result of the more stringent government policies of control and regulation.

In both Japan and Korea offices and classrooms are located together in their own building, but this is usually not the case in Taiwan. As described, *buxiban* offices in Taiwan are concentrated in 'cram streets' like boutiques, but their classrooms are in office buildings elsewhere. Of Taiwan's *buxiban*, while one-quarter had their own buildings, more than half only leased one floor. Using leased space, as shown in Table 5.4, had become a trend in the past years. In the Cram district of Taipei, one may notice a constant flow of boys and girls in blue uniforms, especially during the evening. Always carrying a satchel on their shoulders, they squeezed in and out of elevators in multi-purpose buildings for one or two hours of intensive tutoring classes.

Taiwan's *buxiban* impressed me with their more calculated cost-efficiency management. First of all, leasing a floor of the office building was much cheaper and more flexible than having their own building. The money thus saved, plus profit gained from large classes, made it feasible to have better quality in facilities, remodelling and faculty. The financial situation of *buxiban* might not be better than *juku* or *hakwon*, but they seemed to have done a better job.

---

[10] To arrange seating in classrooms in accordance with the order of achievement is a Japanese practice traceable at least to the fief schools or private Dutch schools during the Tokugawa era (1603–1867). The '*Dasseki-kai*' or 'group meeting for seizing the seat' was a typical embodiment of this competition in a Tokugawa private school. It consisted of a group of 10 to 20 students and a student 'monitor' from grade seven or above. Students sat according to their scores at previous sessions, with the top student seated in the centre of the group. Students asked questions in turn and the goal at every point was to oust the student in the centre in order to secure that position for oneself, for the centre seat was the only position from which one could score points. Disputed points were settled by the monitor. Refer to Rubinger (1982: 140) and Dore (1965: 143, 163, 182–6, 209).

Table 5.4 Ownership of Taiwan's *buxiban* classrooms by number and percentage, 1990 and 1992. *Source: Taiwan Diqü Gelei Duanqi Buxiban Gaikuang Tongji Diaocha Baogao* (Report of statistical survey on short-term *buxiban*), (Taipei: Taiwan Ministry of Education Statistics Office, 1993b), 12.

	Owned		Leased		Owned/ Leased		Borrowed		Others	
	No.	%	No.	%	No.	%	No.	%	No.	%
1990	283	25.5	609	54.7	34	3.1	118	10.6	68	6.1
1992	375	24.8	989	65.3	50	3.3	58	3.8	42	2.8

Classroom and class organization

In the major Japanese *juku*, especially *juku*-cum-*yobiko* companies, the class size is far larger than the classes in middle and high schools (around 40-odd). The full capacity as counted by seating is approximately 100–150. An average class would be 75, though it varies from 50 to more than 100. The large classes and subsequently the large architectural design are the main features of the major *juku* industry, which result from a combination of reasons. First of all, due to economies of scale, the large size is profitable. The larger the classes, the more money can be earned. Second, large classes are manageable because there are no questions and answers in *juku* classes, and the teaching, very much like religious speech, is a one-way dissemination of knowledge. Third, large classes are manageable because computer technology radically reduced the amount of labour used for the grading, correcting and commenting of test papers.

Another important factor is the unification of the exam system. In 1979, after a concentrated investigation and some try-outs, the Joint First-Stage Achievement Test (JFSAT) was instituted to evaluate applicants' attainment in basic and general studies at upper-secondary schools (Tadashi, 1988). The JFSAT is administered in January each year, jointly given by the Japanese Ministry of Education and universities. An identical set of questions would be given to several hundred thousand student applicants throughout Japan over two days. These questions were standardized in their scale of difficulty and area coverage, and they also became more related to the school curriculum. In that sense, the centralized exams were less unpredictable than university-based exams. Research institutes are regressing them based on past test papers, in a similar way to how stockbrokers predict market price undulation. The uniformity of exams made preparation for them in large *juku* classes possible.

The JFSAT or Center Test given at the national level was not a substitute for the exams given by universities, however. The national/public universities still hold their second stage entrance exams, and the private universities have never given up their autonomy of selection. In view of their variability, organizing classes attuned to these different challenges is not easy. One way to solve this problem is to find the common factors among individual university exams. *Juku* schools divide the universities into a number of groups according to these common factors, and then organize classes oriented particularly to certain groups. The private universities, for instance, are often clustered into the following groups:[11]

- Waseda University + Keio University[12]
- Meiji University + Chûo University + Hosei University[13]
- Japan University + Tôyô University + Komazawa University[14]
- Jôchi University + Rikkyô University + Aoyama University[15]

The standardization of the national exams, plus the 'grouping' approach, enable the major *juku* companies to open fairly large classes and expand their business.

As a result, in major *juku* corporations like Sundai or Yoyogizemi, classrooms can be as big as a meeting hall. A course of enormous size is often nicknamed a 'mammoth' class in Japanese. The 'mammoth' is not only 'normal' in the business, but it often suggests the popularity of its teacher or school. By my observation, a regular class could have eleven rows of desks, with fourteen seats per row. Altogether there are 154 seats in a classroom. A class often has only 60–70 students, but my judgement is that at least one in three classes is fully seated. The size of a class depends on its teaching quality, the fame of its teacher, and also the number of applicants for universities to which the class is linked.

In major *juku*, the interior design of the classroom reflects the large market demand. The desk is a long one serving three or four students. Chairs are similar to those in movie theatres: they are foldable and hinged onto the front side of the desk structure. According to the seat assignment maps, a class usually consists of more than 100 students.

The podium in the classroom is high, because the room is quite long and the ground is flat. The top of a seated student's head is on the same level as the knees of the lecturer on the podium. Because of the long distance from the last row to the front, reading the words on the chalkboard could be very difficult. What is more, copying what the teacher writes on the chalkboard is

---

[11] The sources for the information on universities given here and subsequently are: Asahi Shinbunsha (1994a) and Kawaijuku and Tôyô Keizai, eds (1993).

[12] Waseda University, founded by the famous politician Okuma Shigenobu (1838–1922) in 1882, located in Tokyo. Keio University, founded in 1858 by an early educator, Fukuzawa Yukichi (1834–1901), the oldest private school in Japan.

[13] Meiji University, founded in 1939, located in Tokyo. Chûo University, founded as the English Law School in 1943. Hosei University, founded in 1938.

[14] Nihon University, founded in 1947, located in Tokyo. Tôyô University, founded in 1945. Komazawa University has a history of 400 years.

[15] Jôchi University, founded in 1913. Rikkyô University, founded by an American missionary in 1874. Aoyama University, founded in 1874 by an American missionary.

vitally important in a Japanese class. It is interesting to see a *juku* class through the eyes of an American high school principal, a visitor in Japan:

> Akiyama [a *juku* teacher] has learned to write words 10 to 12 inches high. Before erasing a full board, he pauses and briefly steps aside so that students, in surreal parody of themselves, jump up to photograph the contents before his wisdom becomes chalkdust. (Pettersen, 1993)

The 'photographing', if true, is an extreme example. The fact of the matter is, however, that in Japan, great importance is attached to a teacher's notes.

The *juku* chalkboard is wall-to-wall wide, and in some *juku* like Kawaijuku, it is concave-shaped so that students on either side can see better. The felt erasers were unusually huge and efficient, perhaps because Japanese teachers generally need to write and erase a lot in class. The janitors regularly replaced the dirty erasers with clean ones. They collected the dusty erasers in a bucket and cleaned them regularly, using a special machine. The queen-size erasers thus always worked as softly and cleanly as new ones, leaving no whitish trace of powder residue behind.

In Seoul, the *hakwon* schools were similar to *juku*, and so were the classrooms. But the minor contrast is worthy of note. One *hakwon* I visited was a five-storey building overlooking a busy intersection of Shinsôl-dong, the '*Hakwon* Town'. After 6:00 p.m., students who were finally dismissed from school began to show up here in the still empty classroom. This classroom is about half the size of a Yoyogi *juku* room in Japan. There were about 60 seats, as compared to 150 in Yoyogi. On both sides of the blackboard, a 20" TV set was fixed to the ceiling by an iron frame.

Once the class had begun, instead of satellite transmission of simultaneous lectures, the screen showed a pre-recorded lecture of advanced algebra from videotape. About nine students sat randomly at their discretion, scattered. This class was smaller than average, perhaps because its time was too close to regular school hours. One male student in his late twenties was following the class attentively. The rest were all girls. One was washing down her sandwiches with chocolate milk. A couple of others were murmuring merrily to each other. Others were gazing motionlessly at the TV. Neither the teacher nor the assistant was around.

In the room, there were fluorescent tubes on the ceiling; each tube was bright enough, but there seemed not to be enough of them. So the lighting appeared high and slightly dim and shadowy. Dusty ceiling fans were fixed next to the lights. On the switch panels near the door, two of the three switches were broken. They seemed to have been unrepaired for a long time, and were covered with thick transparent tape to prevent electric shock. A big smeared garbage can was placed in the middle of the left aisle. Most of the desks and folding chairs were badly worn out through use, although they were not broken.

In Taiwan, many of the *buxiban* classrooms are even larger than 'the mammoths' in Japan. The classes that I attended had about 200 students each. This was partially due to the higher degree of unification for the entrance exams in Taiwan. In Japan, a major *juku* company had to deal with both the nationally held Center Test, and a great diversity of exams given by individual universities, which altogether amounted to more than 500. In Taiwan, it is *Yikao ding zhongsheng* (one exam determines everybody's entire life), and the national exam system is the only 'Dragon Gate' that students need to pass. The uniformity of the required knowledge, I would argue, makes it possible to organize classes even larger than Japan's *juku* or *yobiko* class. However, this does not mean that *buxiban* had a larger school size than the *juku*. On average, a *juku* company opened many more classes than a *buxiban*. Therefore, compared to Japan, Taiwan's *buxiban* had larger class sizes, but a smaller school size.

Buxiban classes might be huge in size, but their order was extremely good. In an advanced maths class I visited, the 200-capacity room was fully occupied. Students sat shoulder to shoulder, yet there was no detectable noise, no disturbance and no distraction. Everyone was listening and jotting down notes. Judging from their appearance, students belonged to either high schools or the 'tribe of repeaters (*Chongkao zu*)'.

It was a scorchingly hot summer, but inside was cool and comfortable, because of the noise-free central air conditioning. The lighting was perfectly bright and soft, as the source of illumination was in the opaque glass ceiling and on the walls. The inside was well designed and well maintained. The only weakness seemed to be that the space was too narrow: each person had a compact desk and a compact chair, and he or she did not have much elbow room or leg room.

Walls, in human society, provide a prominent space where people exhibit art, philosophy or ideology. In *juku* classes, most classroom walls were clear of unnecessary words or graphs. Only terse notices painted in big *kanji* (Chinese characters), aimed at keeping things in order, ever lined the walls:

– No food or drinks.
– No smoking.
– No talking.

Or, they may directly concern the interests of individuals:

– Please keep your belongings at hand.
– In case of an earthquake, please (1) do not make hasty or risky moves, (2) use the fire exit only, (3) stay away from the glass windows, (4) avoid falling electric lights.

Seldom did I meet anything as ideological as the two inculcating slogans I found in the Yoyogi school:

– Kind and personal guidance.
– Every day is a decisive battle.

In Korea's *hakwon*, the walls were almost blank, except for the class schedules; there was not even the *Taegûkki* (national flag), which was omnipresent in offices and schools. As the harsh winter for extracurricular tutoring had just elapsed, no ideology is legitimately available. The lack of a rudimentary ideology explains the politically cautious, self-effacing profile that the *hakwon* industry still maintains.

Taiwan's *buxiban* is just the other way round. The academic competitiveness is in line with tradition, which has not been fatally battered by government policies, unlike in Korea. The *buxiban* walls that I observed were decorated with greenish artificial ivy leaves, a replica of a European oil painting of classic romance, and a Chinese water colour. Aphorisms are posted in calligraphic art. Some examples were:

> – The Gongjian *buxiban* will escort you to go through this bitter journey of ordeal [i.e. cram].
> – Do not let your heart be shattered, do not give up, because persistence pays in the end.
> – It is the early bird that catches the worm.
> – Only after a freezing snow will the plum flowers bloom.[16]

Around the class, this kaleidoscope of buzzwords and art creates a vivid diversion for the students. Otherwise, the air could have been so tense that one might cut it with a knife.

A main difference among the cram schools of the three countries is that the Japanese *juku* school is larger and more syndicated, but the class in Taiwan is larger. As so many students were crammed into one room, problems occurred. One problem was visibility. There were fourteen rows of students in the classroom. The view of those at the back was blocked by the people in front. The ceiling was about 2.6 metres high, a little too low for the vast area it covered. The podium was only 0.4 metres from the ground, because if it was higher, the teacher's head would touch the ceiling. To tackle this problem, the fourteen rows of desks/chairs had a gradient increase in their heights as they approached the back of the room, as sketched in Figure 5.3.

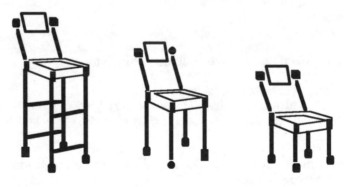

Figure 5.3 Chairs used in Taiwan's big *buxiban* classroom to solve the visibility problem.

---

[16] The plum flower, '*meihua*' or '*lamei*', is a favourite flower in Chinese culture. The flower pattern is composed of five pink, white or red petals. Perhaps because *meihua* generates a delicate fragrance in the cold winter season, it becomes a metaphor of success after hard work against harsh times. Chinese paintings and poems on plum flowers abound, and like other themes, such as bamboo, these symbols also imply an appreciation of certain personal characteristics.

In the picture, you can see that chairs for the front row were of normal size, but those in the back row were as high as almost one metre. When I climbed onto one myself, I felt like I was straddling on top of a fireman's compact ladder, or performing some sort of acrobatics. These high chairs were matched by high desks, four in one. Although they might look thinner and cheaper, they feel perhaps even better, because they were covered with a smooth protective plate.

Modern facilities

The modern facilities that a school is equipped with are an important indicator of its condition and its growth as an enterprise. Overall, an examination of a school's facilities can also show the disparity between schools or areas. The data in Table 5.5 compare modern facilities in two Taiwan cities and Taiwan as a whole. The lighting of *buxiban* in Taipei was twice as good as in the whole of Taiwan, and three times that of Kaohsing. Apart from that, the facilities of *buxiban* across Taiwan seemed to be not much different from the big cities, which means that the tutoring business was quite modernized all over Taiwan.

As shown in Figure 5.4, lighting in Taipei is much brighter than other places. The air-conditioning, however, is quite similar to most of the other cities or even counties, which may be due to the hot climate and living standards. The computers used for teaching are an interesting index.

Taipei's *buxiban* computerization is lower than half of the counties. This may result from the fact there are fewer *buxiban* there than in Taipei. In brief, the overall conditions of *buxiban* in Taiwan were not as good as in Taipei, especially lighting. Yet, if we take air-conditioning and computerization as two major indicators, the difference did not seem that great. The great disparity in lighting may be explained by the high price of electric power. In Korea, the undesirable lighting may also be a result of a power conservation policy.

Table 5.5 The percentage of *buxiban* equipped with modern facilities in Taipei, Kaohsing and Taiwan, 1992. *Source*: TMOE, *Taiwan Diqü Gelei Duanqi Buxiban Gaikuang Tongji Diaocha Baogao* (Report of statistical survey on short-term *buxiban*), (Taipei: Taiwan Ministry of Education Statistics Office, 1993b), 91–3.

Place	Computer	Air-conditioning	Lighting[a]
Taipei	18.0	98.7	25.1
Kaohsing[b]	17.6	97.2	7.3
Taiwan	17.5	92.2	10.3
Total	17.6	94.4	12.8

Notes: a. Measured by watts per sq. metre. b. Kaohsing, the second largest city in Taiwan, located in the south of Taiwan.

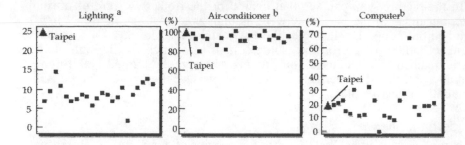

Figure 5.4 The facilities of *buxiban* in different cities of Taiwan, 1993.
Source: Based on TMOE, *Taiwan Diqü Gelei Duanqi Buxiban Gaikuang Tongji Diaocha Baogao* (Report of statistical survey on short-term *buxiban*), (Taipei: Taiwan Ministry of Education Statistics Office, 1993b), 91–3.
Notes: a. Measured by average watts (light) per sq. metre for all *buxiban* in a city. b. The percentage of *buxiban* in a city that are equipped with the facilities.
▲ is Taipei city.
■ is one of the 16 counties and six major cities, in no particular order.

The steadily growing size of *juku* posed two practical problems. An urgent one is the inadequacy of lavatories. The other may be less urgent, but a lot more important: fire prevention equipment. In Japan and Korea, where cram schools are similar to a school building, lavatories are not much of a problem. In Taiwan, this seemed to be a minor problem. Overall, every 100 students shared 4.26 bathrooms. Fire prevention measures and equipment, however, are more or less a potential problem in all three countries. In Japan, the hallways in the old buildings became narrower after remodelling, and the fire exits were hard to find. In Korea and Taiwan, it posed a potential threat to students' safety. Most of the hallways that I visited were too narrow for so many students. These buildings were not designed to serve such a large number of people. One of the great concerns shown in the concluding remarks of Taiwan's Ministry of Education is: 'As referring to the fire fighting equipment, although 94 per cent of *buxiban* were equipped with fire extinguishers, only 55 per cent had a fire exit facility, and 49 per cent had a fire alarm system. Urgent measures thus need to be taken in this respect' (TMOE, 1993b). In one *hakwon* in Seoul, I noted that not only was the staircase meandering and narrow, but the only fire exit on each floor was bolted up and locked. A red bucket was hung on the wall beside it. I could only pray in my heart for the children here that nothing would happen.

THE CRAM WORLD: STUDENTS

They are learning extensively, and having a firm and sincere aim; inquiring with earnestness, and reflecting with self-application – virtue is in such a course.
– *Zixia, the disciple of Confucius, in* Analects

Attendance ratio of tutoring schools: Statistics at the national level

Japanese *juku* are after-school tutoring establishments that give students hope of entering universities, the equivalent of tactical weapons in what is frequently referred to as the 'college entrance war'. In the past decades, the attendance ratio of cram schools has shown a steady increase, as a result of this 'arms race'. This intensification is charted in Figure 5.5.

By 1993, the *juku* attendance rate was 23.6 per cent for primary school students, and 59.5 per cent for middle school students. As for G9, the rate reached as high as 67.1 per cent, as compared to only 47.3 per cent in 1985 (see Table 5.6). To see the change in the actual number of students, I created Table 5.7 on the basis of data from the Japanese Ministry of Education's *1995 Gakushûjuku tô ni kansuru Jittai Chôsa Hôkokusho* (Report on the survey of the issues related to the academic *juku*) (JMOE, 1995) and the *1994 Monbu Tôkei Yôran* (Monbushô statistics handbook) (JMOE, 1994d), which provide evidence of the further development and intensification of *juku* schooling (see Table 5.7).

This 'craze' phenomenon would be more obvious if we keep in mind that during 1985–93, due to demographic changes, the total number of G1–9 students actually decreased from 17,085,555 to 13,619,018, a four million difference. And yet, the number of *juku* attenders still expanded by 463,821. According to a number of Japanese researches, this demographic impact is most painfully felt by private universities and colleges (Obunsha, 1994), but not so much by *juku*. In much contrast, 'jukurization' is still going on in Japan, as if towards a 'universalizing' prospect.

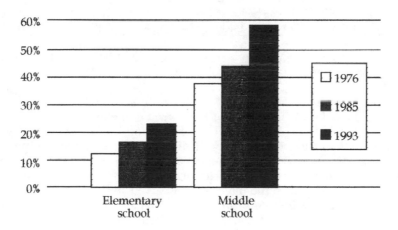

Figure 5.5 The *juku* attendance ratio (by percentage) of elementary and middle school students in Japan, 1976, 1985 and 1993. *Sources*: Based on JMOE, *Jidô Seito no Gakkôgai Gakushû Katsudô ni kansuru Jittai Chôsa Hôkokusho* (Survey of the extracurricular activities of children/students), (Tokyo: Ministry of Education, 1985), 6; JMOE, *Gakushûjuku tô ni kansuru Jittai Chôsa Hôkokusho* (Report on the survey of the issues related to the academic *juku*), (Tokyo: Japanese Ministry of Education, 1995), 5.

Table 5.6 The *juku* attendance ratio for different school levels in Japan, by percentage, 1976, 1985, 1993. *Sources*: JMOE, *Jidô Seito no Gakkôgai Gakushû Katsudô ni kansuru Jittai Chôsa Hôkokusho* (Survey of the extracurricular activities of children/students), (Tokyo: Ministry of Education, 1985), 6; JMOE, *Gakushûjuku tô ni kansuru Jittai Chôsa Hôkokusho* (Report on the survey of the issues related to the academic *juku*), (Tokyo: Japanese Ministry of Education, 1995), 5.

	G1	G2	G3	G4	G5	G6	G7	G8	G9
1976	3.3	4.8	7.5	11.9	19.4	26.6	37.9	38.7	37.4
1985	6.2	10.1	12.9	15.4	21.1	29.6	41.8	44.5	47.3
1993	12.1	14.1	17.5	23.6	31.1	41.7	52.5	59.1	67.1

Table 5.7 The change in the number of *juku* attenders against the total number of G1–9 students, 1976, 1985 and 1993. *Sources*: Data are calculated on the basis of JMOE, *Jidô Seito no Gakkôgai Gakushû Katsudô ni kansuru Jittai Chôsa Hôkokusho* (Survey of the extracurricular activities of children/students), (Tokyo: Ministry of Education, 1985), 6; JMOE, *Gakushûjuku tô ni kansuru Jittai Chôsa Hôkokusho* (Report on the survey of the issues related to the academic *juku*), (Tokyo: Japanese Ministry of Education, 1995), 5; and JMOE, *Monbu Tôkei Yôran* (Monbushô Statistics Handbook), (Tokyo: Ministry of Education, 1994d), 24–5.

	G1–9 students		Juku students	
Year	Total number	Increase†	Total number	Increase†
1976	15,443,887	n.a.	3,119,665	n.a.
1985	17,085,555	+ 1,641,668	4,493,501	+ 1,373,836
1993	13,619,018	– 3,466,537	4,957,322	+ 463,821

Note: † For the 1985 data, the increase = total of 1985 – total of 1976, for the 1993 data, the increase = total of 1993 – total of 1985.

Japan's Ministry of Education is not the only agency that collects data on *juku* attendance. Other organizations have been collecting their own. In June 1994, for example, the Japanese PTA Association, or Nihon PTA Zenkoku Kyôgikai (JPA) conducted a survey of 4000 people of public primary and middle schools across Japan. The subjects included students and their parents from either G6 or G9, the terminal levels for primary and middle schools. A summary of some major data is given in Table 5.8. Some other sources, such as *Yomiuri Shûkan*, a major Japanese weekly journal, and Kawaijuku also have their statistics, as presented in Table 5.9.

These statistics show some interesting disparities. Interesting because all the non-governmental sources, such as the JPA, *Yomiuri Shûkan* and Kawaijuku, provide a *juku* attendance ratio higher than that given by the government. This could result from a more thorough and balanced sampling with regard to rural and less populated areas. The non-governmental statistics could have taken urban areas as their main survey target. While it is difficult to verify my explanation, let us only assume that the Ministry's data were more authoritative, although the reason for the difference has yet to be determined. What is essentially confirmed with certainty here is that enrolment in the academic *juku* has been on a steady rise in the midst of demographic decline.

In Korea, the government played an active role in education, and the cramming practice is a typical manifestation of the power that the central authority held in regulating and controlling academic behaviour. In 1980, the government imposed the Prohibition Policy of Private Tutoring, which constituted one of the most severe measures for normalizing schooling. Nine years after its promulgation, the Prohibition Policy was alleviated in 1989, but cram practices, in terms of either tutoring or learning, are still not adequately legitimized. For that reason, the attendance ratios of *hakwon* in Korea are arbitrarily conditioned and contained by the harsh enforcement of government laws. In 1989, when prohibition had just been relaxed, the attendance ratio for high school students was only about 20.4 per cent (Shin *et al.*, 1991). The meaning of this figure can be questionable, because, first, due to prohibition the number could be under-reported, and second, it is noted that many students received tutoring at home instead of attending *hakwon* to avoid trouble. Soon after prohibition was liberalized, however, the attendance ratios rose radically, as indicated in Table 5.10.

The statistics on attendance ratios for both Korea and Taiwan are less systematic than those of Japan. Furthermore, whenever data were available, they came from less reliable sources. If judged on the data we have, the attendance ratio of *buxiban* in Taiwan does not differ greatly from that of Japan or Korea (see Table 5.11 for the data on Taiwan).

Table 5.8 Attendance ratios of academic *juku* for G6 and G9 students, 1987–94. *Source*: Based on 'PTA Kyô ga Chôsa' (Survey by Japan PTA Association), quoted in 'Juku kayoi: Machimurabu ni Kabudai' (Attending *juku*: an expanding rate in small towns and villages), *Asahi Shinbun*, 19 August 1994b.

	1987	1994	Increase of 1994 over 1987
G6	39.5%	38.8%	0.7%
G9	63.3%	73.3%	+ 9.4%

Table 5.9 *Juku* attendance by school level in Japan, by percentage, 1976, 1985, 1993. *Sources*: a. JMOE, *Gakushûjuku tô ni kansuru Jittai Chôsa Hôkokusho* (Report on the survey of the issues related to the academic *juku*), (Tokyo: JMOE, 1995), 5; b. Kawaijuku information, 1993; c. Robert Delfs, 'All work and no play: cram schools keep alive education nightmare', *The Far Eastern Economic Review*, 12 March 1992: 21–3.

Data source	Year of survey	Average of elementary school	Average of middle school
Monbushô[a]	1993	23.6%	59.5%
Kawaijuku[b]	1992	37.2%	65.7%
Yomiuri Shûkan[c]	1991	51.0%	80.9%

Table 5.10 *Hakwon* attendance ratios of school students in Korea, by percentage, 1990. *Source*: Se-Ho Shin *et al.*, *Kwawe Sueop Siltae Bunseok Yunga* (A study of private tutoring in Korea), (Seoul: Korea Education Development Institute, 1991), 43.

Grade	Hakwon *students*			df
	Yes	No		
G7	68.1	31.9		
G8	67.2	32.8	***	2
G9	61.4	38.6	14.24	
Middle school average	64.8	35.2		
G10	71.9	28.1		
G11	61.0	39.0	***	2
G12	57.2	42.8	65.26	
High school average	63.3	36.7		

*** p<0.001

Table 5.11 *Buxiban* attendance by school level in Taiwan, by percentage. *Sources*: Data from G1 to G7 are based on Li-fen Wu, 'Guoxiao Xüesheng Buxi Zhuangkuang Wenjüan Fenxi' (An analysis of the questionnaire survey of cramming practice among elementary school students), *Renben Jiaoyü Zhaji* (Journal of humanistic education) 43 (15 January 1993): 12–21; data for levels from G8 to G13 are provided by Taipei-shi Buxijiaoyü Shiye Xiehüi (Taipei *buxiban* association), 1994.

Grade	G1–G2	G3–G4	G5–G6	G7	G11	G12	G13
Ratio (%)	18.2	38.7	51.7	80.9	35	40	60

Human behaviours analogous to the 'cram phenomenon' are found in the crazes of, for example, stock purchases, the Florida land boom, or the tulip buying in seventeenth-century Holland. The urgency to act lies in the possibility that purchases by others will drive up the price or will exhaust the supply, i.e., the land, the tulip, or in our case, the chance of upward mobility through higher education. The major premise here is that if the gain the potential investor expects is more than the opportunity cost of the use of the money, then it is rational for him to buy (Coleman, 1990). To pay the *juku* cost is certainly a case in point. University is the entry point of a narrow channel to success, that is a fact. That *juku* can be a necessary escalator to university is also a fact, although a contesting hypothesis exists.[17] The folk rationality, however, is not totally directed by statistical truth. In forming a judgement about the wisdom of an investment, each person uses others as advisory intermediaries, and using others' actions as evidence about the probability of gain can produce the explosive phenomenon.

---

[17] One statistical study of the effects of extracurricular tutoring in Japan is Stevenson and Baker (1992).

Figure 5.6 The countdown for the date of Taiwan's *Liankao*, written on the chalkboard of a high school classroom.

That collective psychology becomes more and more observable as exams approach. Students are the patrons of the cram industry. Statistics show that 93.2 per cent of the cram industry's income came from students' tuition fees (TMOE, 1993b). Money, however, is not a warranty for success. The university entrance examinations test not only what students learned in the final grades, but almost everything they are supposed to know. In theory, this means all the way from Grade 1 to Grade 12. Because the review is so wide in scope, preparation becomes very time-consuming, and a good 'strategic' plan dealing with priorities, sequence and timeline for preparation is crucial.[18] As the entrance exams come nearer, life becomes tenser for the students and families, although a very few grow indifferent: they have already given up. In Taiwan, a prevailing practice in some G12 classrooms is to write on the chalkboard the number of remaining days before *Liankao*, Taiwan's national entrance exams (see Figure 5.6).

The countdown in Taiwan throws into relief an intensified test anxiety, which is shared by students in all three countries. The effect of the 'craze' phenomenon is not only seen in the exam 'arms race' and the students' tight schedule. It also affects the location of *juku* schools and their business. To attend cram school, students had to run from place to place. One Korean student told me that she had to stop at a subway station for her dinner, then rush to another train station to cram for English. The location of the cram school is therefore very important in attracting students. A cram school that is far from the bus or train station is fighting a losing battle.

Here, a typical example is found on the Kawaijuku campus in Tokyo. During my visits to Japan, its campus impressed me with its slack business, despite its prestige. Its location was too far away from the nearby train station, which is under the total control of the Yoyogizemi Yobiko. Also, its classroom buildings were scattered in a maze of back lanes, unnoticeable and hard to find. As a result, it has hopelessly lost its clients to Yoyogi. During my second visit to Kawaijuku in Tokyo, I was surprised to find that there seemed to be much less going on there than two years before: many

---

[18] The *rônin* repeaters and high school students have quite different life-study patterns. This is shown in various reference books that discuss the optimal schedule for exam preparation, which is a major concern for college applicants. Please refer to Yoshiaku Tomiyama (1994); Fujimori (1992); and Yell Books (1994).

rooms were not used; certain classes, including the satellite lecture, did not have enough students at all. The lobby was deserted, and staff were hard to see. Kawaijuku in this case slowly lost its competitive edge, although it could still be kept open with support from its Nagoya Headquarters.

The attendance ratio of tutoring schools: A comparison of metropolitan and local areas

In the previous pages, we discussed the gradual increase in the attendance ratio of the cram schools. We now look at the geographical distribution of that increase. What we want to know is: which locations were most responsible for the increase, big cities or local areas? This information is available in the Japanese Ministry of Education statistics.

Table 5.12 lists the top five prefectures that had the greatest attendance ratio increase. To my knowledge, most of these top prefectures are either on the remote islands or in some peripheral areas, rural or 'less developed'. In comparison, most of the metropolitan areas had a lesser increase: Tokyo (4.7 per cent), Kanagawa (8.3 per cent), Kyoto (7.2 per cent), Osaka (6.3 per cent), Hiroshima (6.5 per cent), Kumamoto (7.6 per cent). This generalization is confirmed by the JPA statistics. According to a JPA survey, the enrolment ratio of G9 students in the large metropolises of Japan remained at around 80 per cent, and there was not much change from seven years ago. In the average medium-sized cities, the figure increased from 66.3 per cent to 77.6 per cent; in the town and countryside, it increased from 49 per cent to 62.2 per cent. In other words, 'statistical evidence showed that the rapid increase of the *juku* enrolment ratio was found mainly outside of the big cities' (*Asahi Shinbun*, 19 August 1994). This may indicate that, although jukurization in big cities has not yet stopped, it was subject to a certain 'saturation effect' there. The main thrust of this 'fever' spilled over into the medium and small-sized towns and perhaps the countryside. This shift, and the so-called 'High in the West, and low in the East' phenomenon, is characterized as a 'local-level boom' (*Nikkei Shinbun*, 30 July 1994).

It is interesting to note that this development is also reflected in the answers to a JPA survey question: 'Do you think *juku* attendance is excessive?' In the metropolitan areas, the percentage of 'yes' answers declined from 78.5 per cent to 69.8 per cent (1987–94), but in 'the other places', the percentage climbed up from 55.2 per cent to 62.3 per cent.

A direct interpretation for this would be that, in the big cities, people have already grown accustomed to the 'evil', but in the other areas, it just began to attract more concern and worry. A hyperbolic journalist in the *Nikkei Shinbun* (19 August 1994) reports that many Japanese children now travel farther than their father for *juku* education and often come home latest in the family.

In sum, jukurization has been rapidly on the rise despite the decline of the cohort population in Japan. One of its dimensions is localization, which is especially found in the east part of Japan. According to my observation of the subculture in the milieu of the *juku*, being a *juku* teacher has been increasingly popular. My impression was confirmed by a major newspaper article about the promising job future of the *juku* industry.

In Korea, the available data afford a comparison between the *hakwon* attendance ratio of the capital Seoul, the other metropolitan cities, and local counties.

Table 5.12 The increase in the *juku* enrolment ratio among school students: the top five prefectures, 1993 over 1985. *Sources*: Based on JMOE, *Jidô Seito no Gakkôgai Gakushû Katsudô ni kansuru Jittai Chôsa Hôkokusho* (Survey of the extracurricular activities of children/students), (Tokyo: Ministry of Education, 1985), 60–1; JMOE, *Gakushûjuku tô ni kansuru Jittai Chôsa Hôkokusho* (Report on the survey of the issues related to the academic *juku*), (Tokyo: Ministry of Education, 1995), 64–5.

Ranking of ratio increase	Prefecture	1985	1993	Increase[a]
1	Tokushima	20.8%	57.1%	36.3%
2	Saga	18.2%	44.0%	25.2%
3	Nagano	19.4%	37.4%	18.0%
4	Aomori	8.0%	25.1%	17.1%
5	Gifu	26.0%	42.1%	16.0%

Note: a. Increase = 1993 ratio − 1985 ratio.

Table 5.13 Hours used weekly for cramming practice by middle and high school students in Korea, 1990–1. *Source*: Se-Ho Shin *et al.*, *Kwawe Sueop Siltae Bunseok Yungu* (A study of private tutoring in Korea), (Seoul: Korea Education Development Institute, 1991), 74.

School level	Capital Seoul	Big cities	General cities	Local counties	Average
Middle school	6 h 17 min.	6 h 30 min.	6 h 46 min.	7 h 32 min.	6 h 46 min.
High school	6 h 10 min.	7 h 10 min.	6 h 10 min.	7 h 6 min.	6 h 49 min.

Table 5.13 shows the evenly distributed cramming activities across the nation. As indicated, the local students in Korea spent as much (sometimes more) time on cramming as the students from big cities.

Three portraits of students: Case studies

The foregoing section about *juku* students describes students' academic behaviours on the basis of statistics. This quantitative description is necessary, because it helps us to generalize and conceptualize about students as a social group. While the individual cannot detach himself from social life, individual life is too complex to be totally accommodated by a macro-level analysis. A better understanding of these students is impossible, if we treat them as faceless components of a social mechanism. In other words, we need to look at individuals.

Portrait One: Matsuda: a Japanese high school student. Matsuda was a tall, polite boy from Kawasaki City, Kanagawa, located to the south of Tokyo.[19] In 1993, as he was terminating his high school education, he had

---

[19] Pseudonym is used whenever necessary.

planned to take university entrance exams and get into college. This was a
hot morning in mid-July. Matsuda was wandering in a decent classroom
building of Yoyogizemi Yobiko. The corridor was soft-coloured, clean and
wide, bathed in the tranquillizing chill of powerful air-conditioners. More
and more students began to gather, and two young men wearing the dark-
brown armbands of 'Yoyogizemi' started to check the student passes. Very
soon, people filed in, but Matsuda was still leaning idly against the wall as if
he was expecting his friends. As the administrators saw the lecturer walk up
to the podium and start the class, they closed the door noiselessly and left.
At this time, Matsuda picked up his satchel from the floor, and entered the
classroom with a couple of other latecomers. He was one of those students
who needed to cram for the university entrance exams but had not paid for
it. Instead of registering at a cram school, they usually just 'walked into' a
particular class that interested them.

This is a two-hour morning class in English especially designed for those
who want to improve their basics. 'I think my English is not really a problem
for me', Matsuda told me later after we made friends in the cafeteria of the
juku, 'I just want to further enhance it during the summer. I check the class
schedule to find out the class I like. Then I just go there and sit in. Generally
there is nobody to check your pass. Today it was bizarre.' Every day, he
weathered the blistering heatwave of summer and travelled all the way to
Yoyogizemi for some English 'enhancement'. Yet, he had not registered for
any schools that might provide him an insured service. It was quite
obviously a practice of economy. What is not clear to me is whether he
could afford it but preferred not to; or whether the tuition was a great burden
to him. He only told me that his father worked in a small shop, but the
business had not been doing well for a long time. His story made me recall
some old Chinese stories of celebrities, all of which have a meritocratic
touch to them: A boy could not go to school as his family was poor. So he
squatted under the window of the classroom to 'steal knowledge'. The
hardship of life whetted his motivation and built his character, which made
him a man of note later.

In May 1994, Matsuda wrote to me from Japan. The first sentence was: 'I
passed all the examinations!' (His exclamation mark was drawn large and
outlined, like ¡.) He was, as he told me in the letter, accepted by the Physics
Departments of both Chûo and Aoyama Gakuin Universities, two good
private universities. He at first oscillated between the two. Then, he made his
choice. What made him uncomfortable in Aoyama Gakuin was its atmosphere: 'its Christian colour is thicker than what I thought [sic]'. He also told
me that he attended Kawaijuku in December and January, where he thought
English teaching was far better than at Yoyogizemi. However, he did not
specify if he continued 'sitting in' as he successfully did before.

In Japan, the *juku* and *yobiko* do not impose many disciplinary requirements upon the student population. Unlike in regular middle and high
schools, students do not have to wear uniforms. They do not have to change
their shoes before they enter a classroom building of the *juku*, either. In
brief, students, whether they are current school students or *rônin*, are treated
in a way very similar to college students. There is no social, moral or
normative regulations that tell them how they should behave in the cram
world, as long as they do not disturb the class. Everybody is brought and
stratified here by the university entrance examination system. In this micro-

society, scores, as the reification of meritocratic order, are very much thought of as the sole concern; life is essentially free from control or disciplinary imposition. The nexus between *juku* companies and their clients is mainly composed of money and academic accountability.

Portrait Two: Cheng Li and his two years of cramming in Taipei. If, in Japan, cram schools mean a sort of relief from the stringent rules of school, it is just the contrary for Taiwan's *buxiban*. The relationship between the *buxiban* and a student applicant is more than the educator and the educated. An experienced cram entrepreneur said: 'Today, *buxiban*'s management is a world of difference from the past. Service has become commoditized, the emphasis on teaching style and teaching content is gone.' As a result, the student–teacher relationship has evolved into one of trading partners. Even if the student gets into university, he or she does not feel grateful to *buxiban* or cram teachers (ZS, 16 September 1994). Strong legal responsibility comes into effect after registration. In Japan, to register at a *juku*, one needs only to pay, to fill out the registration form, and, for most classes, to pass a placement test, etc. To register at a *buxiban*, however, it is obligatory for either the student or his or her parent(s) to sign a binding contract, which is, to my knowledge, unheard of in Japan.

In legal terms, the *buxiban* contract forces the student to follow a whole set of rigidly stipulated patterns of academic life and behaviour. The 'Contract and Commitment Document' (*Heyüe baozhengshu*) of the aforementioned 'New Dragon' *buxiban* stipulates that a student, as the contracting party, is strictly prohibited from smoking in the *buxiban*, and a violator may be expelled without refund. No absence is allowed. Tardiness and early departure should not exceed five times a year. Sick leave is permitted only with a certificate provided by a public hospital, and it should not exceed 24 sessions annually (40 minutes per session). The student should not be absent from a morning test, weekly test, period test, final test or mock test. The student should not insult the teacher, or commit theft, fight, gamble or commit any other offence against the rules made by the *buxiban*. If the student fulfils all the requirements, the *buxiban* 'guarantees that the student as the contract party will pass the university entrance exams and be admitted into a daytime university, otherwise the student is entitled to a full refund of the entire payment of the fee and tuition'. Both the regent of the *buxiban* and the student need to sign this legal document. According to my investigation, most of the *buxiban* required students or their parents to sign a contract of this nature. Although there always exists a gap between what is said and what is done, it seems certain that the relationship between cram companies and their clients is more complicated and stressful in Taiwan than in Japan; and, in cram schools, Taiwanese students are legally obliged to work harder and follow stricter rules than their Japanese counterparts. Here, the story of one student test-taker might help us to have some empirical perspective in this comparison.[20]

Cheng Li is an exam repeater (*Chongkao Sheng*) living in Taizhong, Taiwan. Having graduated from a famous private school, he took the

---

[20] The case study given here is based upon a special report about Taiwan's cram schools, Jiang and Gong (1994).

national university entrance exams in 1993 and failed. In 1994, he left his home to study at a *buxiban* in Taipei for a year. Unfortunately, after one year of preparation, he failed again. Now he decided to go home, even if he might try again for the third time.

Li planned to cram in Taipei because he had too many close friends in Taizhong, and it was truly hard to sit down to study. In Taipei, he would not only benefit from a wide choice of *buxiban*, he could also get rid of his friends and focus on his study. Besides, he also had a sister-in-law in Taipei, who might give him some help. The point was, so long as the environment was good, it would not be necessary to think too much about money.

Li's father requested his sister-in-law to find him a place to live. His family was well-to-do, and room rent was thus not a big problem. From August 1993, Li began his cram life in Taipei as a total stranger. He had to get up early, as he had to arrive at his *buxiban* at 7:00 a.m. and he spent the whole day there until 9:00 in the late evening. During the daytime, he would review his lessons with the teacher, and, in the evening, he would study by himself. Each student was assigned a designated seat, and what is more, an adviser stayed with them all the time. In the case of absence, the adviser would call up and inquire about it. Li felt the disciplinary control here was rather tight.

Li had an easy-going character. But since he had never left home and lived all by himself, he was quite lonesome. His spirits were low, especially when he became homesick. His mother had asked him to call home every day, which he did faithfully. This could both make him feel better, and remind him of why he was there.

Taipei was full of temptations for Li, especially as his family could easily afford to pay his expenses. So he was still not that serious about the exams. It would not matter much to him even if he did badly. In the words of the students, he had not *jüewu* (woken up, or become enlightened) yet. He thought it was no big deal that his family was paying for his cram. Here, he quickly made friends again and they often went to play basketball together, ignoring his studies. The night life of Taipei also appealed to him greatly. In his home city, it was quiet at night. But here, it was still bustling and busy in the street at midnight. His Taipei-born friends, who were also repeaters, took him to their homes to spend the night there. They would say they were doing homework together. But they spent a lot of time chatting.

What Li could never understand was that children from Taipei seemed to be good at both work and play. He felt he had worked hard enough. His friends often told him that he did not have to learn everything and spend too much time on it. But each time, his scores were always far worse than theirs. By and by, his ambition started to dissolve, and he almost took his second failure for granted. And yet, he found that he spent NT$ 10,000 (1 dollar = NT$ 26) for the two-quarter cram fee, NT$ 100,000 for living expenses, and a large sum for housing, which altogether amounted to more than NT$ 200,000 for a year (about US$ 7700). His parents started to regret sending him to Taipei, and he felt sad at not being able to make it. However, he knew exactly what his problem was: he needed more determination and focus.

Portrait Three: The after-school life of Bing-je Kim, Seoul. For Korean students, the Prohibition on Extracurricular Tutoring in the 1980 reforms is a historical divide. Before 1980, cram study took three basic forms: (1) paying one's regular school teacher to hold after-hours classes, (2) attending a separate cram school in the evening taught by well-educated persons, especially the regular teacher, and (3) hiring a private tutor. The most common and available tutors are students at the major universities, who have proven their merit by making it through the entrance process. Such tutoring by university students can be extremely lucrative – enough to earn one's way through school if necessary – and is known in Korea, as in Japan, by the German term for 'work', *arbeit* (*arûubait'tû*). The Prohibition forbade elementary, middle and high school teachers from doing tutoring. It forbade university students from doing *arûubait'tû* for non-relatives, and it made private academies return fees after 1 August 1980 to those students who were currently enrolled in school (Sorensen, 1994).

Although everybody wants the competition for university to slow down, pressures to get ahead through education are such that the government could not make the reforms really work and stick. It was impossible to police *arûubait'tû* when such arrangements were made, as they always are, privately between a family and a university student. As competition for admission to prestigious universities and good high schools continues, schools cannot help but respond to parents' and students' anxiety about entrance examinations. Schools gradually have set up programmes of extra-curricular 'autonomous study' and 'supplementary classes'. 'Autonomous study' is optional study done in schools under the supervision of teachers but without explicit lessons. It is normally done one hour before the regular school day and sometimes after school as well, until nine or ten o'clock at night. Many schools offer an additional hour of 'supplementary classes' for students who are not doing well. Although teachers cannot directly receive fees for supervising 'autonomous study', they can get extra fees for 'supplementary classes'. In addition to these more or less public subterfuges, many other kinds of extracurricular and irregular study are found (Sorensen, 1994). What are these 'legal' and 'normative' ways of tutoring students? Are they more wholesome than life in the cram schools? While there is no solid statistical comparison at hand, the following narrative can help us to form a perception.[21]

This was around 12:00 midnight. The lights were still on in a room on the fifth floor of an apartment in Pangbae-dong, Kangnum-gu District, in the southern part of Seoul. A lady in her early forties stood on the balcony, awaiting her child. The chilly wind of autumn was blowing towards her from the misty, expanded Han-gang river bank. Her 13-year-old son, Bing-je Kim, was a second-grader in the Pangbae Middle School, one of the local élite. Under the pressure of the entrance exams, he had to leave home at 6:30 in the morning, and return about 12:00 o'clock at night. School lasted from 8:00 a.m. to 5:00 p.m.. After class was over, there was one hour of 'complementary teaching' (extracurricular tutoring). Then, according to school rules, he had to stay at school for self-study until 10:00 p.m.

The day for him was however not over. On their way back, he and some of his friends went to the so-called 'Reading studio' – a place that rents rooms to students for self-study – to do some reading before they dragged

---

[21] The following is a translated report excerpt from Chu (1989).

their exhausted bodies home. Each morning, before Kim bade farewell to his mother, she prepared two boxes of *bendô* (meal) for his lunch and supper. After some snacks, Kim went to bed and slept immediately.

Kim entered Grade 2 of the middle school in March this year. In order to get into the Kinggi High School, the best élite school in Seoul for boys, he put his full weight into his study for one and a half years. His mother had high hopes for him. She wished he could graduate from Seoul National University and take up a career in the financial business, which is seen as a 'gold rice bowl' in Korea.

The background of this narrative report was a newly built area housing a large proportion of professionals and their families, and the pressure to succeed is imaginably more intense than in other places. However, since those courses are arranged at school, their participation ratio should be higher than the voluntary-based *hakwon*. It is interesting to note that, while school-based tutoring seemed to be normative in Korea, in Taiwan the government has been opposed to it, because some teachers were found to withhold certain teaching content for after-school tutoring, thus affecting the regular teaching process.

THE CRAM WORLD: KNOWLEDGE

Learning as though you would never be able to master it;
holding it as though you would be in fear of losing it.
– *Confucius,* Analects, *sixth cent.* BC

There is little doubt that *juku* differ from normal schools in teaching and learning. But how, and why? To start with, I will look at school textbooks and the changes in them, if any. While this may be a convenient point of entry, these instructional materials are doubtless also noted for their role. Textbooks are central tools and the central objects of attention in all modern education. The implicit and explicit tasks they prescribe define the core work of the school. As givens in particular situations, the textbooks that teachers have are both the resource for their teaching and the limiting force they face (Westbury, in Elliot and Woodward, 1990). One example of that limitation is provided by the breadth and depth of the curricula affected by textbook revisions.

The gap of knowledge

In his study of Japanese textbooks, Komiyama (1991) finds that, contrary to the general judgement, in recent years textbooks have become easier than previously. First, the content was reduced. The maths textbooks of 1990 were thinner than the 1975 versions, as shown in Table 5.14. A further examination of the content shows two changes. First, some of the content was removed. Second, some content was moved into higher-level textbooks. Compared with the 1975 maths textbooks, in 1990, 12 minor items were deleted from the G6 textbook, and 11 minor items were moved into the next level (G7). Similarly, eight items were deleted from the G7 textbook, and five moved up to G9; eight items were deleted from G9. Deleted items included the cubic function (algebra), circle and globe (geometry), standard deviation and correlation (statistics). The textbooks, on the whole, were easier in 1990 than in 1975. This is also true of other subjects, and for the elementary school (Komiyama, 1991: 66–80; Inamura and Ogawa, 1986: 61–72). However, the entrance exams of middle and high schools did not become easier. To show that disparity, let us look at some maths problems sampled from the entrance exams for six middle schools:[22]

(a) $1\frac{4}{5} - 1\frac{3}{5} \times 0.125 + 0.875 \div \frac{1}{8}$

(b) $0.3 \div 1\frac{1}{5} + (1 + 0.5 - 0.3 \div 1\frac{1}{3}) \times 0.2$

(c) $231 - \{35 \times 6 - (87 - 19) \div 17\}$

(d) $2\frac{5}{18} - 1\frac{7}{18} \times \frac{3}{5} + \frac{1}{4} - 2\frac{7}{9} \times \frac{7}{15} \div 6\frac{2}{3}$

(e) $\frac{11}{56} + (3\frac{3}{44} - 0.7) \div 70$

(f) $36 \div 3\frac{3}{7} + \frac{8}{11} \times 3\frac{5}{24}$

Now, compare the above with those given in the G6 textbook (for the terminating year of primary school), given in the left-hand column below. Then look at the questions in *juku* for G5 students, given in the right column. What we can see is that textbook questions are too simple for the middle school entrance exams; and that the *juku* questions match the entrance exam questions well:

Questions in the Grade 6 school textbook	Questions in the Grade 5 *juku* course
(a) $(8 + 6) \div 7 + 5$	(a) $2 \times (13 - 4) \div 3 + 5 \times \{8 - (13 - 9)\}$
(b) $\frac{9}{2} \div 0.25 \times 1/6$	(b) $(7\frac{1}{2} - 2\frac{1}{4} + \frac{2}{3}) \div 24$
(c) $(\frac{2}{3} + \frac{1}{4} - \frac{1}{2}) \div \frac{5}{12}$	(c) $48 - \{25 \times (4 + 3) + 35\} \div 7$

What Komiyama (1991) and Inamura and Ogawa (1986) find in their studies is a growing gap between what is taught in school and what is tested for the next, higher level of schooling, all the way up to tertiary level. That, according to their argument, has brought *juku* to the fore to fill the curricular gap (see Figure 5.7).

---

[22]The maths questions given here and in the subsequent text are taken from Inamura and Ogawa (1986), 62.

Table 5.14 The change in the total number of pages in maths textbooks in Japan's middle schools. *Source*: Hirohito Komiyama, *Kashikoi Gakushû-juku no erabikata* (How to select a good academic *juku*), (Tokyo: Shinryôron, 1991), 67.

	Number of pages		Page reduction	
Grade	1975	1990	Number	Percentage†
G7	266	190	76	28.6%
G8	240	202	38	15.8%
G9	227	196	31	14.7%
Total	733	588	145	19.8%

Note: † Percentage of reduction = (1990 − 1975) ÷ 1975 × 100%

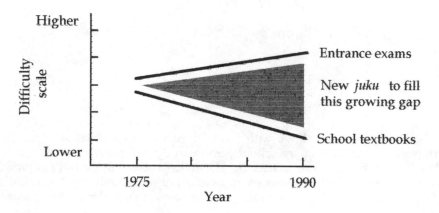

Figure 5.7 A schema of the function of *juku* as a supplementary educational system.

Table 5.15 Percentage of Japanese schools whose entrance exams exceeded the scope of the curriculum as stipulated by the 'Monbushô Study Guidance' (*Gakushû Shidô*). *Source*: JMOE, 'Izen mirareru Nanmon Shuddai' (Too difficult questions are still in the exams), *Mombu Kôhô* (Ministry of Education official report), 15 June 1994, 936: 6.

Category	1992	1993
Middle schools		
National	11.8	11.8
Private	47.6	66.7
Subtotal	42.5	55.8
High schools		
National	57.1	14.3
Private	58.4	77.3
Subtotal	58.3	74.1

That gap is particularly salient at the high school entrance level. A study of the entrance exam questions for middle and high schools, undertaken by the Japanese Ministry for Education in 1993, found that the discrepancy between teaching and testing remained a problem in both national and private schools. The results of that analysis are presented in Table 5.15. That discrepancy between what is taught and what is tested is likely to be the most critical factor in the entrance exams. Table 5.15 suggests that, had the entrance exams not been as competitive as they are now, *juku* would still have been necessary to meet the requirements of the higher level in Japan. That gap and the emergence of the *juku* industry also have some self-perpetuating effects. It is observed that teachers in regular schools 'agreed to give minimum homework to students to allow them some private space and time after school'. Meanwhile, some teachers assigned students little homework as *juku* schooling leaves them little time afterwards (Shimahara and Sakai, 1995). This phenomenon is similar to what I found in Korea. *Juku* are also nibbling away the academic responsibility that regular schools were unable to take full charge of. In a sense, some tacit contract was formed between regular schools and *juku* on how to carve up education.

The typology of the average *juku* and their teaching style are documented by Thomas Rohlen (1980), Merry White (1987), B. Feiler (1991), Mamoru Tsukada (1991) and Robert August (in Leestma and Walberg, 1992), for instance, in their ethnographic or sociological classics. The findings of this literature prompted people to take note of some constructive roles that *juku* may play:

> ... many critical influences on learning lie outside of the schools. The success of Japanese secondary students, for example, is partly attributable to the extensive tutoring they receive, their study in the *juku*, and the intense exam system that determines senior high school as well as university admission. (Stedman, 1994)

Thomas Rohlen (1980) counts the '*juku* phenomenon' as a heavy price that Japanese paid for the 'distinction of being the world's most educated people' (207). He casts light upon the ambivalence that Japanese hold toward juku due to the multiple roles it may play:

> Whether left, right or center, public leaders tend to bemoan exam pressures and the rise of *juku*. Privately, for their own children, however, exams are a reality and *juku* are options to be taken seriously – not only for their potential value at exam time, but because they may indeed encourage character development and spur personal ambition. Part of the paradox of child rearing in Japan is that parents seek outside mechanisms to counterbalance the dependency they have encouraged and in doing so, they continue the pattern of 'oversocialization'. (233)

In the sections that follow, I will delineate that function of *juku* in institutional detail: How are *juku* classes organized? What kind of knowledge is taught? And how is it taught? While relevant data are very thin or unavailable in general, the fairly complete information collected on Kawaijuku in Japan makes it possible for me to focus on this major company as a case study. While it is not typical of an average *juku*, it is typical of the corporate industry, which caters for almost all graders and repeaters, a combination of the academic *juku* and *yobiko*.

Knowledge as sorter

As a corollary of the entrance exam system, the cram school is permeated with the test culture. To illustrate the point, I will take Kawaijuku as a case study whenever appropriate in the following text. Students often take the *Senbatsu* (selection) Exams or *Moshi* (mock test) Exams to enter Kawaijuku. These are placement tests serving as sorters rather than as gatekeepers, which distinguishes them from the real entrance exams. The Kawaijuku coursebook lists a dazzling variety of classes, several of which require no qualification exams. For those that do, a student's *hensachi* scores will place him or her in different classes. These classes are arranged in hierarchical order based on the nationwide intra-school mock test administered by the Kawaijuku. Table 5.16 gives an example of the selection system.

The role of these initial or entrance exams is purely diagnostic. They assess students' academic proficiency, and then assign them to· classes accordingly. Unlike the regular schools, the curricula of these *juku* courses exhibit a pronounced range of diversification finely attuned to individual levels. The instruction is, however, based not on individualization but on groups. Each and every one who comes needs remediation. The compelling need to give a particular remediation diversifies *juku* curricula in terms of the difficulty level, intensity and orientation.

Kawaijuku is not an institute of academic exclusion. It accommodates virtually anyone who applies. The manifold channels testify to the flexibility of the *juku* in giving help and promise of success. This is, needless to say, led by the principle of profit maximization. The entrance channels for middle school students are:

1. Entrance by selection test (*Senbatsu nyûshitsu sei*). For Grade 7, the subjects tested are Japanese and arithmetic; for Grades 8 and 9 English and maths. The test results will be used to assign students to different courses according to their *hensachi* scores. The courses covered by this method are advanced ones, requiring *hensachi* scores not less than 55.0.
2. Entrance by interview (*Mansetsu nyûshitsu sei*). This method is mainly used for the courses that render scholastic assistance to students who worry about their low GPA scores in middle school. The interview is brief, and basically of a fact-finding nature. The students or parents will be asked about the GPA scores and about compatibility between the *juku*'s textbook and that of the students' curriculum.
3. Entrance without any exam (*Mushiken nyûshitsu sei*). In contrast to most of the rest of the courses which teach the core subjects of English, maths and Japanese, this entrance method is limited to physics and social science courses.

The courses accessible through the three methods have only one purpose: to get students into academic high school. Helping students with such a wide range of ability is by no means an easy task. One hidden means of doing so seems to be more lectures for poor achievers. Most of the courses for middle school students are open only at weekends (only one class is scheduled in the evening on Thursday and Friday). The élite Selection Course, for instance, is scheduled for 3:40–7:50 p.m. on Saturday, and 1:50–6:00 p.m. on Sunday. That makes about seven and a half hours of instruction per week. Those who do not take an entrance exam, on the other hand, spend a total of almost 10 hours at the weekend.

Curricula are also designed differently. The top-level class stresses competitiveness. The pattern that instruction follows is: (1) The teacher first reviews the basics, based on the textbook. (2) Students take the class exams. (3) The teacher comments on the major points in the exams. The 'Interview' class, on the other hand, spends more time on instruction in the fundamentals. The focus is on primary concepts, with some time-efficient comments on drills at the end of each lesson in the textbook.

I should add quickly here that Kawaijuku promises no unrealistic miracle in making changes. As the course brochure indicates, courses with higher *hensachi* scores at the entry points are targeted at better schools, which are not generally expected for the 'Interview' course. However, it is possible for individuals to transfer from one course to another through evaluative and administrative arrangement.

Table 5.16 The Kawaijuku high school courses requiring placement exams, 1993. *Source*: Kawaijuku, *Kawaijuku Green Course Nyûjuku Yôkô* (The outline information about registration into Kawaijuku 'Green Course'), (Nagoya: Kawaijuku, 1993b), 5.

Course category	Minimum hensachi scores
Top-level class	Above 65.0
High-level class	Above 60.0
Prestigious university class	Above 60.0
High-level private university class	Above 60.0
General regular class	Above 52.5

Approach to knowledge

Kawaijuku is not where laws such as grammar rules or Pythagorean theory are preached upon as canonized knowledge. Neither are they to be explored.[23] Kawaijuku is only interested in bringing knowledge to bear on solving problems. The exposition of pure theory is kept very brief, under the presumption that, first, the basic textbook concepts, such as π, or the fact that the area of a circle is πr^2, are not esoteric or inaccessible to students, and second, students are very much expected to know the theory in concept before the class or at school. *Juku* does not and cannot pour knowledge into a student's brain and press a lid on it. It only helps students to plug knowledge into the problem, and put it to work. For Kawaijuku, this 'plug in and put it to work' is the hard core of the business.

Consequently, Kawaijuku is vitally dependent on the expertise of teachers who excel at putting theory into practice. It is beyond any shadow of doubt, therefore, that classes are teacher-controlled and lecture-centred. The prototypical scenes I got so used to are: A teacher (mostly a man) is on

---

[23]I have, in passing, visited one or two *juku* in Tokyo where curious kids use decent little labs for exploring science. However, conceptual application rather than exploration is the designated role of most preparatory schools.

the podium, immaculately attired, often in a business suit, speaking with resolve and vigour through a wireless microphone he is holding. His lecture is fast-paced, but meticulously measured. His flow of speech is glib but with staccato. His humour, if any, is extremely dry, jerky, and apologetic in tone. In class, there is seldom or never a long embarrassing pause, or humming and hawing, or stumbling over unexpected surprises. This could not be achieved without two prerequisites: first, scrupulous, near-perfect preparation on the part of the instructor, and second, the role of students as receptacles of knowledge: listen very attentively, follow the sequence of logic, take full and neat notes and, last of all, ask no questions.

All told, however, the English word for *juku* or *buxiban*, 'cram school', is a grave misnomer. To wit, *juku* lectures are not designed to make knowledge digestible so that it can be crammed into students' brains. The lecture is intended to help students to crack difficulties in problem solving, whether it is English reading, classic Chinese, maths or physics. Principles are referred to for organizing and rationalizing this effort and making it structured. In consequence, a course generally starts with a mini-lecture on the concept to be covered. This is done with the help of examples written on the chalk-board. Then, the instructor will switch to the main part of his pedagogy. He presents, analyses, explains, and then proceeds to solve the problems step by step, one after another. These problems are either selected from the mock tests given earlier, or based on the home assignment that students should have prepared.

In class, students were never, or very seldom indeed, asked to pose questions or to respond. In all the classes I attended, *juku* or not *juku*, with or without prior arrangement, it was apparent that, at the instructor's wish, the class proceeded as smoothly as silk. Teaching was a one-way free flow of knowledge. The pace of academic progress was well maintained, and the teaching plan was accomplished to the letter, which might well be a source of envy for American teachers. Digression did occur in class, especially after a tedious elucidation, but it was kept minimal. Not a single student asked the teacher to repeat or elucidate, even in places where I was certain that the students would be baffled or confused. Japanese students were very quiet, and virtually silent in class. There was no teacher–student interaction.

The teacher's explications in class are aimed at guiding students through the barriers in surmounting the problem. The effort is directed toward opening up a path for the students to follow. In so doing, many Japanese teachers use quite a lot of symbols or signs, occasionally to the extent of abuse. Metaphorically, it is like laying down a marker along that 'path' as a reminder. During my class observations, I noted a dazzling number of signs that the teacher used on the chalkboard: triangles, arrows, straight underlines, wavy underlines, transposition, all shapes of brackets, big frames, and so on. They were used to chop up and analyse long-winded sentences, or multiple-procedure maths computations. To the students, these are vital clues to what is covered in the class. They copy them down exactly, and a good set of notes may become the master copy for others to photocopy. Each Japanese student had a bunch of coloured pens in his or her pencil box. They made the notes a little more cheerful to read, and less tangled when many arrows or lines criss-crossed one another.

Kawaijuku students could choose the teacher they wanted. In the classroom, the instructor acted as the central role model. What qualified him for this role was the amount of content knowledge he possessed, his superb pedagogical preparation and skill, and his fluency in tackling a problem in an organized, lucid and voluble fashion. The students observed their role model cracking the problem, following his logic, and copying down the details of the whole process. By doing so day in and day out, while they learned from the role model the application of the specific theories, they also emulated the role model intellectually. In this learning process, high-order intellectual ability is unconsciously learned. The pedagogic style in Kawaijuku reflects Japanese notions of teaching. In discussing the concept of *shidô*, or guidance, Gerald LeTendre (1996) asserts that *shidô* implies that there is 'a' way, not a variety of equally acceptable approaches, and it is the teacher who leads the way on the path.

The faith upon which Kawaijuku was built can be expressed in the English cliché that 'practice makes perfect'. Apart from the assignments and drills, the class schedule was dotted with mock tests. For the middle school course, for instance, there were altogether six nationwide mock tests for the Grade 9 level in a calendar year. The recurrent mock tests are the crux of success. Our cognitive abilities may be divided into those that are resource-consuming or controlled and those that are relatively resource-independent or automatic (Shiffrin and Schneider, 1977). Certain types of cognitive skill may become automatic with practice. What is initially difficult and resource-consuming becomes, with practice, automatic and relatively resource-independent (Anderson, 1982). Experience can make people perform tasks effortlessly. A daily life example is given by Sternberg and Joseph (1995). The expert driver does not need to think about fundamental driving skills like steering, changing gear and braking. Indeed, most of us are experts in this respect and can plan the day's work while we are behind the wheel. For the novice driver, however, the basic driving skills can be applied only with conscious effort – 'to let one's thoughts turn to events later in the day would be to court disaster'.

'Keeping up with the textbook', as Thomas Rohlen (1983) illustrates, 'leaves little time for classroom debate, or for considering the contemporary relevance of a topic. Discussions are inherently inefficient if information loading is the central goal. Other factors, such as large class size and profound reluctance by most students to express their opinions before a group also inhibit discussion. Japanese students prefer the comfort of passive and relatively anonymous listening to active participation.' Even for the purpose of exam-cramming, lack of interaction might be a big problem in Japanese teaching, because it is hardly imaginable that students could learn anything new, without having their weak points or mistakes pinpointed and tackled during the course. It is interesting to note that many teachers were conscious of this weakness and asked, sometimes very earnestly, if the students were following him. An instructor in a Kawaijuku class inquired:

'*Yorosii deshô ka* (Good)?'
'*Miemashô ka* (Can you see it)?'
'*Tsuzukimasu ka* (Shall I go on)?'
'*Okei desu ka* (Is it OK)?'
'*Mada mimasen ka* (Still not see it)?'
Or simply, '*Deshô* (Isn't it)?' '*Darô* (Isn't it)?'

A teacher of English kept using '*Ii* (Good)?' at the end of each sentence. In response, however, there was never an answer from 50–100 students; they did not even nod or shake their heads, although, on occasion, they were given time to do that. A Kawai official explained that nobody ought to raise questions in class even if the teacher asked, because otherwise normal progress would be affected. In Kawaijuku, there were special places for students to meet the teacher after class. I did not see much consultation there. Oral question and answer seemed to be excluded as a viable way of learning, by a tacit compact between teacher and students.

In Japan, as in East Asia, in the interplay of teaching and learning, the learner always assumes final accountability. In his study of Tokugawa education, Ronald Dore (1965) reveals the Sino-Japanese belief in diligence which can provide its own eventual reward. Dore cites a Chinese phrase: 'If one reads a passage a hundred times the meaning becomes clear of itself (*Dushu baibian, qiyizijian*).' Implied in this concept is that knowledge can always be self-evident, and thus can be self-taught. According to this logic, the questions and answers are not really indispensable. They may even be suspected as a waste of time or even a source of unnecessary debate and confusion.

To excel in Kawaijuku tests and entrance exams presupposes the mastery of basic formulas and laws by heart. In no exams are books allowed. Inevitably, impeccable memorization is the primary requirement. 'Memory trace' is the necessary change that occurs as a result of learning. It consists of three principal phases of intellectual process: acquisition, storage, and retrieval of the memory trace. The memory trace is rehearsed; it involves storage maintenance and acquisition, which in turn consolidates the memory trace unconsciously (Wickelgren, 1977). Recall and recognition founded on memory are the basis for learning. Victor Hori (1993) casts the issue in a religio-metaphysical light. To show the relationship between rote memorization and logical insight, a parallel of ritual formalism and mystical insight, he produces the following example:

$$\frac{25 \times 500}{50 \times 10} = 25$$

If you can calculate the above problem in your head, states Hori: 'you can do so because you have already memorized the multiplication tables and can "just see" that 50×10 is the equivalent of 500 and that therefore 500 and 50×10 can be cancelled out of the top and bottom of the fraction. Without this piece of rote memory, the insight in "just seeing" would not be possible.' To one who has not memorized the multiplication tables, the ability to 'just see' the answer here must seem exceedingly mysterious, something like mystical insight. Hori argues convincingly that much the same can be said for the ability to 'see' a solution in all forms of maths and many other forms of organized learning.

The need to split up knowledge

Kawaijuku courses show how the challenge of the entrance exams is met through a drastic reorganization of knowledge. They are just the opposite of holistic education which combines and fuses subjects in order to take advantage of their interrelationships. *Juku* courses divide up maths, English or Japanese, thus giving rise to a plethora of separate subjects. For instance, Kawaijuku categorizes maths for preparing the university entrance exams into the following discrete subjects:[24]

Courses for Japan's National Center of Entrance Examinations Test
    Center Test Maths (I)
    Center Test Maths (II)
    Center Test Maths (I and II)

Courses for Human Science Major
    General Mathematics (Series α, β, γ)
    Graph (Series α, β, γ)
    Analytic Geometry and Numbers (Series α, β, γ)
    Probability and Statistics for Human Science
    High-level Maths for Human Science
    Maths for Human Science of Tokyo University
    Maths for Human Science of Kyoto University
    Maths for Hitotsubashi University[25]

Courses for Natural Science Major
    Graph
    Analytic Geometry and Numbers I
    Analytic Geometry and Numbers II
    Differential and Integral (Series β, γ)
    General Maths (Series β, γ)
    Graph (Series β, γ)
    Analytic Geometry and Numbers (Series β, γ)
    Probability and Statistics for Natural Science
    High-level Maths for Natural Science
    Seminar on Differential and Integral
    Seminar on Maths for Natural Science
    Maths for Natural Science at Tokyo University
    Maths for Natural Science at Kyoto University
    Maths for Tokyo University of Industry
    Maths for Medical Science
    Maths for Natural Science of Waseda and Keio Universities

Each of the above subjects is taken as an autonomous course with its own instructor (*Tandô kôshi*), its own textbooks produced by Kawaijuku publishing house, and its own curriculum. For a student at Kawaijuku, some of these subjects are required, others are optional. Although the titles of some courses might be very similar, they differ in terms of specific content, problems chosen, centre of focus and scale of difficulty. Broadly, the complex pattern of the subjects and courses is shaped by two factors: one is to meet

---

[24]The source for the following is Kawaijuku, Kawaijuku Green Course (Nagoya: Kawaijuku, 1993).
[25]Hitotsubashi University, a national university located in Tokyo. Founded in 1875.

the very specific requirements and emphases of departments and/or universities; the other is to meet the needs of certain groups of students.

The segmentation and refinement of knowledge is not limited to mathematics. There are other disciplines available in Kawaijuku:

Fine Art
Biology
Chemistry
English
Geography
Geophysics
History, Japanese and Global
Japanese
Mathematics
Physics
Political Economics

Each of the above disciplines has a number of separate subject courses, although their number may vary. As a comprehensive cram corporation, Kawaijuku runs courses for students at virtually every level (except university), catering for students from primary school level to the *rônin* repeaters, and each level has its own set of courses.

As regards knowledge, the relationship between regular schools and *juku* schools bears some resemblance to oil fields and petroleum refineries. While the 'crude' form of knowledge comes from regular education, schools like Kawaijuku extract, refine and process it. Prep schools are, of course, best known for their basic function of furnishing students with academic competence. Kawaijuku, however, is not narrowly confined to that role. Apart from after-school *juku* and *yobiko* courses, it has an entire system related to education in other fields.[26]

- *Kawaijuku International Education Exchange*. Kawaijuku International Education Center is Kawaijuku's headquarters for international exchange. Pre-courses for US colleges, teenager exchange visitor programmes, TOEFL preparatory courses, together with a Japanese language school, are some of the main educational activities. Counselling for overseas-bound students is also available. SAT preparation is included along with cross-cultural studies.
- *Business Training Programmes*. To comply with the changing needs of society, Kawaijuku established a special college to provide business training tailored to actual needs. The sophisticated teaching approach and many overseas learning opportunities are reasons they are favourably accepted.
- *Japan Information Center for Examinations*. Kawaijuku provides more than two million students in Japan with yearly practice sittings for university entrance exams. The Center has access to a huge database with which it conducts teacher guidance programmes dealing with how they

---

[26]The following information is drawn from the 'Profile of the Kawaijuku Educational System', the information sheets printed by Kawaijuku in 1990.

can assist students with cram preparations. Local Kawaijuku directors handle this important task very systematically all over Japan.

- *Children's Education.* Kawaijuku Maki Kindergarten and Dalton Schools are opened for toddlers through primary school youngsters. Their goal is to make school a delightful milieu by making learning experiences fun. For primary school students, personalized instruction in a supportive and nurturing environment, discovery, testing and independence are stressed. Field trips and many outside activities are included.
- *Institute for Culture and Education Research.* Research is conducted in the Institute on teaching methods, basic issues in the educational field, and college entrance exam systems of other countries. The Institute has sponsored numerous symposia and lectures in the relevant field.
- *Art Education.* Besides preparing students to take exams for academic higher education, Kawaijuku also prepares students for art college. Kawaijuku has its own art gallery where students may display their own work. The atelier is open for use by local artists.

It will be interesting at this point to compare briefly our information about *juku* with how they are generally portrayed. A good many scholars see *juku* as no more than a place where students spend time 'ingurgitating facts and refining their test-taking techniques', which is why 'Japanese students are the world's champion exam takers' (Woronoff, 1990). This argument, very typical in presenting *juku* schools, is inaccurate for Kawaijuku on at least two counts. First, as shown in our discussion, while memorization is crucial, the main thrust in Kawaijuku courses is indubitably problem-solving competency. Second, the key to success in exams, I would argue, is a true understanding of the subject, the recall and recognition capacity of problem-related memory trace, and efficiency and accuracy in application, computation and finally cracking the difficult problems. While mastery of test skill is needed, to my knowledge and experience, it is only secondary and peripheral to the matter. I concur with G. Martz, J. Katzman and A. Robinson (1992) that even such powerful techniques as calculated guess-work, POE (Principle of Elimination), etc., will be meaningless and futile without a solid foundation in the subject. The multiple-choice form of examination, widely used in entrance exams, is only deceptively easy. The futility of such techniques as guessing can be shown by some probability research. Suppose we have the following three exam questions:

Question A	Question B	Question C
a. --------	a. -------- (Correct)	a. --------
b. --------	b. --------	b. --------
c. --------	c. --------	c. -------- (Correct)
d. -------- (Correct)	d. --------	d. --------
e. --------	e. --------	e. --------

If one relies on a guessing technique, getting the correct answer d for Question A is one out of five, or 1/5 probability. Getting answer a for

Question B carries the same probability. Statistically, getting the correct answers for both A and B is $1/5 \times 1/5 = 1/25$, which is only 4 per cent probability. Likewise, getting the correct answer to all three questions is $1/5 \times 1/5 \times 1/5 = 1/125$, a hopeless 0.8 per cent probability.

Another powerful technique, Principle of Elimination (POE), is also a precarious last resort. POE is a procedure which involves crossing out all the wrong answers, thus being left with the correct one. The dilemma is that POE takes a long time. This is because rather than pick the right answer straight away, POE needs to weigh all five stems of the answer carefully, calculate and compare them, and take out the most unlikely four one by one (Martz, Katzman and Robinson, 1992). In a race against time, that could lead either to time loss, or to rushing to finish the questions, thus making careless mistakes. My argument is that machine-readable exams, such as multiple choice, hold significant reliability. Techniques are helpful, but they cannot increase the scores significantly without real improvement in achievement. The trouble people meet in exams may appear technical, but it often reflects academic problems. Techniques, in the final analysis, do not work miracles. Only achievement does that.

A DISCUSSION

Our study of the cram schools throws into relief an obsession with education, and an obsession with university entrance exams, in East Asia. The institutionalization of either *juku*, *buxiban* or *hakwon* is first of all the institutionalization of the consumption of time and effort. Its bottom line can be measured by attendance at regular school, which registers the willingness of the student to learn. A comparison of data from the USA and East Asian countries shows a marked contrast. Between 1975 and 1991, high school drop-out rates in the USA changed from 17 per cent to 15 per cent (NEGP, 1992: 23). In Japan, the rates were kept at no more than 2.2 per cent during 1985–92, falling to 1.9 per cent in 1992 (Jiji Tsûshinsha, 1994: 80). In Korea, the average high school drop-out rate for 1980–90 was 4 per cent (KEDI, 1993). If we add to this the extracurricular attendance ratio in the academic *juku*, which in 1993 was 23.6 per cent for elementary school students and 60 per cent for middle school, we have an idea of that obsession with education. The whole growth of the cram world stems from the kernel of that obsession, a meritocratic drive embodied in the entrance exam system.

The exam subculture is, as I remarked in the Introduction and discussed in detail in other chapters, the confluence of two main factors: cultural heritage and the institutional structure of credentialism. Since these two factors are fairly stable over time, they do not have much to tell about why there has been a notable increase in the growth of *juku* attendance rates and the *juku* industry. In recent years, furthermore, the steady increase in *juku* attendance has been quite anticlimactic in Japan, given the demographic decline and the shortage of students that plagued private universities.

A number of reasons have been put forward to explain the stable growth in Japan. First, as Komiyama Hirohito (1991) contends, the growth of *juku* presupposes healthy economic development. Some of the large academic *juku* were founded in the early 1970s when the economy grew at the high rate of 11.64 per cent on average (1991: 122–30). In the following years, cram schools proliferated rapidly, as indicated in Figure 5.8.

That drastic increase paralleled the improvement in living standards. One indicator of that improvement was the popularization of consumer commodities among Japanese families, especially the so-called 3 Cs, namely Car, Colour TV and 'Cooler' (air-conditioning), as shown in Figure 5.9.

What accompanied the improvement in the quality of life, as shown in Figure 5.9, was the rise in the advancement ratio at different levels of education. The better standard of living, and the increased chance of education, caused people to be more interested in investing in better education for their children. This generated a thrust in the development of the cram industry.

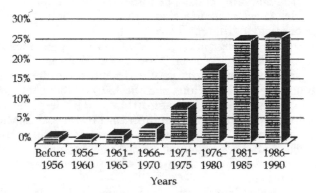

Figure 5.8 The years when the academic *juku* were founded, by the percentage of academic *juku* among the total, taking 1993 as the base year. *Source*: Based on *Gakushûjuku tô kansuru Jittai Chôsa Hôkokusho* (Report on the survey of the issues related to the academic *juku*), (Tokyo: Japanese Ministry of Education, 1995), 46.

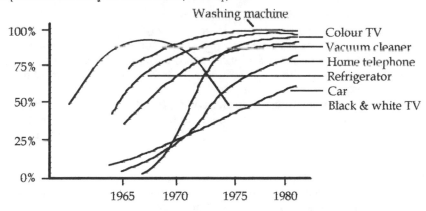

Figure 5.9 The popularization of the main durable consumer goods, by percentage of families, 1965–93. *Source*: *Kokumin Seikatsu Hakusho* (The White Paper of citizens' life), quoted in Hirohito Komiyama, *Gakureki Shakai to Juku* (Credentialistic society and *juku*), (Tokyo: Shinryôron, 1993), 129.

Another explanation of the increase in cram schools is the curricular gap between textbook knowledge and tested knowledge. When the textbooks became easier and the entrance exams became harder, the gap became wider.

What I also found in both Japan and Korea (probably not so much in Taiwan) was a reduced amount of school-assigned homework, an almost inevitable trend of liberal schooling. As a result, this turned into a kind of spiral process: as the cram schools filled the gap in teaching, regular schools began to give less homework to give students more free time. As more schools tried to do so, more *juku* were needed to fill that gap.

Other explanations for the increase in the cram business are also put forward. For instance, it is argued that, to achieve academic excellence and to beat the highly specialized competition, family or community education is not longer sufficient. The craze phenomenon as a collective psychology seems plausible as well. In the exam race, if somebody started to run, nobody might remain indifferent for very long.

The competition among individual students to excel does not seem to vary significantly between Japan, Korea and Taiwan. The competition among cram schools, however, is very different in the three countries. It is first conditioned by the regulations and the laws of the state concerning the legitimacy of cram schools, which are different. This hypothesis echoes the postulation of Orrù, Biggart and Hamilton (in Powell and DiMaggio, 1991: 390–422) of an internal 'organization isomorphism' within Japan, Korea and Taiwan. The industries within an East Asian country, according to their theory, have a common national pattern, which differs from other countries in the East Asia region.

It is hard to recapitulate the minutiae in my study of the school culture shown through the physical plant and equipment of major cram schools in three countries. In describing classrooms, desks and chairs, lighting, air-conditioning, etc., I try to convey to readers what impressed me when I visited those schools. It may be summarized as follows:

1. There is a large demand for cram schooling.
2. Cram schools become prosperous in accommodating that demand.
3. The scale economy is perhaps the only viable answer to that demand.
4. The service is by no means always satisfactory, especially in terms of physical conditions, although the quality of the teachers and teaching is generally very good.
5. There are some indications of an increasing trend towards localization of cramming. This is shown, in particular, in the growing *juku* attendance at local level (Japan), and the improving condition of cram schools in non-metropolitan areas (Taiwan).

Finally, exams are the only cause and *raison d'être* of the vast cram industry. These exams require meticulous analysis of twists and turns of logic. They require students to unravel knotty problems with speed, vigour and composure. Mastering encyclopaedic knowledge, persevering, practising and excelling demands character. In the cram world, this knowledge, rationality and character are uniquely enshrined. What is equally enshrined is the role model of the teacher in cracking the problems of the exam system.

CHAPTER 6

With help from the gods: prayer, luck and spiritual strength: the desecularization of entrance exam systems

The two figures, one ecstatic and the other crest-fallen, belong together. They symbolize in the popular imagination the rewards and suffering Japanese must face in the pursuit of educational distinction, which is followed by a good job, economic security, respect, and status in a technocratic world.
– *Thomas Rohlen*, Japan's High Schools, *1983*

Every religious conception of the universe implies a distinction between the sacred and the profane ... It is from the sacred, in effect, that the believer expects all succour and success. The reverence in which he holds the sacred is composed equally of terror and confidence. The calamities that menace and victimize him, the prosperity that he desires or gains, is attributed by him to some principle that he strives to control or constrain.
– *Roger Caillois*, L'homme et le sacré, *1959*

In ancient China, the supernatural lore that grew around the state civil service examinations (*keju*) created a host of gods and spirits that were patrons of both the literati and the system itself. They had the effect of producing a lasting respect for the status structure moulded by the *keju* system (Yang, 1961). On a considerably lesser scale, but with quite similar fervour to that of the fledging candidates for official literati, that worship bore its ancient coordinates in Korea and Japan as well.

Today, however, secularization has become a fact of our new social life. All religions, as Arnold Toynbee states, have been losing their hold on the population, and the foundations of faith have been subject to critical scrutiny by social sciences and ideologies (Cogley, 1968). The emancipation from economic traditionalism, concedes Max Weber, has been one major factor that greatly strengthens the tendency to doubt the sanctity of the religious tradition (Weber, 1958). In consequence, one may reasonably assume that meritocratic cults, as noted, are now passé. The question this chapter attempts to pursue is: does or does not religion still play a role in the exam-centred system, which, it could be argued, is one of the most rationalistic aspects of modern life? In the following pages, I first describe the ecclesiastical dimension of the 'exam wars', manifested through rituals, talismans, pilgrims and worshipped deities. Then, I scrutinize a Japanese occult charm, *ema*, or 'painted horse', to study a totemic means of communion with the supernatural force. The *ema* is chosen here, because, unlike other religious objects, it carries a rich, and on occasion subtle, record of the students' yearning, motivation, and concern. The *ema* lays bare the inner world of college-bound youth, their reverie, sincerity and fear, which are rarely openly discernible in a society where views or 'truth' are expressed with social agreement in mind. Finally, I recapitulate the theme in a comparative perspective, and conceptualize these findings.

This dissertation does not dwell on how pious the young generation can be today, although that may be a fascinating topic in itself. Instead, I look into the effects of the university entrance exam systems which are the main gateway to socio-academic mobility in Japan, Korea and Taiwan. For me, the study of religion is intriguing, because it yields unique revelations of how intense and powerful a driving force the entrance exams could be in a credentialist culture.

OLD ASIAN MECCAS OF MERITOCRACY AND A NEW PILGRIMAGE OF STUDENTS

In all history, asserts Emile Durkheim, there is no religion without a church, which is, as he defines it, a community formed ethically by all the believers in a single faith, laymen as well as priests (Durkheim, 1965). One major purpose these organizations serve is facilitating and validating hopefulness (Greeley, 1982). Taking entrance exams involves a number of factors. Technically, it involves many unpredictable factors, such as unexpected focuses in test items, mental and/or physical conditions, effects of test venue and time, impromptu performance, and, last but not least, the variable which is customarily termed as 'luck'. Some of these factors are not amenable to control. In his case study of a small community in Japan, Ezra Vogel highlights that unknown factor in exams in the midst of particularism:

> The cause of examination worry is not only the finality of the results but the fact that examinations are impersonal and therefore unpredictable. ... By having properly placed friends and keeping up a good relationship with them, one previously could be virtually assured of success. But there is no such assurance when one is evaluated on the basis of competency by some impersonal authority. Examination questions might be different from what one had anticipated, or one might not feel well, or one's nervousness might inhibit performance (Vogel, 1971).

Given that unpredictability, even the best cram schools had no warranty for a student's success.[1] To shore up hopefulness for something as fateful as it is insecure, churches often can give spiritual guidance, impart confidence, and offer consolation. From 1968 onwards, the Japanese mass media began to focus their attention on the *juken sensô* (exam war), as from 1966 to 1976,

---

[1] For a detailed statistical study of the effects of extracurricular preparation for exams, see Stevenson and Baker (1992).

student prayers at Shinto shines radically increased from 10,000 to 100,000 (Aoki, 1977: 24–5). Among the students from Keio University, Kawai cram schools, or elsewhere with whom I had interaction, about 15–20 per cent had visited a Shinto shrine for their entrance exams (generally for getting into high school). Another 40 per cent of them explained that their parents went to a temple to make a wish on their behalf.

In Japan, the sect of Shinto religion that dedicates itself to the business of exams is called the 'Temmangu (literally Heaven-Filling)' Church. Its deity has the full title of *'Temman Daijizai Tenjin'*, or 'Heaven-Filling Great Self-Sufficient Deity', who is known more affectionately as 'Mr God (*Tenjin-sama*)'. Only shrines to Inari, the god of the harvest, and Hachiman, the god of war, are more numerous (Borgen, 1994). There are 12,000 big or small monasteries of the Temman Church in Japan. Among them, the branch shrine, Yushima Jinja in Tokyo, where I observed the meritocratic religion, is not the central or even the major one (Shimizu, 1991). However, it opened for me a narrow but very revealing perspective on how university entrance exams stir up students' academic motivation and behaviours. Located in the vicinity of Tokyo University and Ochanomizu where students gather, Yushima Shrine, due to its easy access, has long become a Mecca for student exam-takers and their parents to evoke a holy blessing. Even in the Yoyogizemi cram school, sometimes the school principal would borrow such sacred objects as *shiamoji* (wooden spoon) from the monastery to bless the students' victory in mock exams (NHK, 1983a). Each year, from New Year's Day to the dates of entrance exams (15 January through early March), 700,000–800,000 students and/or their families would come to this temple alone for an auspicious visit (Shimizu, 1991).

According to the five-yearly NHK surveys on religious attitudes, from 1973 onwards, the number of teenagers who carried religious charms and talismans steadily grew. A detailed 1981 NHK survey indicates that 77 per cent of teenagers 'often' or 'sometimes' carried charms with them. While this reflected a prevalent custom in Japan, for the teenagers it was mainly influenced by the heavy involvement of this generation in educational matters, especially examinations (Reader, 1991: 182–3). To investigate how prevalently students resorted to religion for academic matters, Ian Reader (1991) conducted a brief survey of a total of 151 students at two universities. He finds that 75 per cent of the students bought talismans (*omamori*), 33 per cent purchased *ema* for writing prayers, 57 per cent stated their talismans were helpful in exams, and 61 per cent said their praying was helpful for exams (pp. 182–3).

The praying scripture (*norito*) and the services at Shinto are categorized into a number of rubrics, such as fortune, health, safety and domestic harmony. With the passing of time, the education-related *norito* showed a gradual contraction onto exams due to their central role in the school-to-workplace linkage. In his 1965 study of the Temmangu Church, Takuchi Yusaku finds that over 70 per cent of the academic-minded prayers came for their exams, and only 20 per cent wished to improve their study in a broad sense (Aoki, 1977). The key words used in the academic *norito* were once phrased in a diffused spectrum of choices: *juken* (exams), *seiseki kôjô* (GPA improving), *juken tesuto* (mid-term test), or *gakki tesuto* (term test) etc. (Aoki, 1977). Now, they have come under a more 'unified', unequivocal label, *gôkaku kigan* (prayer for success in exams). This critical success in competitive exams has become the core of concern.

In Japan, the most desperate manifestation of Shinto devotion to exams is probably the 'One Hundred-Time Homage (*Ohyakudo-mairi*)'. It aims to win sympathy from the deity through self-inflicted torment. To perform *Ohyakudo-mairi*, a parent or student would climb up the flight of stone steps leading to the shrine, pass through the *tori'i* – an archway that represents the division between the secular and divine worlds – walk over to the shrine, shake a thick rope to toll the *suzu* – a bell rung by worshippers to announce the visit to the god, and then pray. This procedure needs to be repeated a hundred times to fulfil the *Ohyakudo-mairi*. Despite its torments, according to H. Hattori and T. Kamezawa, the two Japanese students I interviewed, the *Ohyakudo-mairi* for exams is not that rare among Japanese parents, although no statistics in this regard exist. In a Japanese family, it is the father that exerts pressure on children for achievement. The mother, on the other hand, 'interferes' less. Instead, the Japanese middle-class as well as lower-class mothers will make countless sacrifices, such as taking on extra work, to provide the money necessary for tutors and other additional educational expenses so that their children will be in a better competitive position (De Vos, 1973). As part of that division of responsibility, conducting the *Ohyakudo-mairi* ritual is said to be one of the sacrifices on the part of the mother.[2]

While the *Ohyakudo-mairi* is perhaps the most exhausting way of praying for the exams, the most expensive one is paid ritual supplication. To apply for it, patrons must fill out a sheet known as the 'Scholastic Prayer Application Form' as shown in Figure 6.1.

Scholastic Prayer Application Form
Prayer category: A   B
Purpose: Continuous study   New enrolment   Entrance examination
Name of Applied School: ————————————————
Address: ————————————————
Applicant's name (with furikana)   ————————————————

Figure 6.1 A sample of the 'Scholastic Prayer Application Form' used in Yoshimajinja Shrine, Tokyo.

---

[2] I would like to thank H. Hattori, a Japanese student I interviewed, for his conceptual analysis of the *Ohyakudo-mairi*. The ritual practice of *Ohyakudo-mairi* may vary greatly, however. See, for instance, the description of 'circumambulation practice' by Reader (1991), 173–4 and 189.

Depending on the payment for the service, US$30–50 on average, the priests would chant the supplication *norito* of about 300 words. Natsuko, a law student at Keio University, said her parents paid the priests ¥3000 to pray for her, which, in her words, was the most effective way of evoking an occult blessing.[3]

There are, however, some other less expensive, simplified ways of communicating with supernatural powers. Amongst them, '*ema*' is worth mentioning here. Literally 'a painted horse', *ema* is a wooden tablet on which a visitor can write a prayer. It is available at most shrines for ¥200–¥1000 per piece; *ema* mirrors the deepest well of a wish, anxiety and craving in its writer's mind. During the Russo-Japanese War, 1904–5, as I will discuss below in detail, the Japanese expressed their ultranationalist fervour and wish through drawings and texts in *ema*.

In Taiwan, an amazingly parallel version of the Japanese *ema* is the so-called *Guangming deng*, or the 'Brilliance Lamp', in the Longshan Monastery. Located in the west of Taipei City, the commercial, industrial and political capital of Taiwan, is the temple where I most closely observed exam-minded ritual behaviours in Taiwan. Being a Buddhist temple, it houses an array of polytheist deities, many of which can be traced to Taoism, a major form of Chinese religion, or other more decentralized Chinese origins.

Not far from the main river that flows around Taipei, the Longshan Monastery stands out amid the modern buildings with its glittering, yellow glazed tiles, wing-like upward gables, and the roof ornament packed with colourful sculptures of heavenly creatures and indeterminate flowers. As the hub of a bustling market and sprawling shops, it is thronged with pious pilgrims, foreign tourists and local loafers who idle away time in the sun. All were draped in a floating veil of incense aroma.

The Longshan Temple was built in 1740, during the reign of Emperor Qianlong (1736–70), when the Qing Dynasty reached its peak of prosperity and expansion. Here, the main deity enshrined is the Buddhist Goddess of Mercy. In the past years, this church has been seen as the authority to compromise lawsuits and settle disputes, and any revelation from the gods was strictly obeyed by the parties concerned. With the 'relocation' of the Chinese Nationalist Government to Taiwan island in 1949, the temple was greatly renovated. In the front yard, in addition to the Goddess of Mercy, or Guanyin Buddha, there are also images of the Preacher of Buddha Truth (Weituo), Mountain God (Shanshen), King Dragon in East Sea (Donghai longwang), and the God of Earth (Tudishen).

The Brilliance Lamps were erected in the rear quarter of the temple. They had a long tradition of serving exam-takers, money-seekers, and so forth. Devotees of the God of Scholarship needed to apply for a Lamp one year before the exams were given. To do so, they needed to give their names, addresses and other information. They also had to pay a minimum of NT$ 600 (23 US dollars) as the application fee. Then, these personal files would be put into the computer, which produced plastic labels for each and every one. The administrators of the monastery would attach these name labels to

---

[3] One US dollar is about ¥100.

the so-called 'Brilliance Lamp'. This was an approximately 1.5-inch wide, 2.5-inch high miniature niche box with a transparent door. The background inside was a sage icon in relief. The name, address and the prayer text were visible outward through its glass door. A tiny electric bulb was fixed inside the niche to light it up day and night.

If judged by sheer appearance, the Japanese *ema* and the Taiwanese Brilliance Lamp did not have much in common, as shown in Figure 6.2. However, the main functions of *ema* and *Guangming deng* were significantly similar to each other. Both were some sort of courier, or letter of request, addressed to the Gods of Examinations, and both were posted for about one entire year before a new batch took them over.

All the Lamps were permanently fixed neatly on several huge cone-shaped Lamp stands. They were two metres in diameter, five metres high, resembling some large-sized Christmas trees inside the monastery. Twenty-four hours a day, these 'Christmas trees' revolved gently around their axis driven by motors, with thousands of niches glimmering golden rays of hope. While Taiwanese 'trees' were put indoors, Japanese *ema* were hung on a wooden shelf in the open yard of the shrine. They looked like merchandise packages displayed on racks in a convenience store. Rains or melting snow might soak them badly and blur the text. However, either indoors or out-doors, a common principle for their location was: these sacred messages are put as close as possible to the gods so that they can bask in their celestial radiance. Even in a Japanese shrine, the *ema* racks are generally found in front of the open entrance of the hall, or in its close vicinity. The large shrine windows, always ajar, put the thick *ema* plates within the visual field of the deities, as seen in Figure 6.3.

In the same vein, according to the Longshan administrators, the reason that Taiwanese 'Lamp Trees' were kept revolving day and night was that every applicant wanted to have an equal 'exposure' to the gods' blessing.

Praying texts on the Brilliance Lamps were uniformly formatted, very likely from a template of a word-processor. They were then printed out on computer labels. A label would include data as shown in the sample (see Figure 6.4). Except for the name and address, all the praying texts of Brilliance Lamps are duplicates of this sample. The *norito* (praying scriptures) for *ema*, on the other hand, were written by individuals themselves in a variety of idiosyncratic styles. Given their complexity, and the immense amount of information they contained, I will return to examine *ema* specifically later.

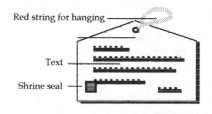

Japan's *ema*: 'Painted Horse'

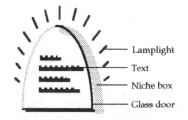

Taiwan's 'Brilliance Lamp'

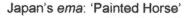

Figure 6.2 *Ema* and *Guangming deng*, as two examples of exam-oriented religious instruments for prayer used in East Asia.

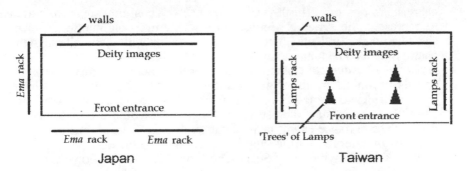

Figure 6.3 A comparison: layout of *ema* in a Japanese Temmangu church and Lamps in a Taiwanese polytheist temple.

BRILLIANCE LAMP

Name: Daishe Chang   Application No. 5900
Address: Apartment 194, Fushing Rd.,
       Shinchuang City, Taipei
Date: 20 June, 1994   Time of prayer: 7.00 o'clock, Chinese hour

Pray for my success in passing the entrance examinations with honour and brilliance (*Guangming jidi*)

Figure 6.4 A sample of the content of the 'Brilliance Lamp' in Dragon Mountain Temple, Taipei.

The means of communication with the gods are not limited to the above. Local variations and peculiarities are found in different temples. The Temmangu church of Tasaifu in the Fukuoka Prefecture of Japan is one example. Tasaifu is perhaps the No. 1 Mecca for exam-driven student pilgrimage, as Sugawara Michizane, the Japanese God of Examinations and Literature, was sent on exile and died at that place. There, a special gourd is used as the *ema*. Students can jot down their wish for exams on a piece of paper, put it into a tiny gourd they buy, and hang it up in the shrine just like they would do with an *ema*. Most religious objects of the sort are standardized and sold in Japan, available at the shrine-run gift shop. The following are some of the commodities used for worship directly related to entrance examinations. As the list is based on my own observations only, it is by no means an exhaustive one:

- *Hachimaki* (Headband). The headband that I found at the Tokyo Yushima Shrine, for instance, had a scarlet plum-flower in the middle. Four black Chinese characters were inscribed across it: '*nyûshi toppa*', literally, 'breaking though entrance exams'. It may also be '*hisshô* (fight to win)', a Japanese cliché of optimism. As always, *hachimaki* can hardly fail to remind one of the determination of a WWII *Kamikaze* pilot.
- *Omamori* (Protective charms). These are made of red-and-gold embroidery inscribed with auspicious wishes. There are also more individualized

charms, *eto omamori* (birth-year charms). Twelve animal signs were used to represent the Oriental Zodiac (*juni-shi*) corresponding to different calendar years. Students often carry the *Omamori* with them, although the charm may also be hung up in the car or at home.

- *Gakugyô jôju enpitsu* (Pencil set for scholarly achievement). These are pencils produced by the shrine. Each is printed with a motto such as: 'Self confidence comes from diligence', 'Make progress step by step', 'Work hard every day', and so forth. Examinees would use these pencils during their entrance exams in anticipation that the 'sacred' stationery can ward off blunders and bring superior scores against the odds.

- *Kigan shinji* (Praying Holy Seal). The Holy Seal is traditionally one of the three treasures of the Japanese Shinto, together with the Sword and the Mirror. It can be used for erecting a religious altar of entrance exams back at home. I noted some students attached a *kigan shinji* to their *ema* plates to enhance their appeal to gods.

- *Gôkaku orei* (Gratitude gift to gods). After going through the thick and thin of the 'exam inferno', if the student passed the entrance exams, he or she would purchase a *gôkaku orei*, a token gift, and tie it onto the *ema* rack as a return to indebtedness. *Gôkaku orei* is just a version of the *ema*. Unlike *ema*, on its reverse is generally printed the Chinese characters, *orei* (gift) and the *Daruma*, a cultural image used for celebrating the fulfilment of a goal.

- *Hamaya* (Exorcizing arrow). In Japanese culture, *Hamaya* is a charm promising to ward off errors and evils. It looks like the ordinary arrow of archery, with three different sizes, small, medium and large. While the *Hamaya* used to go together with the *Hamayumi* (exorcizing bow), it is not necessarily so now. The exorcizing arrow is used specifically at the beginning of the year, which coincides with the schedule of the Japanese entrance exams just one month later. In Yoyogizemi, one of the largest cram corporation in Japan, *Hamaya* is one occult object used to boost students' confidence. On New Year's Day, Yoyogizemi will give all its students an important lecture on how to cope with the exams. To tune up the students for the final challenge, the lecture is ritualized, and every student is awarded a *Hamaya* with the words '*gôkaku hisshô*' – the inevitable victory for the entrance exams – attached.

In Taiwan, there are perhaps fewer talismans produced specifically for entrance exams than in Japan. But that does not mean people have no channels of communion. The following scene, reproduced from the field journal I kept, shows how a Taiwanese student prayed:

14 Dec. 1995, Thurs. The sky was lead-coloured, drizzling. In the Dragon Mountain Monastery (*Longshan si*), a chubby girl of 13 or 14 in a blue uniform of middle school stepped over to the front of Wenchang, the God of Literature. She tossed NT$15 (about 58¢) into the collection box, backed down, and then stood still, praying in silence. Moments later, she took out two thin bundles of vegetables – Chinese celery and spring onion – from a flimsy plastic grocery bag, and laid them in parallel on the altar. She prayed again, but very briefly, and retreated. The two greenstuffs, I was told by a priest, were used as puns: the celery, '*qin*', could mean in Chinese diligence or hardworking. The Chinese spring onion, '*cong*', stands for intelligence or quick-wittedness.

The ritual was anything but sophisticated. Nevertheless, its hidden symbolism encapsulated an abridged version of meritocracy in folk concepts. Its was a 'recipe' for success. Its 'ingredients' included 'onion' (intelligence), 'celery' (diligence), and money (symbolized by the 58¢). One also needs some sort of supernatural help, which was why she was there.

In Taiwan, the high season for exam-related pilgrimages is June and early July each year, when the entrance exams are imminent for both university and high school. As the sweltering summer solstice begins, preparation shifts into high gear, and test anxiety mounts along with the temperature. The temples are then teeming with the student – and parent – pilgrims. They generally buy a bundle of incense sticks, light them up, and hold them high with both hands before their faces while praying. Some students kneel on the floor, some just stand. Many students bring their exam permit and show the attached photos to the gods during the ritual. In one minor accident during the 1995 Taiwan entrance exams, a student lost his exam permit because his parents used it during a religious visit and could no longer find it (ZS, 2 May 1995). Some, I learned, bring their nearly expired student ID cards from high school. They set the cards on fire and burn them to show their determination. The ritual message is explicit: this is the exam of exams, the final judgement of adolescent school life. With all the perspiration, all the sacrifice and endless exercises, all the loving care, worry and expectation from the beloved ones, everybody will be soon left alone for the Final. The time has come. There is no retreat.

If a cram school is a place to learn what students did and sacrificed for their success, churches lend us an entirely different perspective which allows us to detect some desecularized components in exam-driven motivation. First, these exams generate tremendous anxiety as well as tremendous hope, and religion is a response to both. Secondly, religiosity expresses one's wish to rise above oneself in order to attain some superior power, confidence and composure through ritual experience (Greeley, 1982), and thirdly, self-transcendence, as described, is not necessarily an escape from the real world. For many, it reflects a desire to jump-start through ritual one's own untapped potential.

Every religion implies a distinction between the sacred and the profane. This polarity of the universe originally derived from the sacred–profane dichotomy in the social order. The domain of the sacred is one of fear and hope, a powerful force in life, but evanescent in its qualities. It is susceptible to dilution, dissipation or debasement by the profane. Rites are therefore designed to control its impact (Durkheim, 1965; also Caillois, 1959). In East Asian cultures, as elsewhere, the social hierarchical structures embody that sanctified division; in pop theory, success or failure in the high-stake exams is perhaps the best imaginable legitimate criterion that justifies that hierarchy. In Chinese society, for instance, passing competitive exams implies an achievement that glorifies and illuminates one's ancestors (*Guangzong yaozu*). This is perhaps the most valued mandate a Chinese is born with. In the eyes of the common populace, the exams have always been a ruthless but impartial sorting device. The young thus grouped, those who enter college and those who do not, are evaluated very much with that sacred–profane bifurcation.

While the folk culture is often elusive to grasp, it is still traceable not only in the way people behave and in what they say, but also in pop literature as well. In her bestseller, *Hensachi Diary* (*Hensachi Nikki*), Fuyoko Murasaki, a Japanese mother of a middle school student, depicts her alarm and shame when she learnt that her son earned only 50 *hensachi* (a deviation grade) scorepoints.[4] Seated beside the other parents, she felt all the quandary and pain. She commemorates the day when she got the score report as 'Hensachi Memorial Day' (Murasaki, 1991). In a Taiwanese short story, 'Fright in the Examination Hall (*Kaochang papa*)', a boy who believed he would flunk the exam wrote a mental letter to the girl seated next to him in the exam hall. It reads:

> Here, we two are only separated by an aisle. But our future courses of life will be so different from one another. I can just imagine, amid the rejoicing of your family and friends, you will enter with flying colours the Foreign Languages Department, Taiwan University. After 'all play and no work' for four years there, you will then study overseas, MA, PhD, and then return home to honour your ancestors (*Guangzong yaozu*). ... For me, I can only visualize right now my dad's flames of fury, my mum's brimming tears, my teacher's sigh of despair, and disdain cast from my classmates. I will be a failure, a loser wandering around the 'Cram Street', and then end up as a drafted soldier ... (Kuling, 1994: 208)

The fact that the merit system simply moulds two worlds with different prospects and promises has something in common with the structuralistic nature of religion. Similar to religious affiliation, working hard for the exam system underlies the sanctification of that social grouping. By going to church, a student is aligned to, and becomes a reserve member of, the Sacred 'clan' – the social élite class. Those gods are role models in the 'clan', and the students who enter university constitute its extended membership. To evoke spiritual force and to obtain membership of the Sacred élite are the religious dimensions of exam competition between Pass and No-Pass, as schematized in Figure 6.5.

This dedication to 'Pass', or to enter the technocratic core class, has a forceful impact on and lasting potential for academic motivation. When it rises to the religious level, the religious affiliation, be it enduring or just exigent, tends to correlate powerfully with behaviour and attitude (Greeley, 1982).

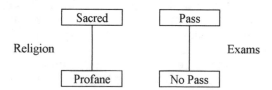

Figure 6.5 A comparison: the system of religion and the system of exams.

---

[4] See Chapter 3, note 8.

Their preoccupation with the Sacred nature of meritocratic success in exams seemed for many students to be more immediately important, and more obsessive than money. The following text, reproduced from a Japanese *ema* tablet, illustrates the point:[5]

> Example
> *Pray for success (gôkaku kigan)*
> Education Dept. of Aoyama University
> Law Dept. of Aoyama University
> Seijo University[6]
> I must succeed in passing exams. *If I can, I will require nothing more, not even money. Of course, I do not need tears any more, either. How about that?* [italic added]

The indifference to material gains stated in this Japanese *ema* cannot be taken seriously. Nonetheless, it is equally true that meritorious attainment actually means a lot more. A further illustration of that point is found in the proportion of Brilliance Lamps in Taiwan's Dragon Mountain Monastery. The temple of the God of Examinations, Wenchang, was next to two other deities: Empress of Heaven (Mazu), worshipped for safety in voyages and also for getting children; and the God of Riches or Wealth (Guandi). All three are enshrined in the rear temples, which are separated from the Buddhist pantheon in the front. Each image of the three main deities, God of Examinations, Empress of Heaven and God of Riches, is accompanied by a flock of minor deities, including God of Farsightedness, God of Sun, Goddess of Moon, Goddess of Obstetrics, Goddess to Secure Foetus, God in Red Coat, God of Horse. The layout of the temples, as shown in Figure 6.6, is centred on the three main holy figures, which are a lot larger in size than the rest.

The service of the Brilliance Lamps is available for all the gods for the same price. However, the number of applicants is not evenly distributed among the three, as it depends entirely on the interests of the pilgrims. By my estimation at the time I did the investigation, the numbers of Lamps for the three gods were:

Empress of Heaven	None
God of Riches	6400 Lamps
God of Scholarship	30,000 Lamps

What happened was that the temple for the God of Scholarship did not have enough space for exam-driven prayers. So the Lamp niche-boxes for the God of Scholarship 'intruded' into the territory of the Empress of Heaven and occupied its entire temple space, expressed in Figure 6.7.

---

[5] Unless indicated otherwise, the main source of *ema* texts quoted later in this chapter is Aoki (1977).

[6] Aoyama University, a private school in Tokyo, founded in 1874 by an American missionary. Seijo University, a private school located in Tokyo, founded in 1917.

God of Riches	Empress of Heaven	God of Examinations

Front entrance

Figure 6.6 The structure of the rear temple at the Dragon Mountain Temple.

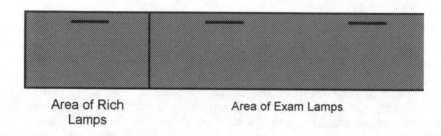

Area of Rich Lamps   Area of Exam Lamps

Figure 6.7 The ratio of the Rich Lamps and the Exam Lamps in the rear temple at the Dragon Mountain Temple.

This does not imply that Taiwanese were less interested in making a fortune. A better explanation is that academic success has been such a hallmark of status in an Asian Newly Industrialized Country (NIC) that educational achievement became more and more important, and access to a better life via exams was accorded a first priority here. To understand why people throughout the ages came to those churches to entrust their spiritual dependence, evoke fortitude or solicit consolation, it is indispensable to know who are worshipped and why, which I turn to now.

THE PORTRAYAL OF GODS OF EXAMINATIONS

The highly visible ecclesiastic aspect of exams is not confined to Taiwan alone. In Korea, the self-inflicted tribulation during religious ritual on the part of the parents could be as torturous as the 'Hundred-Time Homage' performed by Japanese. It is reported that mothers bow 3000 times a night at a Buddhist temple for their children's success in exams or pray for a hundred days at Christian churches (Cho, 1922). In Japan, the Shinto shrine has long been a resort for Japanese students for a blessing of the entrance examinations. Each year, it is estimated, several hundred thousand students visited Shinto churches for their entrance exams (Shimizu, 1991). In Taiwan, in the monastery I observed, the number of registered prayers for passing exams far exceeded that for wealth-earning.

To know a people, asserts Edward Werner, one has to know their gods, as knowledge of them is essential for an adequate understanding of the minds of their adherents. The people named in religion live, or lived, in that Other World and are honoured or worshipped by those in this world. They are usually, though not always, human beings who have died, but deified and thus still living and continuing to lead a 'theanthropical life', honoured and worshipped (Werner, 1961). Who are honoured, and why and how they are honoured in an imagined world, is a reflection of those who are living.

Why have some people become gods, while most others do not? Emile Durkheim supplies an answer: 'In the present day just as much as in the past', he writes, 'society is constantly creating sacred things out of ordinary ones. If it happens to fall in love with a man and if it thinks it has found in him the principal aspirations that move it, as well as the means of satisfying them, this man will be raised above the others and, as it were, deified' (Durkheim, 1965). A deity thus crystallizes and personifies values of a particular society which it treasures as adorable or useful. This is also true for the origin of the Gods of Examinations, Literature and Scholarship.

Japan's God of Examinations was Sugawara Michizane (845–903). During his lifetime, as a Confucian, he did not establish any religious organization, although he performed, on occasion, ritual activities at both Buddhist and Shinto shrines (Borgen, 1994). However, after his death, a whole Shinto sect, 'Temman Church (*Temmangu*)', was founded after him. This Church renders specialized service to the *jukensei* (students of examinations), who are its main patrons.

Shinto is an ancient native religion consisting of a set of traditional rituals and customs involving multiple services. To generations of schoolchildren, however, the meaning of the Shinto shrine has long been embodied in the god Tenjin-sama, the 'saint of learning' worth praying to before examinations (Dore, 1965). From 1968 onwards, Japanese mass media began to pay closer attention to the 'Exam War' (*juken sensō*). From 1966 to 1976, student prayers at Temman Church radically increased from 10,000 to 100,000 (Aoki, 1977). To date, the reasons for praying have expanded to various sorts of exams. According to Kenni Shimizu, there are altogether 12,000 big or small monasteries of the Temman Church across Japan, catering to that gigantic demand (Shimizu, 1991).

The real person behind Japan's God of Examinations, Michizane, was a highly successful literati-official during the Heian Era, known for his unparalleled accomplishment in Sino-Japanese literature and culture. His works included, among others, a 200-volume history, *Ruiju Kokushi* (The Categorized National History of Japan). His success in the civil service exams led him to a series of careers in university, provincial government and as Minister of Ceremonial. At the pinnacle of his power, Michizane authorized all orders from the Council of State together with his rival, Fujiwara no Tokihira (871–909).

After his patron Emperor Uda abdicated in 897, however, Michizane's situation became precarious. In 901, Michizane was charged with two offences. One was that he had an ambition to dominate the court, the other, more specific one was that he was plotting to depose the emperor, and replace him with his own son-in-law. Historical study shows that the charge was groundless (Shimizu, 1991). Michizane was, however, persecuted in a political frame-up and demoted in 901 AD. Two years later, on the 25th of the second month, 903, he died in grief in exile.

His integrity and excellence, as well as the injustice that befell him, were followed by a series of calamities. In 909, his rival Tokihira, who attacked him, died in his prime at the age of 39. Thirteen years later, the crown prince, then only 21, also passed away. He was Tokihira's nephew, the child of Emperor Daigo and Tokihira's sister, whose marriage had followed Michizane's exile. The crown prince's demise was blamed on the wrath of Michizane's vengeful ghost, and so one month later Michizane was belatedly pardoned. Still, this did not placate the wronged minister and troubles at court continued, particularly among Tokihira's descendants. A series of ensuing accidents made people believe that the effect of onryô (a vengeful ghost) was at work.[7] As a result, in 947, a shrine was dedicated to Michizane at Kitano, just north of the capital. Forty years later, it was recognized by the government, and Michizane was known as 'Temman Tenjin', the 'Heaven-filling God'. This history later won him the titles of God of Literature, Calligraphy, Scholarship, Honesty, Benevolence, and so on.

Michizane's deification was the result of an intricate synthesis of Shinto and Buddhist ideas, and an intermingling of popular and aristocratic cultures. This diversity of origins explains Tenjin's rapid acceptance as one of the most widely worshipped gods in Japan's pantheon of deities (Borgen, 1994). To the exam takers of modern ages, however, Michizane has been best known as the God of Entrance Examinations. One reason was that Michizane himself had occasion to give four civil service examinations. Also, he showed his concern for the fairness and effectiveness of the exam system in three proposals written in 883. His recommendations included a limit on the length of the examination, a lifting of the ban on some forbidden subjects used in exams, and clearer standards for the grading system.

Scant and scattered descriptions are found in Dore's *Education in Tokugawa Japan* about religious ceremonies in education in pre-modern Japan. Many schools before the Meiji propagated faith in Michizane as the God of Scholarship (Dore, 1965: 95, 273, 286). In the Edo period, Tenjin Lectures were conducted in school. Pupils presented offerings of food and drink before an image of Michizane while praying for success in their studies and in their calligraphy. Idolization of Michizane epitomized an early prototype of Japanese values in scholastic excellence and, above all, meritocracy.

During the Meiji era, 'Michizane worship' in no way diminished its popularity. At least one early Meiji leader, Okuma Shigenobu, was a devoted follower of the Tenjin cult, and the story of Michizane's virtues continued to appear in textbooks. His image might be less supernatural, but more nationalistic. The image was, however, as fanciful as those of the

---

[7] The belief in the after-effect of injustice began at the end of the Nara period, which formed the *onryôshisô* concept (Theory of vengeful ghosts made by injustice) during the Heian period. According to some other more legendary sources, the natural calamities evoked by the death of Michizane also included solar eclipses, earthquakes, meteors, draughts, floods, epidemics, conflagrations, and so forth (Kenni Shimizu, 1991). Some Confucian rationalists, like Kaibara Ekken, however, denounced stories of divine retribution in form of *onryôshiso* arguing that Michizane was noted for his virtues of honesty, purity and moderation (Borgen, 1994).

medieval priests who wrote of his journey to China. In higher schools, student assemblies were held before an image of the God of Exams, during which the 'God Sutra' (*Tenjin kyo*), similar to a Buddhist sutra, was recited (ibid.). In the First Higher School, the *de facto* Tokyo University, for instance, the giant portraits of Michizane and Sakanoue no Tamuamaro[8] in school were a powerful reinforcement of the Minerva and Mars symbols on the school badge, a unity of the 'way of letters' and the 'way of the warrior'. At matriculation ceremonies (*nyûgaku shiki*) in the First Higher, these two portraits hung majestically above the podium, symbolizing martial vigour and scholastic competency (Roden, 1980).

There are however few, if any, ethnographic or statistical studies of the religious dimensions of exam culture in the prewar era. Yet, there did exist some informal evidence that indicates the continuity of students' resort to shrines, even in the heat of the War. The following piece of humour, written by a *rônin* (repeater) and published in 1939, was an illustrative example. It took the form of a dialogue between a brother and his younger sister:

The Exam God Doesn't Know English

Brother (*rônin*): 'Early this morning, I went to the Shrine to pray.'
Sister: 'What did you pray for?'
Brother: 'Well, I asked the Exam God to let me do well in my English exam tomorrow.'
Sister: 'My goodness, how could the ancient God understand English?!'
Brother: 'Oh yeah, that is why every year it did not work!'

– Obunsha, *Juken Junhô* 9(34) (Dec. 1939).

If we put the humorous part aside, we may say that evoking supernatural power almost became a tradition attached to high-stake exams. Religiosity is a thread of continuity passing almost uninterruptedly through modern history.

As soon as World War II was over, the God of Scholarship quickly fell from favour as stories of his loyalty to the emperor lost their appeal. First of all, the state Shinto, where the God of Scholarship belonged, was abolished in order to 'prevent a recurrence of the perversion of Shinto theory and beliefs into militaristic and ultranationalistic propaganda'. The sponsorship and support of Shinto by the Japanese government or public employees were prohibited and ceased immediately, although private Shinto activities were still permitted. But public educational institutions were forbidden from disseminating its doctrines.[9] The Occupation authorities removed the portrait of Sugawara Michizane from the five-yen note where it had first appeared in

---

[8] Sakanoue no Tamuamaro (758–811), a Japanese military hero, spearheaded a campaign against the Ainu in northern Honshu.

[9] For further details, see 'Memorandum to Imperial Japanese Government from GHQ and SCAP' issued by General Headquarters of the Occupation, dated 15 December 1945, in Beauchamp and Vardaman (1994), 68–9.

1888 and had remained until the war ended. The play about him, 'Sugawara Secrets of Calligraphy', was banned for being too 'feudalistic'. But gradually after the Occupation was over, as the Japanese began to re-examine their ancient past more objectively, leading specialists in Japanese literature and history began to write about him as a human as well as divine figure (Borgen, 1994).

Michizane monopolized the worship of scholarship in Japan. In Taiwan, however, deity apotheosis associated with examinations is manifold, stemming from at least four sources.[10] First of all, there is Wenchang, the God of Literature. His secular name was Zhang Ya; he was born during the Tang Dynasty (618–907 AD) in the Kingdom of Yue (modern Jiangsu Province), and later lived at Zitong, in Sichuan Province. Like Japan's Sugawara Michizane, he was a brilliant writer, and held an appointment in the Board of Rites (*libu*). In his latter days he suddenly disappeared, or was killed in battle.

The above is the account accepted as historically authentic, but other versions exist. First, the date of his birth differs in different works, with the earliest going back to the Qin dynasty (221–206 BC). One of them refers to him as the God or Spirit (*shen*) of Zitong, who held office in the Jin Dynasty (265–316 AD), and was killed in a fight. Over a period of three thousand years, Wenchang, as the God of Literature, accumulated as many as seventeen reincarnations. The God of Exams also has a position in the celestial world, i.e., the third star in the Ursa Major group.

Wenchang, the supreme god, has two main companions. One is a Star God, Kuixing, in the constellation Andromeda but later transferred to one in the Ursa Major group. The other source is Zhuyi (Mr Redcoat), originally Zhu Xi, a Confucian scholar of the Song Dynasty. In the Longshan Temple, the Star God stands to the left of the God of Exams. He has the visage of a demon, holding a writing brush in his right hand and a dipper (*dou*) in his left, one of his legs kicking up behind. His figure is intended as an impersonation of the Chinese character '*kui*', which means 'excellence in the academic field' (see Figure 6.8).

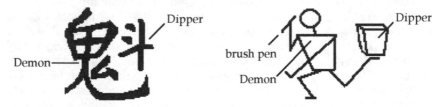

Chinese character 'kui', which is composed of demon and dipper

The posture of Kuixing, the Star God, in emulation of the Chinese character 'kui'

Figure 6.8 The impersonation of the Star God (Kuixing) in Chinese religion.

---

[10] Unless otherwise specified, the following historical account of the Chinese God of Literature is essentially based on the information collected from the Dragon Mountain Temple, and Werner (1961).

This Star God of Scholarship is regarded as the distributor of literary degrees, and is invoked above all in order to obtain success in competitive examinations. Mr Redcoat, on the other hand, helps backward and dull scholars to pass examinations (Yang, 1961). He represents Zhu Xi (1130–1200 AD), the famous writer and commentator, whose works were an orthodox exposition of the Confucian classics. Apart from being the protector of weak candidates, he is also the purveyor of official posts. Mr Redcoat is sometimes accompanied by another personage, named Jinjia, Mr Golden Armour. He is charged with the interests of scholars.

The deities of Chinese gods of literature are not limited, however, to these three. The long history of culture produced quite a number of minor attendants to Wenchang, such as four acolytes. Deities of other categories, such as the God of War (Guan Yü), also have some power in this field. As a famous warrior, Guan Yü has been worshipped by the literati because he was traditionally credited with the ability to repeat some Confucian classics from beginning to end.

'PAINTED HORSE': INTERPRETING STUDENTS' MESSAGES WRITTEN ON SHINTO TALISMAN *EMA*

The Japanese *ema* is, as noted earlier, a square wooden board sold at Shinto shrines for student pilgrims to write down their greatest wish. Like Taiwan's Brilliance Lamp, it is an occult charm with protective powers. Also like the Brilliance Lamp, it is supposed to convey personal messages to the omniscient beings. However, unlike the Brilliance Lamp which is rigidly uniform in its format and content, one can write whatever one wants on *ema*. This difference makes *ema* a telltale source, a courier that may reveal the innermost world of its writer. Communion between the pilgrims and gods has some other means as well. Takehiko Aoki, for instance, writes about a grandma who donated money into the *saisen-bako* (collection box) at the shrine. On the paper used for wrapping the coins, she wrote: 'Please let my grandson pass the exams gloriously even at the cost of my life' (Aoki, 1977). Thus, what makes *ema* unique is its far richer messages, its variety of styles, and its unchecked freedom of self-expression.

The *ema* is an approximately 5"× 4" unpainted wooden tablet, purchasable at most shrines for ¥200–¥1000 ($2–$10) each. Visitors can write their wishes on *ema*, usually with a black felt-tipped pen, as if jotting down notes on a one-page writing pad. The tablet is made from cypress – a member of the evergreen family that produces fragrant, light but durable wood. Its decoration generally includes a totemic picture, the name of the Shinto temple, and, on many occasions, a red shrine seal stamped in the corner.

Using the *ema* as a courier to the gods is not confined to the Temman Church. It is widely used in all Shinto churches. The scope of its service may relate to personal luck or fortune, financial prosperity, excellent health, domestic security, harmonious marriage, child-bearing and safe birth, love and courtship, abandoning gambling, drugs and alcohol, academic success, etc.. While the *ema* of the Temman sect are uniquely related to entrance exams, I also noted in my study that the *ema* in other churches might also be germane to *gôkaku kigan* (prayer for exams) in all sects. How great a proportion did exam-related *ema* amount to in general Shinto, then? This question is almost impossible to answer, as there were no statistics available to me, and I doubt there are any at all. They are also exceptionally difficult to collect, because as there are thousands of big or small Shinto temples across Japan, their *ema* are countless.

I picked two shrines at random, and sampled their *ema*. These two shrines were Enoshima Jinja and Hase Kannon, both in the Kanagawa prefecture. Both were the average type of shrine, medium-sized and moderately well known. According to the guidebook to Shinto shrines, Enoshima Jinja promotes 'good business, family harmony, and traffic safety', and Hase Kannon, 'good luck, and good commercial business' (Nakajima, 1994). Neither of the two specializes in exams or academic affairs. The statistics from my *ema* sampling are presented in Table 6.1. In the two non-academic shrines, exam-related *ema* accounted for about half the total *ema*. Admittedly, the figures given above were not obtained through strict statistical method. They do, however, give some idea about how people used generic shrines to ask for success in exams.

According to Sato and Tamura (1978) and Iwai (1979b), the largest number of today's *ema* are related to scholastic achievement, especially supplications for entrance exams. This has not always been true, however. In the history of *ema,* its main theme and totemic decorations have been transformed under the sway of social concerns, trends and culture.

The ancient Japanese believed that deities came to the human world on horse-back, and as a result, the horse became a divine animal. During religious rites, a horse was used to carry sacred or spiritual objects (*shinrei*). Farmers used a black horse to pray for rain, and a white horse to pray for sunshine (Sato and Tamura, 1978). Archaeological evidence shows that horses were employed during the Nara period for religious purposes, and there was a custom for devotees to donate horses to the church. However, as a horse was expensive and also needed to be fed during religious activities, people started to use earth horses, wooden horses, or a picture of a horse instead. These alternatives brought into the foreground the *ema* which means literally 'a painted horse' or 'a picture of a horse'. The early *ema* was still related to agriculture, just like the real horse previously.

Later on, the artistic themes of *ema* expanded from the horse to a number of other motifs. Different animals, human or deity figures and natural scenes found their way into *ema*. Also, as the Shinto shrine became the 'spiritual nexus' of the villages, *ema* became the emblem of unity, representing the collective local interest (Iwai, 1979a, 1979b).

Table 6.1 Percentage of exam-related *ema* in Enoshima Jinja and Hase Kannon, two non-academic Shinto shrines in Japan. *Source*: My compilation.

	Exam-related ema	Total number of ema	Percentage[†]
Enoshima Jinja	17	33	51.51
Hase Kannon	41	68	60.29

Note: † Percentage = number of exam-related *ema* ÷ total number of *ema*.

This function of the *ema* motif as an emblem or logo for the local community gradually superseded the incipient animal worship. This feature bore a close resemblance to the nature of the totem (Durkheim, 1965; Leach, 1967).

Since then, happiness, health and love have been perpetual themes of *ema*. However, as the local or national concerns changed, so did *ema*'s function. The typical examples were great natural disasters such as the famine of 1886 and the devastating earthquake of 1923, which became the topics of *ema* during those years. War topics became popular during the Meiji Restoration, Russo-Japanese War, and World Wars One and Two. People donated for *ema* which depicted navy battles engraved with the nationalistic cliché '*hitsshō*' meaning 'fight with a firm conviction to win'.

Whether during a time of war or peace, one significant value of *ema* lies in its frankness, as opposed to *tatemae*, or views that have been adjusted to social norms and acceptance. The *ema* is entirely a genre of personal work, not meant for publication. One does not need to register to put up an *ema*, and it is not subject to censorship. Therefore, it vents the real voice, and embodies '*honne*', the real intentions or sentiments of its 'authors'. One example given by Iwai (1979b) is the so-called 'deserter's psychology' (*torei shinri*). On the back of some war *ema*, family members wrote in tiny characters: 'Only pray that he come home safe and in peace.' That was unacceptable and antithetical to the 'dying-on-the-battlefield' ultra-nationalist heroism.

During the period 1966–76, student prayers at Shinto shrines multiplied from 10,000 to 100,000 a year, and the *ema* began to take up its new role. The *ema* was often used for a year until January. If a student was too busy to come to the shrine, his parents, his family members, or his boy/girl friends would come to pray in his stead. There was thus a 'total mobilization of family' in this 'exam war'. With the passing of time, the contents of *ema* for *juken kikan* expanded from college entrance exams to those for high and middle schools, and then to those for kindergarten, a process which is termed as '*teireika* (trend of lower age)'. As academic *ema* grew in number, these prayers and wishes began to underscore major features of both the exam system as well as *ema per se*.

First of all, what is shown in *ema* is that exams have become a highly symbolized system, due to their perceived rewarding function and their dramatic effect in shaping individual destinies, as illustrated by Thomas Rohlen (1980). They resemble a bull's-eye: easy to aim at, easy to focus on, and even easy to hate. And yet, it is too fair and too deep-rooted to be abolished. Partially for that reason, the system is powerfully correlated to academic behaviour. The warlike nature of the exams generated great intensity and focus of motivation. This is shown in the request and promise *ema* writers made to God:[11]

---

[11] All the italics are added in the subsequent examples.

Example I
For the Metropolitan Air Aviation Special School:[12] *Absolute* Success!
Constant effort brings success.[13]

Example II
In order to succeed in passing exams for metropolitan high schools,
please let me study hard with all my might (*issyô kenmei*).
... *Succeed. Succeed. Succeed. That is my lifetime wish.*

Example III
To enter Group 61, I will work hard for it *as a life-or-death aim*.
I will do my best during the exams. Please help me.

The above textual excerpts taken from *ema* were typical in the way that
words like 'absolute', 'succeed', 'work hard as a life-or-death aim' were
used. Praying does not seem to be an action of passing responsibility over to
the deities. Everybody knows that for exams this simply will not work.
Therefore, to pray is to let determination and confidence bounce back, so
that the writer feels recharged. 'I've never been one', claims Eva Bowring,
'who thought the good Lord should make life easy; I've just asked Him to
make me strong.' This idea was echoed in many an *ema* as the tenet. The
determined emotion involved was sometimes shown through the word
'death', as in the above example. Similar examples were not hard to find:

Example I
God, please, HELP ME [sic in English].
As my wish is getting into high school,
God, please, fulfil my *once-in-a-lifetime dream* ...

Example II
Enter high school *or death* (*shinde mo*)!
To achieve that, I will fight with all my might.

Example III
God, I will study till *victory or death* (*hisshi ni*). Therefore, let me enter high
school please.

This 'death' was not a moribund promise. However, it did reflect the
keynote for the resolution of these children. These were not simply

---

[12] Metropolitan Air Aviation Special School, a Tokyo vocational high school. Its
hensachi range in 1994 is 56–59. Twenty per cent of its graduates go to university,
and 80 per cent go to work in the aviation industry.

[13] A proverbial equivalent in English for it is 'If at first you don't succeed, try, try
again.'

evanescent pledges. They matched the motivation and behavioural pattern of students.[14]

Secondly, '*honne*', or frank expression of the author's real thoughts, marked the content of *ema*. Without much need for a persona mask, *ema* displayed the gamut of real feelings as exams came near: fear, anxiety, stress, strain and disillusionment.

Example I
Agriculture Dept. of Shinshu University:
It has been a long time! Oh, shall I still go on trying then?
Please take care of us....

This was apparently an *ema* that belonged to a *rônin*, a student who failed in passing the entrance exams and intends to try again. One can almost hear the sigh of dismay and hesitation. The next ones are just forthright:

Example II
No matter what, I just want to get into Edogawa High![15]

Example III
Pray for success (*gôkaku kikan*)
Education Dept. of Aoyama University
Law Dept. of Aoyama University
Seijo University[16]
I must succeed in passing exams. *If I can, I will require nothing more, not even money*. Of course, *I will not need tears any more, either*. How about that?

The above does not mean that the writer was less interested in making a fortune. A better explanation is that academic success has been such a significant hallmark of status that it was often thought of as the most important.

Thirdly, entrance exams are both high stake in their socio-economic ramification, and challenging in their encyclopaedic scope. For that reason, they need high concentration, time, effort and sacrifice on the part of students and their families. Thus, what permeated most of the *ema* was a kind of Stoic spirit, self-control and a willingness to postpone gratification:

---

[14] The academic behavioural pattern motivated by entrance exams is perhaps most demonstrated in the extracurricular activities of Asian students. See Chapter 5, 'The cram world: why so large in East Asia?'

[15] Edogawa High School, one of the top metropolitan schools in the 6th district of Tokyo. Its *hensachi* are 55–59 points.

[16] See note 6.

Example I
To pass exams and enter metropolitan high schools, to improve *hensachi* scores, please take care of me. *I will not be discouraged, not lazy, and I will be industrious in my academic life*. Please help in these also.

Example II
To enter the school of my choice, I promise:
• *Not to read comic books*
• *Not to listen to radio*
• *Not to watch TV*
Please help me to be able to achieve all those.

Example III
I will listen to my parents and study very hard. I will spend more than five hours on my work. Therefore, please absolutely, absolutely, let me enter Matsudo county High School.

It is not very clear how efficient the spirit of 'all work and no play' could be. The above does show a tendency of self-denial patterns in behaviour. This, again, suggests that to come to the shrine was not to entrust accountability to heaven entirely. On the contrary, it was an occasion on which people tried to enhance their determination. Expressions of self-sacrifice, such as *'isshyô kenmei'* (fight with all one's might, throughout one's life), *'ganbaru'* (work with perseverance), etc., are so much used that they became clichés in *ema*.[17]

Life in middle school or high school, however, did not consist only of grinding one's head on books. This was also a time of friendship, love and courtship. One *ema* carried such words:

Example
... No matter what, my God, do not let him be a lordless *rônin* (repeater) forever.
– From his lover (*koibito*). ...

To the Japanese, deferred gratification of love may not necessarily be an anticlimax. In Asian literature, as is true in real life, that may add a bittersweet taste to the romance. A true story of love recorded in *ema* is recounted by Aoki (1977). Yasuko was the girlfriend of Saito, who was in the thick of preparing for the university entrance exams. Yasuko liked Saito so much that she was considering getting married to him in the future. However, Saito had never told Yasuko which university he had chosen, because he did not want her to worry, and he promised not to see her until he passed. This left Yasuko perplexed, and she talked with her friend Kadaiko about the matter. Kadaiko assured her that Saito would never change his heart. She assured that what he needed was to devote his 'youth (*seishun*)' to his cause, his

---

[17] Amano (1993) reveals that no parent would not say *'ganbare'* to their children, particularly during the exam preparation. The phrase has turned into a word for people to greet each other (*aisatsu*). To describe this workaholic phenomenon, Amano describes Japan as *'ganbaru no sekai'*, or a 'hardworking world'.

future. As a result of their meeting, the two girls came together to a Shinto shrine and they co-authored this *ema*:

A Prayer for Academic Achievement

Saito San (Japanese for Mr) has been devoting all his young life to the university entrance exams. I, however, have no idea which university it is. ... No matter what may happen, please let Saito San study so that he can get in.
– Kadaiko
Until Saito enters into that university, and fulfils his hope, I will not stop waiting for him. In my dream, I saw we two were together, I am longing for that day.
– Yasuko

We do not know if there was a happy ending to this true story. But the sacrifice on both sides of the story as a result of the high priority of exams in life is quite clear.

Fourthly, a fact demonstrated in *ema* was that exams concern, before everything else, competition and elimination. This might be carried to a superstitious extent in students' psychology. Some students tended to hang *ema* tablets above the rest: the higher, the better. This tendency is also found in Taiwan. To register for a Guangming Lamp at Taiwan's Longshan Temple, one usually paid NT$ 600 ($23). But, the price at the top of the Lamp stand was different from that at the bottom. To buy a niche at its apex would cost a maximum of NT$ 1000 ($38). In Japan's shrine, however, there is no cost implication in putting the *ema* higher. Some students used their umbrellas to hang their *ema* tablets on the high branch of plum trees in the courtyard, although that was not really allowed.[18] When a student found another *ema* author was applying for the same university as his, he drew an arrow on his *ema* pointing in the direction of that *ema* board, and wrote: 'I will absolutely not be defeated by this neighbour of mine!'

The rite of *ema* prayer is seasonally cyclical. In Japanese Shinto, it is generally assumed that the effective life of a charm as an agent of good luck is one year. For students, the calendar runs from April to 31 March the next year. By January and February, the *ema* racks were laden heavily with *ema* of anxious prayers. After a period of silence, these were suddenly replaced by a new batch of *ema*: the Gift *ema* for success (*gôkaku orei no ema*). Those whose dream of entering college came true would return to Jinja and show their thanks to the god. In most cases, the writing on 'gift *ema*' would start with an expression of rejoicing and gratitude for the heavenly protection. Then, students would show their determination to continue working as conscientiously as before in the new school, and would request the God of Scholarship to give them further strength for doing so. This type of *ema* is described as 'killing two birds with one stone'. Etsuko, an unknown

---

[18] The plum tree in Eastern culture is a symbol of intellectual detachment and nonchalance to worldly gain. It also suggests academic attainment resulting from hard work. Probably for that reason, Shinto Temman churches often plant plum trees. History has it that Japan's God of Examinations, Sugawara Michizane, rhymed at 11 a famous line on plum flowers.

student, wrote the following to the God of Entrance Examination, as reproduced in Figure 6.9. Like it or not, entrance exams followed students like a growing shadow and drove them to study harder and harder throughout their school years, until university.

Gôkaku orei, or the Gift *ema*, differs from the Prayer *ema* in its design of graphic prints on the back of the *ema*. As discussed earlier, *ema* originated with worship of the horse. Later, the images used diversified, and demonstrated a marked characteristic of Totemism. The *ema* images of the Temman Church included buffalo, roosters, hens, etc. They have since become more of a collectively religious label, rather than an animal cult (Durkheim, 1965; Leach, 1967). They are emblems of the Sacred group, logos of an 'intellectual clan'. The Gift *ema*, then, is a sub-totem, which circumscribes a consummation after all the ordeal. Its totemic symbol is the *Daruma*, a Japanese version of the exaggerated face of Bodhidharma (? – circa 530 AD), Indian founder of Zen Buddhism.[19] His visage, though austere, is one of the most favourite and congenial to Japanese, with large, glaring eyes, heavily bearded jowls, a prominent nose, and an overall severe countenance. In Japan, the *Daruma* is a traditional image used for celebrating the attainment of a goal. In the Temman Church, the *Daruma* marks a special occasion when a cycle is fulfilled. The Dragon Gate is passed (*Tô-ryûmon*), and the Sacred and their new members come together.

The Sacred–Profane contrast of those who passed and those who did not is portrayed by Thomas Rohlen: 'The two figures, one ecstatic and the other crest-fallen, belong together. They symbolize in the popular imagination the rewards and suffering Japanese must face in the pursuit of educational distinction, which is followed by a good job, economic security, respect, and status in a technocratic world' (Rohlen, 1983: 78).

Etsuko

EMA GIFT TO GODS FOR SUCCESS (Gôkaku-orei)
I've passed the entrance exams for the Affiliated Middle School of Wayo Women's College. Thank you very much.

PRAYER & WISH (Kigan)
In the next six years, I venture to solicit your blessing again so that I can make progress successfully and graduate from my high school.

Figure 6.9 An example of the written content in the Japanese *ema* gift given to the Examination God.

---

[19] Whether *Daruma* was a historical person or just a creature of imagination is the subject of a rather sterile scholarly dispute. So-called biographies in Chinese sources are too sketchy and too late in composition to provide reliable evidence of his career. One the other hand, there are no compelling reasons to doubt the existence in sixth-century China of a venerable Indian monk named Bodhidharma who made seminal contributions to the redirection of Buddhism. For further details, see McFarland (1987).

When those who made it come back to the shrine to express their gratitude, their joy is not hard to understand. After all the work that 'de-humanized' and 'alienated' the candidates for quite some time, life became colourful once more, free from severe competition, anxiety and tribulation.

One 1994 issue of the Sundai journal, *Ascent*, reported interviews with students at the Tokyo Yushima Shrine after the exams were over. They were asked about their feelings and their motives in visiting the shrine.[20] Standing in the tranquil, breezy open space of the shrine, they all felt elated. The past year that had engaged them so tensely was over like a trance.

One student being interviewed was Yoki, a boy of 19, now a student in the Maths Department of Japan University. At first, he thought so badly of the mistakes he made in the exams that he did not even bother to go and check his exam scores. Nevertheless, he was accepted by all five universities of his choice. He went to the university, browsed around, fascinated by everything he saw. He was especially impressed by how clean the restrooms were. At the shrine, he said that his success did not come from fate (*un*) but from the 'solid power' (*jitsuryoku*). Nevertheless, standing on the sacred field, in the middle of the bronze *tori'i* (the *inari*-style gate), the weather-beaten *Toshogu* (the main sanctuary of a shrine), the age-old plum trees and the cooing flock of doves, he said he felt like floating in the ethereal air. Yoki hoped his university would make him a maths teacher.

Junko, an 18-year-old female student of International Relations in Tsudajuku University,[21] was another typical Japanese disclaimer. She said she did not have much confidence of success, either. However, she was accepted by five out of the seven universities to which she applied, and Tsudajuku was her first choice. This was what she articulated at the shrine:

No sooner did I see my student number [on the board] than I started to cry for joy. I went immediately to a play, *The Four Seasons of an Opera Troupe*. I enjoyed myself immensely. I had wanted to see it for a long time. But I could not afford to go until I passed the exams. At the university, I will work hard at my English and German, and my dream of travelling around the world using my own foreign languages will come true.

Keiko, a female student of 19, was a first-year student of American-English Literature, Aoyama Gakuin University. Her motto in life was 'work hard, play hard'. At the shrine, like everybody else, she bought a gift *ema*, and tied it up on the *ema* stand in homage. She promised that at university she would study hard at her favourite subject: Western Literature. She also wished to make a lot of friends on campus. She felt that her life had been narrow indeed, and now it was time to widen it.

To those who succeeded, the experience felt like the rite of passage. They were ecstatic, even though the school might not be élite and the job would

---

[20] The following interviews were taken from Sundai monthly journal, *Ascent* 20: 4 (14 May 1994), 3–5.

[21] Tsudajuku University, located in Kodaira City. Founded in 1900 as a girls' school.

not be that rewarding. And yet, despite their symbolism, the exams were not an empty ritual: a larger percentage of students failed.

The *ema* are not meant to be displayed in the shrine for ever. Each year, when an exam season is over, they will be ritually burnt (*Otakiage*), and the racks will soon be laden with new cypress-made totems and new wishes. This circulation pumps life, money and faith into Shintoist meritocracy. In the Tokyo Yushima Shrine, a new temple hall, far more solemn and stately, is currently under construction. According to the plan, this new hall will be put into use in 1996, which just happens to mark the 1150th posthumous birthday of Japan's God of Exams, Sugawara Michizane.

A DISCUSSION

This chapter scrutinizes the entrance exam system and its effects in the light of religion, which is not customarily employed in the study of East Asian education. In this endeavour, an interpretative key to the religious component of meritocracy I detected is the sacred–profane dichotomy, the primary classification of society in religion (Durkheim, 1965; Caillois, 1959). 'It is the basic idea of religion,' writes Henri Hubert. 'Myths and dogmas characteristically comprise its content, ritual reflects its qualities, religious ethics derive from it, priesthoods embody it, sanctuaries, holy places and religious monuments enshrine it and enroot it' (Caillois, 1959). That bifurcation brings religion and the entrance exam system together with a common value system, as schematized in Figure 6.5.

Like religious affiliation, the effort devoted to the exam system argues for the sanctification of meritocratic grouping in society. By going to church, a student is aligned to, and becomes a reserve member of, the sacred 'Clan'. Those gods are role models in the 'Clan', and students who enter university constitute its broad membership. To evoke spiritual force, and to obtain membership of the Sacred, is the religious dimension of exam competion between Pass and No-Pass. This has significant potential for academic motivation, and religious affiliation tends to correlate powerfully with behaviour and attitude.

The sanctification of the meritocratic effort and fate can be dated back to the pre-modern era. It is a part of the time-honoured tradition in local culture. The churches, deities and priests (mainly in Japan) are serving the new generation as they have done for about a millennium. Only the universalization of schooling breathed new life on an unprecedented scale into the classical religion.

The symbiosis between the merit system and religion is observable in the three countries. Most of the students from Japan, Korea and Taiwan I talked with acknowledged visiting the church, either going themselves or having their parents/friends go on their behalf, for evoking sacred power and consolation in the face of entrance exams.[22] While the important role of

---

[22] The people I interviewed concerning the visit to church for entrance exams include students of Keio University in Japan, students of Fu Jen University in Taiwan, and some Japanese, Korean or Taiwanese students or teachers who were at Stanford University.

religion is very similar in the three meritocratic societies, how that role is played out differs immensely. The complexity and differences are shown in the list given in Table 6.2. This is not an exhaustive source for the institutional structure of exam-related religions in Japan, Korea and Taiwan. It only shows the rich complexity of the religious practices that have stemmed from the meritocratic tradition in Asia. Noteworthy here is the high degree of theological specialization of the sects, deities, monasteries, talismans and religious objects in Japan and Taiwan in different ways, but not in Korea. That specialization is summarized in Table 6.3.

As shown in Table 6.3, exam-related religions differ in form in the three countries, although there is no difference in the nature of their services. The variety of specific occult materials, such as protective charms, as well as the totem imagery is abundant and unique in the Japanese Shintoist service. No parallel is found in either Korea or Taiwan. Taiwanese, on the other hand, have inherited many of their meritocratic deities from mainland China. That polytheism has resulted from, first, the peculiar features of Chinese religion. The populace prayed to different gods for different purposes (Yang, 1961). It is also attributable to the centuries-old history of the *keju* civil service exam system. The data also show that religious activities attuned to exams are not specialized in Korea, unlike in Japan or Taiwan. Parents or students usually go to Western churches or Buddhist temples.

The forms of religious activities for high-stake exams differ immensely between Japan, Korea and Taiwan. The main religions and deities patronized are totally different in the three countries, and their religious objects and services have little in common. Confucianism, though dynamic in the three countries as an undergirding mentality, did not serve as a major religion in this regard. The emergence of religious services dovetailed to the merit system was almost independent within the three countries, although they serve the same function.

This study suggests that exam-centred religious forms stemmed from local religions. Therefore, they are largely defined by the religions they are affiliated to, such as Shinto and Chinese polytheist religion. For that reason, in comparison to the entrance exams *per se*, which have a lot in common in their systemic structure, the exam-related supernatural activities are as different in their pattern as the aboriginal religions. If there is any common denominator among these activities, it would be that each of them is a corollary of the high-stake exam system.

Confucianism has been a value system for East Asian meritocracy in both theory and *praxis*. It laid down the structural principles for developing the exam system through which people were raised to power and prestige on the basis of achievement, at least in ideal, rather than birth. Nonetheless, orthodox Confucianism, as C. K. Yang concedes, 'is not a full-fledged theistic religion, since it poses no god or supernatural dogma as the symbol of its teachings' (Yang, 1961: 224). Historically, the Confucian literati were not interested in breaking away from irksome mundane life. In spite of its religio-mystical garb, Confucianism was marked with rationalistic and agnostic qualities. It also fell short of systematic revelation or futurism. Apart from an incorporated Buddhist-world salvational spirit, throughout Chinese history there have been no Confucian churches, priesthood or creed (Chan, 1953: 15). As a result, Confucius is far less deified, and has thus less supernatural force to offer to exam-taking students.

Table 6.2 The main features of exam-related religions and their services, Japan, Korea and Taiwan. *Source*: My compilation.

	Japan	Taiwan	Korea
Religion	• Shintoism • Buddhism • Confucianism	• Chinese polytheism • Buddhism • Confucianism	• Buddhism • Christianity • Confucianism
Church institution	• *Temmangu* temple • Buddhist temple • Confucian temple	• *Wenchang* temple • Buddhist temple • Confucian temple	• Buddhist temple • Christian church • Confucian temple
Deity	• God of Exams: Sugawara Michizane	• God of Scholarship: Zhang Ya • Stellar Deity: *Kuixing* • Mr Redcoat: Zhu Xi • Mr Golden Armour	• Buddha • Christ
Priesthood	• Special priests in Temmangu Palace	• No special priest	• No special priest
Scriptures	• Special prayers	• No special prayer	• No special prayer
Totem	• Different animals, scenarios, humans, etc., printed on *ema*	• Buddhist image	
Occult objects	• Painted horse (*ema*) • Headband (*Hachimaki*) • Charms (*Omamori*) • Pencil set for scholarly achievement (*Gakugyô jôju enpitsu*) • Praying Holy Seal (*Kigan shinji*) • Gratitude gift to God (*Gôkaku orei*) • Exorcizing arrow (Hamaya)	• Brilliance lamp (*Guangming deng*) • Charms (*Omamori*)	• Special Buddhist beads/rosary

Table 6.3 A summary of specialization of exam-related religions and their services, Japan, Korea and Taiwan. *Source*: My compilation.

	Japan	Taiwan	Korea
Religion	+	+	−
Church	+	+	−
Deity	+	+ + + +	−
Priesthood	+	−	−
Prayer	+	−	−
Totem	+ + + + + +	+	−
Occult objects	+ + + + + +	+ +	+

Note: + indicates scale of specialization. − indicates no specialization.

In all three countries, Confucius is enshrined. And the architecture of his temples is spectacular, sublime and well funded. Yet, as I observed, they were much secluded, and their 'business' was slack compared to elsewhere. The Confucian temples fall short of 'powerful' occult services, especially divination, which have been the main reason of all the bustle and rustle in other churches. The voice uttered in the name of the gods tends to resolve an emotional conflict and produce confidence (Yang, 1961). In Taiwan, for instance, when the entrance exams are finally over in July, the fortune-tellers, palm-readers, astrologers and oracles suddenly become hectic and overwhelmed by anxious examinees or parents. During the brief period before notification, their clients want them to figure out their score results, and the probability of their college life (ZS, 20 July 1995).

This book attempts to illustrate how the merit systems motivated the young generation to work hard. The number of people who resorted to religious power for exams has been on the rise, although no statistics have ever been collected about that frequency. Our fragmentary knowledge is therefore predicated mainly on mass media coverage, the scholars' estimation, and my own observations. Some evidence lends support to my proposition that sacred protection for exams has been a top priority in the wishes of the worshippers. Most college students that I talked with have had the experience of visiting temples for their entrance exams at certain phases of their schooling, either by their families or themselves.

In a broad sense, religion is the reference of life to divine power. For the entrance exams, that reference is expected to generate spiritual guidance, confidence and consolation. In Japan, Korea and Taiwan, the evocation of the occult force for exams is based on the individual or on the family instead of socially organized. But its institutionalization and the great commonality found among students' behavioural patterns justify the present study as a socio-cultural thesis rather than a psychological one.

The religious aspect of the study opens up the possibility of revealing how the entrance exams influenced young people, which is hardly assessable otherwise. The obstacle comes from the so-called '*tatemae–honne*' difference of 'truth'. *Tatemae* refers to the way things are presented, or official motives, the facade. *Honne* is, in contrast, genuine motives, observed reality, the truth one knows or senses. While this double standard may be taken as a necessary morality, it may also be treated as hypocrisy or 'socially sanctioned deceit' (Condon and Saito, 1974; van Wolferen, 1990). At any rate, there is a great gap between reality and how it is presented in Japan. In the other two East Asian countries, we see less fondness for unanimous agreement, but the *tatemae–honne* disparity is still true in terms of the great differ-ence between reality and how it is presented. For an outsider, therefore, *tatemae* becomes an impermeable wall, behind which lies hidden what has been going on, and what has been really at work, the *honne*.

If we keep in mind that particular cultural dilemma, the Japanese *ema* (painted horse) is truly a blessing. It is telltale, gaining us insight into what we wish to know about the effects of university entrance exams. Its value lies in its frankness, which makes it possible to fathom the *honne*, the truth. The *ema* is not meant for publication. Instead, it records in telegraphic brevity its author's utmost wishes, unfettered by censorship or social norm.

The *ema* shows that, due to their perceived rewarding function, and their dramatic effect in shaping individual destinies, exams have become a highly symbolized system, a conspicuous focus of attention, even of unpopularity, but impossible to abolish. Partially for that reason, the exam system is powerfully correlated to academic behaviour.

Secondly, '*honne*', or the candidness of the author's real thoughts, marked the content of *ema*. Without much need of a persona mask, *ema* displayed a gamut of real feelings as exams came near: fear, anxiety, stress, strain and disillusionment.

Thirdly, the entrance exams are both high-stake in their socio-economic ramification, and challenging in their encyclopaedic scope. For that reason, they need high concentration, time, effort and sacrifice on the part of the students and their families. Thus, what permeated most of the *ema* was a kind of Stoic spirit, self-control and a willingness to postpone gratification.

Fourthly, a truism demonstrated in *ema* was that exams were about competition and elimination. This might be carried to a superstitious extent in students' psychology. In *The Life of Reason: Reason in Society*, George Santayana contends: 'The combative instinct is a savage prompting by which one man's good is found in another's evil.' The competition engendered by universalistic rules for education embraces an unprecedented number of contestants. As a result, elimination, and the fear of it, almost seems to be inevitable.

Overall, what we have found is a cultural continuity for students to invoke the Gods of Examinations as a result of the traditional emphasis on education and the high-stake association of the meritocratic system of exams with social mobility. The study demonstrates the great importance of exams and reinforces belief in their significance. By literally opening to all a pathway to success, this system has tapped the spiritual strength and dynamics that help to reaffirm the veneration for learning, to renew the intellectual profile of the new generation, and to recast the meritocratic core of the élite.

Is religion an inexorable companion of the merit system of exams? The independent development of cult patterns in Japan, Korea and Taiwan seems to suggest a positive answer. It might also be useful to look at what has happened in Mainland China. There, though pseudo-meritocratic access to university had been set up in the late 1970s, it has since been elusive and vulnerable, heavily swayed by erratic political situations. Nonetheless, compared to earlier times, the social ladder via university has been taken as a regular avenue to a hopeful and decent life. According to the report of a Taiwanese correspondent, there has been a surging trend (*weiwei fengchao*) of religiosity amid middle school students in Mainland China (ZR, 9 July 1995). Many students became interested in praying to gods for augury (*qiushen wengua*) or consulting the diagrams in the classic Confucian work of divination, *The Book of Changes* (*yijing*), for guidance. Among them, most did it for their entrance exams (*kaoshang lixiang-Daxüe*). In a Hangzhou-bound tour group that was interviewed by chance, for instance, 40 per cent of the group were pilgrims who were not there for scenic wonder or other pleasure.[23] The specific purpose was to pay homage to Buddhas for their children's success in entrance exams. In a Communist regime, where the freedom of religion had been virtually deracinated, the advent or revival of meritocratic cults suggests that, when a screening system's high stakes are so relentless and impartial, an appeal to the supernatural is always needed in one form or another.

---

[23] Hangzhou, the capital of Zhejiang Province, famous for its scenic spots and religious temples, often considered as one of the most beautiful cities in China.

CHAPTER 7

Time, effort and money: mobilizing private resources to gain social status

The elementary actor is the wellspring of action, no matter how complex are the structures through which action takes place.
– *James S. Coleman,* Foundations of Social Theory, *1990*

Nothing comes from nothing.
– *Lucretius,* On the Nature of Things, *first cent.* BC

As time goes on, new and remoter aspects of truth are discovered, which can seldom or never be fitted into creeds that are changeless.
– *Clarence Day,* This Simian World, *1920*

The level of educational achievement in Japan has been long known, and well discussed (Rohlen, 1983; Lynn, 1988; Stevenson and Stigler, 1992; Medrich and Griffith, 1992). On international tests of both science and maths, for instance, Japanese mean scores are higher than those of any other country. The degree of variation in ability among Japanese students is also shown to be very low, meaning that equality of achievement is notable (Rohlen, 1983: 3).

The achievements of Taiwanese and Korean children, however, are much less known, and less researched. For that reason, I reproduce some essential statistics (see Figure 1.1). The data in Figure 1.1 are based on the 1991 International Assessment of Educational Progress (IAEP) Tests, in which fifteen countries, mostly Western, participated. Among 13-year-olds, Koreans and Taiwanese tied for first place in maths. In science, Koreans were placed first, followed by Taiwan. Among 9-year-olds, South Koreans were placed first in maths, with Taiwan in third place. In science, South Koreans were again placed first, followed by Taiwan.

From the series of assessments sponsored by various sources, what is generalizable for Japan, Korea and Taiwan appears to be the great similarity in their world rankings. It indicates that the salient achievement is not limited to Japan alone: it is an 'East Asian phenomenon'. That academic pre-eminence evokes a question that sparked off this chapter: why did the students from those three countries have high achievement? To answer this, I examine in a cross-national perspective two essential variables in this chapter. One can be termed as the 'capital factor', which refers to the investment in education and the economic status. The other is the 'labour factor', which measures how much effort and/or time students exert on their academic work. This pair of variables, labelled, in economic terminology, as investment and inputs, will be used for the analyses both at the international dimension and within a particular society.

By analogy or metaphor, or a blend of both, education is valued by many educators as a scarce commodity (Blaug, 1976). It can be a consumption good or a production good (Phillips, 1992). Partially following that human-capital approach, I intend to find out (1) is there more time and money invested in East Asia? (2) is this due to the exam system? (3) what can money buy? (4) how much money and time are 'wasted'? (5) what combination of time, money, ability and location is optimal? (6) how does the gender factor work? Underlying these questions are two major concerns. First, how much of achievement is attributable to money: how far is education purchasable through family expenditure, and how much is achievement affected by economic status, such as income level? Second, how far is achievement composed of human labours, for example measured by the labour hours allocated to school-instruction, homework and extracurricular study? The second concern underscores the fact that students have an active role to play in their own education. Their family milieu, their environment, their social grouping, and so forth, are very informative about what they will be. On the other hand, students are not incarcerated by that 'ecology' in a deterministic fashion. How the ascribed and achieved factors played their parts to forge the education outcome in East Asia is one theme of this chapter.

In approaching that theme, one must bear in mind that education is context-specific. In our cases of Japan, Korea and Taiwan, the entrance exams form such a context. While this context resembles a setting, the students are the '*dramatis personae*', the term used by Thomas Rohlen (1983) in describing students in education. The earlier chapters dealt mainly with that setting. In this chapter, however, the spotlight will be placed on the *dramatis personae*. In so doing, I give some special attention to the '*rônin* (Japanese warrior without lord)', or repeaters for university entrance exams. This is a phenomenon found not only in Japan, but also in Korea and Taiwan (k. *Jai su saeng*; c. *Chonkao sheng*). Given the paramountcy of access to higher education as a mobility path, each year a large number of students became '*rônin*'. In 1990, for example, there were 820,000 *rônin* altogether in Japan, Korea and Taiwan, accounting for more than one-third of the total number of university applicants. The issue of *rônin* has drawn grave social concerns. Is the exam-driven behavioural pattern a manifestation of the power of money? Or an act-out of meritocratic virtue? Or, perhaps both?

In tradition, the question posed here is tangentially related to the comparative importance of ascribed and achieved status in determining access to higher learning, a key concern in the world of education. Ascribed status refers to gender, place of residence and socio-economic background, and achieved status is often symbolized by the achievement scores. Stratification research, in this regard, is an untiring quest to ascertain whether the influence of family background declines with modernization and mass education, or conversely, it is stable or increases. Bourdieu and Passeron (1964, 1977), Boudon (1974) and Collins (1971, 1979) argue for cultural and economic reproduction, as inequalities between classes and status groups combine to produce educational inequalities among their children. Educational credentials therefore mirror the class structure and help legitimize inequality of job opportunity. On the other hand, Lenski (1966), Parsons (1970) and Treiman (1970) posit the lowering of financial and social thresholds, suggesting that education plays an increasingly important role in the process of status attainment. Today, these two perspectives – customarily labelled as reproduction and modernization theories – diverge mainly on the mobility of the higher-level educational hierarchy rather than the lower.

Two caveats are necessary here. First, this chapter is not a meta-analysis of the mobility-stratification of the society at large. Instead, given the nature of my study, it is only confined to the mobility pathway via the university entrance system. For that reason, previous stratification studies are sifted, but they are cited only when relevant to that focus. Second, my analysis attempts to explain achievement not only on the basis of the effects of such conditions as social background and educational expenditure. 'Labour hours', i.e., measurement of time on work, is also taken as an essential factor. Input of labour is vitally important in the economic production function (Blaug, 1976). However, in the economics of education, the labour variable is seldom factored into the model, although theoretically it should have been (Carroll, 1963; Carroll and Spearritt, 1967; Levin, in Bidwell and Windham, 1980). To express the division of students as a result of the two variables, I have the configuration shown in Table 7.1. Simply, Cell 1 refers to hard-working 'rich' children, Cell 2 is the hard-working 'poor' children, Cell 3 is 'rich' children who do not study hard, and Cell 4 is 'poor' children who do not study hard. We are pretty certain that Cell 1 (rich children working hard) would succeed, and Cell 4 (poor children that do not study) would fail. To test the modernization against reproduction hypotheses, what interest me more perhaps are Cells 2 and 3: Can 'poor' children offset their background through more serious study? And, will 'rich' children still succeed without studying hard for the entrance exams?

Table 7.1 Categorizing students according to parents' economic status and students' effort.

Parents' economic status

		High	Low
Students' efforts	High	1	2
	Low	3	4

In the following pages, I first discuss students' time allocation to study in Japan, Korea and Taiwan in contrast to some other countries, mainly Western. I then turn to the *rônin* population, examining their failure, their lifetime decision to repeat, and their time allocation. Next, I study how much students are financed by state and family. Finally, I discuss how effort and money work together as a pair of major factors in the process of inter-generational status transmission.

SEIZE THE DAY, SEIZE THE HOUR: TIME AS A FACTOR IN STUDENTS' ACADEMIC LIFE

A round man cannot be expected to fit a square hole right away. He must have time to modify his shape.
– *Mark Twain*, Following the Equator

One crucial factor in achievement is how much time students spend on study. Extensive studies have also been conducted on the correlation between the amount of time on academic work and their results, which generally confirm that the positive correlation between time/effort and achievement is as valid for the Asian as it is for the American. A study of time on school work in 15 Western countries indicates a high correlation between hours of homework/instruction and achievement (Passow, 1976). In the United States, Paschal *et al.* (1984) state after an analysis of 15 studies that homework had a positive effect on academic achievement, especially when commented and graded. More recently, based on an extensive 70 correlation studies through manipulated experiment, Cooper (1989) could report a positive relationship between homework and attainment. It is observed that the gains at high school level were higher than at the junior high and elementary levels. One of these researches was done by T. Keith utilizing the massive High School and Beyond dataset (Keith, 1982). Analysis of the 1989 A-level Information System (ALIS) has found that for A-level students, the amount of homework is positively correlated with their grades, even when students of the same ability were compared, and there is no evidence of variation across socio-economic groupings (Tymms, 1992). The findings from 20 years of the National Assessment of Educational Progress (NAEP, 1988) further confirms that the amount of reading that students did for school was positively related to their reading proficiency. In Table 7.2, Grade-12 average proficiency in the subjects assessed in 1988 is analysed according to the amount of time spent on homework. The results show a 'consistent, positive relationship between proficiency and the amount of time spent on homework. The startling fact remains, however, that more than two-thirds (71 per cent) of the high school seniors typically do one hour or less of homework each day' (NAEP, 1988: 74–5).

In Japan, the association between time on work and academic achievement is indicated in the 1992 FKK Research Institution Survey of 2450 middle school students.

As the FKK Survey shows, to achieve very good scores, 40.2 per cent of students studied 1–2 hours per day, and 35.8 per cent had to study 2–5 hours or even more.

Table 7.2 Average proficiency by the amount of time spent on homework per day, 1988: Grade 12 in American schools. *Source*: National Assessment of Educational Progress, *America's Challenge: Accelerating Academic Achievement: A Summary of Findings from 20 Years of NAEP* (Washington, DC: US Department of Education, 1990), 75.

Time on homework daily	Percentage of students	Reading (0–500)	Writing (0–400)	US history (0–500)	Civics (0–500)
None assigned	9	269 (2.6)	210 (3.3)	281 (2.0)	281 (2.4)
Did not do	9	281 (2.4)	202 (2.9)	292 (2.5)	285 (3.2)
1 hour or less	53	288 (1.8)	225 (1.7)	296 (1.4)	298 (1.8)
2 hours	19	293 (1.6)	232 (2.5)	299 (1.6)	302 (1.6)
More than 2 hours	10	296 (2.4)	236 (2.8)	302 (3.5)	304 (2.4)

In the low achiever group, 57.8 per cent studied less than one hour. In the two studies introduced above, one in the US, the other in Japan, the association of time on work with achievement scores is manifest. With that association in sight, we next study time devoted to schooling, to school-assigned homework, and to other extracurricular activities as directly germane to strengthening academic proficiency.

It is not immediately apparent, as Clark Sorensen (1994) remarks, why children in South Korea and Taiwan should be so successful in science and maths. Neither subject is a traditional strength of East Asian intelligentsia.

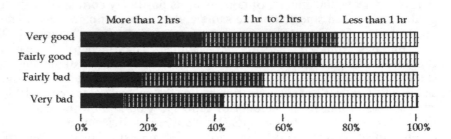

Figure 7.1 Time on academic study per day and the achievement scores, by the percentage of middle school students, 1992. *Source*: Based on Fukutake Shoten Kyôiku Kenkyûjo, *Monografu: Chûgakusei no Sekai* (Monograph: The world of middle school students), Vol. 43, *Tsukareteiru Chûgakusei* (Exhausted middle school students), (Tokyo: Fukutake Shoten Kyôiku Kenkyûjo, 1993), 18–21.

In the meantime, while 'lip service' has long been given to education in those countries, there has been a stark disparity between rhetoric and reality in terms of state commitment to education, which I will discuss in the section on educational expenditure. These reasons justify a close scrutiny of time and effort institutionalized by the education/examination system.

Instruction, school-assigned homework, and other extracurricular activities, especially in *juku*

In the modern world, instruction in school has been the primary method of academic learning. Modern school teaches a real sense of time in terms of an extraordinary need for regularity that centres on the clock. In school this is especially embodied in the school calendar and schedule:

> Time is thoroughly segmented and defined, with the curriculum serving as the central gear in a complex machine of time-compartmentalized activities. Because time is precious, order is reinforced, and social organization achieves a high level of immutability. (Rohlen, 1983)

The universality of mass education and growing interest in creating statistics at the international level have made it possible to compare schooling worldwide. Japanese go to school for 60 days more each year than their American counterparts; using the American five-day week as a standard, this means that Japanese students get three months' more schooling each year. Altogether, over the twelve years of elementary and secondary education, the Japanese student receives four more years of schooling (Rohlen, 1983).

For the Korean and Taiwanese students, the IAEP data furnish a reliable resource for wide international comparison of time used for instruction (see Table 7.3). In Table 7.3, the calendars of East Asian countries are longer than other countries. That discrepancy probably resulted from the same reason as raised by Rohlen, as just cited. East Asian countries used more days for school instruction than Western countries.

Table 7.3 Average days' instruction in school for 13-year-olds in selected countries, 1991. *Source*: US Department of Education, *Digest of Education Statistics 1993* (Washington, DC: US Government Printing Office, 1993), 414.

Country	Average days in school year	Average minutes of instruction in school day	Total time (by hour)[a]
Korea	**222 (2.5)**[b]	**264 (2.4)**	**976.8 h**
Taiwan	**222 (2.5)**	**318 (6.9)**	**1176.6 h**
England	192 (1.8)	300 (4.4)	960.0 h
France	174 (1.7)	370 (3.4)	1073.0 h
Israel	215 (2.2)	278 (6.5)	996.2 h
Spain	188 (2.3)	285 (3.2)	893.0 h
US	178 (0.4)	338 (5.0)	1002.7 h

Notes: a. My calculation based on the data given. b. Standard errors appear in parentheses.

Table 7.4 An international comparison: hours for school-assigned homework, weekly quiz, and IAEP maths scores for 13-year-olds in selected countries, 1991. *Source*: US Department of Education: *Digest of Education Statistics 1993* (Washington, DC: US Government Printing Office, 1993), 414.

Country	Average per cent correct on IAEP maths test	Students with 2 hours or more homework daily	Students who take a science quiz at least once a week
Korea	**73 (0.6)**	**41 (1.7)**	**17 (1.0)**
Taiwan	**73 (0.7)**	**41 (1.3)**	**32 (1.1)**
France	64 (0.8)	55 (1.6)	81 (1.0)
Israel	63 (0.8)	50 (1.9)	36 (2.2)
Canada	62 (0.6)	27 (1.0)	50 (1.1)
Spain	55 (0.8)	64 (1.5)	31 (1.7)
US	55 (1.0)	29 (1.6)	90 (1.1)

Note: Standard errors appear in parentheses.

What may deserve our further attention is that, due to the difference in daily schedule, Korea and Taiwan, although known for the high academic achievement of their children, did not necessarily keep students in the classroom for longer hours. The total instruction hours for Korea are less than France, Israel, Spain and even the US.

When we compare time spent on school homework, we have some similar findings, as shown in Table 7.4.

The two East Asian countries achieved much higher scores than the others in IAEP maths test, yet their students did not necessarily spend more time on school-assigned homework. The proportions of Korean and Taiwanese with more than two hours on maths were less than France, Israel and Spain. Also, surprisingly, Koreans and Taiwanese took fewer weekly quizzes than most of the other countries, including the US.

To sum up the two sets of time data here, we see that time spent by East Asians was more than that spent by the Americans, but not necessarily so as compared to the other European countries. Put otherwise, comparatively East Asian kids did not necessarily spend more time in school or on their school assignments in a global context. Still, they achieved decisively higher results than most of the rest.

One set of data that was significantly missing in the IAEP survey is extracurricular activities besides the homework assigned by school. In this regard, a practice prevailing in Japan, Korea and Taiwan but seldom found elsewhere is the highly institutionalized, out-of-school tutoring or cramming at *juku* academies. Other extracurricular activities, such as private tutoring, video-audio aids and regular mock examinations, did exist and generated a large business. But cram schools were far more tangible and important for our investigation. The large attendance ratio of students in prep schools is discussed in Chapter 4. What I need to investigate here, however, is how much time did students in East Asia spend attending cram schools? The data in Table 7.5 are for middle school students in Japan.

In Korea, the overheated competition for university entrance exams affects local students perhaps even more than metropolitan children. As indicated in Table 7.6, the *hakwon* attendance ratio may be high in almost all parts of Korea.

What I may sum up briefly from the above is that cramming for entrance exams, especially in the *juku*, but also in other forms, consumes a considerable amount of time. This is unparalleled in many other countries in its popularity, institutionalization and perseverance. This is a significant missing datum in the IAEP survey results. The contrast would become salient with this part of the timetable if cramming were counted. Jon Woronoff (1990), a sober critic of Japanese education, puts it thus:

> During the school year, there is the normal homework, which can amount to two or three hours a day. On top of that, any special courses in cram or prep schools, which can add another hour or two a day plus, for the most determined, Saturday and Sunday during the final phase. Nowhere in the world do you find kids who spend half that much time. So they cannot help but 'learn' a lot. (113)

Table 7.5 The hours used per day by middle school students who attended *juku* studies, Japan, 1976, 1985. *Source*: JMOE: *Jidô Seito no Gakkôgai Gakushû Katsudô ni kansuru Jittai Chôsa Hôkokusho* (Survey of the extracurricular activities of children/students), (Tokyo: Ministry of Education 1985), 12.

Year	Less than 1 hour	1–2 hours	2–3 hours	More than 3 hours
1976	11.8%	75.7%	21.3%	2.5%
1985	10.8%	66.6%	25.5%	5.1%

Note: Because there were students who attended more than one *juku*, the total of the percentage exceeds 100.

Table 7.6 Hours used weekly for cramming practice by middle and high school students in Korea, 1990–1. *Source*: Se-Ho Shin *et al.*, *A Study on Private Tutoring in Korea* (Seoul: Korea Education Development Institute, 1991), 74–5.

School level	Capital Seoul	Big cities	General cities	Local counties	National average
Middle School[a]	6 h 17 min.	6 h 30 min.	6 h 46 min.	7 h 32 min.	6 h 46 min.
High School[b]	6 h 10 min.	7 h 10 min.	6 h 10 min.	7 h 6 min.	6 h 49 min.

Notes: a. Data for 1991. b. Data for 1990.

Table 7.7 An international comparison: total hours used daily for out-of-school academic studies at age 10–13, by percentage of students, 1979. *Source*: Based on Sôrifu (Office of Japanese Prime Minister), *Kokusai Hikaku: Nihon no Kodomo to Hahaoya* (International comparison: Japanese children and mothers), (Tokyo: Sôrifu, 1981), cited in Keimei Kenkyûkai, *Kyôshi no tame no Data-Bank* (Databook for teachers), (Tokyo: Keimei Kenkyûkai, 1987), 18-9.

Country	More than 3 hours	2 hours	1 hour	Less than 30 mins	No time
Japan	20.1	30.9	32.9	13.0	3.1
Korea	15.5	35.9	35.4	11.4	1.0
US	4.7	21.5	47.8	20.4	5.6
France	3.5	18.5	49.7	25.3	3.0
UK	3.9	15.4	46.5	23.0	10.7
Thailand	5.1	17.0	39.5	31.9	6.6

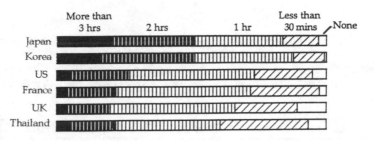

Figure 7.2 An international comparison: total hours used daily for out-of-school academic studies at age 10–13, by percentage of students, 1979. *Source*: Ibid.

The same can be generalized to the children in the three countries under review. Compared to the entire hours used out of school for academic matters, as shown in Table 7.7, Asian students worked much longer. These data are plotted in Figure 7.2.

The foregoing study puts a spotlight on the effects of high-stake exams in extracting time from students in East Asia. I now start my clarification by discussing entrance exams as a powerful motivation, which is in part responsible for making East Asian children Parkinsonian students.

Exams as a motivation to study

Achievement motivation has been an important theme in educational productivity research and theories (Fyans, 1980). Recent large-scale empirical research (Uguroglu and Walberg, 1979) in America suggests that motivation is a highly consistent positive correlate of achievement but that it is associated with only about 11 per cent of the variance in achievement on average. This is because, first of all, an array of other factors were also at work, such as socio-economic status, family investment, innate ability, etc. Secondly, motivation, in the final analysis, is only a willingness to act. It does not count much unless and until one sets motivation into motion. Only through time and effort can the motivation-to-motion link be connected. The three traits of motivated behaviour, especially persistence, are no more than time and effort.

For East Asian students, test anxiety may affect motivation in terms of direction, intensity and persistence. Here, we must bear in mind the interplay of factors for learning. For instance, exams motivate not only students, but also family and school, which, in turn, creates conditions for them through a better environment for study, and financial and academic support. These factors often function as a catalyst, and they won't take effect unless combined with students' own time and effort. Rohlen (1983) succinctly revealed the difference in time utilization between Japanese and American students. R. Lynn, Stevenson and Stigler, and M. Barrett basically pursued this line of inquiry. Time utilization is often treated as one of the crucial factors of achievement, and used as an index for cross-country comparison.

Higher achievement is correlated to different sources of motivation. A six-country study of student motivation underscores the effects of different motivations to learn in Japan (see Table 7.8).

In an effort to pinpoint the source that compelled students to absorb knowledge instead of having a more enjoyable time, an investigation was made to compare elementary school students who needed to take exams for middle school and those who did not. Such study points to a bifurcation of lifestyles of children, as suggested in Table 7.9. Exams, as reflected in Table 7.9, applied a vital brake upon students' daily behaviour. They had to have less sleep, watch less TV, and go to bed later, in order to spare enough time for the entrance exams. The experience of Haruko, a Japanese female student from Kyoto whom I interviewed, is a testimony to that different lifestyle. While in elementary school, she had to work hard for two or three hours a day before she could enter a very good private middle school. In the last year of elementary school, she attended a Spartan *juku*, the best in Kyoto. Then, she always needed to achieve highly, because, perhaps as an extreme case of *juku*, corporal punishment was waiting for a low achiever. A *juku* student whose test scores went below 85 percentage points would be spanked three times with a ruler by a male teacher. The private middle school she entered was an 'escalator'. As a result, she said that she did not work or cram all the way through both middle and high schools. It carried her eventually into university.

The compelling effect of entrance exams can also be seen in the marked contrast in the time spent on work before and after the entrance exams. Figure 7.3 compares study hours at different levels of schooling.

As shown in Figure 7.3, a Japanese college student spent only half the time that middle or high school students used for study. In fact, he or she studied even less than an elementary school student. This phenomenon finds its striking parallel in both Korea and Taiwan.

Table 7.8 Scale correlation between three main motivations and higher achievement for Japanese students. *Source*: Based on H. Azuma *et al.*, 'Student learning orientation: The Japanese study', chapter 6 in *Why Do Students Learn? A Six-Country Study of Student Motivation*, edited by SLOG (Brighton, England: Institute of Development Studies at the University of Sussex, 1987), 99.

| | *Higher achievement* | | | | |
| | *Sex* | | *School type* | | |
	Males	*Females*	*Public*	*Private*	*Pooled data*
Extrinsic motivation	**0.51**	**0.51**	**0.50**	**0.49**	**0.49**
Intrinsic motivation	0.31	0.17	0.26	0.28	0.26
Parental expectation	0.34	0.34	0.32	0.35	0.34

Note: the study was conducted at Grades 8 and 11 in both private and public schools, Tokyo and Hiroshima. Total student subjects for sampling is N = 733 (390 males and 343 females).

Table 7.9 A comparison of daily schedule: students who needed to take exams for entering middle school versus students who did not. *Source*: Data based on FKK, *Monografu: Shôgakusei*, Vol. 11-8, (Tokyo: Fukutake Shoten Kyôiku Kenkyûjo, 1991); cited in *Nihon Kodomo Shiryô Nenkan*, Vol. 3, edited by Nihon Sôgô Ai'iku Kenkyûjo (Tokyo: Nihon Sôgô Ai'iku Kenkyûjo, 1992).

Activities	*Students with exams*	*Students without exams*
Time to get up	7.05 a.m.	7.07 a.m.
Time to go to bed	11.18 p.m.	10.42 p.m.
Hours spent sleeping	7.58	8.08
Hours spent watching TV	1.78	2.78
Hours spent studying at home	3.8	1.3
Hours spent reading comics	0.4	0.55

In Taiwan, a jocular transliteration of the English word 'university' is *'yuni wan sinian'*, literally, 'university allows you to play for four years'.[1] This is not, of course, to disclaim the fact that some students might work with even more diligence in East Asian universities. Furthermore, in recent years, as it became harder to get a job in Japan, Korea and Taiwan, university students started to work harder than before. Still, the larger picture of university life is a much more relaxed one after all the ordeal of exams. That relaxation stands in contrast to university life in the US, where longer hours begin to be consumed academically, as plotted in Figure 7.4. What

---

[1] For further description of the lax atmosphere at universities, see for Japan, Zeugner (1984); for Taiwan, Huang (1994) and Li (1994).

might be appalling in the chart is that 80 per cent of American students studied for more than two hours; in comparison, 35 per cent of Japanese students of university did not do anything academic at all! For a vast population of the young and restless, the intrinsic motivation for learning apparently has its limitation.

Getting into university requires great sacrifice. A very popular concept about that sacrifice is found in a Japanese proverb, 'Yonto goraku', literally, 'sleeping four hours will succeed, and five hours fail'. Its equivalent in Korea is 'Sadang ohrak', with precisely identical meaning and also written in the same Chinese characters. Some people I interviewed claimed that was just what they did. But for the entire population, it is perhaps exaggerated. Statistics presented in Table 7.10 show that students slept much longer.

Although, compared with 20 years ago, a student did have less sleep, on average they slept more than seven hours daily. This pattern seems to be quite stable, confirmed by statistics from a different source (see Table 7.11). But, of course, some students might sleep much less than others. It is also plausible that, as exams loomed near, most students would stay up very late, and some claimed that they virtually worked round the clock.

Burning the midnight oil is, however, not a guarantee of success. Even with high-calibre intelligence, and a heavy investment in time, effort and money, one may still flunk the exams. Those who do not yield to fate then turn into rônin, or 'lordless warriors' – the topic of the ensuing pages.

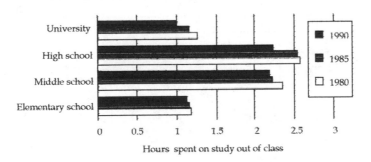

Hours spent on study out of class

Figure 7.3 Time spent after school on academic study daily by students of elementary, middle and high schools and university, 1980, 1985 and 1990. *Source*: Based on the data from NHK, *Nihonjin no Seikatsu Jikan 1990* (Japanese' time spent in daily life, 1990), (Tokyo: Nihon Hôsô Kyôkai, 1992), 131–51.

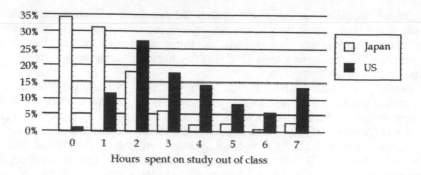

Hours spent on study out of class

Figure 7.4 Time spent on academic study by university students in Japan and the US, 1991. *Source*: Based on Japan External Trade Organization, *US and Japan in Figures II* (Tokyo: Japan External Trade Organization, 1992), 35.

Table 7.10 The sleeping hours of middle and high school students in Japan, 1970, 1990. *Source*: NHK, *Nihonjin no Seikatsu Jikan 1990* (Japanese' time spent in daily life, 1990), (Tokyo: Nihon Hôsô Kyôkai, 1992), 139, 143.

School	1970			1990		
	Mon.–Fri.	*Sat.*	*Sun.*	*Mon.–Fri.*	*Sat.*	*Sun.*
Middle	8 h 03 mª	8 h 13 m	9 h 21 m	7 h 52 m	7 h 50 m	9 h 08 m
High	7 h 18 m	7 h 32 m	8 h 49 m	7 h 17 m	7 h 22 m	8 h 49 m

Note: a. measured in hours (h) and minutes (m).

Table 7.11 The average study hours used for preparing the university entrance exams (outside of school and *yobiko*), 1956. *Source*: Yoshiro Shimizu, *Shiken* (Examinations), (Tokyo: Iwanami, 1957), 64.

Period	*High school students*	Rônin
April–August	7.4	7.5
September–December	7.0	7.2
January–March	6.9	7.3

BECOMING REPEATERS AFTER A TWIST OF FATE: TRY IT, AND TRY IT AGAIN

The Law of Inertia: Once the exam taker fails, he will continue to fail and will never succeed;

The Law of Reaction: Once the exam taker fails, due to its reaction, he will succeed later.

– *'The New Newtonian Laws'*, *A humour of 1933, Obunsha*, The 50-Year history of Japan's Humour in Exams, *1985*

Exam-repeaters are those students who do not gain admission to any university or those who do not gain admission to the university they wish to attend. They thus take a year or more to prepare solely for university entrance exams and often attend full-time cram schools. The exam-repeaters are notoriously known in Japan as *rônin*, or 'lordless warriors'. They are called *'Jai su saeng'* in Korea, and *'Chongkao sheng'* in Taiwan. The salience of this *rônin–Jai su saeng–Chongkao sheng* phenomenon in East Asia is shown in the sheer number of these students. This refers first of all to their stable proportion in the annual applicants for entrance exams, as shown in the data for the past 23 years (see Table 7.12).

In the past 20 years, exam-repeaters amounted to 30–50 per cent of university applicants in the three countries listed. Jobless, traumatized but unyielding, they spent an entire year whetting their competitive edge for the next trial. Some *rônin* in Japan simply stayed at home and prepared for the next round of exams. They are occasionally called *tokurô* (residence *rônin*) in Japanese.

Table 7.12 The number of exam repeaters and their percentage of total applicants to university, Japan, Korea and Taiwan, 1970–93 (by 1000 students). *Sources*: JMOE, *Kokukôritsu Daigaku Nyûgakusha Senbatsu jisshi jôkyô* (The actual implementation of selecting entrants for national and public universities), (Tokyo: National Center for University Entrance Examinations, 1994c), 1–2; TMOE, *Daixüe Duoyuan Ruxüe Fang'an* (Multiple university entrance programme), (Taiwan: Taiwan University Entrance Exam Center, 1992), 78–81; KEDI, *Educational Indicators in Korea* (Seoul: KEDI, 1982), 69; Liangdan Jin, *Zhong-Han Liangguo Shengdaxüe Chongkaosheng Chongkao Wenti de Bijiao Fenxi* (A comparison of the repeaters for the university entrance exams in Taiwan and Korea), MA thesis (Taiwan Normal University, 1982), 22–39.

	Japan			Korea			Taiwan		
Year	Repeaters	Total	R_j/T_j	Repeaters	Total	R_k/T_k	Repeaters	Total	R_t/T_t
	R_j	T_j	(%)	R_k	T_k	(%)	R_t	T_t	(%)
1970	179	539	33.2	46	121	38.0	–	–	–
1972	167	550	30.4	56	163	34.4	–	84	–
1974	169	602	28.1	64	195	32.8	–	93	–
1976	191	650	29.4	76	254	29.9	44	95	46.2
1978	198	654	30.3	117	320	36.6	32	95	33.4
1980	185	637	29.0	184	502	36.6	49	97	50.0
1982	188	644	29.2	239	732	32.6	–	96	–
1984	204	674	30.3	250	702	35.6	–	98	–
1986	206	724	28.5	234	669	35.0	54	110	49.2
1988	252	811	31.1	341	962	35.5	54	112	47.9
1990	278	888	31.3	485	1289	37.6	57	120	47.2
1992	279	921	30.3	570	1400	40.7	–	–	–
1993	275	917	30.0	543	1353	40.1	–	–	–

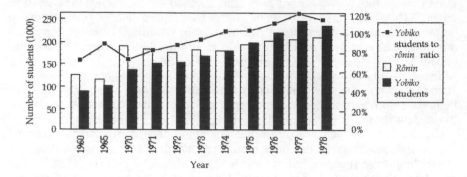

Figure 7.5 Numbers of *rônin* and their ratio to the *yobiko* preparatory school attendees in Japan, by percentage, 1960–78. *Sources*: JMOE, *Kokukôritsu Daigaku Nyûgakusha Senbatsu jisshi jyôkyô* (Actual selection of entrants for national/public universities), (Tokyo: National Center for University Entrance Examinations, 1994c), 1–2; Yoshiko Ikeda and Fumiko Yabana, *Daigaku Rônin no Shinri to Byôri* (A psychological and pathological study of *rônin* for university), (Tokyo: Kinko, 1982), 14.

In Taiwan, those who just stayed at home to cram for the next exam were sarcastically nicknamed *jiadun sheng*, or 'students who squat at home'. However, most of the *rônin* attended the prep schools specially designed for their needs, as shown in Figure 7.5.

It is interesting to note that, in the 1960s, the *yobiko* students were about 70 per cent of the total number of *rônin*. In 1978, *yobiko* students totalled more than the total number of *rônin* that took the entrance exams, probably because regular high school students also attended *yobiko* in some numbers, which were mainly founded for *rônin*. *Yobiko* was thus an essential institutionalized way of life for most repeaters. The importance of the *rônin* phenomenon is also shown in their large ratio among the entrants to universities, especially the élite ones (see Table 7.13).

Data for the *rônin* ratio in élite university entrants in Taiwan are not available. However, a survey (Jin, 1982) shows that an estimated 70 per cent of the applicants for university in Taiwan wanted to enter élite national universities. That credentialistic tendency may suggest a similarly high ratio of repeaters in élite universities in Taiwan as well.

Table 7.13 The distribution of *rônin* entrants among élite universities in Japan (1983) and Korea (1971–6). *Sources*: Mamoru Tsukada, *Yobiko Life: A Study of the Legitimation Process Stratification in Japan* (Berkeley: University of California, 1991), 98; Liangdan Jin, *Zhong-Han Liangguo Shengdaxüe Chongkao Sheng Chongkao Wenti de Bijiao Fenxi* (A comparison of repeaters for university entrance exams in Taiwan and Korea), MA thesis (Taiwan Normal University, 1982), 40.

	Name of university	Proportion of rônin entrants
Japan[a]	Tokyo University	51%
	Kyoto University	53%
	Waseda University[b]	62%
	Keio University	68%
Korea[c]	Seoul National University	34%
	Korean University	34%
	Yong sei University	31%

Notes: a. Data for Japanese universities are for 1983. b. Datum for Waseda is for 1992. c. Data for Korea are average for 1971–6.

Why did they become repeaters?

The impact of failure in high-stake exams cannot be overstated. Years of tightly scheduled school life were brought to a nihilistic close. A student found he or she was in the middle of nowhere. Crestfallen, at the beginning they lost interest in everything. A politician well known in Taiwan writes about his own setback in the exams in these words:

> The failure of *liankao* not only made me ashamed. My whole family lost face. It seems that, whenever a kid is taking *liankao*, all his neighbours know it, all his relatives know it, and everybody was waiting for the result. As soon as he failed, his family would feel a kind of 'pressure' from all of them. Upon reflection, my first reaction to failure was to stay away from people. I felt like the sky had collapsed, the future was lightless, and I experienced a big blow. I did not go outside. I shunned my friends and stayed indoors in gloom. (Kuling, 1994: 208)

The failed students soon found themselves at a crossroads in life. They could either start a career at a low level, go to a college that was not hard to get into, or prepare for the exams independently or at a *yobiko* (Tsukada, 1991). Starting all over again is a tough decision. They have to step out from the normal progression of their lives, bear the stigma of failure, and struggle against their ill fate. Their inferiority complex is comparable to the jobless during the Depression (Goffman, in ibid.). For some people, however, the fact that many of their classmates also failed was some solace and at *yobiko* most students were facing the same *rônin* struggle. Therefore, for some first-year *rônin*, their shock or depression lasted only a short time.

The decision to become a *rônin* is strongly related to how they interpret their past failure. In Japan, *rônin* considered the results of exams to be a reflection of their efforts to push themselves to their limits. Success justified the pain and effort they expended, failure revealed that more effort was needed (Tsukada, 1991). In his comparative survey, Liangdan Jin (1982) finds that, among repeaters, 40.9 per cent of Koreans and 46.1 per cent of Taiwanese thought that 'inadequate preparation for the exams' failed them; 25.5 per cent of Koreans and 23.3 per cent of Taiwanese attributed their failure to the 'inappropriate method of their preparation'; 21.8 per cent of Koreans and 18.7 per cent of Taiwanese believed they failed because 'the high school did not institute proper curricular guidance'; 4.5 per cent of Koreans and 4.1 per cent of Taiwanese thought they performed badly because 'they were too nervous during the exams'. Only 0.9 per cent of Korean and 1.7 per cent of Taiwanese attributed their failure to reasons other than effort and preparation. In the minds of many *rônin*, they failed because they did not work hard enough. What is alluded to here seems to be that, with more painful preparation and self-sacrifice, they could have made it.

Some *rônin*, according to my interview, were less depressed. To them, the first failure was an accident, and passing exams was only a matter of time. Therefore, they might spend even less time on preparation, since they only needed to concentrate on the subjects that they flunked. Others even chose to be a *rônin* although they were selected by an élite school, because they did not like the department. A mayor in Taiwan recounts that he became a repeater in 1969. Although he was admitted by the top élite Taiwan University, he wanted to enter the Law Department instead of business management. Cases like his, however, account for less than one-fifth of the *rônin* population, as indicated by the statistics in Table 7.14.

From the above, we can see that the majority of *rônin* needed to try again simply because no school accepted them due to the cut-off scores. About 30–40 per cent of repeaters were accepted but they or their family did not like the school or the department. In that sense, *rônin* are composed of (1) those who opt to repeat in order to have a better choice, and (2) those who had to repeat as they did not reach the lowest acceptable scores. That difference might explain, in part, the polarity of *rônin*: some of them ended up in very good universities, and others never made it.

The above study only clusters *rônin* by their achievement versus their choice. It does not, however, reveal the underlying factors that influence a student's decision to become a *rônin*. To repeat implies not only to endure and to redouble one's effort and time. It is an important decision affecting and affected by a number of factors other than scores. These were included in the study by David Stevenson and David Baker (1992) – see Table 7.15.

In the table, family resources have a modest influence on becoming a *rônin* after high school. Students whose families have more money and whose parents have more education are more likely to continue in the *yobiko*. These effects are small, however, adding only about 5–6 per cent to the likelihood that a student undertakes the *rônin* year (Stevenson and Baker, 1992: 1650–1).

Data also show that students from prestigious high schools tend to become *rônin*, most likely because they are taking the most competitive entrance exams. However, family expenditure and student sacrifice are far more motivated by the student's gender. Males dominate the ranks of *rônin*. Males are 49 per cent more likely to become *rônin*.

Table 7.14 Reasons for becoming exam repeaters in Korea and Taiwan. *Source*: Liangdan Jin, *Zhong-Han Liangguo Shengdaxüe Chongkao Sheng Chongkao Wenti de Bijiao Fenxi* (A comparison of repeaters for university entrance exams in Taiwan and Korea), MA thesis (Taiwan Normal University, 1982), 74.

Reasons for becoming rônin	Korean		Taiwanese		
	No. of students	Percentage in total	No. of students	Percentage in total	Z-score
1. The department that accepted me last time does not suit me.	72	16.4	96	20.9	1.56
2. Parents expected me to enter a better school and department.	96	21.8	45	9.9	5.14**
3. I did not pass and was not accepted.	266	60.5	307	66.6	1.90
4. Others	6	1.3	12	2.6	1.51
Total	440	100	460	100	

Note: ** $p < 0.01$.

Table 7.15 Influences of student, family and school characteristics on becoming a *rônin* after high school among students with college plans in Japan. *Source*: David L. Stevenson and David P. Baker, 'Shadow education and allocation in formal schooling: transition to university in Japan', *American Journal of Sociology* 97(6) (1992): 1651.

Independent variables	Maximum-likelihood parameters	SE
Background factors:		
Gender (1 = male)	1.97†	0.20
Academic standing	−0.08	0.05
Father's education	0.10	0.11
Mother's education	0.17*	0.08
Family income	0.23†	0.06
High school's reputation	0.24†	0.08
Pass examination (1 = pass)	−3.78†	0.20
Rural/urban (1 = urban)	0.43*	0.19
Hazard rate (follow-up correction)	0.98†	0.27
Intercept	−1.75†	0.48
Model compared to model with intercept only	796.38	
df	9	
N	1586	

Notes: * Coefficient is twice its SE.
     † Coefficient is larger than two and a half times its SE.

Table 7.16 Who influences the decision to repeat the university entrance exams? Answers given by exam repeaters. *Source*: Liangdan Jin, *Zhong-Han Liangguo Shengdaxüe Chongkao Sheng Chongkao Wenti de Bijiao Fenxi* (A comparison of repeaters for university entrance exams in Taiwan and Korea), MA thesis (Taiwan Normal University, 1982), 120.

	Koreans		Taiwanese		Z score
	Number	Percentage	Number	Percentage	
Student	192	43.6%	218	47.4%	1.146
Parents	92	20.9%	54	11.7%	3.779**
Teacher	74	16.8%	86	18.7%	0.758
Classmate	52	11.8%	51	11.1%	0.339
Friend	24	5.5%	38	8.3%	1.639
Others	6	1.4%	13	2.8%	–
Total	440	100%	460	100%	–

Note: ** $p < 0.01$.

Naturally, students who failed examinations during the first year are more likely and students from rural areas less likely to become *rônin*, because of the higher costs of sending a student to live in the city to attend a *yobiko* (Stevenson and Baker, 1992).

The male–female difference in Japan, as cited, and to certain extent in Korea, reflects a male-dominating socio-cultural context. That was reified in parental attitudes towards a daughter's education. The four-year universities led to more valuable jobs upon graduation. Men in Japan spend their lives at such jobs; women are not expected to do so and in fact rarely pursue careers. Therefore, male students are much more intensely supported and pressured to enter a good university, regardless of family finances and the psychic costs. As Rohlen (1983) observes, nothing reflects this better than the fact that about 85 per cent of all students doing *rônin* were male in 1974.

When the background factors are compared to the individual factor, however, the importance of a student's own decision to repeat is shown (see Table 7.16). While about 21 per cent (Korea) and 12 per cent (Taiwan) of students decided to repeat under the sway of their father or mother, 44 per cent (Korea) and 47 per cent (Taiwan) reached that decision by themselves. Hence, to be a *rônin* is first of all an individual decision and then a family matter, which suggests an internalization of credentialism on the part of the children. Yet, that is not to underestimate the importance of family. To the contrary, one or more years of *rônin* implies a substantial investment of time and money. Its risks, anxiety and challenge were intimately felt by the whole family. That decision is unimaginable without the consensus of the family. But, as implied in the data, it was above all an individual plan, since it was the student who had to bear the brunt of the ordeal.

The life of repeaters: Their schedule and hours of learning

Surveys on the population of repeaters across any of our three societies are virtually non-existent. In the world of cram schools in Japan (*yobiko*), an immense amount of data has been collected through surveys focused on their enrolled students. A wide variety of questions are thus covered – such as favourite newspapers or comics, personal hobbies, personality charac-teristics, and the hours spent daily on work. While it is not necessarily true that all repeaters attended *yobiko*, as noted previously, the majority do take courses in *yobiko*. For that reason, the *yobiko* survey could be quite informative about the repeaters.

In 1993, the Kawaijuku, one of the three giant *yobiko* corporations in Japan, conducted a comprehensive survey of a total of 9190 *rōnin* students matriculated in its courses geared towards university entrance exams. Figure 7.6 plots the distribution of average hours Kawaijuku students spent on study out of class. The survey covered the academic year 1993, including three terms, the summer and the winter, as presented in Figure 7.6.

In the scatterplot of Figure 7.6, the dots for each column represent the aggregation of the average hours spent by the students in each course. In the Todai Course (Tokyo University), for example, the dots indicate the hours used for after-class study in three terms and two seasons, as expressed in detail in Table 7.17 (I stands for weekdays, and II stands for weekends and holidays).

It is noteworthy that, despite their different orientation, the time students spent on their study had amazingly small deviation from the average for all courses. The slightly outlying ones are perhaps the Medical Science Course, which took more hours, and the Basics Course, which took fewer hours than the rest. The *yobiko* students worked from four to eight hours or so daily to prepare themselves for their second attempt at the exams. Table 7.18 sum-marizes the above data, and presents a clear picture of Kawaijuku students' time allocation. In Term One, students worked on homework longer on weekends than on weekdays, probably because instruction took away a lot of time during weekdays.

As exams approached, the difference between weekdays and weekends became smaller. Typically, they would study for 7–8 hours at home on the eve of the exams in addition to their *yobiko* classes. The data for the life of Japanese students in 1956 suggest some consistency in the hours that they needed for perfecting their knowledge. The data are not easily comparable with that for 1993 Kawaijuku students, since their units of period differ. And yet, roughly speaking, they seem to be quite close to each other, although a Japanese *rōnin* might spend even longer hours for university entrance exams in the earlier period.

Table 7.17 Study hours spent by the students of Kawaijuku course for Tokyo University, 1993. *Source*: Ibid.

Term 1		Summer		Term 2		Winter		Term 3	
I	II	I	II	I	II	I	II	I	II
3.8	5.9	6.9	7.3	4.5	6.7	7.3	8	7.1	7.9

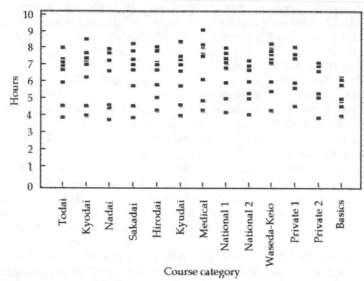

Course category

Figure 7.6 Scatterplot of average hours spent on after-school study per day by Kawaijuku students, 1993, by course category. *Source*: based on Kawaijuku, ed., *1993 Daigaku Juken to Gurîn Kôsu no Ankêto Chôsa* (1993 Survey on the students taking the courses of University Entrance Exams), (Nagoya: Kawaijuku, 1993a).
Note: The total number of student respondents at Kawaijuku was 9190.

Table 7.18 Average hours spent on academic homework per day by Kawaijuku students in the academic year 1993. *Source*: Ibid.

	Weekends/Holidays		Weekdays	
	Home	Outside	Home	Outside
Term 1	4.4	1.4	2.8	1.3
Summer	4.6	2.8	4.0	3.1
Term 2	4.8	2.0	3.3	1.8
Winter	5.4	2.6	4.7	2.9
Term 3	5.7	2.2	5.0	2.3

Table 7.19 The average study hours spent on preparing university entrance exams (outside of school and *yobiko*), 1956. *Source*: Yoshiro Shimizu, *Shiken* (Examinations), (Tokyo: Iwanami, 1957), 64.

Period	High school students	Rônin
April–August	5.5	6.8
September–December	6.2	8.0
January–March	7.5	8.9

How did the repeaters' year(s) pay off?

How did the *rônin* year pay off? That can be answered by checking how many of those surveyed were admitted to university. The acceptance rate of *rônin* in Japan shows the historical changes in the distribution of regular college entrance ratios to those for *rônin* with one, two or more years of extra study. The overall college entrance rate increased steadily until 1975 and has remained about 36 per cent since then. The proportion of entrants with *rônin* experience was 39.5 per cent in 1964 ($N = 128,131$) when the Ministry of Education began gathering data on the *rônin* phenomenon. According to Tsukada (1991) it rose and fell periodically over the next decade and then stabilized at about 30 per cent. Students with two or more years of *rônin* life showed the same pattern as those with one *rônin* year. Those with two or more *rônin* years constituted about 25 per cent of the total number of college entrants with *rônin* experience historically.

The above data about Japan show that the accepted *rônin* ratio in the total of accepted students was stable. They, unfortunately, do not reflect the success ratio within each repeater group, such as 1-year repeaters, 2-year repeaters, etc. In this regard, data given in Table 7.20 on the case of Korea shed some meaningful insight.

Unlike the data for Japan, the Korean data given here break the repeater population down into different years. If we look at their share in the total number of either applicants or those accepted, we find a decline as the years of *rônin* increased. If, as hypothesized earlier, exam-repeaters consist of two types, the ambitious, high achievers and the low achievers, those who were eliminated repeatedly mainly belonged to the second type. Their repeated failure pointed to some 'incorrigible' problems in their academic life.

On the other hand, this also shows that the East Asian entrance system is not an empty ritual. It did select, eliminate and control the quality of education cruelly. While there is no investigation of what exactly caused their failure, I would think the majority who were eliminated belonged to the second type. What is more informative, however, is the acceptance rate for *rônin* of particular years, 1-year, 2-year, etc. In the B/A column, we find that the 1-year *rônin* acceptance rate (50.93 per cent) was very close to that of high school students (51.85 per cent), which is roughly 1 in 2. That rate declined 7 per cent for the 2-year *rônin*. For the 4-year *rônin*, 1 in 3 could be accepted.

For Taiwan, the acceptance ratio for the entire repeaters group is given in Table 7.21.

The overall acceptance ratio in 1981 was 28.21 per cent. The ratio for graduating school students was 5.5 per cent higher than the average for repeaters. Considering that repeaters were a group of students who already bore the stigma of failure, we would say their performances were in general pretty good. That rate of success could well work as a confidence-building agent, recruiting new members into the repeaters' population.

For students and their families in all three countries, it is an effort to overcome the setback of initial failure, especially for males. For the government, however, the phenomenon of repeaters was perceived as an unintended effect of an impartial selection process, the 'necessary evil' to use a common expression. To curtail it, the Korean government once adopted a punitive grading method. For those who took university entrance exams more than once, a certain number of points would be deducted from the total scores. However, it was to no avail in dissuading failed students from repeating.

Table 7.20 The acceptance rate of different categories of student applicants in Korea's preliminary university entrance exams, 1976. *Source*: Liangdan Jin, *Zhong-Han Liangguo Shengdaxüe Chongkao Sheng Chongkao Wenti de Bijiao Fenxi* (A comparison of repeaters for university entrance exams in Taiwan and Korea), MA thesis (Taiwan Normal University, 1982), 38.

Years of Rônin	Number of applicants A	Number of applicants accepted B	Acceptance ratio B/A	Percentage of the total number of applicants	Percentage of the total number of accepted
Students†	170,211	88,261	51.85 %	67.71 %	69.46 %
1-yr Repeaters	55,096	28,063	50.93 %	21.82 %	22.08 %
2-yr Repeaters	17,630	7508	42.59 %	7.01 %	5.91 %
3-yr Repeaters	4769	1948	40.85 %	1.90 %	1.53 %
4-yr Repeaters	3674	1292	31.17 %	1.46 %	1.01 %
Total	251,380	127,072	50.46 %	100 %	100 %

Note: † Students refer to those who have just completed high school, equivalent to the Japanese term *genyakusei* (at-school students).

Table 7.21 The number and ratio of acceptance in Taiwan's *Liankao* university entrance exams, 1981. *Source*: Liangdan Jin, *Zhong-Han Liangguo Shengdaxüe Chongkao Sheng Chongkao Wenti de Bijiao Fenxi* (A comparison of repeaters for university entrance exams in Taiwan and Korea), MA thesis (Taiwan Normal University, 1982), 39.

Type of students	Number of applicants A	Number accepted B	Ratio B/A
School students	57,729 (42.08%)	18,136 (46.86%)	**31.42%**
Rônin	79,469 (57.92%)	20,569 (53.14%)	**25.88%**
Total	137,198 (100.00%)	38,705 (100.00%)	**28.21%**

MONEY AND MERIT: EXPENDITURE FOR THE ENTRANCE EXAMS-CENTRED EDUCATION

This section attempts to answer the question: does money matter? In other words, how do resource inputs affect children's educational achievement and success? How are the achievement levels related to inputs from different sources? To start with, a note about currency exchange rates is in order. The units of currencies for the three Asian countries are Japanese yen (¥), the Korean won (W) and the New Taiwanese dollar (NT$). Because their exchange rates are subject to market fluctuations, I will keep the value of expenditures reported here in local currencies rather than converting them to dollars. At the same time, to give an approximation of their equivalent in US dollars, the rates of exchange for each were, as of April 1994 (quoted from the *Asian Journal*, 21 April 1994):

One US dollar = W807;
One US dollar = ¥103;
One US dollar = NT$26.

Public expenditures in education: An international comparison

If we look at the educational expenditure in Gross National Product (GNP) per capita, the share of education was not necessarily higher for the three East Asian countries (see Figure 7.7). In the data, the percentage of education in GNP is not that impressive for the Asian countries. Japan was lower than the UK and USA. Korea was the lowest here: 3.3 per cent in 1991. As a matter of fact, contrary to our impression, Korea's percentage (3.3 per cent in 1991) was lower than quite a number of other developing countries, such as Mexico (4.1 per cent in 1990), Costa Rica (4.6 per cent in 1990), Algeria (9.1 per cent in 1989), Egypt (6.7 per cent in 1989), or Kenya (6.4 per cent in 1988). Clark Sorensen (1994) observes that the state in South Korea does not devote an extraordinary amount of money to education. Furthermore, there was actually a decline in the GNP percentage of education expenditures. In Korea, it decreased from 3.7 per cent in 1968 to 3.6 per cent in 1991 (Bae, 1991). In Japan, that figure decreased from 5.8 per cent in 1980 to 4.7 per cent in 1989 (UNESCO, 1993).

The educational expenditure of Taiwan (7.0 per cent) was comparatively higher in its GNP proportion, next only to Canada (7.4 per cent) in the chart. However, when we examine PPE (Per Pupil Expenditure), the 'most general measure of resource inputs' (Hedges, Laine and Greenwald, 1994), we find that PPE was so low for Korea and Taiwan that it could not possibly be used as a good predictor for their national academic achievements (see Figure 7.8 and Table 7.22).

The low expenditures on education, as cited, plus some other adverse conditions, such as the larger class size (average 40–50, almost twice the average class size in most developed countries) and a teaching force with limited higher education, are 'typical of East Asian countries that score well on international test in science and math' (Sorensen, 1994).

Even when compared to the Third World, the national financial commitments to education in Japan, Korea and Taiwan are not impressively high. In fact, they might be lower than certain developing countries, as shown in Table 7.23.

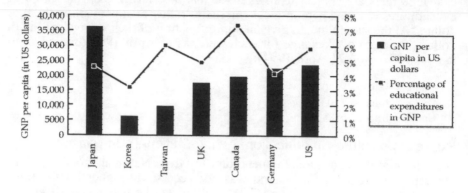

Figure 7.7 An international comparison: GNP per capita and percentage of public educational expenditure in GNP. *Sources*: Based on UNESCO, *Statistical Yearbook* (Paris: UNESCO, 1993); US Department of Education, *Digest of Education Statistics* (Washington, DC: US Department of Education, 1993), 404; KMOE, *Korea Handbook of Education Statistics* (Seoul: KMOE, 1992); TMOE, *Education Statistical Indicators* (Taipei: TMOE, 1994), 63; *Yazhou Zhoukan (Asian Journal)*, 2 January 1994: 35. *Note*: Year of data: 1990 data for Japan, Germany, UK, US, Canada; 1992 data for Korea; 1993 data for Taiwan.

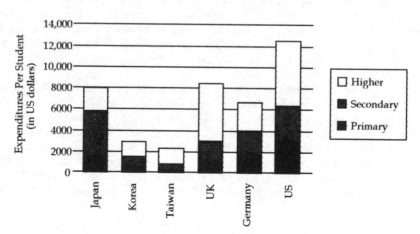

Figure 7.8 An international comparison: educational expenditures per student, or PPE (per pupil expenditures), by school level. *Source*: Based on KEDI, *Education Indicators in Korea*, (Seoul: KEDI, 1989).
Note: 1983 data for Japan, 1987 data for Korea, 1983 data for Taiwan, 1983 for UK, 1983 for Germany, and 1985 for US.

Table 7.22 An international comparison: educational expenditures per student, or PPE (per pupil expenditures), by school level (in US$). *Source*: Cited from KEDI, *Education Indicators in Korea* (Seoul: KEDI, 1989).

	Japan	Korea	Taiwan	UK	Germany	US
Primary	1618	479	301	1140	1689	3173
Secondary	4175	1049	545	1794	2377	3173
Higher	2110	1484	1555	5542	2624	6255
Total	7903	3012	2401	8476	6690	12,601

Table 7.23 A cross-national comparison: public educational expenditure as a percentage of GNP, 1970, 1980, 1989. *Source*: UNESCO, *Statistical Yearbook* (Paris, UNESCO).

Country	1970	1980	1989
Japan	**3.9**	**5.8**	**4.7**
Korea	**3.7**	**3.7**	**3.6**
Algeria	7.4	7.8	8.1
Egypt	4.8	5.7[a]	6.7
Brazil	2.7	3.6	4.6
Chile	5.1	4.6	3.7[b]
Panama	5.4	4.9	6.1
Iran	2.9	7.5	3.7
Jordan	3.9	3.5[c]	5.9

Notes: a.1981 data. b. 1988 data. c. 1977 data.

Credentialism and family investment in education

To understand how much parents invested in their children's education, we need first to understand the differences in earnings resulting from the level of educational achievement in the three East Asian countries. In Japan, income differentials among males in the first year of their first employment for three groups – college, high school and middle school graduates – are given in Table 7.24.

Although the intervals among these indexes have been considerably narrowed in the fifteen years between 1960 and 1975, the college graduate has an undoubtedly greater advantage over the other two groups. In terms of longitudinally computed career income, when the indexes for the college graduate are held constant at 100, the indexes of high school and middle school graduates are 71.4 and 61.5 in 1966, 73.9 and 66.7 in 1970, and 77.2 and 69.2 in 1974. What these statistics show is that the differentials in the groups' initial incomes are, by and large, reflected in their career incomes.

The income differentials between levels of education appeared larger in Taiwan than in Japan, as shown in Table 7.25. While in Japan the index of income for middle school, high school and college graduates had increased up to about 69–84–100 in 1975, in Taiwan those differentials were much larger. During 1978–82, the index was kept at around 55–65–100.

The data for Korea, given in Table 7.26, are better designed than the other two above in that the working years after leaving school are factored in for regressing wages on the level of education attained. As indicated in the table, high school graduates with a 5–9-year work experience were paid less than 4-year college graduates with only 1-year experience, as may be better visualized in Figure 7.9.

Table 7.24 Index of income differentials among males in the first year of first employment in Japan, 1960–70. *Source*: From Makoto Asô and Morikazu Ushiogi, eds, *Gakureki Kôyôron* (The utility of academic credentials), (Tokyo: Ûhikaku, 1977), 139.

Year	College	High school	Middle school
1960	100	62.4	45.2
1965	100	71.8	57.2
1970	100	75.8	63.7
1975	100	84.0	69.4

Note: The wage of four-year college graduates is the base value of 100.

Table 7.25 Income differentials according to level of education, by New Taiwan dollar (NT$) and Index Value, Taiwan, 1978–82. *Source*: BASEY and CEPDEY: *Report on the Manpower Utilization Survey Taiwan, Republic of China, 1993* (Taipei: BASEY and CEPDEY, 1994), 128–31.

Year	College	High school	Middle school
1978	28,360 (**100**)	17,885 (**63.1**)	15,341 (**54.1**)
1979	31,253 (**100**)	19,503 (**62.4**)	17,456 (**55.9**)
1980	34,278 (**100**)	22,345 (**65.2**)	19,834 (**57.9**)
1981	37,501 (**100**)	24,261 (**64.7**)	22,093 (**58.9**)
1982	41,570 (**100**)	26,628 (**64.1**)	24,471 (**58.9**)

Note: Figures in parentheses are indexes, taking the college graduate level as 100 for each year.

Table 7.26 Wages according to the level of education and experience in Korea (in won). *Source*: Byong-sun Kwak, '"Examination hell" in Korea revisited', *Koreana* (Seoul, 1991) 5(2): 45–55.

Years of work	4-year college	2-year college	High school
Less than 1 year	418,000	291,000	235,000
1–2 years	468,000	332,000	265,000
3–4 years	538,000	376,000	307,000
5–9 years	662,000	462,000	395,000

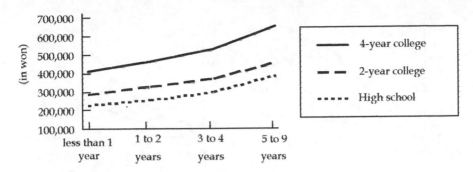

Figure 7.9 Wages according to level of education and experience in Korea. *Source*: Byong-sun Kwak, '"Examination hell" in Korea revisited', *Koreana* (Seoul, 1991) 5(2): 45–55.

With such a disparity of wages between middle and high schools and college graduates, it is natural that everyone tries to go to college at all costs. This wide gap in earnings in line with the educational level is a critical factor in escalating competition among Korea's youngsters for higher education.

How much money do parents pay for their children's education?

In Korea, in past years the government, industries, social organizations and even educational foundations kept their purse strings tight. Compared to that faltering public commitment, or perhaps just in consequence of it, parents have greatly increased their investment in their children's education (Bae, 1991). In Korea, for example, public educational expenditures declined from 3.7 per cent in 1968 to 3.6 per cent in 1991. However, the share of education in family expenditure rose from 5 per cent in 1965 to 10 per cent in 1987. In fact, many families spent up to 30 per cent of their household expenditure on education to cover expenses related to schooling as well as various private tutoring (Bae, 1991). Compared to 1968, the average educational cost to Korean parents for each elementary school student multiplied tenfold in 1990, middle school student 3.9 times, high school student 2.9 times and college student twice. Parents are shouldering as much as 87 per cent of the total educational expenses both in and out of school (Bae, 1991).

The underfunding of schools in Korea, as discussed previously, plus the high competitiveness in the university entrance exams embodied in cultural concepts and societal and industrial structure, are often cited as the causes of heavy family investment. Figures for 1990 indicate that parental and student outlays totalled 9.4 trillion won, or 1.7 times more than the 5.6 trillion won in government expenditures on education during the same year. A large percentage of that was used for entrance-exam-oriented preparation. In metropolitan areas, parents may spend from 200,000 to 300,000 won (US$276–414) monthly on outside tutoring for each child.

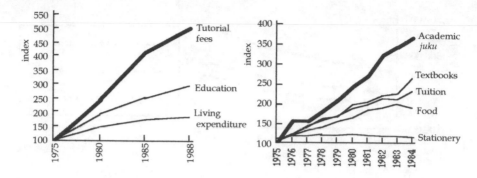

Figure 7.10 The index of tutorial fees and expenditure on academic *juku*. *Sources*: Based on (a) JMCA (Japan Management and Coordination Agency), *Annual Report on the Family Income and Expenditure Survey* (Tokyo: JMCA, 1988), 107; (b) JMOE, 'Hogosha ga Shishutsu shita Kyôikuhi no Sui'i' (The change in family expenditures on education) in *Kyôiku*, edited by Ministry of Education (Tokyo: Ministry of Education, 1986), 282–3.
Note: Index taking expenditure of 1975 as 100.

Investment in tutoring is particularly geared towards the university entrance exams. Again, in Korea it is taken for granted that the chances of admission to good universities increase in proportion to the amount of money spent on private lessons. The national average of annual spending for private education of each high school student in the high-income class is estimated at 983,000 won (US$1357), which is more than the 797,000 won (US$1100) spent for each student in the middle-income class. The average spending reached 1,051,000 won (US$1452) in Seoul, compared with 751,000 won (US$1037) in townships (Bae, 1991).

In Japan, in 1975–90 tutorial fees increased more rapidly than total living expenses and educational expenses. As Figure 7.10 (a) shows, if 1975 is taken as 100, in 1988 the living expenditure index is 184, education expenditure index 293, and tutorial fee index 502. If we break educational expenditure down further, it is obvious that the cost index for *juku* (363) increased faster than for textbooks (258), tuition (226) or stationery (112).

Preparing children for the entrance exams: Who paid more, who paid less?

Families in each nation invested differently to prepare their children for the entrance exams. In Japan, parents of different ages bear burdens of different weight. The heaviest burden fell on families where the family head was aged 40–49, where children are of school age, as shown in Table 7.27.

Also, expenditure on tutoring differed in accordance with urbanization. Again in Korea, it cost more for a family in a bigger city to get tutoring than in a smaller one, as indicated in Table 7.28.

Earlier, in the part about time spent on academic work, we found that Korean students in smaller cities and towns spent more time on study than those in large cities. Here, in terms of investment, we find families in large cities spending more money on their children. That might result from (1) the higher standard cost in the big cities, and/or (2) higher family income in the big cities, which would enable the parents to afford more expensive tutoring.

Tutoring, as discussed, exacted an increasing share of family expenditure in Japan and Korea. In consequence, it became not only a barometer of the commitment to education, it was also an index of the family's disposable income. In Japan, it rose with the family's income. The data for 1988 of the tutorial cost by different economic status are shown in Table 7.29. In 1988, the families in the highest quintile of income were spending almost ten times as much as families in the lowest quintile. A similar case is shown in the findings for Korea (see Table 7.30).

In 1980, the higher-income group accounts for 45.5 per cent of all middle school students who had tutoring studies. Only 14 per cent of students tutored belonged to the lower-income group. In 1991, the pattern changed greatly. The middle-income groups, including the higher and the lower middle-income, increased from 54.7 per cent to 70.1 per cent (the higher and lower income groups combined). The higher-income group declined slightly.

Table 7.27 Annual average of monthly expenditures on tutorial fees by age groups of household head (all households), 1988 (in yen). *Source*: JMCA, *Annual Report on the Family Income and Expenditure Survey* (Tokyo: JMCA, 1988), 199.

Average	Age groups				
	~ 29	30 ~ 39	40 ~ 49	50 ~ 59	60 ~
2855	67	1775	6770	1951	380

Table 7.28 Average monthly expenditure for tutorial fees, by areas in Korea (in won). *Source*: Se-Ho Shin *et al.*, *A Study on Private Tutoring in Korea* (Seoul: KEDI, 1991), 79, 81.

Areas	Middle school	High school
Seoul	90,520	281,898
Other big cities	69,365	160,969
Counties	50,905	128,971

Table 7.29 Monthly expenditure per household on tutorial fees, by yearly income quintile groups in Japan (all households), 1988. *Source*: JMCA, *Annual Report on the Family Income and Expenditure Survey* (Tokyo: JMCA, 1988), 186.

		Yearly income quintile group				
	Average	I	II	III	IV	V
Annual income (¥10,000)	595	256	339	525	684	1110
Tutorial fee (¥)	2855	557	1550	2710	4039	5416

Table 7.30 The ratio of middle school students who took tutoring classes in Korea, 1980 and 1991 (%). *Source*: Se-Ho Shin *et al.*, *A Study on Private Tutoring in Korea* (KEDI, 1991), 63.

Income group	1980	1991
Higher income	45.5	39.9
Higher-middle income	33.3	39.6
Lower-middle income	21.4	30.5
Lower income	14.0	13.7
Total	20.3	31.0

The power of money: How well did the tutoring activities prepare children for university?

There are a number of ways to prepare for entrance exams in Japan; the currently prevailing ones include: mock tests, correspondence course, private tutor, after-school *juku*, and the plans to be a *rônin* after high school termination (Stevenson and David, 1992). As the costs of these cramming methods differ categorically from one another, a comparison of them is thus a convenient and valid approach to the effects of money on the university entrance exams. To begin with, an explanatory note is in order for these main types of tutoring activities:

1. Mock tests (*Mogi shiken*): provided and graded by private firms, these assess a student's chances of being admitted to university. Students receive a report comparing their performance with national norms, are notified of subject areas that require greater study, and are given an estimate of their chances of being admitted into one university.
2. Correspondence courses (*Tsûshin tensaku*): purchased from mail-order companies, these provide exercises for entrance examinations that are mailed back and then returned graded.
3. Private tutors (*Katei kyôshi*): are primarily used for staying abreast of regular schoolwork and used less for examination preparation.
4. Academic *juku* include *gakushû juku*, which are remedial classes, and *shingaku juku*, for preparation for the university entrance examinations.
5. *Rônin* year(s): full-time preparation following high school is a strategy used by students who do not gain admission to any university or by those who do not gain admission to the university they wish to attend. *Rônin* take a year or more to prepare solely for university entrance exams and often attend *yobiko* (ibid.).

The participation ratios for each of the tutoring activities found in the sampling of Stevenson and Baker (1992) are given in Table 7.31.

Stevenson and Baker examine the consequences of participation in tutoring activities for university attendance at two points in time: (1) the first and (2) the second year out of high school. The first point includes all base-year students with university plans and the second point includes only those follow-up-year students with university plans who did not attend university after high school. The findings are summarized in Table 7.32.

Because there is no measure of the actual improvement, the analysis provides a limited assessment of the effect of participation in shadow-education activities on university attendance.

Whether or not a student attends university is regressed twice for each time point. The first logistic equation includes just the block of background variables and the hazard rate for sample attrition and the second equation adds participation in shadow education. Since various background factors predict participation, Stevenson and Baker assess the difference between the total effects of background factors and direct effects of background and shadow-education factors to indicate possible indirect effects of background factors that work through tutoring activities on university attendance.

Participation in high school tutoring activities increases the likelihood of university attendance and adds significantly to a model with only background factors. However, the effects of tutoring did not increase in proportion to cost. The cost of private tutoring is more expensive than academic *juku*, and *juku* more costly than mock tests or correspondence.

According to the findings, the direct effects of mock tests and correspondence courses are significant and positive, adding 16 per cent and 25 per cent respectively to the probability of entering a university after high school. In comparison, after-school *juku* have only a small and non-significant effect on attendance. Using a tutor decreases one's chances of attendance, which most likely reflects the remedial character of most tutoring compared with the preparatory character of the other forms of tutoring activities. While the causes of these differences remain to be determined, it was amply evidenced that the positive effects of tutoring did not necessarily increase with cost.

In the remainder of the direct effects equation, family background, academic ability and school reputation all influence university entrance. Mother's education clearly works through tutoring activities indirectly, since adding the shadow-education block drops this coefficient to zero. Males are more likely than females to enter university, probably because of the emphasis placed on males' educational attainment.

Table 7.31 Japanese students' participation in tutoring activities during high school (base-year sample). *Source*: David L. Stevenson and David P. Baker, 'Shadow education and allocation in formal schooling: transition to university in Japan', *American Journal of Sociology* 97(6) (May 1992), 1646.

Type of activities	Students participating[a]	Students with university plan[b]
Mock tests	54%	68%
Correspondence courses	30%	43%
Private tutors	8%	11%
Academic *juku*	35%	46%
Plan to be a *rônin* after high school	29%	32%
N = 7240		

Notes: a. A student might take more than one type of tutoring activity.
b. Students with college plans account for 74 per cent of the total number.

The second set of equations in Table 7.32 compares the effects of background facts and tutoring activities on those students who had plans for college but did not attend immediately after high school. The dependent variable is university attendance in the second year out of high school. Added to the list of high school tutoring activities is whether or not the student had undertaken the *rônin* year (Stevenson and Baker, 1992).

Among students two years out of high school with college plans, high school tutoring activities had a diminishing effect on attending university, but the effect of being a *rônin* is dramatic because it increases university attendance by 80 per cent.

Table 7.32 Influence of tutoring activities on university entrance for students with college plans (follow-up sample). *Source*: David L. Stevenson and David P. Baker, 'Shadow education and allocation in formal schooling: transition to university in Japan', *American Journal of Sociology* 97(6) (May 1992), 1646.

Independent variables	University after high school		University two years after high school	
	Total effect	Direct effect	Total effect	Direct effect
Background factors:				
Gender (1 = male)	2.69 (0.17)	2.70 (0.18)	0.96 (0.24)	0.16 (0.30)
Academic standing	0.20 (0.05)	0.14 (0.06)	0.28 (0.07)	0.27 (0.07)
Father's education	0.19 (0.07)	0.15 (0.07)	0.02 (0.07)	−0.04 (0.08)
Mother's education	0.20 (0.10)	0.16 (0.10)	0.14 (0.11)	0.09 (0.12)
Family income	0.13 (0.05)	0.12 (0.06)	0.17 (0.07)	0.14 (0.07)
High school's reputation	0.59 (0.07)	0.52 (0.08)	0.43 (0.10)	0.33 (0.11)
Rural/urban (1 = urban)	0.06 (0.19)	0.01 (0.20)	0.39 (0.24)	0.28 (0.27)
Hazard rate	1.28 (0.22)	1.08 (0.24)	0.43 (0.33)	0.16 (0.38)
Tutoring activities:				
Mock tests		1.01 (0.22)		0.58 (0.43)
Correspondence course		0.64 (0.17)		−0.03 (0.22)
Private tutor		−0.30 (0.25)		−0.79 (0.32)
After school *juku*		0.30 (0.17)		0.01 (0.24)
Rônin				3.22 (0.57)
Intercept	−0.37 (0.43)	−1.69 (0.49)		−1.83 (0.85)
Model compared to model				
of intercept only	505.99	554.64	80.86	154.11
df	8	12	8	13
N	1135	1135	511[†]	511[†]

Notes: Entries are maximum-likelihood parameters from logistic regression with SEs in parentheses.
† Students in the follow-up sample with college plans in high school who did not attend a university immediately after high school.

There is a strong association between the *rônin* year and continued competition in the race for university; among this part of the follow-up sample 86 per cent became *rônin* and of these 72 per cent entered college compared with only 6 per cent of the non-*rônin* from this group. This is particularly true among the males, who are much more likely than females to become *rônin*. A further 19 per cent of the original *rônin* continued for a second year to prepare for another round of university exams. Even though the dominant effect in their model is that of the *rônin*, tutoring activities as a group of activities still adds significantly to the background model.

HOW DID EFFORT AND MONEY WORK TO-GETHER? AN EXAMINATION OF THE FAMILY BACKGROUND OF UNIVERSITY STUDENTS

Our use of the idea of equality of opportunity woven into a meritocratic social order rests on the premise that human beings are comparable and finite, that their use-value can be measured and that such measurement is a legitimate basis for stratification.
– *Michael S. Schudson, 'Organizing the Meritocracy'*

In his comment on the history of Japanese education, Thomas Rohlen (1983) writes: 'Despite an unconvincing start, the education system contained the seeds of a meritocratic order. The key was the objectivity of the entrance exam system.' The relationship between education and inter-generational class mobility is an important theme here. This is the comparative investigation of the effect of educational achievement on university enrolment versus the effect of family economic background. In past years, one major testing gauge to measure this 'meritocratic order' is to analyse family incomes of students in universities. Findings made by scholars vary, defying simplified generalization. Rohlen (1977, 1983), Cummings (1980) and James and Benjamin (1988) accentuate the meritocratic and egalitarian qualities of Japan's exam-based education, although they are also disturbed by an augmenting impact of family income on access to the university during 1961–76. Based on the 1975 Social Stratification and Mobility National Survey, Ishida (1993) finds a strong determinant of income inequality for social mobility. Spaulding (1967), Kubota (1969) and Rosenbaum and Kariya (1989), however, suggest a weakening dependence of social mobility on family background both prior to and after World War II due to credentialism in both the bureaucracy and corporate companies. Along similar lines of inquiry to those of Rohlen, Cummings, and James and Benjamin, this article attempts to update the early research through 1978–90.[2]

---

[2] Unless noted otherwise, the major source of statistical data used here is the *Monbushô Gakusei Seikatsu Chôsa Hôkoku* (Report of the Ministry of Education student life survey), carried in the journals *Kôsei Hodô* (Welfare guidance) and *Daigaku to Gakusei* (University and students); both are publications of the Japanese Ministry of Education.

The case of Japan: A follow-up study, 1976-90

Prior to the study of stratification and mobility through entrance exams, three points warrant mentioning, but in brief only, as they are analysed elsewhere in my writing. First, the entrance exams in Japan are an indispensable requirement for national universities, whereas in private universities, generally a large portion of students are admitted without them. Second, overall, the national universities are taken as élite while the majority of private universities are not. As a result, national versus private universities form a 'binary pair' that contrasts the two types:

1. *The national university*: élite-ranked, high *hensachi* level, with the gatekeeping exams anonymous, objective, strictly controlled;
2. *The private university*: mostly non-élite, low *hensachi* level, with admission methods much more lax and less objective.

Due to that contrast, by looking at and comparing who were in these two categories, we will learn how the family income affected the entrance exam system and the trend of that influence. The data for the analysis are drawn from 1978–90 'Report of the Ministry of Education student life survey', *(Gakusei Seikatsu Chôsa Hôkoku)*, published by the Japanese Ministry of Education in its journal *Daigaku to Gakusei* (University and students). Table 7.33 presents the annual family income of students, by national, public and private universities in Japan during the period 1976–90.

Table 7.33 shows that: (1) the average family income for both national and private universities increased, but, as the index shows, the figure for national universities increased faster; (2) despite (1), throughout the period 1976–90, the average annual family income of students from private universities was more than one million yen higher than that of national universities: the difference was ¥1,281,000 in 1976 and ¥1,229,000 in 1990. That gap is shown in Figure 7.11.

Figure 7.11 shows a constant difference in students' family economic background between private universities and national universities. In the meantime, the achievement level of students as expressed by *hensachi* value among the aggregate national university students is higher than the average for the private.[3] What is portrayed here is that, overall, students in national universities came from families with an income ¥1,000,000 lower than those of private universities; but their achievements were higher.

The previous study of Japanese higher education relies essentially upon the statistics of the Japanese Ministry of Education. It has been my intention to do a similar national–private comparison of family incomes at the college level, but so far without success. While the data of the best national universities, such as Tokyo University and Seoul National University, are

---

[3] For a detailed analysis of the difference between the national and private universities in Japan, see Chapter 3, 'A comparative history of university entrance examinations: from 1945 to now'.

obtainable, it appears prohibitively impossible to access any meaningful data on income in any private university in Japan, Korea or Taiwan.

Table 7.33 Annual family income of students, by national, public, and private universities in Japan, 1976–90 (in ¥1000). *Source*: Based on JMOE, 'Gakusei Seikatsu Chôsa Hôkoku' (Report on student life survey), *Daigaku to Gakusei* (Tokyo: JMOE), 1978–92.

Year	1976	1978	1980	1982	1984	1986	1988	1990
Real value in 1000 yen								
National	3760	4443	5100	5360	6011	6277	7038	7617
Public	3769	4685	5059	5594	5878	6354	7231	7780
Private	5041	5677	6189	6748	7322	7835	8166	8846
Total	4748	5401	5927	6405	6983	7432	7880	8539
Index value†								
National	100	118	136	143	167	167	187	202
Public	100	124	134	148	156	169	192	206
Private	100	113	123	134	145	155	162	175
Total	100	114	125	135	147	157	166	180

Note: † Index taking the value of 1976 as 100.

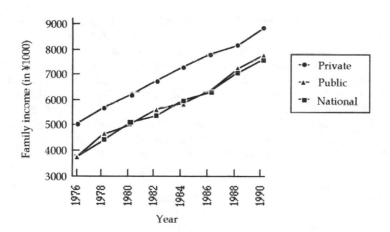

Figure 7.11 Annual family income of students, by national, public and private universities, Japan, 1976–90. *Source*: Based on JMOE, 'Gakusei Seikatsu Chôsa Hôkoku' (Report on student life survey), *Daigaku to Gakusei* (Tokyo: JMOE), 1978–92.

However, by marshalling some skimpy data that are available, I can compare for Japan the top-rank national universities with the private ones. It is shown that the average level of students' family income of the top four and top eight former imperial universities was lower than the average level of all the private universities (see Figure 7.12).

The data in Figure 7.12 lend themselves to an assessment of the élite national universities as a group. Their exam system is strictly objective and anonymous. Compared with the average of private universities, they selected students with higher scores, but their overall economic status is lower. The cause of their better achievement level is motivated by the future mobility. The more immediate, economic reason, however, comes from the fact that the national university is cheaper than the private (see Table 7.34).

As seen in Table 7.34, over the years, private universities cost a lot more than national or public universities because of the difference in tuition fees. The cost of private universities posed an economic barrier to lower-income children; this barrier became higher and higher as compared to national and public universities, which is shown clearly in Figure 7.13.

Thus, the cost advantage of national universities was an important factor that attracted students, especially those with fewer resources. The mobility pathway through university is apparently narrower for them than for students from more affluent backgrounds. It is plain that lower-income families and their children face a greater challenge in getting a college education. But, the honest and almost simplistic selection system had a unmistakable message: so long as they performed better, they could make it. The general income data also show that. The above analysis poses an empirical challenge to the hypothesis that 'access expands but is socially controlled by institutional differentiation so that élite universities (... ex-Imperial Japanese universities) remain the cultural possession of traditionally advantaged groups' (Halsey, 1992).

A comparison of average family income, as discussed here, generates a picture too large for us to study the issue of mobility. We need to know further who benefited from the entrance system, who less so. To that end, one way is to investigate the chances of each socio-economic stratum in getting higher education (Rohlen, 1977, 1983; Cummings, 1980; James and Benjamin, 1988) . The ensuing study is largely a follow-up of that tradition. The source for the data used is '1978–1990 Report of the Ministry of Education student life survey' (*Gakusei Seikatsu Chôsa Hôkoku*), published biennially by the Japanese Ministry of Education in *Daigaku to Gakusei*. The Japanese government divides its population into five quintiles by family income. Each quintile represents 20 per cent of all households, with Quintile 1 the lowest income stratum, and Quintile 5 the highest. Table 7.35 summarizes the ratios of these five quintiles in college students from 1978 to 1990.

To perceive the changing trend in quintile ratios over time, Figure 7.14 produced from the data given was helpful. A couple of points may be made here. First of all, in all sectors, the lowest income stratum, Quintile 1, went up to a varying extent. Secondly, in the national and public universities, students from poor households had been doing well.

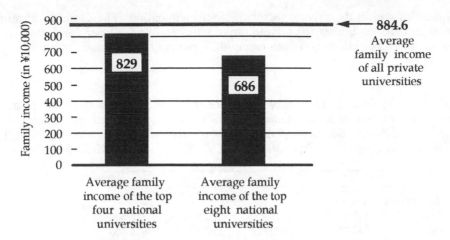

Figure 7.12 The average student family income: top four and top eight national universities versus all private universities, 1991. *Source*: Sanawa Yano, *Kôtô Kyôikuhi no Hiyôfutan ni kansuru Seisaku Kagakudeki Kenkyû* (A study of the policy science concerning the cost of higher education), (Tokyo: Tokyo University of Industry, 1993), 182.
Note: The national university ranking used here is based on the average student family income. The top four are Tokyo University, Kyoto University, Nagoya University and Kyushu University; the top eight include the top four plus Tokushima University, Nagasaki University, Oita University and Kumamoto University.

In fact, starting from 1980, they came to have a large representation, although with undulation, as seen better in the figure. It is worth noting that 1979 was a year of important reform in the university entrance system. The national-level JFSAT started to be used for the first time as the primary gatekeeper for all national/public universities.

Within this new selection system, the lower-income Quintile 1 rose from 22 per cent to 25.3 per cent for national universities and from 18.4 per cent to 24.4 per cent for public universities.[4]

Thirdly, the majority of private universities have been known to be less strict and less objective in entrance screening.

Until very recently, all the private universities were outside the jurisdiction of the national system JFSAT. Their Quintile 5 students had a decisively higher ratio (around 30 per cent on average) than the other

---

[4] Japan's National Center for University Entrance Examination (JNCUEE) was instituted in 1977. In December, together with 120 national/public universities, JNCUEE instituted a simulation Joint First Stage Achievement Test (JFSAT) for upper secondary school third-year students. In January 1979, JFSAT was used as the entrance requirement for both national and public universities. Refer to Chapter 3, 'A comparative history of university entrance examinations: from 1945 to now'.

quintiles within the private sector of higher education. The Quintile 5 ratio was also much higher for private universities (around 30 per cent) than for national and public universities (around 20 per cent on average for both).

Table 7.34 Cost of university education to a student, by national, public and private universities in Japan, 1976–90 (in yen). *Source*: Based on JMOE, 'Gakusei Seikatsu Chôsa Hôkoku' (Report on student life survey), *Daigaku to Gakusei* (Tokyo: JMOE), 1978–92 (especially 1992: 120–33).

	1976	1978	1980	1982
National universities				
Tuition	146,700	206,500	265,900	315,500
Living costs	446,900	514,500	580,100	654,400
Total	**593,600**	**721,000**	**846,000**	**969,900**
Public universities				
Tuition	153,200	203,400	254,800	319,100
Living costs	402,200	473,200	512,500	564,200
Total	**555,400**	**676,600**	**767,300**	**883,300**
Private universities				
Tuition	341,300	449,300	565,500	679,000
Living costs	446,300	505,600	593,900	642,100
Total	**787,600**	**954,900**	**1,159,400**	**1,321,100**

	1984	1986	1988	1990
National universities				
Tuition	347,900	371,500	409,100	445,900
Living costs	684,800	738,600	776,500	876,400
Total	**1,032,700**	**1,110,100**	**1,185,600**	**1,322,300**
Public universities				
Tuition	372,200	404,900	444,000	493,600
Living costs	590,200	650,400	678,000	758,200
Total	**962,400**	**1,055,300**	**1,122,000**	**1,251,800**
Private universities				
Tuition	776,000	855,400	941,300	999,500
Living costs	650,500	679,600	702,200	755,500
Total	**1,426,500**	**1,535,000**	**1,643,500**	**1,755,000**

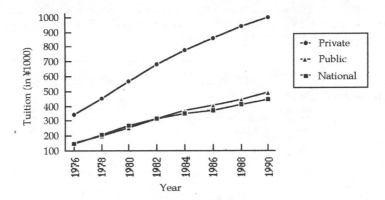

Figure 7.13 The cost of university tuition in Japan, by national, public and private universities, 1976–90. *Source*: Based on JMOE, 'Gakusei Seikatsu Chôsa Hôkoku' (Report on student life survey), *Daigaku to Gakusei* (Tokyo: JMOE), 1978–92.

Here, a major caveat is necessary, concerning the validity of the surveys. There is a major difference in data collection in the Japanese Ministry of Education's Student Life Survey before and after 1977. Earlier, distribution of college students by family income quintiles included the entire population of Japan. One example of the data created thus is shown in Table 7.36.

The data are puzzling because they conflict with other information we have about access to education in Japan. For example, virtually all Japanese children in the relevant age group attend school for the nine years of compulsory education, and 99 per cent of them are in public schools. Thus, there can be no income bias operating at the primary or junior high school levels, overall or in the public sector. Yet, Table 7.36 appears to show an 'income bias'. It seems that poor or middle-income families are heavily represented in kindergartens, rich families in universities, but 'this will simply be telling us about the relationship between income and age, not about the educational access of different lifetime groups' (James and Benjamin, 1988).

Compared to the US or the European countries, this methodological problem may be more serious in Japan, where earnings rise steeply with age. The earnings of a 55-year-old male may be four times those of a 20-year-old male, especially in large firms and government employment. Therefore, the difference stems more from seniority bias than lifetime income bias, although the latter is what interests us most (James and Benjamin, 1988).

One way to circumvent this problem is to consider only the age group or cohort relevant to each level of education. According to Jyoji Kikuchi, well researched on this issue, fathers of junior college and university students are aged 40–59 (ibid.). In the Japanese Student Life Survey, the household heads for four-year university students are aged 45–54.

Table 7.35 Students from five quintiles of family income by national, public and private universities, by percentage, 1978–90[a]. *Source*: JMOE, 'Gakusei Seikatsu Chôsa Hôkoku' (Report on Student Life Survey), *Daigaku to Gakusei* (Tokyo: JMOE), 1978–92.

	Quintile 1[b]	Quintile 2	Quintile 3	Quintile 4	Quintile 5
National universities					
1978	22.0	19.0	18.9	19.1	21.0
1980	23.8	19.9	16.9	18.6	20.8
1982	25.9	19.9	16.9	18.8	18.5
1984	24.4	17.8	17.5	19.6	20.7
1986	25.4	19.8	18.1	18.8	17.9
1988	27.4	17.3	19.1	16.6	19.6
1990	25.2	18.4	18.8	16.8	20.8
Public universities					
1978	18.4	19.1	22.3	19.1	21.1
1980	21.0	20.8	18.1	20.0	20.1
1982	23.2	20.6	18.7	18.6	18.9
1984	22.8	20.0	18.6	18.9	19.7
1986	24.6	20.0	18.3	19.1	18.0
1988	26.3	17.6	19.1	17.2	19.8
1990	24.4	17.1	17.6	19.0	21.9
Private universities					
1978	11.1	16.8	19.9	20.5	31.7
1980	15.6	17.5	16.0	20.3	30.6
1982	16.2	17.6	17.0	19.9	29.3
1984	17.2	15.1	17.1	19.7	30.9
1986	17.8	16.3	17.4	20.1	28.4
1988	18.6	14.5	17.1	19.4	30.4
1990	16.9	16.4	17.2	19.5	27.9

Notes: a. For full-time university students whose household heads (*setaishû*) were 45–54 years old. b. Quintile 1 is the lowest quintile of family income, and Quintile 5 the highest.

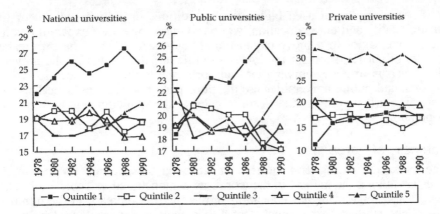

Figure 7.14 Students from five quintiles of family income by national, public and private universities, by percentage, 1978–90. *Source*: JMOE, 'Gakusei Seikatsu Chôsa Hôkoku' (Report on student life survey), *Daigaku to Gakusei* (Tokyo: JMOE), 1978–92.
Notes: For full-time university students whose household heads (*setaishû*) were 45–54 years old.
Quintile 1 is the lowest quintile of family income, and Quintile 5 the highest.

Table 7.36 Distribution of students by family income quintiles, all households in Japan, 1976. *Source*: Based on Sôrifu (Office of Prime Minister of Japan), *Annual Report on the Family Income and Expenditure Survey, 1976*, quoted in Jyoji Kikuchi, 'Access to education and the income redistributive effects', in *Allocation of Educational Resources in Japan*, edited by Shogo Ichikawa (Tokyo: National Institute for Educational Research, 1978), 152–7.

	Quintile I	Quintile II	Quintile III	Quintile IV	Quintile V
Kindergarten	16.3	23.1	25.5	20.7	14.4
Primary school	14.7	19.3	23.8	23.8	18.4
Junior high school	12.7	15.0	20.5	25.1	26.6
High school	12.4	13.9	17.6	24.9	31.1
University	8.6	9.0	11.6	24.6	45.9

Hypothetically, Jyoji, James and Benjamin appear to be plausible in arguing for the need for age grouping in studying college students. While it exceeds the scope of this book to decide which age range is more accurate, it appears unlikely that their difference would alter entirely (1) the contrast in quintile-ratio patterns between national and private universities or (2) the basic trends of change in the quintile ratio for each category of university respectively.

To sum up, Japan used high unit expenditures in the national sector to ensure quality and élite education, while relying on low unit expenditures in the private sector to achieve expansion (Magnussen, 1975). The difference in rates of participation for the lowest quintile at national and public universities versus private universities supports the popular conception that national and public universities are the poor person's ticket out: the Dragon Gate. The private universities seem to cater to the wealthier segments of the population.

The case of Korea

The expansion of higher education in Korea is outstanding. Its enrolment rates are among the highest in the world, as demonstrated in Table 7.37. The historical change in higher education shows that the increase in the number of college students grew much faster than that of the teaching faculty or material conditions.

In the past 50 years or so, the number of college students expanded more than 200-fold, while both schools and faculty members increased by only about 30-fold (Table 7.38). Due to this salient feature of higher educational expansion, learning the trends in the effects of family background factors is important in understanding how education and the social structure in the Newly Industrialized Countries (NICs) changed. The study here is largely drawn upon the statistical findings concluded by Young-hwa Kim (1990). Their data source is the samples of the 1970, 1975, 1980 and 1985 Korean Population and Housing Census. The census records the basic characteristics of all individuals living in the households surveyed, such as their sex, birth dates, educational levels, occupations and places of residence. Kim examines trends in the effects of background factors on the transition to college education. Youths in Korea enter college at age 18 on average. However, since many youths who have failed their first college entrance exams repeat the exam the next year (*Jai su saeng*), one has to wait until at least two years after high school graduation in order to know whether a student entered college or not. Therefore, the samples for the analysis are restricted to those youths aged 20–22, who lived with their father and whose head of household was a father, which is the normal family structure in Korea.

Table 7.37 International comparison: enrolment rates in higher education in Korea, 1991. *Source: UNESCO Statistical Yearbook* (Paris: UNESCO, 1992).

Areas	Year	Enrolment rate
Korea	**1991**	**40.5**
World total	1990	12.7
Asia total	1990	6.5
Developed countries	1990	38.8
Developing countries	1990	6.9
Taiwan	1991	37.9
Japan	1989	30.7

Table 7.38: Expansion of higher education, by school, faculty and enrolment in Korea, 1945–93. *Source*: KMOE, *Education in Korea 1993–1994* (Seoul: KMOE, 1994), 30.

	1945	*1960*	*1970*	*1980*	*1990*	*1993*
Number of schools	19	85	232	357	556	655
Index	100	450	1220	1879	2926	3447
Number of faculty	1490	3808	10,435	20,900	41,920	51,227
Index	100	260	700	1400	2813	3438
Number of students	7819	101,041	201,436	615,452	1,490,809	2,099,735
Index	100	1290	2586	7871	19,066	26,854

Note: The index takes the values of 1945 as 100.

Unlike the survey source used for Japan, household heads for Korea were limited to the father, but were not confined by age cohort. The sample size is given in Table 7.39.

Background variables included in the analysis are father's education and father's occupation, recoded into six social class variables: upper middle class, new middle class, old middle class, working class, urban marginal class and farmer class. These classes correspond to the following:

- *Upper middle class*: high-level professional, technical, administrative and managerial workers
- *New middle class*: low-level professional, technical and administrative workers, clerical workers
- *Old middle class*: self-employed low-level professional and technical workers, self-employed sales and service workers, and self-employed production workers
- *Working class*: sales, service and production workers
- *Urban marginal class*: maids, cleaners, street vendors and unskilled labourers
- *Farmer class*: agricultural, animal husbandry and forestry workers, fishermen and hunters

In the study, years of schooling is used for the linear regression models and the log-odds of transition to college is used for the logistic models. The results from linear regression analysis show that the explained variance by all background variables from linear regression models decreased from 39 per cent for those born in 1948–50, to 34 per cent for those in 1953–5, to 28 per cent for those in 1958–60, and to 20 per cent for those in 1963–5, as shown in Table 7.40.

The reduction of the explained variance by all background variables implies the diminishing effects of background variables on educational attainment. In general, we see an obvious downward direction. For the 1948–50 cohort, 39 per cent of the years of schooling can be explained by family background. For the 1963–5 cohort, however, it only explains 20 per cent of the years of schooling.

Table 7.39 The sample size: number and the proportion of respondents aged 20–22 whose household head is father. *Source*: Young-hwa Kim, 'Consequences of higher educational expansion in Korea: trends in family background and regional effects on higher educational attainment, 1967– 1984' (Seoul: Korea Educational Development Institute, 1990), 141.

1970 census	1975 census	1980 census	1985 census
5123 (34.1%)	6272 (42.9%)	19,323 (45.7%)	26,130 (49.2%)

Note: The number in parentheses shows the percentage of the entire population of the census.

The regional effects on educational attainment have been substantial, but they also show the diminishing pattern of trends for both males and females (Y. H. Kim, 1990: 148–9). Living in cities provides additional benefits for educational attainment compared to living in rural areas. Conversely, handicaps from living in rural areas have been substantial across all cohorts. Yet, as data show, the effects of the place of residence have declined over time. The overall pattern of trends indicates that the effects of father's education, social class origin, and place of residence on educational attainment have tended to diminish over time.

The foregoing study on the effects of family background on school years should, in theory, include college education. What is more germane to my interest here is the logistic regression analysis, claimed to be more appropriate to the study of the effects of independent variables on the log-odds of transition probability to college. The result is reported in Table 7.41.

The logistic regression coefficients are conceptually difficult to understand. Unlike the linear regression, no consistent trend is discernible except that the advantages of upper middle class origin have declined for the most recent three birth cohorts (Y. H. Kim, 1990). This is confirmed by comparing statistically the chances of college education between social classes. Table 7.42 presents the result of this comparison and shows that, when the upper middle class is taken as a base, all the other classes had increased in the recent cohorts. Meanwhile, when the new middle class is taken as a base, all other classes had declined. On the other hand, the relative disadvantages of the working class and urban marginal class compared to the new middle and old middle classes appear to have increased, although they gained some advantages compared to the upper middle class.

To wrap up the above, two conclusions appear to be less controversial. First, the effects of place of residence on educational attainment diminished over time; this is found in both the linear and the logistic regressions. Also, as the linear regression shows, the overall dependence of educational attainment on social origins declined categorically.

However, when examining the chances of higher education using logistic regression, the picture is less straightforward. No decline of the effects of family background is perceivable in absolute terms, except for the upper middle class. The family background effects continued to offset the expansion of college education. Despite that correlation, to declare simply that the inequality persisted obscures some crucial facts.

Table 7.40 Linear regression analysis of years of schooling by birth cohort: coefficients in Korea. *Source*: Young-hwa Kim, 'Consequences of higher educational expansion in Korea: trends in family background and regional effects on higher educational attainment, 1967–1984' (Seoul: Korea Educational Development Institute, 1990), 145.

	Year of birth			
	1948–50	*1953–5*	*1958–60*	*1963–5*
Father's education	0.22	0.22	0.21	0.14
Social class				
Upper middle	1.91	1.63	0.94	0.42
New middle	1.59	1.29	0.75	0.41
Old middle	1.40	1.28	0.93	0.61
Working	0.31[b]	0.35[a]	0.30	0.18
Urban marginal	0.16[d]	0.03[d]	0.01[d]	−0.03[d]
Place of residence				
Seoul	1.46	1.09	0.83	0.52
Large cities	0.92	0.82	0.75	0.53
Small cities	0.93	0.92	0.54	0.33
Intercept	6.89	7.25	8.08	9.94
SE	2.39	2.41	2.29	1.77
R^2	**0.39**	**0.34**	**0.28**	**0.20**
N	5039	6207	19,168	25,831

Note: a: $0.0001 < p$ 0.001, b: $0.001 < p$ 0.01, c: $0.01 < p$ 0.05, d: $0.05 < p$, others (no mark): p 0.0001.

Table 7.41 Logistic regression coefficients of four-year university transition for high school graduates by birth cohort in Korea. *Source*: Ibid., 147.

	Year of birth			
	1948–50	*1953–5*	*1958–60*	*1963–5*
Father's education	0.16	0.15	0.15	0.16
Social class				
Upper middle	0.86	1.04	0.95	0.86
New middle	−0.0[d]	−0.03[d]	0.17[b]	0.19
Old middle	0.18[d]	−0.14[d]	0.07[c]	0.18
Working	−0.25[d]	−0.30[b]	−0.26	−0.30
Urban marginal	−0.29[d]	−0.12[d]	−0.23[a]	−0.35
Place of residence				
Seoul	0.64	0.62	0.42	0.25
Large cities	0.66	0.53	0.40	0.39
Small cities	−0.63[b]	−0.47[b]	−0.19[b]	−0.13[a]
Intercept	−2.87	−2.68	−2.62	−2.05
N	1691	2542	10,250	19,366

Note: a: 0.0001 p 0.001, b: 0.001 p 0.01, c: 0.01 p 0.05, d: 0.05 p, others (no mark): p 0.0001.

Table 7.42 Predicted probability ratios of four-year college transition by social class and by birth cohort. *Source*: Ibid., 150.

	Upper middle class = 1				New middle class = 1			
	1948 –50	*1953 –55*	*1958 –60*	*1963 –65*	*1948 –50*	*1953 –55*	*1958 –60*	*1963 –65*
Upper middle	1	1	1	1	2.26	2.61	2.01	1.75
New middle	0.45	0.38	0.50	0.57	1	1	1	1
Old middle	0.54	0.35	0.40	0.57	1.21	0.90	0.81	1.00
Working	0.36	0.30	0.33	0.37	0.81	0.77	0.67	0.65
Urban marginal	0.35	0.35	0.34	0.36	0.77	0.92	0.70	0.62
Farmer	0.45	0.40	0.43	0.49	1.02	1.03	0.86	0.85

The exposition of the data cited shows: (1) for the upper middle class, the chance of getting into university declined compared to the rest of society; (2) that chance had increased for the new middle class, composed of low-level professional, technical and administrative workers, and clerical workers, showing the growing social dynamics of low-rank 'white collar' workers.

The case of Taiwan

To study the changes in access to élite education in Taiwan, I draw upon two statistical studies, one at the national level (Tsai and Chiu, 1993), the other at the school and district level of the city of Taizhong (Broaded, 1994). The first study was part of the large-scale project concerning persistent inequality in thirteen countries. Their methodology was very similar to that for Korea introduced earlier. In order to investigate cross-cohort trends in educational stratification in Taiwan they made two parallel analyses. The first breaks the data down into five ten-year-interval birth cohorts and the second into three major birth cohorts, which have experienced three critical stages of formal education development. Comparisons across these three cohorts clearly reflect the impact of educational expansion. As in the case of Korea, in reviewing their report, I take into consideration both the original statistical descriptions and their conclusion, which are summarized in Table 7.43.

Table 7.43 shows that parameter estimates vary by cohort. Among the oldest, father's education and occupational status both have a significant impact on their sons' schooling. In contrast, father's education and farming origin have approximately the same effect, but in the opposite direction, on highest completed school grade for the second cohort. Among the youngest, educational attainment is directly and significantly influenced by father's schooling alone. Looking at the trend in the impact of social background rather than its size, we see a sharp decrease in the effect of father's schooling in the two oldest cohorts, and a slight increase in the youngest cohort.

A similar pattern can be found for the effect of father's occupational status (Tsai and Chiu, 1993: 206–7). For access to higher education, again as for Korea, a logistic analysis was made; the resulting data are in Table 7.44.

It is difficult to tease out of the statistics given here any clear pattern of trends. The effects of father's schooling and father's SEI underwent great changes in the most recent three cohorts, and the direction of these changes just went in opposite directions to each other, as shown in Figure 7.15.

Table 7.43 Linear regression analysis of years of schooling completed in the extended model, Taiwan, coefficient. *Source*: S.-L. Tsai and H.-Y. Chiu, 'Changes in educational stratification in Taiwan', in Yossi Shavit and Hans-Peter Blossfeld, *Persistent Inequality: Changing Educational Attainment in Thirteen Countries* (Oxford: Westview Press, 1993), 215.

	Year of birth		
	1919–45	*1946–55*	*1956–68*
Father's schooling	0.34 (0.06)	0.17 (0.07)	0.21 (0.05)
Father's SEI[†]	0.12 (0.06)	0.03 (0.06)	0.03 (0.04)
Farming origin	0.67 (0.61)	−1.27 (0.74)	0.08 (0.47)
Mother's schooling	0.13 (0.08)	0.20 (0.08)	0.13 (0.06)
Urbanization	3.18 (0.80)	1.30 (0.94)	1.18 (0.69)
Taipei City	0.90 (0.52)	0.83 (0.67)	−0.20 (0.52)
Kaohsing City	1.43 (1.15)	1.91 (0.94)	0.42 (0.90)
Ethnicity	0.58 (0.45)	0.29 (0.81)	−0.20 (0.57)
Constant	−3.97	6.43	6.64
R^2	**0.35**	**0.30**	**0.28**

Notes: The value in parentheses is the standard error.
† SEI: Social Economic Index, which is constructed on the basis of father's occupational status.

Table 7.44 Logistic regression of social background factors in transition to post high school education, given senior high school completion, Taiwan. *Source*: Ibid., 216.

	Year of birth		
	1919–45	*1946–55*	*1956–68*
Father's schooling	−0.06	0.06	0.04
Father's SEI[†]	0.13	−0.10	0.06
Farming origin	1.58	−1.72	0.88
Mother's schooling	0.08	0.03	0.04
Urbanization	0.08	0.14	0.37
Taipei City	0.82	0.84	−0.03
Kaohsing City	−6.96	0.79	−0.88
Ethnicity	0.41	0.98	0.08

Note: † SEI: Social Economic Index, which is constructed on the basis of father's occupational status.

From the 1919–45 cohort to that of 1956–68, the coefficient of father's schooling rose from −0.06 to 0.04, whereas father's SEI fell from 0.13 to 0.06. The two family effects, when plotted, form two 'V' shapes, inverse to one other. They defy interpretation, begging as many questions as they solve.

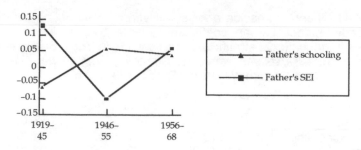

Figure 7.15 Logistic regression of social background factors in transition to post high school education, given senior high school completion, Taiwan. *Source*: Ibid.

In that regard, empirical findings at the school level reported by Montgomery Broaded (1994) are very informative. Broaded studied the role of the entrance exam system in the transition to the differentiated structure of education opportunities at the senior high school level in the central Taiwan city of Taizhong.

In Taiwan, the transition from junior high to senior high is an important part of the weeding-out process, very similar to the university exam system. At the end of their nine-year compulsory schooling, entrance examinations distribute young people to stratified educational opportunities. On the one hand, this process is meritocratic and enjoys widespread public support as the fairest sorting device yet devised. On the other hand, other features of the education system have a potentially inegalitarian thrust. Since children are expected to attend neighbourhood schools at both elementary and junior high school levels, patterns of residential segregation on the basis of income, social class or ethnicity may be reflected in the composition of the schools' student body.

To investigate that issue, extensive questionnaire data gathered from 1564 third-year junior high students were combined with school records about their high school entrance examination scores and actual high school enrolments. These students belong to four public schools selected to reflect variation in their rates of advancement into academic senior high schools.

School 1 has the highest transition rate into academic senior high schools of the four schools in the sample. School 2 has the lowest transition rate into academic high schools of the four in the sample. School 3 has a higher transition rate into academic scenario high schools than School 2, but still falls a bit below the national average. School 4 has transition rates into academic senior high schools slightly above the national average (Broaded, 1994). The findings about the association between parental characteristics and high school placement are reported in Table 7.45.

In the above, none of the associations within individual schools is strong, and most of them are in fact quite weak. In Taizhong's public junior high schools, differences in parental characteristics account for a rather small part of the variation in senior high school placement outcomes. Overall, modest associations are observed with father's occupational prestige (0.10) and father's income (0.10).

Table 7.45 Family background variables by senior high school placement. *Source*: Montgomery Broaded, 'Social origins, ability group placement and educational outcomes in urban Taiwan', presented at CIES Annual Meetings, San Diego, March 1994.

	Income		Education		Occupation prestige	
	Father	Mother	Father	Mother	Father	Mother
School 1						
D	0.04	−0.03	0.05	0.06	0.03	0.07
r	0.03	−0.03	0.07	0.10	0.04	0.09
School 2						
D	−0.01	0.03	0.00	0.06	0.03	−0.02
r	−0.05	−0.02	−0.02	0.01	0.06	−0.05
School 3						
D	0.06	0.06	0.12	0.09	0.03	0.03
r	0.04	0.06	0.15	0.08	0.04	0.03
School 4						
D	−0.05	−0.03	0.11	0.09	0.02	0.12
r	−0.08	−0.06	0.15	0.14	0.04	0.15
Total D	0.10	0.02	0.18	0.20	0.10	0.21
r	0.09	0.01	0.22	0.23	0.12	0.24

Note: Zero-order correlations, asymmetric Somer's D with high school placement dependent, and Pearson's r.

The associations with mother's occupational prestige (0.21), mother's education (0.20) and father's education (0.18) are stronger. Because of a host of factors, such as the mechanism of three objective entrance exams, the diffusion of educational achievement values, the relatively equal provision of basic education, etc., 'talented children from less advantaged social origins face considerably fewer impediments to educational advancement than they would in a different educational and societal context' (Broaded, 1994: 26).

A DISCUSSION

'Does money matter? Does time/effort matter?' These are two questions that the preceding pages tried to answer. A model with the two questions blended together is hardly conventionally framed. Skimpy data about time spent on work are available. But in the myriad of statistical studies regressing achievement or stratification, very seldom has time spent on work been factored in as an explanatory variable. The lack of this juxtaposition splits my discussion methodologically, one for 'time', the other for 'money'. I synthesize the two in a final discussion of the educational outcomes by examining the stratification represented in university students.

In the first part of this chapter, time is treated as an alias of effort. In a multinational comparison, the educational achievements of Japan, Korea and Taiwan were at the top, and their academic calendars were longer than those of other countries, especially the US. It is found that, when measuring time spent on academic activities, such as schooling hours and homework, the difference between East Asia and many other countries starts to dwindle. That is not, however, to deny that difference. In my argument, (1) that difference was substantial, and (2) it came largely from the institutionalized cramming for exams. That difference was dramatized and typified by the experience of exam-repeaters, which stretched pre-college school years from the American 6-3-3 system into a *de facto* structure of education in Japan, Korea and Taiwan:

           6-3-4
    Or, 6-3-5
           6-3-6
           6-3-7
           ...

The phenomenal salience of exam-repeaters stems from their being a high proportion of the applicants for entrance exams as well as in the élite universities. The majority of exam-repeaters believed they failed because they did not work hard enough rather than because of lack of natural ability. Data also show that most exam-repeaters attended prep schools, indicating high-degree institutionalization of time and effort and a fully developed genre of knowledge transmission. The acceptance ratio of exam-repeaters – 30–50 per cent in Korea and 25 per cent in Taiwan – shows that pain and perseverance did pay off for a portion of them.

In a sense, the exam-repeaters' years were only the 'tip of the iceberg', as they were the conspicuous part of college preparation. Equally time-consuming were routinized mock-test exercises, *juku* life, and other means of extracurricular cramming. The credentialistic structure of East Asia and the impartiality of the entrance system grind into the heads of young people the knowledge they need to learn. One common denominator among Japan, Korea and Taiwan is that the bottom line of the entrance exams requirement has been translated into the bottom-line quality for the entire school system.

In the second part of the chapter, I discuss the factor of 'money'. An international comparison of public expenditures reveals that Japanese, Korean and Taiwanese regimes were not as exemplary in education as they have been assumed to be. Whether measured in absolute terms (per pupil expenditures) or in relative terms (share of educational expenditure in total GNP), they are not ranked top in the IAEP countries. Even compared to some non-IAEP countries of the Third World, Japan, Korea and Taiwan were not that impressive. A disparity is found between rhetoric and reality in the national commitment to the educational goal.

In a way, the commitment to education in the three East Asian countries is more tangibly at non-governmental social level, or local cultural level, manifested in parental expectation and support. 'Education', says Milton Sapirstein (1955), 'like neurosis, begins at home.' This is not to deny the effect of the system. Quite the contrary, meritocratic virtue and behaviour to date are defined and confirmed by a larger context, including the credentialist structure of workplaces and the state-controlled university entrance system.

Studies show that family investment in education is correlated with family incomes, and that investment differed significantly between urban and rural areas. These provide the germ for potential inequality. However, educa-tional behaviours and outcome are not uni-dimensionally subject to economic determination. The costly decision to repeat entrance exams was cited as a case in point. Students from richer families and whose parents have more education are more likely to continue in the most extensive forms of cramming. However, these effects are small, adding only about 5–6 per cent to the likelihood that a student undertakes the *rônin* year (Stevenson and Baker, 1992).

While there is ample evidence for the unequal investments in extracurricular education, the cost-effect of that investment is mixed. Findings (Stevenson and Baker, 1992) about the so-called 'shadow education', i.e., cramming for exams, in Japan, show that the costs of tutoring activities were not statistically correlated with success in entering college. This tends to suggest that performance is a multivariate outcome, for which the economic factor is only one of the factors. The comparison between the NICs and the developed world also lent some support to that point.

In the concluding part of the chapter, I factored in both money and effort in analysing educational achievement. Economic status or investment in education has been taken as a significant variable in the input–output study, generally expressed by the educational production function (EPF). EPF treats education as an enterprise analogous to modern industry, typically demonstrated in this EPF formula taken from Henry Levin (1980):

$$Y = a + b_1 X_1 + b_2 X_2 + \dots + b_n X_n + e$$

In this linear equation, Y is the educational output, and X represents the various inputs such as the characteristics and number of teachers and other personnel as well as instructional materials and faculties. The bs signify the regression or slope coefficients for each input, showing the estimated effect of a unit increase in each input on output. The intercept term or constant, a, refers to that level of educational output that is not dependent on the inputs, and the residual or variance in Y that is unexplained by the equation is symbolized by e (Levin, 1980). In its application, the independent variables for EPF are generally those which can be termed as conditions for students, closely relevant to but extraneous of students' behaviours. In regression for educational attainment, as shown in the study of the case of Korea, variables such as parents' educational level, income, occupation, residence, etc. are also taken into account. School inputs may also include such measures as class size, teacher experience, education, verbal score, library facilities, and other indicators of educational resources, as a formula in Fägerlind and Saha (1991: 201):

$$Y = f(F,I,P,S)$$

where the educational output Y is a function (f) of various inputs, including family background (F), pre-school ability (I), peer group influence (P) and school factors (S) (Fägerlind and Saha, 1991). This type of equation has been estimated for micro-levels, such as individual students, schools or districts, or for the macro-level at international level.

In spite of rapid development of this type of research, according to Henry Levin (1980), the 'investigations have been more successful in demonstrating the inherent complexities of the phenomenon than in producing useful results'. Little commonality has been found among the researchers' conclusions. Few studies have provided results which would suggest that feasible policy differences in the magnitudes and types of educational resources would change appreciably the existing patterns of educational outcomes. As Levin acknowledges, a major deficiency in these researches is the lack of a guiding theoretical framework, with the inevitable result.

In that regard, one major deficiency underpinning the EPF model, I would argue, is the absence of the temporal variable in their regression. EPF is a derivative application or a metaphor of economic production. A production function defines a boundary in the input–output space, specifying the maximum physical output that can be obtained from every possible combination of physical inputs, given the existing level of technical knowledge (Blaug, 1970). A production function lays great stress on time, as shown in a Cobb-Douglas production function:

$$Q = AN^{\delta}K^{\beta}$$
where
Q = physical output,
N = inputs of labour measured in man hours,
K = inputs of capital measured in machine hours,
A, and δ, β = constants to be estimated.

Time spent on work is, as succinctly shown, a vitally important measurement of output. In the same vein, time was once hypothesized as equally important in the educational production function as well. In conceptualizing the economics of education, the model by John Carroll (1963), to take one example, is considered as exemplary (Levin, 1980). Carroll proposes five components, three relating to the individual learner and two pertaining to the learning conditions. Individual factors include (1) student aptitude, defined as 'the amount of time needed to learn the task under optimal instructional conditions'; (2) student ability to understand instruction; (3) student perseverance, which is the amount of time the learner is willing to engage actively in learning. Factors external to the students are (4) time allowed for learning and (5) the quality of instruction. Carroll attaches great importance to the time spent on work as a variable in the 'economics' of the educational production function. Very unfortunately, that variable has rarely been factored in the analysis of student achievement, despite its paramountcy.

As noted, the weakness of the EPF model also appears in international comparison. Drawing on the IAEP cross-national assessment of achievement, Passow et al. (1976) rank educational achievement by developed and developing countries (see Table 7.46), omitting the Newly Industrialized Countries (NICs), such as South Korea and Hong Kong (Fägerlind and Saha, 1991). That major exception is apparently applicable to Taiwan as well.

Table 7.46 Country rank order correlation coefficients between level of economic development and achievement, IEA countries. *Source*: H. Passow *et al.*, *The National Case Study: An Empirical Comparative Study of Twenty One Educational Systems* (Stockholm: Almqvist and Wiksell, 1976), 174. Cited from Ingemar Fägerlind and Lawrence J. Saha, *Education and National Development: A Comparative Perspective* (Pergamon, 1991), 199.

Achievement	Population I (10-year-olds)	Population II (14-year-olds)
Aggregate achievement	0.62* (N = 12)	0.45 (N = 13)
Science	0.37 (N = 15)	0.26 (N = 17)
Reading comprehension	0.55* (N = 13)	0.44 (N = 14)

Note: * Significant at 0.05 level.

Table 7.47 Interrelationship between educational achievement and economic status of different countries.

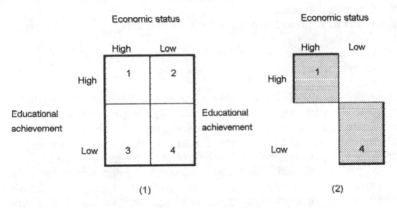

(1)　　　　　　　　　　　　　(2)

In my study, neither GNP nor educational expenditure sufficed to explain the high achievement of Korea and Taiwan. The disparity in time allocation to academic work, especially the enormous effort and family support generated by exam preparation, should thus be taken as a major explanatory factor. The matrix in Table 7.47 is used to illustrate the four possibilities for a country's educational performance against its economic status.

The four cells in Table 7.47 (1) represent four hypothetical possibilities of educational achievement for the countries at different stages of economic development. Cell 1 = developed countries with high achievement; Cell 2 = developing countries with high achievement; Cell 3 = developed countries with relatively low achievement; and Cell 4 = developing countries with low achievement. Granted that Cells 1 and 4 are normative, the IAEP findings highlight the possibilities in Cells 2 and 3. That is, a country might achieve higher even if its economic status (GNP) was lower, and vice versa. Cell 2 can refer to the East Asian NICs, and Cell 3 may, in relative terms, indicate the low achievement of some countries in the First World. These two possibilities result from the reciprocity of capital and labour, to use the terms of classic economics again. Input of labour hours in education may include school hours, time spent on homework, and time spent on other extra-curricular studies, etc. Other things being equal, labour measured in study hours could have tremendous effects in augmenting the educational output. This is not reflected in the earlier model, $Y = f(F,I,P,S)$, because it truncates that major factor.

To apply that point of argument to the societal level, the combination of family income and students' effort may be schematized (see Table 7.48).

In the final analysis, the neglect of 'labour hours' unduly dismisses the dynamic role that students can play in their achievement. It blurs the fact that education acts both as an agent for the reproduction of the social order, and as a producer of social mobility (Fägerlind and Saha, 1991). A modified EPF model which accommodates the circumstances expressed in Cells 1–4 of Table 7.48 may be written as:

$$Y = f(F,E,I,P,S...)$$

> Where Y = the educational output is a function (f) of various inputs,
> F = family background,
> **E = effort of student learners, measured in hours,**
> I = pre-school ability,
> P = peer group influence,
> S = school factors.

In my argument, a model like the above can reach a better fitting for the findings of my study with regard to the mobility-and-reproduction analysis. Let me recapitulate those findings in the following paragraphs.

In Japan, the average achievement of national university students, as expressed by *hensachi*, is higher than that of private university students. Yet, the family income of national university students has been lower than the latter. Furthermore, it is shown that the average level of students' family income of the top four or eight former imperial universities was lower than the average level for all the private universities. Empirically, that argues against a major hypothesis of David Phillips (1992) claiming 'an increase in concentration of students of advantaged class origin in the Japanese ex-Imperial universities'. Overall, national universities have served as a more efficient agent of mobility than private universities. In examining the historical trend of the stratification of college students, previous studies find ample evidence for the lessening egalitarianism of Japanese universities during 1966–76. The follow-up study, as I present here, suggests a more meritocratic turn in 1978–90. The change, in my hypothesis, has a major bearing on the centralization of access to higher education, which was a major step toward universalism in sorting via test standardization, and an enhancement of impartiality, anonymity and objectivity.

For Korea, the effects of place of residence on educational attainment diminished over time. As linear regression shows, the overall dependence of educational attainment on social origins declined categorically.

Table 7.48 Matrix of two variables for achievement: time/effort of students and their family income.

Family income

		High	Low
Time/effort of	High	1	2
students	Low	3	4

However, when examining access to higher education with logistic regression, no decline in the effects of family background is perceivable in absolute terms, except for the upper middle class. Family background effects continued to offset the expansion of college education. However, two points warrant our attention. First, for the upper middle class, the chance of getting into university declined as compared to the rest of society. Second, that chance increased for the new middle class, composed of low-level professional, technical and administrative workers, and clerical workers. That shows the growing social dynamics of the expanding low-rank 'white collar' strata.

The dichotomy of the new middle class as opposed to the old middle class has also drawn research interest in Japan. Vogel (1963) distinguishes between the old middle class (small independent businessmen and land-owners) and the new middle class (white-collar employees of large business corporations and government bureaucracies), a distinction made earlier by Aonuma (1962), Hazama (1960) and others. Ohashi (1971) and Horie (1962) suggest the decline of the old classes in entrepreneurial activities, and the growing number of the white-collar strata. Kawai (1973) suggests that the most important phenomenon of modern life is the ever-growing expansion of the white-collar strata. Therefore, the growing status of the new middle class in Korea could well find its parallel in Japan.

The statistical procedure used for analysing Taiwan is similar to that for Korea. Linear regression analysis shows that father's education and occupational status have a significant impact on children's schooling. However, there was a 'sharp drop-off' in the effect of father's schooling. A similar pattern can be found for father's occupational status as well. The statistical descriptions for the chance of college, however, are confusing and self-contradictory. The patternlessness of the result defies interpretation. Preliminary findings from a different study conducted at the subnational (high school) level indicate that, in Taiwan, the correlation between high school entrance exams and family background was insignificant. That study was analysed here because in Taiwan high school and university entrance exams have a lot in common. Unfortunately, no research is readily available on the correlation between university entrance exams and family background.

CHAPTER 8

The news media and the dark side of the exam systems

> One of the most valuable philosophical features of journalism is that it realizes that truth is not a solid but a fluid.
> – *Christopher Morley*, Inward Ho, *1923*

The wide diffusion of the media of mass communication is one of the best indicators of modernity. The 'consumption' of news and the other messages disseminated by the mass media seems to rise markedly before the rise in consumption of other 'goods' typically in great demand (Inkeles and Smith, 1974). Newspapers are one of the most efficient sources of information, education and influence. By 1989, there were 125 newspapers in Japan, as compared to 1626 in the US. However, that does not mean the circulation of Japanese papers is less than American ones. It only means that they are more concentrated in a small number of major papers in Japan, as shown in Table 8.1. That concentration has perhaps made it relatively easier to reach a socially sanctioned interpretation, a consensual frame of reference, necessary for a homogeneous society, though it might exist quite separately from personal views of the world.

Table 8.1 Leading newspapers ranked according to their circulation (by 1000 copies). *Source*: JETRO, *U.S. and Japan in Figures: Part II* (Tokyo: JETRO, 1992), 108–9.

Rank	Japan		US	
1	Yomiuri Shimbun	9785	Wall Street Journal	1857
2	Asahi Shimbun	8249	USA Today	1347
3	Mainichi Shimbun	4046	Los Angeles Times	1196
4	Nihon Keizai Shimbun	3008	New York Times	1108
5	Sankei Shimbun	2028	New York Daily News	1098

In this milieu, the press-amplified intellectual disapproval and cynicism of the exam system, admittedly a rigorous apparatus of competition and elimination, is thus easy to hold in sway. In that regard, two most typical examples are discussed in the succeeding case studies, one on suicide, the other on cheating in exams. I first introduce the problems as they were presented, and then analyse the relating data.

YOUTH SUICIDE AND THE UNIVERSITY ENTRANCE EXAMS

To be, or not to be, that is the question:
Whether 'tis nobler in the mind to suffer
The slings and arrow of outrageous fortune
Or to take arms against a sea of troubles,
And by opposing end them.

– William Shakespeare, Hamlet, *Act III, Sc. 1*

Sadder still are suicides of very young people, adolescents and even children. And the plunge is deeper: they reject not just a few last bitter moments, but life, all of it and at once, with all its myriad possibilities, as if they had the somber courage to hearken to Silenus' oracle to king Midas: 'What is the greatest good for a man?' 'Never to have been born. Or failing that, to die at once.'
– Maurice Pinguet, Voluntary Death in Japan, *1993*

In Japanology, the connection between suicide and the system of entrance exams seems to be a self-evident fact, a near truism. Illustrative are two books, dramatically antithetical to one another by their titles: *Japan As Number 1* and *Japan As Anything But Number One*. Despite the large difference in their views, the exam–suicide causality is referred to by both. In the latter, Jon Woronoff remarks:

It is not hard to imagine what happened to children who were brought up in this rat race. And the grind of 'examination hell' only intensified with the years, requiring ever greater efforts to get into the top schools. Polls showed that students thought of this in terms of 'exertion', 'mental anguish', and 'uncertainty'.... Meanwhile, suicide took a depressing toll among youngsters year after year. (1990: 119)

In comparing Japan with the US, Ezra Vogel writes in *Japan As Number 1*:

The student who does not enter a desired high school or university may be equally miserable. Suicide rates are high among Japanese youth, and those who are discouraged by not making the proper organization may be more depressed than their American counterparts, who will have a variety of later options open to them. (1979: 240)

Critics may be euphemistic and cautious in their phrasing while conveying the same unmistakable message:

Stories about suicides in connection with examination worry or failure receive much publicity and create the impression that *shiken jigoku* is a major cause of death among school-age children. It is not, but aberrations in personality development and difficulties in parent–child relations are undoubtedly aggravated by chronic exam anxiety. (van Wolferen, 1990: 88)

A more authoritative, and hence oft-cited source in confirming that connection is found in an OECD document, *Reviews of National Policies for Education: Japan*, which concludes:

The pressure on the individual student becomes so great that it probably is even reflected in the suicide curve, which has a life-cycle maximum for both sexes at the age of university examinations and an annual maximum for boys in the month the results of the examinations are known. (Beauchamp and Vardaman (eds), 1994: 207–8)

In none of the above citations did the authors bother to present the data to show the high suicide rate caused by the exam system. Their self-assurance is typified by a footnote attached to the statement: 'The Japanese media have been so full of this not even a shallow observer could miss it' (van Wolferen, 1990: 123).

Japanese youth suicide is notoriously well known. Less well known, but equally disquieting is youth suicide in the US. The alarming tone is found in both passages given below:

Japan

[The suicide rate of young people under the age of nineteen] suddenly jumped by 44 percent from 557 to 802 in 1986. Suicides by teenage girls rose an alarming 77 percent. These figures are most prominent in a rising wave of suicide throughout Japan, where the incidence in the population as a whole rose 8 percent to 25,524, the highest level in postwar history.
'Unlike American children,' said Tamotsu Sengoku, director of the Japan Youth Research Institute, 'Japanese kids hold in all their frustrations. They are under a lot of pressure from school and need to vent their energy in some way.' He continued by saying that when everything else fails, suicide is the final outlet. (Schoolland, 1990: 108)

US

In an epidemic, the statistics become stupefying. Killing oneself is the third leading cause of death of America's youth, superseded only by automobile accidents and homicide, both of which, more often than we suspect, may be suicide masquerading. The rate of adolescent suicide rose 66 percent in the 1970s, 200 percent since 1950. For every suicide among teenage girls, there have been some 50 attempts; for boys, 15 to 20. Girls attempt suicide much more frequently than boys, but boys complete their attempts four times as often. (Peck *et al.*, 1985: vii)

The suicide of a young person is a profoundly tragic event. To understand the suicide-mortality among the young, we need to know at least three dimensions of the issue: (1) what percentage of youth suicide can be imputed to the exam system? (2) how does the youth suicide rate compare to other nations? (3) how does Japanese youth suicide change over the past years? These questions will contribute to an empirical verification of what factor exams have played as causes of youth suicide. To do so, a comparative perspective is necessary. In his study of suicide, Emile Durkheim argues:

> Only comparison affords explanation. A scientific investigation can thus be achieved only if it deals with comparable facts, and it is the more likely to succeed the more certainly it has combined all those that can be usefully compared. (1958: 41)

Therefore, it is highly desirable not only to find out the youth suicide rate of Japanese, but also to compare it with other countries both in the West and in East Asia. The comparative data on Korean suicide are, as usual, not readily available (Peng and Tseng, 1992). Fortunately, we have statistics for Taiwan and a number of Western countries. It is worthy of note, before we begin, that the focus of both the critiques, as just quoted, and our concern is not the link between suicide and certain ethnic traits, Japanese or Taiwanese, but the link between suicide and a system, the university entrance exams.

Japan: Some major discrepancies between facts and critical hypotheses

If the pressure of the exam system is a major factor in youth suicide, as implied in the critique cited previously, we would expect a rise in youth suicide if the entrance exams became more competitive, and the pressure mounted higher. A review of the 'competition ratio' would help us to figure out if getting into university has become harder or easier in the past years. Competition ratio just means the ratio of the applicants for a place in university. It is calculated by 'number of applicants ÷ number of entrants'. If the competition ratio is '4.9', the number for all universities in 1960, as shown in Table 8.2, it means that there were more than four people competing for one place in the university (see Table 8.2).

Table 8.2 The competition ratio for entrance into Japanese universities, 1960–90. *Source*: JMOE, *Kokukôritsu Daigaku Nyûgakusha Senbatsu jisshi jyôkyô* (The actual implementation of selecting entrees for national/public universities), (Tokyo: National Center for University Entrance Examinations, 1994c), 4.

	1960	1965	1970	1975	1980	1985	1990
National	5.6	5.6	5.8	6	3	2.9	5
Public	8.6	9.8	10.2	9.8	6	5.6	9.7
Private	4.4	4.3	5.7	6.5	7.4	7.7	10.6
Total	4.9	4.8	5.8	6.5	6.4	6.6	9.4

Note: The competition ratio = number of applicants ÷ entrants.

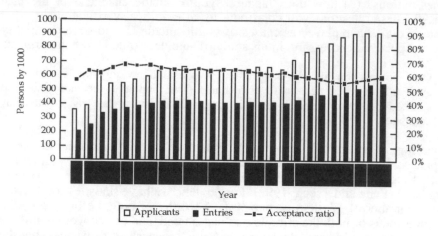

Figure 8.1 Trends in applications and enrolments in Japanese universities, 1960–90. *Source*: JMOE, *Kokukôritsu Daigaku Nyûgakusha Senbatsu jisshi jyôkyô* (The actual implementation of selecting entrants for national/public universities), (Tokyo: National Center for University Entrance Examinations, 1994c), 4.

From 1960 to 1990, the average competition ratio for all universities increased from 4.9 to 9.4. As shown in Table 8.2, the most notable increase in competition was for the private universities, which grew from 4.4 to 10.6, while for public universities it increased from 8.6 to 9.7. With the growth in the number of university applicants, the actual acceptance rate reached a peak of 68.2 per cent in 1972, and then dropped afterwards (see Figure 8.1).

The increasing competitiveness of the entrance exams can be ascribed to demographic growth and the folk culture of meritocracy, together with the improvement in living standards. The effort in the past several years to reform the exam system has generated so little result that it is described as 'immobilism' (Schoppa, 1991) and is ridiculed as 'tinkering with the hell' (Frost, 1992). Noteworthy is the 'Joint First-Stage Achievement Test' (JFSAT, *Kyôtsû Ichiji Shiken*), instituted in 1979 by the National Center for University Entrance Examination. The national and public universities and some private universities require applicants to take both the JFSAT and their own exams. The burden of preparing both made a typical student's workload harder (Frost, 1992). Meanwhile, a study of the history of test papers shows no sign of relaxation of competitiveness in the exam questions themselves.[1]

---

[1] See Chapter 4, 'What kind of exams? Questions of world history and mathematics in the three countries', for details of the change in form and content of exam questions.

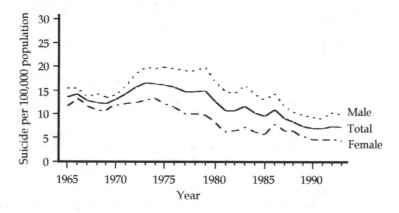

Figure 8.2 Suicide and self-inflicted injury among the 15–24 age group in Japan, 1965–93 (per 100,000 population). *Source*: Based on the data of WHO (World Health Organization), *World Health Statistics Annuals* (Geneva: WHO).

If youth suicide can be imputable to the entrance exam system, we would find a concomitant trend in suicide in the age group preparing for the university entrance exams. Is that a fact? To pursue this question, let us first examine the suicide rate for 15–24-year-olds. In Figure 8.2, the suicide rate for the 15–24 age cohort in Japan has been steadily falling from 16.5 per 100,000 in 1973 to 6.9 in 1991, and 7.25 in 1993. The 15–24 age group covers the ages of students for both senior high school and university.

How about the age group under 19 or 20, which is exactly the time of entering university? Figure 8.3 may help us to compare the suicide mortality rate for that group between 1955 and 1986.

The tables of suicide rates for the Japanese population between 1955 and 1986 show that the rate for youth under 19 also diminished. The 15–19 age group reached 30 per 100,000 population in 1955. This figure dropped sharply to less than 10 from 1965 onwards. The postwar peak around the age of 20–30 has flattened (Yoshimatsu, 1992). Is this change simply part of a nationwide declining trend? After all, postwar peace and economic prosperity could pull down the curve across the board. This is, however, not the case. The decline in the youth suicide rate has occurred against a background in which the rate for the entire population has increased, as demonstrated in Figure 8.3.

As shown in Figure 8.4, compared to the general drop in the 15–24 group, the suicide trend of the entire population was on the rise: 14.7 per 100,000 in 1965, 18.0 in 1975, 19.4 in 1985 and 22.3 in 1993. The increase in the rate of the middle-aged group (40–50 years old) appears to be responsible for the national increase.

However, one may still assume that, despite the drop in the Japanese youth suicide rate, it remains a serious problem in international comparison. Isn't Japan well known as a suicide nation?

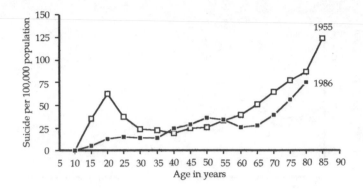

Figure 8.3 A comparison of the suicide rate of all ages in 1955 and 1986 (per 100,000 population). *Source*: Kazuya Yoshimatsu, 'Suicidal behavior in Japan', in Kok Lee Peng and Wen-Shing Tseng (eds), *Suicidal Behavior in the Asia-Pacific Region* (Singapore: Singapore University Press, 1992), 15–40.

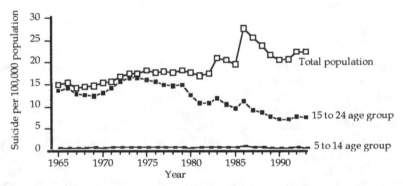

Figure 8.4 The suicide rates of the 15–24 age group and the total population in Japan, 1965–93 (per 100,000 population). *Source*: Based on the data of WHO, *World Health Statistics Annuals* (Geneva, WHO).

In Figure 8.5, we can see that the Japanese rate has been dropping ever since 1973. The US rate, on the other hand, has been rising from 6.2 in 1965 to 21.9 in 1993. It is reported that, from 1955 to 1980, the suicide rate among young people aged 15–24 rose markedly, and has remained high since, ranking among the highest countries in the world in youth suicide rate (Hendin, in Peck *et al.*, 1985; 1995). A similar pattern is also discernible for the 5–14 age group, although, due to the low suicide rate of young children, the Japanese–US disparity is not as wide as for older children (Figure 8.6).

As a matter of fact, data show a growing trend in youth suicide in European countries in the past 30 years as well. Figure 8.7 plots a number of countries for illustration. The data given in the figure are summarized briefly in Table 8.3. During the period 1965–90, youth suicide rates rose for most of the nations listed in the figure. Finland is the extreme case of that growth. Germany was perhaps an exception, but its figures were basically higher than Japan's at all times during this period.

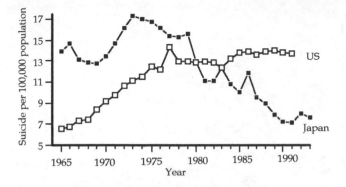

Figure 8.5 Suicide rates among the 15–24 age group, Japan and the US, 1965–93 (per 100,000 population). *Source*: Based on the data from WHO, *World Health Statistics Annuals* (Geneva: WHO).

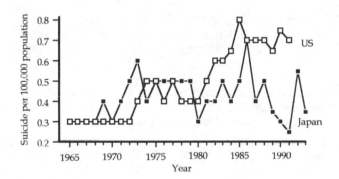

Figure 8.6 Suicide rates among the 5–14 age group, Japan and the US, 1965–93 (per 100,000 population). *Source*: Based on the data from WHO, *World Health Statistics Annuals* (Geneva: WHO).

Table 8.3 Suicide rates among the 15–24 age group: Japan and selected Western countries, 1965–93 (per 100,000 population). *Source*: Based on the data of WHO, *World Health Statistics Annual* (Geneva: WHO).

	1965	1970	1975	1980	1985	1990
Japan	14.0	13.0	16.0	12.5	9.5	6.95
Australia	n.a.	8.6	8.9	11.2	14.5	15.7
Denmark	8.0	8.5	9.4	12.1	12.6	9.05
Finland	9.0	14.7	26.1	23.6	21.8	31.0
France	5.0	7.0	8.6	10.7	10.9	9.25
Germany	13.0	13.4	15.0	12.5	12.8	9.35
US	6.0	8.8	11.8	12.3	12.9	13.0

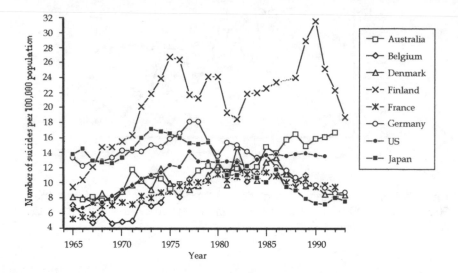

Figure 8.7 Suicide rates among the 15–24 age group: Japan and selected Western countries, 1965–93 (per 100,000 population). *Source*: Based on the data of WHO, *World Health Statistics Annuals* (Geneva: WHO).

Table 8.4 The gender difference for the 15–24 age group in selected countries, 1990 (per 100,000 population). *Source*: based on the data from WHO, *World Health Statistics Annuals* (Geneva: WHO).

	Japan	*Australia*	*Denmark*	*Finland*	*France*	*Germany*	*US*
Male	**9.2**	26.6	14.1	50.9	14.1	14.4	22.0
Female	**4.7**	4.7	4.0	11.0	4.4	4.3	3.9
Difference	**4.5**	21.9	21.9	39.9	9.7	10.1	18.1

Note: Difference = Male – Female.

Another issue which we would wish to consider in relation to exam pressures on suicide is the gender ratio. As the data for the Japanese 15–25 age group show, male suicides have been consistently a lot higher than female. In Japan, boys are more subjected to exam pressure than girls because of both parental expectations and the structure of the gendered division of labour. Logically, we would expect a higher rate of male suicide in this age group due to greater pressure, stress and anxiety. Yet a higher male suicide rate tells us little, because it is common throughout the world and not at all unique to Japan. Let us compare gender difference (Table 8.4).

As the comparative data in Table 8.4 show, the male–female gender difference among the 15–24 age group in Japan is much lower than those for selected advanced Western countries. Among the countries listed here, the highest difference is found in Finland (39.9 per 100,000), followed by Australia (21.9), Denmark (21.9), and the US (18.1). France, where the gender difference is lower than any Western countries given here, was still twice as high as Japan.

To recapitulate, unlike what some critics depict as the relationship between Japan's suicide rate and exam pressures, the facts tell a different story. First, the Japanese youth suicide rate has dropped to a quite stable level which has been unequivocally lower than the average of other advanced nations and this trend runs opposite to the rising competition ratios for university entrance. Second, the gender differences in suicide do not support an argument for linking exam pressures to suicide. On the other hand, more careful studies started to bring to light the gap between critiques and empirical reality. Rohlen (1983) writes:

> The general public thus receives the impression that the causal relation between exams and juvenile suicide is strong. Foreigners writing about post-World War II Japanese education have echoed this theme. The issue has not to my knowledge ever been investigated closely, but merely reviewing the available facts reveals a significantly different story. (327–8)

Given the test anxiety and high-stake ramifications of the university entrance exams, it is not hard to convince an uncritical audience that entrance exams are a major cause of suicide and other pathologies. Yet, many a hypothesis in suicidology may sound plausible but untrue.[2] The foregoing discussion of the exams–suicide relationship also points to the need to further scrutinize how severely exams aggravate youth suicide and how typical that problem was among students.

Month-by-month data should also confirm or deny this relationship. It is observed that the suicide rate of school children tends to rise annually during the examination season from January to May (Kazuya, 1997: 27). April and May could be times of disappointment, but not pressure (Iga, 1986: 33). This is questionable for two reasons. First, the rates for February and March, when exam pressures are greatest and failures become known, are not high. Second, the question of seasons is complicated by the fact that adult suicides in Japan, as in many countries of the northern hemisphere, also peak in April and May (Rohlen, 1983). Emile Durkheim (1958) long ago concluded that in all European countries, 'beginning with January inclusive, the incidence of suicide increases regularly from month to month until about June and regularly decreases from that time to the end of the year' (p. 111).

In other Asian nations, the seasonal pattern of suicide also shows a similar trend. In Thailand, where the educational structure is different from the Japanese, the peak suicide rates occur in April–June (Choprapawon and Visalyaputra, in Peng and Tseng, 1992). The same pattern is found in other countries as well (De Maio et al., 1982). Even in the US the peak is from March to May (Center for Diseases Control, 1985).

---

[2] A typical example is perhaps the finding that the season with the highest suicide rate is not the depressing winter or autumn, but the lively spring and summer. Research into some other possible suicidal causalities, such as war, psychopathic states, ethnicity, etc., also poses challenge to some common-sense concepts in this regard. See for instance, Durkheim (1958) for a classic study of suicidology.

Exams as a cause of suicide: A close scrutiny

The suicide causality of the modern system of exams was focused on and brought to national attention by the modern media. The early news coverage that evoked popular concern for the suicidogenic effect of exams can be traced to the Taisho period (1915–26). In 1922, an elementary school teacher in Yamanashi prefecture committed suicide by *seppuku* (self-disembowelment). The reason, it is told, was that he suffered from the bad scores that his students received in the middle school entrance exams. Three years later, the news media reported another exam-caused suicide that shocked the nation. In Kumamoto prefecture, a wealthy entrepreneur (*shisanka*) and his wife killed themselves by hanging. They suffered a nervous breakdown on learning that their fourth daughter had flunked the entrance exams. These tragic events later became the theme of a special book, *Shinkôsa no Kaisetsu* (Comments on the modern exams), published by Asahi Shimbun, a major news media corporation, in 1939. It was perhaps the first of its kind that began to draw deep concern from the general public regarding exam–suicide causality (Masuda *et al.*, 1961).

Since World War II, every year as examination time arrives, newspapers and magazines have carried reports of student suicides. The tragic image of a diligent student committing suicide due to failing the entrance exams is 'one of the most powerful weapons in the armory of those in Japan and abroad who are critical of Japan's education system' (Rohlen, 1983: 327). That established a strong causal relation between exams and suicide, and made the screening system a major curse of Japanese society. However, as noted earlier, a cross-national comparison reveals quite a number of major discrepancies between critiques and reality. Now, let us find out the suicide rate ascribed to the exam system (see Table 8.5). This set of data comes from the National Police Agency, which categorizes suicide causes as reported. In his investigation, Rohlen (1983) finds that school-related problems are important in at least one-quarter of the cases. School is a more common cause of suicide than either family or peer relationships for youth under age 21. In school-related suicides, exam-related cases are a small proportion: 26 out of 398 (Rohlen, 1983: 327–34). In other words, only 6.5 per cent of the total suicides under 21 were related to the exams (see Table 8.6).

From the data in Table 8.6, we may note that the exam-related suicides have been quite stable, both in number and in its ratio. Its ratio remained the same 5.5 per cent for 1991 and 1992, slightly decreased from 1977 (6.5 per cent). This seems to attest to the Durkheimian view about the consistency of suicide ratio for a group of people within a period of time.

Our findings do not disconnect the pressure of entrance exams from the suicide rate as one causal effect, but they do clarify its weight as compared to the other causes, like love affairs, family relationships, crime or illness.

The findings suggest that (1) to impute Japanese youth suicide mainly to exams is a powerful hypothesis, but one which the facts do not support. The aggravating effect of the exam system on suicide is shown to be a lot less than the impression people got from alarmist reports; (2) given its small percentage of total self-inflicted mortality, exam-led suicides could not be a major factor responsible for the major rise (before 1972) or fall (after 1973) in the under-20 suicide rate.

The causality of adolescent suicide is also discussed elsewhere. Mamoru Iga (1986) studies the suicide motives of Japanese males for April–June 1974 based upon the information in Table 8.7.

If we compare Rohlen's data with those of Iga, we may see a decline in the male suicide rate during the 1974–7 period. In Table 8.8, the youth male suicide rate related to school problems seems to drop drastically. This may imply that school problems dwindled for students. A different source for 1974 furnishes conflicting data for Iga (see Table 8.9).

Table 8.5 Motives for suicides among persons under 21 in Japan, January to June, 1977 (Rohlen's data). *Source:* Japanese National Police Agency; based on Thomas Rohlen, *Japan's High Schools* (Berkeley: University of California Press, 1983), 330–1.

Motives	Number of suicides	Percentage of total
Family related	54	13.6
Illness related	39	9.8
Work related	15	3.7
Relations with opposite sex	52	13.1
School related (with a breakdown into 9 items)	**106**	**26.6**
(1) Lack of motivation to study	49	12.3
(2) Failure in exams	**16**	**4.0**
(3) Entrance exam preparations	**10**	**2.5**
(4) Concern about educational future	4	1.0
(5) Dislike of school	12	3.0
(6) Teacher's scolding	2	0.5
(7) Trouble with school friends	3	0.8
(8) Unable to do homework	4	1.0
(9) Unspecified others	6	1.5
Others (including mental illness)	132	33.2
Total	398	100

Table 8.6 Motives for suicides among persons under 20 or 21 in Japan, January to June, 1977, 1991 and 1992. *Sources:* For 1977 data, Japanese National Police Agency; based on Thomas Rohlen, *Japan's High Schools* (Berkeley: University of California Press, 1983), 330–1. For 1991 and 1992 data, Keisatsuchô (Japanese National Police Department), *Keisatsu Hakusho* (Police White Paper), cited in Jiji Tsûshinsha, *Kyôiku Deta Randdo* (A databook of educational statistics), (Tokyo: Jiji Tsûshinsha, 1993), 84–5; (1994), 86–7.

Causes	1977[a]	1991[b]	1992[b]
Total number of suicides	398	454	524
Exam-related suicides	26	25	29
Percentage of exam-related suicides[c]	**6.5%**	**5.5%**	**5.5%**

Notes: a. 1977 data are for the age group under 21.
b. 1992–3 data are for the age group under 20.
c. Percentage = exam-related suicide number ÷ total number of suicides.

The difference in the suicide rate for males under 19 related to school problems is most likely caused by the column 'unknown': Iga excludes the unknown cases and as a result blows up the percentage for each cause. If we compare Tatai's data with that given by Thomas Rohlen, the youth suicide rates related to school problems were very similar for 1974 and 1977: 27.4 per cent and 27.0 per cent. This tends to confirm the well-accepted hypothesis in suicidology that the suicide rate of a group of people for a particular cause is generally stable for a period of time (Durkheim, 1958; Halbwachs, 1978).

The findings based on the above data and discussion indicate that, as Rohlen summarizes (1983), 'the evidence does not support any simple assertions about the relation of examination pressures to juvenile suicide rates. School-related problems are not inconsequential, but they only account for about one-quarter of youth suicides. Further, exam pressures and the competition for élite high school and university places seem notably less relevant to suicide than the inability of the educational system to cope adequately with students who fall behind' (334).

Table 8.7 Suicide motives of Japanese males for April, May and June 1974 as a percentage of the total (Iga's data). *Source*: Ministry of Welfare: *Jisatsu Shibô Tôkei* (suicidal death statistics), 1977, as reported in Mamoru Iga, *The Thorn in the Chrysanthemum: Suicide and Economic Success in Modern Japan* (Berkeley: University of California Press, 1986), 32.

Motives known	Total 2116 cases	19 and under 126 cases	20–29 395 cases
Illness and physical defect	48.7	13.5	11.9
Marital problem	6.2	1.0	4.5
Family problem	7.6	14.3	21.6
Heterosexual affair	5.6	11.1	17.9
Financial problem	6.7	2.4	4.7
Occupational problem	11.8	9.5	22.7
Schoolwork problem	**3.0**	**34.1**	**5.0**
'Being tired of life'	3.9	9.5	6.8
Other	6.5	4.8	4.9

Table 8.8 A comparison: male youth suicide under 21 in Japan, 1974–7. *Source*: Data of 1974: ibid., 32; data of 1977: Thomas Rohlen, *Japan's High Schools* (Berkeley: University of California Press, 1983), 330–1.

Year	School-related suicide for male youths (%)
1974	34.1[a]
1977	27.0[b]

Notes: a. for young males of 19 and under. b. for young males under 21.

Table 8.9 Suicide motives of Japanese males for April, May and June 1974 (Tatai's data). *Source*: Ministry of Health and Welfare, as reported in Kichinosuke Tatai, 'Japan', pp. 12–58 in Lee A. Headley (ed.), *Suicide in Asia and the Near East* (Berkeley: University of California Press, 1983), 33.

Motives	Total	19 and under	20–29
Invalidism	37.6	10.8	18.2
Marital problems	4.8	0.6	3.1
Other family member	5.9	11.5	4.8
Love affair	4.3	8.9	12.3
Money problems	5.2	1.9	3.3
Employment problems	9.1	7.6	15.6
School problems	**2.3**	**27.4**	**3.5**
Depression	3.0	7.6	4.7
Other	3.8	3.8	3.1
Unknown	24.1	19.7	31.4

The unmistakable drop in the youth suicide rate may baffle early writers who envisioned the worsening or at least the continuity of the situation judging by the intractability of the exam system. To find the reason for that fall, one has to identify the essential factor that disposes youth to kill themselves. An examination of the age distribution curves of suicide in Japan during the years 1947, 1955, 1965, 1975 and 1982 shows that the peak around the young age group has become less prominent. Meanwhile, there is a gradual rise in rates for the middle-aged group of 40–50. Scholars like Kazuya Yoshimatsu (1992) and Maurice Pinguet (1993) consider that phenomenon as part of the aftermath of World War II. Youth during the postwar period and the current middle-aged group are taken as a cohort phenomenon: they belong to the same generation (Yoshimatsu, 1992). This generation, in contrast to other generations, has experienced turbulence because their adolescence was traumatized by WWII. As they grew up and looked for a niche in the competitive Japanese society, they encountered great difficulties and failures. Their past tragic heroism contrasted sharply with the new society 'where everything was for sale' (Pinguet, 1993: 16). This generation lived in the shadow of nostalgic self-identification with an ideal father, dying so far away, so young, for the glory of a vain service, or with an elder brother who perished young. Thus, through the 1950s, just as the economy was taking off, several thousand young Japanese were to die for lack of the sorry courage to forget: they were to perish as if in posthumous tribute to the defunct Minotaur of military self-sacrifice (ibid.). This generation, according to Yoshimatsu (1992), 'continuously chose suicide as one the preferable ways of coping with stresses in life'. The former explanation seem to suggest the high rate of youth suicide in the postwar period was more of an accident.

In their recent work, *Suicidal Behavior in the Asia-Pacific Region* (1992), Peng and Tseng also argue hypothetically that the fact that life is becoming more stimulating and materially satisfactory to the young might have caused their suicide peak to melt down (pp. 253–4). However, researchers elsewhere also take social affluence as an aggravating effect on suicide. The rise of suicide rates in Europe in the past years is a glaring case in point. Even Tseng and Peng themselves concede in the same book that 'suicidal behavior may be relatively low in less prosperous society and high in more affluent ones', which conflicts with their comment on Japan (p. 6). These conflicting hypotheses are presented here only to highlight the need to clarify the significant facts in the field, to match the hypothetical concepts with facts, before the articulation of hypotheses. In hope that a comparative dimension will widen our view and enable us to generalize with more confidence, we now examine the exams–suicide connection in Taiwan, where the competition for university as a status ladder is a lot tougher than in Japan.[3]

Voluntary death in Taiwan

Unlike Japan, little has been written by social scientists or psychiatrists about suicidal behaviour in Taiwan. Therefore, a brief introduction is needed at the outset. Suicide mortality rates in Taiwan in the past 40 years exhibited three distinct periods. In 1948–58, there was a peak in the suicide rate of the population, due to the social disorganization caused by the mass influx of the two million Mainland Chinese who fled to Taiwan. In 1958–68, a second peak accompanied active industrialization and modernization, and the social restructuring as the economy moved from an agricultural to an industrial base, as evidenced by the growth of per capita income of the Taiwanese at this time.

A sharp decline in suicide rates occurred in the period that followed. This was a period in which most inhabitants enjoyed a stable political and economic environment. As Chong, Yeh and Wen (1992) point out, 'this decline was not due to the steady increase in birth rate but to a lower suicide mortality amongst the young'. This is shown in Figure 8.8.

Suicidological studies show that different peoples have their own unique and quite constant pattern of suicide. However, from the overview given above we perceive two things in common between Japan and Taiwan: (1) relevance of suicide rates to the after-effects of wars (World War II and the Chinese civil war between Communists and Nationalists) and macro-level social changes; (2) the drop in youth suicide in the past years.

In the following paragraphs, I will look at youth suicide in detail. The sources of information include Department of Health statistics; vital statistics abstracts; household registration statistics; and the Taiwan Demographic Fact Book and the Suicide Prevention Center, Mackay Memorial Hospital, Taipei, Taiwan. The data we have were collected into two sets according to period. The first set covers 1969–71, and the second, 1972–80. The two datasets come from the records of the Mackay Memorial Hospital, Taiwan. The cases collected are suicide attempts, including both completed suicide (meaning deceased) and incomplete. For that reason, I will first define the term 'suicide attempt'. Most researchers into suicide use the term to describe the condition in which a person attempted to kill himself or herself and did not succeed (Peng and Tseng, 1992).

---

[3] I based that judgement on two major facts: The Taiwanese entrance exam system is narrower and less multidimensional. The recommendatory route is less acceptable and less used than in Japan. The grading system of Taiwan is also harsher. For a detailed discussion, refer to Chapters 3 and 4.

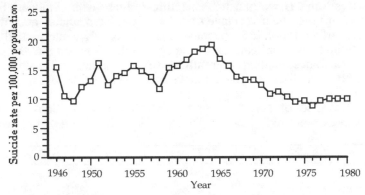

Figure 8.8 Suicide rate of the total population in Taiwan, 1946–80 (per 100,000 population). *Source*: Taiwanese Ministry of Health, 'Vital statistics abstracts', cited in Lee A. Headley (ed.), *Suicide in Asia and the Near East* (Berkeley: University of California Press, 1983), 64.

The difference in the end result between completed and incomplete suicide is often caused by the efficiency and speed of the mode of suicide chosen (Halbwachs, 1978). It is hard to verify to what extent an attempt might be partly motivated by feigning or simple impulsiveness. But the correspondence between committed and attempted suicides is in general acknowledged: both increase or diminish simultaneously (ibid., 1930). The legitimacy or even the advantage of studying attempted suicide is discussed by Maurice Farber (1968):

> At the very outset of the study of suicide, we seem to encounter a curious methodological paradox: As soon as a subject enters the category in which we are interested, that is, he commits suicide, he instantly becomes unavailable because he is dead.

Actually, of course, the dilemma is not hopeless. While the diaries of the victims or the psychotherapy records might help, a better solution, according to Farber, is to study those who attempted suicide but survived.

In the Taiwan data provided by the Suicide Prevention Center, the number of completed suicide attempts is specified in the data of 1969–71: 23 out of 1286; this information is not specified for the data of 1972–80. As we are looking for the causality of the exam system in Taiwan as a suicidogenic effect, we may investigate the severity of that correlation without knowing if the attempt really led to mortality (Table 8.10).

In the cases recorded during 1972–80, four cases were related to academic problems, amounting to no more than 0.2 per cent of the total suicides. The rest consisted of issues concerning sex or love, familial or social relationships, financial or health causes. What percentage of young people did academic suicides account for, then? Unfortunately, there is no categorization by age. But, the data have an occupation breakdown (see Table 8.11). In the occupation list, only the 'Student' column can match the category of 'Academic failure'. The occupation of 'Prostitute' may fall into the age cohort under 20, but prostitutes are unlikely to kill themselves for

'Academic failure'. If we match 'Academic failure' with 'Student' for the same period of time, the percentage of academic-related suicide accounts for 2.58 per cent of a total of 155 student suicides. Even if we interpret all of the academic failures as exam-caused, the empirical data suggest that there were a lot fewer Taiwanese students committing suicide because of exams. This is also reflected in the focus in Taiwan news media (see Table 8.12).

Table 8.10 Cause of suicide attempts of all ages, Suicide Prevention Center, Mackay Memorial Hospital, Taiwan, 1972–80. *Source*: Ibid., 84–5.

Causes	1972–80	Percentage
Marital conflict	542	18.93
Conflict with family	418	14.60
Boy–girl conflict	550	19.20
Conflict with others	20	0.70
Financial problems	122	4.26
Mental problems	105	3.67
Physical illness	64	2.23
Legal problems	6	0.21
Unemployment	1	0.03
Academic failure	**4**	**0.14**
Other	116	4.05
Unknown	916	31.98
Total	2864	100.00

Table 8.11 Occupations of suicide attempters, Suicide Prevention Center, Mackay Memorial Hospital, Taiwan, 1972–80. *Source*: Ibid., 84–5.

Occupation	Number of cases	Percentage
Labourer	238	8.28
Merchant	249	8.66
Government employee	66	2.30
Professional	178	6.19
Prostitute	202	7.03
Unemployed	265	9.22
Housewife	648	22.54
Student	**155**	**5.39**
Farmer	19	0.66
Retired	5	0.17
Unknown	850	29.57
Total	2875	100.00

Note: There is an eleven-case discrepancy between the total number of cases by occupation (2875) and by causes (2864) given in Headley's tables. The reason for that is not clear.

Table 8.12 Reasons given for suicides reported in newspapers, Taiwan, 1969–71. *Source*: Ibid., 73.

Causes reported	Male	Female	Total
Love affairs	17	48	56
Marital conflict	26	56	82
Conflict with family member	30	45	75
Social maladjustment	75	29	104
Physical illness	24	14	38
Mental illness	25	21	46
Criminal and legal matters	51	5	56
Unknown	56	46	102
Total	304	264	568

Note: The newspapers include *Lien-ho-Pao Daily* and four other major newspapers.

In Table 8.12, there is no story about a child killing himself under exam pressure. We do not know if the list is exhaustive, or if things might change in the following years. One thing seems clear: compared to Japan, the Taiwanese news media have given far less priority to suicide victims of the 'Exams Hell' either because (1) there was not that much raw material, or (2) exam-driven suicides would not 'entertain' readers as in Japan.

CHEATING: HOW MUCH HAS THE EXAM SYSTEM BEEN ABUSED?

Vice often rides triumphant in virtue's chariot.
– *Thomas Fuller*, Gnomologia, *1732*

Cheating, when unconcealed, seldom fails to excite and shock a reader, at least for an instant. Not unlike a Sherlock Holmes detective story, its revelation arouses our vicarious curiosity. We want to learn how it might be premeditated, contrived in the dark, and why it was brought to light. In East Asia, news media each year search for attempted abuse of an air-tight entrance exam system. In Japan, examples of well-publicized exam-related scandals include the sale of copies of the Waseda University School of Commerce exam for US$40,000 each in 1979 (Rohlen, 1983). Another case occurred in the spring of 1991. It was found that, amid the student examinees for Meiji University School of Commerce, there were a number of substitute impostors. The news created a stir as one student patron was the son of a famous show business star. The service fee was in the region of US$10,000 per person. The substitutes were played by students from such universities as Waseda, Meiji and Keio (Sato in Bungei Shunjûsha, 1992).

In Taiwan, within the framework of a screening system that has successfully upheld impartiality and indiscrimination, any attempt at abuse through cheating will be grabbed by the journalist world to stun and entertain the readers. *China Daily* (ZS, 20 July 1995) reported a 'Hi-Tech' cheating case. During the national entrance exams for vocation and commerce schools, a proctor saw four student examinees (three female and one male) wearing digital watches, a violation of the rule. Later, it was found that they were not simple watches. They were state-of-the-art transmitters, a brand new product in the market. They had a memory databank, and were capable of transmitting ten digits at a time. At the time they were questioned, the four had already received a number of numeric messages.

Media-exposed cheating in high-stake exams also hit the headlines in credentialistic Korea. For example, in 1993, a high school teacher and two other persons tried to help a student to get into Yang-sei, the top private university in Korea. The parents paid them 2500 million won (equivalent to US$201,000). Through newspaper advertisements, they hired three substitute examinees, students from élite universities, and each was paid between US$6000 and 12,000. During the investigation into the incident, the substitutes also confessed to working for somebody else to pass exams on a previous occasion. The parents who came to them included a member of the district assembly and an official working in the procuratorial institution. In the same year, some administrative staff members of a univer-sity accepted US$500,000 from the parents of university applicants. This news sent shock waves through Korean society. Not only that, the East Asian news media also watch each other. The above was reported in a Japanese paper, *Tokyo Nichinichi Shimbun* (Tokyo Daily News, 5 February 1995), under the title 'The Unhealthy Entrance Exams Shaking Korea'. The article puts forward three reasons: the loosening control of the authority, the 'worship of money (*haikin-shugi*)', and 'entrance examination fever (*nyûshi-netsu*)'.

Cheating is not as serious a problem as youth suicide. But both capture public concern, and both put the exam system into a degree of crisis or jeopardy. While people's attention is riveted by the grave effect of exams on youth suicide, they look to the exams' operation for news of cheating. A story like those given earlier prompts us to want to know: how severely is the system abused? Or to put it another way, are those stories only the 'tip of the iceberg', representing a much more wide-ranging breach of the integrity of the exam system? At the individual level, the study of cheating concerns merely the student's code of conduct. At the larger, social level, however, the study may tell us several things. First, we can learn if the exam system is responsible for abusive behaviour, or if it tempts people to do what they usually will not do. Second, how well the exam system has retained its ideology and legitimacy by being fair to all and invulnerable. Third, and perhaps most crucially, how well the exam system, as a form of meritocracy, is accepted by the young generation, demonstrated by follow-ing the 'rules of the game'. It may be true that newspapers are guilty of muckraking here, as systematic and reliable data are not easy to find or access. As a result, I will focus on Taiwan, due to the availability of data there. The sources include '1967–76 Work Report of the University Entrance Examinations Committee (UEEC)', 'The Minute Proceedings of the UEEC and its branch offices', and the rules and regulations concerning exam administration issued by the UEEC.[4]

---

[4] Unless otherwise specified, the data in the following discussion on cheating in Taiwan essentially come from Yu-Chang Wu (1977).

Statistics on violations of exam rules in Taiwan

Let us start with some basic statistics on the entrance exam-takers whose behaviour violated the rules of exams. Table 8.13 gives the number and percentage of rule violators among the total number of examinees. During the period 1967–76, about one in every 1000 examinees broke the exam regulations. The figure seems insignificant. And yet, there is a quite notable increase when the percentage is plotted (see Figure 8.9). Especially from 1973, the rate of violations more than doubled. What might have affected that change? Does it mean students became less patient with the system, and disgruntled with a rigid set of merit laws? Was it a sign that a growing number of students began to act against the social norm, and in turn, against the legitimacy and authority of a selection system? Any attempt at an answer requires one to dig deeper into those abnormal behaviours.

First of all, judged by their motivations, the violations of exam regulations can be divided into two categories: unintended and deliberate. Generally speaking, the former results from negligence or accident, or *force majeure* to borrow a legal term. For example, a student may be late for the exam because of traffic, or the student's number does not match the exam number due to an administrative error. The latter category refers to an illegal or incorrect action that is taken with a view to improving exam scores. This category may include hiring a substitute to impersonate the examinee, or copying an answer from one's neighbour. In the record of cheating in exams, these two categories have the following types (not exhaustive):

Examples of unintended violations:

- Forget the ID card or the exam pass.
- Arrive late or leave early.
- Take the wrong seat.
- Use a pencil or red ball-pen for essay writing.
- Make marks with pen.
- Besmirch the exam paper.

Examples of deliberate violations:

- The ID photo or signature does not match the examinee.
- A substitute disguises himself as the examinee; or a person cooperates with the examinee to cheat.
- Continue to answer the exam after the time is over.
- Take the exam paper out of the exam room.
- Pass the answer around during the exam.
- Bring written aids into test room.
- Tell another examinee the answer during the exam.
- Make signs to give the answer.
- Peep at or copy the answer from another person.
- Help another examinee to see one's own answer.
- Make changes after turning in the exam paper.
- Attack the proctor physically in a conflict.
- Create disorder in the exam room. (Y. C. Wu, 1977)

While the first category of unintended violations may be as technically disastrous to the student as the intended, it is basically not included in my study here. What I try to understand is the second category, the deliberate violations (both premeditated and improvised) that reflected a deviation from or even rebellion against the rules. Any change in that behavioural pattern at the societal level can indicate acceptance of social control and authority. It is a barometer of how well social control is imposed or internalized. Let us look at some incidents of abuses of the exam system.

Table 8.13 Rule-violating examinees in Taiwan's national-level university entrance exams (*Liankao*), 1967–76. *Source*: Yu-Chang Wu, *Woguo Daixūe Lianzhao Kaosheng Weigui zhi Yanjiu* (A study of the rule violations among the students during the university entrance exams in Taiwan), (Taipei: Tiangong, 1977), 17.

Year	Number of examinees	Number of examinees who violated exam rules	Percentage
1967	55,854	62	0.11%
1968	58,791	39	0.06%
1969	68,930	38	0.05%
1970	74,437	75	0.10%
1971	78,879	64	0.08%
1972	83,971	122	0.14%
1973	98,073	115	0.11%
1974	93,757	234	0.24%
1975	97,859	172	0.17%
1976	94,807	142	0.15%
1977	94,807	142	0.15%
Total	805,358	1063	0.13%

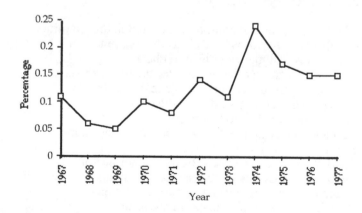

Figure 8.9 Change in the percentage of rule-violating examinees, Taiwan, 1967–76. *Source*: Ibid.

Case studies of deliberate violations of the law

One major type of violation involves a third party who helped the exam-taker to finish the exams. This third party might involve one or more persons, who were friends of the examinee or who were hired. They provided the answers to the examinee through hand signals, code or direct conversation, either in or out of the exam room. In 1974, a student, after turning in his exam paper, helped his brother with the exam. He sat on a lawn and made hand signals to communicate the answer. In the same year, a student who completed his own exam climbed on top of the roof near the window of the exam room. There, he signalled the answers to his friend by displaying a combination of different coloured plastic plates. In the 1975 English exam, a student who had finished his own paper organized a group of people to provide answers to his friend. From outside the window, they sent signals indicated by the different colours of their shirts and by standing up and sitting down.

Another type of violation involved some materials that had the potential answers written on them. These included a self-made card, eraser, ID pass or draft paper. As no books were allowed in the exams, a dictionary or other reference books secretly brought in also belonged to this category. Answers might also be found on hands, on the stem of the pen, or on one's skirt or shirt. As an extreme illustration, on an ordinary ball-pen, a text comprising 800 tiny Chinese characters were carved as an aid to its owner, who must have had microscopic eye-sight. Also, as early as the 1970s, the electric transmitter, a miracle in modern communication, was already being used to cheat the system for high reward at high risk.

In comparison to the common types of deliberate cheating, some behaviours against the rules of exams show an anti-establishment pattern in high degree. Instead of trying to 'outsmart' the system, these actions have a provocative nature, resembling an open challenge to the system. They might take the form of, for instance, a physical attack on the proctors, or creating flagrant disorder in the exam room, or continued rampant cheating even after a warning from the proctor. In the 1974 geography exam, a student beat a proctor who warned him about suspected cheating.

The circumstances of creating disorder often result from (1) receiving a warning about cheating behaviour; (2) shouting out the answer to the exams outside the exam room; (3) non-examinees outside the exam room stirring up trouble when being questioned about possible cooperation in cheating.

If we compare the annual average number of violations during 1967–72 with 1973–6, as shown in Table 8.14, we may see notable increases in certain items, such as 'Cheated by using hand signals', 'Told others the answers', 'Showed answers to others', etc. In Table 8.15, we can see that 1972 was a landmark year.

According to Table 8.15, violations against the regulations from 1967 to 1971 were around 60–70. They increased notably after 1972: 126 cases in 1972; in 1974, they doubled again. What happened was most likely related to a major reform of the exam format. In 1972, Taiwan utilized the machine-readable multiple choice format for the first time. The computerization of the exams was accompanied by an increase in deliberate violations of rules. They were essentially deliberate violations, such as: 'Copied answer from others', 'Substitution or cooperation in cheating', 'Cheated by using hand signals', 'Showed answers to others', 'Put names on the answer sheet', etc.

The violations resulting from negligence were generally unchanged, such as 'Took the wrong seat', 'Answered on the question sheet', etc. One exception is the 'Forgot ID card or exam pass', which resulted from either leaving it at home or losing it on the way to the exam venue. Some deliberate violations decreased, for example, 'ID photo or signature did not match', 'Made changes after turning in the exam paper'.

Overall, it seemed that although the computerized format facilitated the heavy workload of grading papers, it also seemed to make cheating occur earlier and be more tempting. Technically, in cheating, writing out a passage was far more difficult than doing multiple choice questions. As shown in the data, there was a large increase in the number of people who 'Continued to answer after the time is over'. This was again a technical problem. Probably a redesign of the time limit was needed.

Table 8.14 Activities against the rules in Taiwan's national-level university entrance exams (*Liankao*), 1967–72 versus 1973–6. *Source*: Ibid., 44.

	1967–72		1973–6		Difference
Type	Total	Per year	Total	Per year	per year[a]
Forgot ID card or exam pass.	32	5.33	56	14	8.63
Took the wrong seat.	21	3.50	9	2.25	−1.25
Took the exam paper out.	13	2.17	2	0.50	−1.67
Answered on the question sheet.	4	0.67	1	0.25	−0.42
Arrived late or left early.	5	0.83	11	2.75	1.92
ID photo or signature did not match.	29	4.83	7	1.75	−3.08
Substitution or cooperation in cheating.	1	0.16	8	2	1.84
Continued to answer after the time is over.	141	23.50	170	42.50	19
Passed answer aids.	12	2	26	6.50	4.5
Brought in answer aids.	29	4.83	34	8.50	3.67
Told others the answer.	9	1.50	29	7.25	5.75
Cheated by using hand signals.	1	0.17	27	6.75	6.58
Copied answer from others.	81	13.50	166	41.50	28
Showed answers to others.	3	0.50	36	9	8.5
Made changes after turning in the paper.	6	1	1	0.25	−0.75
Attacked proctor physically.	0	0	1	0.25	0.25
Put names on the answer sheet.	1	0.17	43	10.75	10.58
Besmirched the answer sheet.	7	1.17	23	5.75	4.58

Note: a. Difference per year = (1973–6 per year) − (1967–72 per year).

To sum up, violations against exam rules were the results of (1) negligence or (2) deliberate cheating. While the study can show the ethics of students in honouring the code of conduct, attention is given to the second type. It is seen here as a parameter to indicate to what extent students observe the 'rules of the game' of a meritocratic system.

Granted that increase, each year there were no more than two rule violators for every 1000 examinees. If we look only at deliberate violations, their percentage of the total number of exam-takers was only 0.025 per cent (Wu, 1977). That means only two or three persons in 10,000 cheated. For Taiwan, that suggests a pattern of youth behaviour highly confirmative of the principles of controlling access to the social ladder.

Table 8.15 Activities against the rules in Taiwan's national-level university entrance exams (*Liankao*), 1967–76. *Source*: Ibid., 40.

Type	1967	1968	1969	1970	1971	1972	1973	1974	1975	1976
Forgot ID card or exam pass.	8	5	13	3	0	3	8	10	24	14
Took the wrong seat.	7	5	5	0	3	1	4	0	3	2
Took the exam paper out.	3	1	1	5	0	3	0	1	0	1
Arrived late or left early.	0	1	0	2	0	2	3	3	1	4
ID photo or signature did not match.	20	9	0	0	0	0	3	4	0	0
Substitution or cooperation in cheating.	0	0	0	0	1	0	0	7	0	1
Continued to answer after the time is over.	3	9	11	39	23	56	30	49	37	54
Passed answer aids.	2	0	0	2	2	6	2	16	8	0
Brought in answer aids.	2	5	4	2	7	9	12	15	5	2
Told others the answer.	0	0	0	0	2	7	13	16	0	0
Cheated by using hand signals.	0	0	0	1	0	0	2	18	7	0
Copied answer from others.	9	3	4	13	22	30	21	48	52	45
Showed answers to others.	0	0	0	0	1	2	3	17	10	6
Made changes after turning in the exam paper.	5	1	0	0	0	0	1	0	0	0
Answered on the question sheet.	1	0	0	1	0	2	0	1	0	0
Attacked proctor physically.	0	0	0	0	0	0	0	1	0	0
Put names on the answer sheet.	0	0	0	0	0	1	8	23	7	5
Besmirched the answer sheet.	0	0	0	3	3	1	6	6	9	2
Others	2	0	0	4	0	3	6	17	18	30
Total	**62**	**39**	**38**	**75**	**64**	**126**	**122**	**252**	**181**	**166**

A DISCUSSION

Youth suicide and cheating have been two favourite stories for news media. Both, in consequence, draw great public concern as well as interest. Both depart from normative behaviours in an extreme fashion as a result of the exam system. Both are actions marked with abusive anomaly, although a suicide is anomalous in treating oneself, and a cheater is anomalous in treating the establishment. The primary focus of the study of these two outstanding issues concerns not only verifying to what extent the system could be a source of social problems, but also to what extent the exam system could engender a social crisis against its own legitimacy and viability.

Our study shows, first, that youth suicide in Japan has gradually but explicitly dropped, especially since the early 1970s. That happened in the wake of intensified competitiveness in the university entrance exams. That falling suicide rate is counter-evidence to the critique of the severe suicidogenic effect of the exams. Second, in Western nations, including the US, where education is far more liberal than East Asia, youth suicide has been on the rise. Japan's youth suicide rate approximated the average level of Western countries in the 1980s, and became lower than that of most Western nations after 1985. Contrary to what scholars have been trying to convince us of (Schoolland, 1990, for example), more children have killed themselves in the US than in Japan since as early as 1980.

The detailed data for January–June 1977 show that 6.5 per cent of the total number of suicides under 21 were related to the exams in Japan. For Taiwan, where the entrance exams are relatively harsher than in Japan, the statistics of suicide attempts (both incompleted and completed) for 1972–80 indicate that no more than 3 per cent of youth suicides were academic-related. These painstaking investigations challenge the notion that 'exam hell' is a main aggravating factor in youth suicide. That notion is spawned by the amplified news coverage of tragic accidents, the shocking effect of fragmented and truncated data, and the perplexity and little understanding on the part of the general public in the face of voluntary death among the young.

The causes of suicide have been an issue as controversial as it is unsolved. As a result, it is hard to know why the youth suicide rate in Japan fell in the past years. If the exam system is not the major cause of youth suicide, to follow that logic, it could not be responsible for the major fall in its rate, either. In Japan, the fall in youth suicide was accompanied by the rise of suicide among the middle-aged. According to one explanation (Yoshmatsu, 1992), this is a 'cohort phenomenon': the two belong to the same generation which, having experienced turbulent periods during their adolescence, continued to resort to suicide as a way out. Other quite recent research (Peng and Tseng, 1992) ascribes the fall in Japanese youth suicide to material affluence in society. These hypotheses remain to be fully determined.

Cheating is another dark side of the exam system where news media would like to muckrake. The rich variety of cheating styles, as illustrated previously, never fail to excite the curiosity of the audience, in the same way a gripping story of, say, a bank robbery does. In East Asian countries, while reading this news, the general public also want to test or prove a self-fulfilled prophecy: 'There is still justice in this world; despite the accident, the only system that is immune from social corruption and nepotism remains fair and untarnished.'

Violations against exam rules were the results of (1) negligence or (2) deliberate cheating. While the study may disclose how many students dishonoured the code of conduct, in the sociological dimension I am more interested in trying to understand to what extent students followed the 'rules of the game' of a meritocratic system. During the period 1967–76, violations were on the rise, mainly due to, as our analysis shows, the new computerized format of multiple choice questions. While this is not a crisis in the legitimacy of the exam system, it does show that such a technicality could affect people's behaviour. All told, each year there were, however, no more than two rule violators for every 1000 examinees. If we look at deliberate violations, their percentage of the total number of exam-takers was only 0.025 per cent (Wu, 1977). That means only two or three people out of 10,000 cheated. For Taiwan, that suggests a pattern of youth behaviour highly confirmative of the principles in controlling access to the social ladder. Granted that the close watch over exam administration maintained by proctors keeps the cheating rate low, it is unimaginable to keep tens of thousands of people observing the rules unless these rules have been accepted and internalized. 'Internalization of a norm', explains James Coleman (1990), 'will mean that an individual comes to have an internal sanctioning system which provides punishment when he carries out an action proscribed by norm or fails to carry out an action prescribed by the norm.' What the statistics on cheating can tell us is that a high degree of internalization of the exam system is a fact.

CHAPTER 9

Conclusion

The Exam is the engine, not the fuel.
– *A popular Victorian metaphor*

If we look at East Asia, the several elements of education we have covered constitute only a small part of the grand enterprise called 'education'. Nonetheless, they occupy a crucial and in many ways central position in it. The exam system, tested knowledge, test-based meritocracy, the tutoring industry and the attitudes, practices and beliefs related to these institutions are deeply interconnected. Therefore, we should reiterate the basics of that close-knit reality. This seems in every way like a jigsaw puzzle, as we need to consider all the parts, and also to assemble them into one piece. To start our recapitulation, we need to bring out the large picture first. **In this regard, the main question to ponder is: what factors served to make the exam systems in Japan, Korea and Taiwan similar?**

Our study of the exam systems and subcultures, sometimes microscopic in detail, points to the two fundamental factors of explanation: the cultural context and the legacy of history, especially Japanese colonialism. First of all, the primary commonality that Japan, Korea and Taiwan share is East Asian culture. We are dealing with a 'cultural sphere', as far as exam systems and the response of a population to them is concerned.

Culture is a repository of ideals and basic institutional solutions to problems. We all live in culture, although we may not consciously feel it. Culture surrounds us, and we are enveloped by it like fish in the water. There is no such thing as a human nature independent of culture. The increasing reliance upon the cultural systems of significant symbols – such as language, art, myth, ritual – for orientation, communication and self-control all created for man a new environment to which he was then obliged to adapt (Geertz, 1973: 48–9). The term 'cultural sphere' underscores the long cultural interaction between China and its neighbours: the forming of East Asia as a Sinocentric world order. A critical component was the Chinese written form, which carried the Chinese language, Confucianism, Chinese civil laws (*lüling*), Chinese sciences, and a Chinese version of Buddhism to Japan,

Korea, Vietnam and other neighbours. Acknowledging local adaptation and resistance, the essential point is that these became five common denominators for the cultural sphere of East Asia approximately during the Sui–Tang Dynasties period (581–906 AD). Together, they fashioned the mentalities that underlay a common set of institutions: meritocracy, family structure and state legitimacy in East Asia. In Japan, Korea and Taiwan, this cultural legacy then influenced the modern formation of education. This should be the essential reference in our study of the exam systems, past and present.

In the nineteenth century, this cultural sphere was transformed and somewhat temporarily overshadowed by the arrival of Westernization and modernization. But its deep structure survived, and like a zillion-terabyte database, the inner dimension of the cultural sphere remains at work. This is evidenced in the imperial exam system of early Meiji Japan. The Japanese exam system that emerged turned out to be a grand solution to one dilemma arising from the contradiction between modernity and the national culture. As a group-oriented society, Japan easily could 'choke on its own narrow particularism if it does not have well-entrenched mechanisms that counterbalance its powerful tendencies to allocate rewards and favors on the basis of personal affiliation' (Rohlen, 1983). The modernization of Japanese education and examinations is heavily influenced by the West. However, it is also connected to the traditional past. Confucian educational values revived in Meiji through a series of major Imperial Rescripts had profound consequences in Japan, as well as colonized Korea and Taiwan. Japanized Confucianism in fact played a key role in guiding the formation of modern socio-political life. Under colonial rule, Japan also vigorously initiated and promoted local re-Confucianization in Taiwan and Korea. Modernization was thus a process of 'dimorphism', as world culture and local culture together formed a new society (Japan) and its systemic structure and this was then exported to Korea and Taiwan.

Equally if not more important for explaining the parallelism among the three systems is the modern legacy of colonial education. Japan created and popularized public education in its two major colonies, Taiwan and Korea. Furthermore, it also renewed interest in Confucianism, and established a hybrid selection system that mixed meritocratic principles and Japan's selfish interests. Colonization, as elsewhere, left many Taiwanese and Koreans with a passionate post-colonial resolve to match or outdo their former colonial overlords. The very fact that Japan and its former colonies have a common cultural root, as noted, has made this colonial legacy especially unique and noteworthy. It gave Taiwan Chinese and Koreans confidence in their ability to duplicate Japan's economic and educational success. The colonial vestige of meritocracy, the nationalist bitterness and anger towards the Japanese colonizer, and the drive to outperform it, make a volatile mix that has ironically given postwar education in the three countries much in common.

As regards the prevailing importance of exam systems in East Asia, what are other possible competing hypotheses?

In rationalizing the exam-based, highly centralized education in East Asia, different perspectives may exist, however. Ronald Dore (1965), for instance, also underscores the importance of the Confucian tradition, but he is more interested in relating the exam culture to the comparative status of national development. In his 'late development explanation', because the new knowledge and new institutions in Japan were 'imported' from the West, and because of the discontinuity of the former élite system, the 'unbending use of the examination merit principle' was needed to control qualification and merit selection (Dore, 1965: 44–5). While this developmentalist approach appears plausible, several matters are not explained: (1) the many common features that the exam system of Taiwan and Korea share with the Japanese one, which is far more advanced than the rest of Asia; (2) many continued contrasts between East Asian systems and those in other developed (i.e. Western) countries. According to his historicist perspective, credentialism should be seen as an almost immutable property of developing nations. However, the variety of systems and lack of convergence worldwide make his hypothesis untenable. Many countries in the Third World category are mismatches.

The sociological school of institutionalism may also challenge the argument that the local culture plays a major role in moulding the modern system. In their theoretical interpretation of mass state-sponsored schooling, the European model in the world cultural frame is accentuated as a dominating feature of local systems of education. This approach postulates the construction of a mass education system as a major and indispensable component of every modern state's activity. In sum, it argues globalist ideas of rationality and the state control of modern development everywhere.

When considering the exam structure in particular, we have to add that, first of all, the influence of the Chinese *keju* system on the nineteenth-century exam systems in Europe is historically irrefutable (Durkheim, 1938; Têng, 1968; Miyazaki, 1976; Amano, 1990; Huang, 1992). A study of early European education reveals that the fundamental difference between the classic European qualification test and the Chinese *keju* system was competition. Exams were highly ritualized in Europe. Émile Durkheim criticizes this repetitive ritual prevailing in the prototypical model of Europe:

> In the university and the colleges of the Middle Ages the system of competition was completely unknown. In those days, there were no rewards to recompense merit and induce effort. Examinations were organized in such a way that for conscientious pupils they were little more than a formality. (Durkheim, 1938, trans. Collins, 1979: 262)

In Europe, the competitiveness of exams started with Jesuit colleges under the influence of the ancient Chinese system (Durkheim, 1938; Amano, 1990). Accordingly, in evaluating the modern German model and the East Asian one, we need to take into consideration the time-depth of the cross-cultural interplay and understand that influence has run in both directions.

Second, both the modern German model, initiated under Frederick the Great (1712–86), and the Chinese model were aimed at eliminating the power of the aristocracy and avoiding the possible dangers of nepotism and favouritism. However, unlike the *keju* or the modern selection system in East Asia, which was a direct ladder to government office, in the German model applicants still needed to complete a programme of approved courses (Amano, 1990: 11). This is not similar to the systems in East Asia.

Additionally, it is hard to accommodate in a worldwide pattern of generalization the many important peculiarities that mark East Asian exam culture, such as the 'cram phenomenon', the vast army of repeaters (*rônin*), the highly culture-dependent pattern of academic behaviours, and the age-old religious practices specifically affiliated to the exam system.

Chapter 1 traces the origin of the modern exam system back to the Meiji Japan, which was then replicated in Taiwan and Korea during the colonial era. **We ask: why and how did the exam-based system of merit selection come into being, playing a dominating role in the Meiji Japan?**

As the exam system was a solution to the dilemma between modernity and traditional culture, it necessarily incorporated some of both. To build a modern bureaucratic and technocratic élite, to select men of talent and guarantee the quality of education, and, historically, to eradicate the unequal extra-territoriality imposed on Japan by foreign powers, the Japanese deemed it necessary to have a meritocratic system. The exam system also became indispensable because of the surging wave of students preparing themselves for higher education (Amano, 1990: 215–16). The fact that the first model the Japanese leaders had in their minds was the *keju* (Chinese imperial exam system) serves as an ample manifestation of the effects of Sinocentric culture in general, and the ancient (but defunct) Japanese system of *kôkyo* (Japanese for '*keju*') in particular.

Nevertheless, Japanese exams were eventually patterned after the German system for both higher education and the civil service, indubitable evidence of Western impact. The two models, Chinese and German, had common principles: both were impersonal, based on measured achievement, and both deterred hereditary access to bureaucratic status. However, at the end of nineteenth century, the German model was more legitimate, especially since in the nineteenth century the Chinese exam system was in the process of being discredited and destroyed in China itself. Another difference between the two was that the German system was more attuned to the priorities of the modern era. But the cultural continuity is also manifest in the historical evolution of exam systems, the value and virtue reflected in the tested knowledge, and the subculture of examinations unique to the East Asia.

Historically, during this formative process, how did the Japanese examination system initiate the modern relationship between merit and status?

The actual relationship between merit and status was forged and reinforced through the process of legalization. The coupling of education to social status became possible and tightened up through a number of legislative measures in the fields of education and recruitment. First, the 1886 Middle School Ordinance was issued, which ended the muddled passage from compulsory to 'higher' education, and established the public higher school (initially very élite) as a clearly demarcated university prep school (Roden, 1980). Soon afterwards, in 1887, a general examination ordinance was adopted and went into force, which extended exams from the judiciary to all parts of the government. Japan's leaders had eventually concluded that governmental stability depended in large part on a career bureaucracy, and that such a bureaucracy could not be maintained without examinations for all its career fields (Spaulding, 1967).

An important question concerning modern merit exams is: did the exam systems of Japan, Korea and Taiwan originate in the common experience of Japanese colonial administration before WWII?

The answer is affirmative. The exam systems in the colonies were carbon copies of the Japanese one. Our analysis of entrance policy and exam papers has found no major discrepancy among the three systems. Nevertheless, in practice, selection and promotion in the colonies betrayed one difference from the Japanese system. Both documentary evidence and scholarly literature point to a major non-exam channel in the colonies, unlike in homeland Japan. This channel gave convenient leverage to Japanese in favour of Japanese citizens over Koreans or Taiwanese. It was partially due to the centrality of the Japanese language in the colonial system, but other factors also contributed. Empirical data show a yawning segregation in schooling between Japanese and local students in Taiwan and Korea. Despite improvement in later years, children were segregated throughout colonial rule. The merit system was severely twisted by an unofficial, but firmly implemented, quota system in favour of Japanese. Having said that, we have to realize that the system paved the way to advanced education for a small number of Taiwanese and Koreans, and many became leaders. The ethnic discrimination in the colonies only underscores the limitation of the exam system as it was embedded in a larger political context that could not tolerate true meritocracy.

The legacy of Japanese education in Taiwan and Korea was profound. The achievement in school attendance of colonial children was not only unprecedented, but also made American and European colonies pale in comparison. Japanese colonial education built a well-educated and adept workforce in the early stages of development in Taiwan and Korea. Today, élite schools and universities are not only products of the colonial past; their administration and management also had some lasting effects. Confucian values of merit revived during the Meiji era have remained guiding concepts in teaching and learning. Japanese education planted the seed of meritocratic expectations, idealism, and hope for social mobility. Once emancipated from colonialism, the Taiwanese and Koreans aspired to the same ideals that Japanese education left behind. And now they aim to outperform the Japanese.

Chapter 2 turns to a second stage in the modern history of exams. After WWII, the Western impact, especially through the American presence, was notable in East Asia. There was a rapid expansion of enrolments, the implantation of democratization, and some decentralization of education in the three countries. This change can indeed be described as part of a process of Eurocentric globalization, the sweeping tendency to isomorphism that has ritualized many aspects of education worldwide (Ramirez and Boli, 1987; DiMaggio and Powell, 1983). **In this new context, to continue my comparison: what were the commonalities and differences among the three postwar systems? How did they change over the years?**

In postwar East Asia, the systems of high-stake entrance exams (based on objective measures of achievement) re-emerged in Taiwan and Korea. They became gradually centralized, justified by a broadly felt need to regulate quality, weed out corruption and give more chance to bright, low-income students. In Japan, the Occupation sponsored an overhaul of the entire educational system. However, very much contradictory to the large-scale reform effort for decentralization, psychometric assessment and de-emphasis of exams, the achievement-based nature of exams once again became almost the only pathway to university. In a word, meritocracy was valued despite Westernizing trends and this was embodied in exam systems.

In our historical comparison of entrance exam systems, we find a pattern of convergence among the three systems of Japan, Korea and Taiwan in the postwar era. This pattern, in its development, bears certain coordinates with the traditional imperial exams: (1) a hierarchical pecking order of students across the nation, (2) increased state authority in ratifying and empowering core knowledge, (3) a heavy dependence on written questions and answers, (4) strict uniformity and standardization of test form and content, (5) the chronic phenomenon of the huge number of exam repeaters, and (6) the close meritocratic nexus forging schools with power and status. The combination of these characteristics is hardly found elsewhere. To accentuate its cultural basis and context, I coined the term 'Kejurization'. The ancient Chinese system was not the chrysalis of today's exams in institutional terms, however. It merely provided underlying concepts and values for modern Kejurization. It was meritocratic principles and *praxis* adopted by the imperial Meiji that served as the immediate archetype of modern exams in East Asia.

Regarding postwar reforms: why were the exam systems in East Asia largely intact and intractable through numerous reform efforts, starting from the most drastic ones during the immediate postwar period?

Many a reform failed to adapt and dovetail to the local cultural and value system, thus making their receptivity too low to survive. Oftentimes, a reform failed because it threatened impartiality, treasured in East Asia because of the otherwise omnipresent favouritism and particularism. Meritocratic objectivity has helped to maintain social equilibrium and the *status quo*. In this respect, there have been many explanations for the intractability of the exam systems, which substantiate or supplement the foregoing hypothesis. Rohlen (1983), Lynn (1988) and Frost (1992) posit that the Japanese have been focused on the entrance exam system, and that collectively they secretly admire its results, despite their public criticism. This attests to the East Asian conviction that competition brings out the best in people, that it leads to hard work, and that this effort helps keep society competitive. Vogel (1979) and Dorfman (1987) contend that Japanese particularism needs to be balanced by brief but brutal testing mechanisms that do the job of social selection. That is, cooperative and interpersonal emphases need counterweights, such as impersonal, competitive exams. Schoppa (1991) argues that education issues are characterized by certain conflict patterns resulting in certain patterns of policy-making, depending on the question of whether or not the conservatives are in agreement. In case of serious disagreement, for instance, on the reform of university entrance exams, inaction is a likely result. Dore (1975) suggests that, because of the large gap between the limited posts in the realm of the élite and the great mass of highly educated people who long to get the posts, the Japanese government is obliged to guarantee access and mobility in the fairest possible way, i.e., to legitimize the hierarchy. None of these explanations excludes any of the others.

The above explanations for the Japanese system should also serve as a theoretical source for interpreting Taiwan and Korea. In both countries, Japanese colonialism left a meritocratic ideal, which the postwar authorities and people in Taiwan and Korea were highly motivated to strive for. It is true that the *de facto* goal of Japanese colonial education in Taiwan and

Korea was to fashion the lower track of a two-track Meiji education system (Adams and Gottlieb, 1993; Tsurumi, 1977). Yet, as McGinn *et al.* (1980) argue, the Japanese-imposed entrance examinations set up a credentialistic model for both Korea and Taiwan, and this became an integral part of their educational systems.

A discussion of exam history would be 'hollow' if we did not even look at the exam questions proper. For my study of questions, I chose World History and Maths, as they have been normative exam subjects. **In an exploratory approach to the exam questions: What kind of intelligence or knowledge was tested? How much did the examiners expect the applicants to know? What kind of change has taken place over time?**

A study of the prewar exam papers based on occasionally skimpy data gives a clue to a number of contrasts with the postwar exams. In general, the prewar ones involved fewer topics of the discipline and asked fewer questions. They were easier. That generalization is equally applicable to Japan, Taiwan and Korea, because, in the Japanese colonial empire, education was virtually a unified system. Let us first look at the world history exams.

The prewar Japanese exams in world history clearly demonstrate a didactic, utilitarian purpose for studying history. As nationalism prevailed in Japan, the topic of world history became less examined than Japan's national history. Whenever world history was examined, stress was given to such current concerns as the Western imperialist rivalry and colonization. The prewar questions in maths exams were also easier than now. Unlike maths exams today, the university entrance questions then did not evaluate achievements in high school maths, as the maths screening exam was actually administered at the end of middle school. This does not mean, however, that the entrance exams were not sophisticated and tricky. In fact, prewar competition was higher than postwar competition in terms of acceptance ratio. What has not changed since the prewar period, however, is the incontestable dependence upon and importance attached to academic achievement in evaluation.

An intriguing question here relates to the role of the American educators during the Occupation: how much did they change or influence exam design and assessment concepts in East Asia?

This issue might have been dealt with from a policy-making perspective, but it has rarely been addressed in the epistemic–psychometric dimension, such as the form and content of the exams. The Allied Occupation after the War brought with it a flood of new educational concepts and methods. Due to postwar growth, some new techniques, such as machine-readable multiple choices, were accepted willingly and instantly by Japan, Korea and Taiwan. The new psychometric theory and intelligence test were not, however. Achievement quickly became the major criterion, despite academic criticisms and a series of experiments with alternative methodologies.

Both the intelligence test and the achievement test are designed to measure cognitive ability. However, the former is more interested in assessing *g*, or 'general intelligence', the core intelligence behind all intelligence. The latter not only examines intelligence, but centres on measurable learning including such factors as motivation, industry, and complex problem-solving ability. The achievement test has been taken as more legitimate in East Asia, simply because it has a better fit with the Confucian epistemology. In the final analysis, one can hardly deny that the discourse of psychometrics and the interpretation of human intelligence are culturally valued and defined.

In recent years, what commonalities and dissimilarities are found in the exam papers of the three countries?

Today, the primary commonality among exams in Japan, Korea and Taiwan is that, by encompassing and compressing the full scope of a textbook into a highly condensed form of questions, entrance exams become a test of competency rather than criterion-referenced qualification. In that sense, as compared to the prewar period, its utilitarian purpose seems to have been blurred. But this results in kinds of high quality. In exams, the *idiot savant* may score higher. However, rote effort, although important, is merely the prerequisite, the bottom line. It would be simplistic to state that the more one stored in one's brain the greater one's chances. Yet in maths, problem solving needs 'learning by exercising'. Judging ability is vital for multiple choices. Similar to other forms of assessment, high-calibre ability in application, analysis and comparison was needed for high achievers.

Similarities aside, the exams of Japan and Taiwan are not identical. In the past ten years or so, Japan's exams have maintained a uniformity, standardization, and an evenly spread scale of difficulty. The world history questions focus on pallid factual knowledge. The exams of Taiwan show, in contrast, more diversity. The difficulty scale varies greatly with the exam paper. Its grading system is harsher. Taiwan's exams include a blend of conventional questions and some experimental ones, aimed to make answering questions a more playful process, less anchored in rote memorization. It would have been fascinating to have the questions of the Korean exams also in our comparative frame. However, this is unlikely for the time being due to the language barrier and the lack of the necessary information.

In our 'jigsaw picture' of exam culture, one major part is the 'cram world'. Although the issue has been notoriously known, and has captured enormous public concern, not very much has been written about this world in the three countries. **Our interest turns to the origin of the tutoring academies: when did they start in Japan, Korea and Taiwan?**

My study of the early *juku* and *yobiko* in Japan has revealed the symbiosis of the exam system and its subculture. If we limit our interest to the exam-centred *juku/yobiko*, the advent of modern cram schools can be traced to the Meiji era, about 20 years after the exam system was instituted in 1872 (Amano, 1990: 78). Pretty much the same can be said about the '*rônin* phenomenon', the sense of competition and test anxiety, pop literature, and the intellectual critique. This subculture seems to have a life of its own, surprisingly unperturbed either by the ongoing wars or by the Occupation.

In tracing the genesis of academic tutoring academies back in history, their classification becomes ill-defined. This has made dating difficult and arbitrary. For instance, the village *shijuku* (private school) in late Tokugawa Japan took on a role quite similar to that of the modern tutoring school, but they are generally not counted as the early form of academic *juku* or *yobiko*. On the other hand, the preparatory schools that Amano (1990) dates as the earliest *juku/yobiko* were very vague in their boundary with the private middle schools.

That problem becomes even more obvious when we discuss early cram schools in Korea and Taiwan. Taiwanese scholars traced the modern *buxiban* back to the first Japanese language tutoring school of 1895, although its function, purpose and status differed much from the modern cram school. For Korea, in reconstructing the origin of *hakwon*, it becomes obvious how historiography can be affected by ideology. Unlike in Taiwan, when the Japanese annexed Korea Western missionary schools had already grown up in quite large numbers. Nevertheless, the Japanese-built school system was far more influential than the missionary schools during colonial times. However, in the *hakwon* history compiled by the Korean *Hakwon* Association, Japanese-initiated supplementary education is rarely mentioned. The contrast in the historiography of cram schools between Korea and Taiwan is apparently caused by political and ideological reasons.

It is worthy of note that, in both Korea and Taiwan, no evidence is found for the existence of prewar cram academies geared specifically toward entrance exams. This absence, I would hypothesize, was mainly historical. First, the tutoring academies established in the two colonies were harshly confined and controlled by the colonizer. The Japanese rulers would not support and tolerate cram schools which they perceived as a waste of time and energy. Secondly, for a Taiwanese or Korean to enter middle school or university was not simply an academic matter. They faced ethnic and political limitations. Therefore, there was no great impetus for students to cram hard. Thirdly, as the standard of living of Taiwanese/Koreans was lower than that of the Japanese, tutoring would be too expensive to afford. Hence, there must have been very little demand for cram enterprises. This analysis is admittedly very hypothetical due to the limited information I have. As a marginal and occasionally illegitimate business, the tutoring industry has been much less documented than formal education.

When we come to the postwar cram world of Japan, Korea and Taiwan, we want to know the basic facts and figures, as well as their meanings. We ask: What is the cram school attendance ratio among the students, and what can that tell us?

Our study of these schools has thrown into relief an East Asian obsession with education. The institutionalization of the *juku/buxiban/hakwon* is first of all the institutionalization of a pattern of consumption of time and effort. A baseline for measuring this demand can be the completion rate for regular high school, which registers the willingness on the part of students to learn. A comparison of data of the US and East Asian countries shows a marked contrast. Between 1975 and 1991, the US high school incompletion rate fell from 17 per cent to 15 per cent (NEGP, 1992: 23). In Japan, the rate was kept at no more than 2.2 per cent during 1985–92, falling to 1.9 per cent in 1992 (Jiji Tsûshinsha, 1994: 80). In Korea, the average high school incompletion rate for 1980–90 was 4 per cent (KEDI, 1993). If we add to this the extracurricular attendance ratio in the academic *juku*, which, by a conservative estimation, was over 20 per cent for elementary school students (1993 data for Japan) and over 60 per cent for middle school students (1990 data for Korea, 1991–3 data for Japan), we have an idea of the East Asian educational obsession. The whole growth of the cram world stems from obsession, a meritocratic drive embodied in the entrance exam system.

Our second question about the extracurricular study is: Why did the number of cram school students keep growing, and the cram industry remain flourishing?

The exam subculture is, as I remarked in the Introduction and discussed in detail in other chapters, the confluence of two main factors: a cultural heritage and an institutional structure of credentialism. Since these two factors are fairly stable over time, they do not have much to tell about why there has been a notable increase of the growth in the *juku* attendance rate and the *juku* industry. In recent years, furthermore, the steady increase in *juku* attendance has been quite surprising in Japan, for instance, given the demographic decline and the crisis that plagued private universities in getting enough students.

A number of reasons have been put forward to explain why *juku* flourish in Japan. First, as Komiyama Hirohito (1991) contends, the growth of *juku* presupposes healthy economic development. Some of the large academic *juku* in Japan were founded in the early 1970s when the economy was kept at the high rate of growth of 11.64 per cent on average (1991: 122–30). The better lifestyle, and the increased chance of higher education, caused people to be more interested in investing for the better education of their children. This certainly helped the development of the cram industry.

Another explanation for the increase in cram schools is the curricular gap between textbook knowledge and tested knowledge. When the textbooks became easier, and the entrance exams became harder, that gap grew in Japan. What I also found in both Japan and Korea was a slow reduction in the postwar period in the amount of school-assigned homework, a trend of liberal schooling. As a result, the cram schools filled the teaching gap for the ultimate entrance exams and, in time, regular schools began to assign less homework to give students more free time. This interaction meant that more *juku* were needed to fill the gap.

Other explanations for the increase in the cram business also exist. For instance, it is argued that, to achieve academic excellence and to beat the highly specialized competition, family or community education is no longer adequately proficient. A collective psychology is also at work. In the race to pass exams, if somebody starts to run, others cannot remain indifferent for very long.

The competition among individual students to excel does not seem to vary significantly between Japan, Korea and Taiwan. The competition among cram schools, however, is very different among the three. It is first conditioned by the regulations and laws of each state concerning the legitimacy of cram schools, which are different. It also follows the different patterns of local business. This hypothesis echoes the postulation made by Orrù, Biggart and Hamilton (in Powell and DiMaggio, 1991: 390–422) of an internal 'organizational isomorphism', with each Asian country distinct from the others.

It is hard to recapitulate the minutiae in my study of the school culture shown through the physical plant and equipment of major cram schools in the three countries. In describing classrooms, desks and chairs, lights, air-conditioning systems, etc., I have tried to convey what impressed me when I visited those schools. It may be summarized in the following points: (1) there is a large demand for cram schooling; (2) cram schools become prosperous in accommodating that demand; (3) economy of scale is perhaps the only viable answer to that demand; (4) the service is by no means always satisfactory, especially in terms of physical conditions, although the quality of teachers and teaching is generally very good; (5) there are some indications of an increasing trend of expansion in the demand for cramming in peripheral parts of society. This is shown, in particular, through the growing attendance ratio of *juku* in rural Japan, and the improving conditions of cram schools in the non-metropolitan areas (Taiwan).

Teaching and learning are the pivotal activities of the tutoring academies. But, do we know how knowledge is transmitted in the cram world? Despite their bad reputation, is there anything beneficial in their curriculum and pedagogy?

The exam system is the only *raison d'être* for the vast cram industry. These exams require meticulous analysis of logical twists and turns. They require one to unravel knotty problems with speed, vigour and composure. To master encyclopaedic knowledge, to persevere, practice and excel, demands self-discipline and a certain kind of character. In the cram world, knowledge, rationality, persistence and coolness under stress are uniquely enshrined. What is equally enshrined is the role model of the teacher in cracking the tricky problems of the exam system. Some of these aspects are admittedly quite functional and effective, and once were accommodated in the conceptualization of the role and nature of schooling.

Next, we look at the effects of the entrance exam system in the light of religion, which is not customarily employed in the study of East Asian education. **In all three countries, many students go to some religious place for a blessing on the exams. Why do they resort to supernatural or superstitious forces for something as rationally structured as exams?**

An interpretative key to the religious component of meritocracy I detected is the sacred–profane dichotomy, the primary classification of society in religion (Durkheim, 1965; Caillois, 1959). It brings religion and the entrance exams together within a common value system. Devoted effort spent on exams argues for the sanctification of meritocratic grouping in society. To evoke a spiritual force and to obtain a sacred blessing are the religious dimensions of exam competition.

The sanctification of effort can be dated back to the pre-modern era. It is a part of a time-honoured tradition in local culture. The churches, deities and priests (mainly in Japan) are serving the anxieties and hopes of the new generation as they have done for about a millennium. Only the universalization of schooling breathed new life into traditional religion. The forms of religious activities for high-stake exams differ immensely in Japan, Korea and Taiwan. The main religions and deities are totally different in the three countries, and their religious objects and services have little in common. Confucianism, though dynamic in the three countries as an under-girding mentality, did not serve as a major religion in this regard. The emergence of religious services dovetailed to the merit system arose in-dependently within the three countries, although they serve the same function.

This study suggests that exam-centred religious forms stemmed from local religions. Therefore, they are largely defined by the religions they are affiliated to, such as Shinto and Chinese polytheist religion. For that reason, in comparison to the entrance exams *per se*, which have a lot in common in their systemic structure, the exam-related supernatural activities are as different as the traditional popular religions of each nation. If there is any common denominator among these activities, it would be that each of them is a corollary of the high-stake exam system.

What kind of role is played by Confucianism, the orthodox cult and faith in the ancient past of East Asia?

Confucianism has been a value system for East Asian meritocracy both in theory and in practice. It laid down the structural principles for developing the exam system through which people were raised to power and prestige on the basis of achievement, at least in the ideal. Nonetheless, the orthodox Confucianism, as C. K. Yang concedes, 'is not a full-fledged theistic religion, since it poses no god or supernatural dogma as the symbol of its teachings' (Yang, 1961: 224). Historically, the Confucian literati were not interested in breaking away from the irksome aspects of mundane life. In spite of its religio-mystical garb, Confucianism was rationalistic and agnostic. It also fell short of systematic revelation or futurism. Throughout Chinese history, there has been no Confucian church, priesthood or creed (Chan, 1953: 15). As a result, Confucius is far less deified, and has thus less supernatural force to offer to exam-taking students.

In Chapter 6, I discuss two important explanatory factors in the exam competition; time and money. **I first ask: How valid is it when we take time spent on study as one explanatory factor for the achievement of an individual or a population?**

The educational achievements of Japan, Korea and Taiwan are well known. This is correlated with the amount of students' time spent on work. East Asian academic calendars are longer than those of many other countries, especially the US. Out of school, students spent a lot more hours cramming for exams. Extracurricular study was typified by the experience of exam-repeaters. The majority of the repeaters believed they failed because they did not work hard enough rather than because of a lack of natural ability. Data also show that most repeaters attended prep schools, indicating a high degree of institutionalization of time and effort and a fully developed genre of knowledge transmission. The repeaters' acceptance–application ratio in university admission – 30–50 per cent in Korea and 25 per cent in Taiwan – shows that pain and perseverance did pay off for a portion of them.

In a sense, the repeaters' extra years of study are only the 'tip of the iceberg' of time spent on work, as they were the conspicuous part of college preparation. Equally time-consuming were routinized mock-test exercises, cramming life, and other means of extracurricular study. The credentialistic structure of East Asia and the impartiality of the entrance exams focus each generation on the knowledge they need to learn. One common denominator among Japan, Korea and Taiwan is that the bottom line of the entrance requirements has been translated into the bottom line of quality for the entire school system.

My second focus in Chapter 6 is given to 'money'. **I pose the question: How much 'money', private and public, is associated with the academic achievement of the three countries?**

My comparison of public expenditures reveals that Japanese, Korean and Taiwanese regimes were not as exemplary in educational spending as they are assumed to be. Either measured in absolute terms of PPE (per pupil expenditures) or in relative terms (share of educational expenditure in total

GNP), they are not ranked among the top in the IAEP countries. Even compared to some non-IAEP countries of the Third World, Japan, Korea and Taiwan are not that impressive. The commitment to education in the three East Asian countries is more tangibly argued at a non-governmental or social level, in the area of parental expectations and support.

For this credentialism-driven family behavioural pattern, the income differentials between middle school, high school and college is one explanatory factor. However, as the educational disparity of wages is found to be a universal phenomenon, it is apparently not enough in explaining the exceptionally enormous amount of time and effort that students have allocated to their academic work, as well as the significant increase in the educational share of family budgets in East Asia. As noted, that can only be understood with reference to the value system contextualized in a larger cultural milieu.

Studies show, not surprisingly, that family investment in education is correlated to family income, and that investment differed significantly between urban and rural areas. These differences are the potential source of inequality of outcomes, which began to draw more and more sobering concern from educators and critics alike. Yet, we have to acknowledge some very unique features of the entrance exams. The systems of Japan, Korea and Taiwan are depicted as 'meritocratic' in that they are relatively free from appraisal based on factors extraneous to academic matters, such as birth, power, privilege, politico-ideological judgement or philanthropy. I therefore concur with the economists John Fei, Gustav Ranis and Shirley Kuo (1979) in their conclusion that:

> The imperial examination system, institutionalized long ago in traditional China, continues to hold sway. *Rigorous and impartial entrance examinations are annually held at all levels of formal education. Because wealthy families do not have the marked special advantages frequently encountered elsewhere, access to educational opportunities is thus relatively equal for all.* [italic added] (321)

Compared to the university admission process of, for instance, the United States or China, there is relatively less educational inequality in Japan, Korea and Taiwan due to the exam-centred system which is less affected by the ascribed status, and which embodies a high esteem for knowledge and teachers, an epistemology that gives more emphasis to effort than genetically endowed ability, a psychometric evaluation that measure both intelligence and motivation, perseverance and character.

The exam system has long been a cause of intellectual disapproval and criticism, largely due to the unintended effects it generates. For that reason, I complete my jigsaw puzzle picture with a discussion of two case studies of the conspicuous negative sides of the system: youth suicide and cheating. These two have been favourite stories in the news media. Both, in consequence, draw great public concern as well as interest. Both are abhorrent actions. The primary focus of my study of these two issues is to verify whether the exam system is a source of the problem, and also to question whether the exam system could engender a social crisis against its own legitimacy and viability. For the causal association between exams and adolescent suicide, I raise three questions: **(1) What are the ratios of Japanese and Taiwanese youth suicide, and how have they changed**

over time? (2) How do these ratios compare to other nations? (3) What percentage of youth suicide can be imputed to the exam system?

Our study shows, first, that youth suicide in Japan has gradually but explicitly dropped, especially since the early 1970s. That happened in the wake of intensified competitiveness of the university entrance exams. A falling suicide rate is counter-evidence to the critique of exams as a cause of youth suicide. Second, in Western nations, including the US, where education is far more liberal than in East Asia, youth suicide has been on the rise. In the 1980s, Japan's youth suicide rate approximated the average level of Western countries, and became lower than most of Western nations after 1985. Contrary to what some scholars have been trying to convince us of (Schoolland, 1990, for example), children have killed themselves at a higher rate in the US than in Japan since as early as 1980.

The detailed data for January–June 1977 shows that 6.5 per cent of the total suicides under 21 were related to exams in Japan. For Taiwan, where the entrance exams are relatively harsher than in Japan, the statistics of suicide attempts (both incomplete and completed) for 1972–80 indicate that no more than 3 per cent of youth suicides were academically related. These painstaking investigations challenge the notion that the 'exam hell' is a main aggravating factor for youth suicide. That notion is spawned by the amplified news coverage of tragic accidents, the shocking effect of fragmented and truncated data, and the perplexity and little understanding on the part of the general public in the face of media reporting.

Cheating is reputedly another dark aspect of the exam system according to the news media. I first measured the gravity of the violation, and then examine what sociological messages we can draw from our investigation of cheating.

The rich variety of cheating styles, as illustrated previously, never fail to excite the curiosity of the audience. In East Asian countries, while reading this news, the general public also want to be convinced that, despite the incidents, the exam system is still fair and corruption-free.

Investigation showed that cheating, either through negligence or deliberately, although it rose during 1967–76, largely due to technical changes in exam format, remained low, at 0.025 per cent of the total number of exam-takers for deliberate cheating (Y. C. Wu, 1977). This is an indication of a high degree of internalization of the exam system's values.

The history of exams is a history of an institution, a system. On the other hand, this system is not an empty shell, but a structural order governing human behaviour and consciousness. In that sense, what we have been studying is a key behavioural pattern, the history of that pattern, and the power behind that pattern. In *Days of Judgment*, Roy MacLeod writes:

> In an examination, the process cannot be divorced from its product. As Henry Latham of Trinity Hall, Cambridge recalled, using a popular Victorian metaphor, 'the Exam is the engine, not the fuel'. The 'fuel' was selected into different categories, for different social functions. Examinations not only assessed the acquisition of new knowledge, in the language of Bourdieu, they reinforced existing positions of cultural and social capital, enabling both those who set and sat examinations to share in the cultural validation of their educational beliefs. (1982: 5)

What he alludes to here is that, apart from assessment, one vitally important role of exams is comparable to an 'engine'. It is the driving force that actualizes values and beliefs concerning intelligence and knowledge. 'Engine' is the modern metaphor equivalent to the ancient image of the 'Dragon Gate'.

Finally, I would like to discuss some major limits of this book, which, in a sense, also implies the need for future research and elucidation. First of all, my study has left a number of 'empty spaces' unattended. In my analysis of tested knowledge, I mainly compare the exam questions for élite universities in the prewar period. Similarly, for the postwar period, I concentrate on the entrance exams administered by the government at the national level. I have not touched upon the entrance exams administered by the individual universities, especially the non-élite or regional universities: How were their exams different from élite ones in terms of their scale of difficulty and content? As for the tutoring academy courses attuned to the non-élite universities, how much do they differ from the élite-track courses? The pursuit of these questions will contribute to a more comprehensive understanding of the issues we have addressed.

Key to abbreviated citations

BASEY	Budgetary Accounting and Statistics Executive Yuan of Taiwan
CEPDEY	Council for Economic Planning and Development Executive Yuan of Taiwan
CET	College-based Entrance Test
CSNG	Chôsen Sôtôkufu Naimubu Gakumukyo (Educational Bureau of the Government-General of Korea)
DIKG	Dai Ichi Kôtô Gakkô (The First Higher School)
DNSS	Daigaku Nyûshi Sentâ Shiken (Questions and annotated answers to the exams given by the National Center for University Entrance Exams)
ET	Essay Test
FKK	Fukutake Shoten Kyôiku Kenkyûjo (Fukutake Shoten Educational Research Institute)
FPC	Foreign Press Center
HHCY	Hankook Hakwon Chong Yunhaphwe (Korea Unified Association of *Hakwon*)
HSS	High School Scores
JETRO	Japan External Trade Organization
JMCA	Japan Management and Coordination Agency
JMOE	Japanese Ministry of Education
JTS	Jiji Tsûshinsha (News Correspondence Agency)
KBS	Kokusai Bunka Shinkokai (Japan Cultural Society)
KEDI	Korea Educational Development Institute
KMOE	Korean Ministry of Education
KOIS	Korean Overseas Information Service
NAEP	National Assessment of Educational Progress
NAGP	National Education Goals Panel
NET	National Entrance Test

NHK	Nihon Hôsô Kyôkai (Japan Broadcasting Corporation)
NPT	National Preliminary Test
NSAT	National Scholastic Achievement Test
NSDR	Nihon Shiritsu Daigaku Renmei (Japan Association of Private Colleges and Universities)
NSMS	Nyûgaku Shiken Mondai Shôkai (Entrance examination questions and answers)
NUT	National Unified Test
SLOG	Student Learning Orientations Group
TBX	Taiwan Bijiao Jiaoyü Xüehui (Comparative Education Association of Taiwan)
TMOE	Taiwan Ministry of Education
UNESCO	United Nations Educational, Scientific and Cultural Organization
USAMGIK	US Army Military Government in Korea
WHO	World Health Organization
YKK	Yano Keizai Kenkyûjo (Yano Economics Research Institute)
YTH	Yomiuri Terebi Hôdôbu (Yomiuri Televised News Department)
ZR	Zhongyang Ribao (The Central Daily)
ZS	Zhongguo Shibao (The China Daily)

References

References in English

Adams, Donald K., and Esther E. Gottlieb. 1993. *Education and Social Change in Korea*. New York: Garland Publishing.

Altbach, Philip G., and Gail P. Kelly. 1978. *Education and Colonialism*. New York: Longman.

Altbach, Philip G., and Gail P. Kelly. 1986. *New Approaches to Comparative Education*. Chicago: The University of Chicago Press.

Amano, Ikuo. 1990. *Education and Examination in Modern Japan*. Translated by William Cummings and Fumiko Cummings. Tokyo: University of Tokyo Press.

Amsden, Alice H. 1989. *Asia's Next Giant*. New York: Oxford University Press.

Anderson, Charles W. 1982. *The Use of Codified Knowledge in Five Teacher Education Programs: A Comparative Analysis*. East Lansing, Mich.: The Institute for Research on Teaching, Michigan State University.

Asian Journal.

August, Robert. 1992. '*Yobiko*: prep schools for college entrance in Japan'. Chapter 8, pp. 267–308 in *Japanese Educational Productivity*, edited by Leestma, Robert, and Herbert Walberg. Ann Arbor, Mich.: Center for Japanese Studies, The University of Michigan.

Azuma, H., K. Kashiwagi, and H. Ohno. 1987. 'Student learning orientation: the Japanese study', Chapter 6 in *Why Do Students Learn? A Six-Country Study of Student Motivation*, edited by Student Learning Orientations Group. Brighton, England: Institute of Development Studies at the University of Sussex.

Bacon, Jacqueline, and Heather L. Carter. 1991. 'Culture and mathematics learning: a review of the literature'. *Journal of Research and Development in Education* 25(1): 1–9.

Bae, Chong-keun. 1991. 'Education top reason behind rapid growth: schooling for economic takeoff'. *Koreana* 5(2): 56–62.

Beauchamp, Edward R., and James M. Vardaman, Jr. 1994. *Japanese Education Since 1945: A Documentary Study*. New York: Sharpe.

Bee, Robert L. 1974. *Patterns and Processes: An Introduction to Anthropological Strategies for the Study of Sociocultural Change*. New York: Free Press.

Biggs, J. B., and Collis, K. F. 1982. *Evaluating the Quality of Learning: The SOLO Taxonomy* (structure of observed learning outcomes). New York: Academic Press.

Bishop, John L., ed. 1968. *Studies of Governmental Institutions in Chinese History*. Cambridge, Mass.: Harvard University Press.

Blaug, Mark. 1976. *An Introduction to the Economics of Education*. London: Allen Lane.

Bloom, Benjamin S. 1956. *Taxonomy of Educational Objectives, Handbook I: Cognitive Domain*. New York: David McKey.

Borgen, Robert. 1994. *Sugawara no Michizane and the Early Heian Court*. Honolulu, Hawaii: University of Hawaii Press.

Borthwick, Mark. 1992. *Pacific Century: The Emergence of Modern Pacific Asia*. Boulder, Col.: Westview Press.

Boudon, R. 1974. *Education, Opportunity and Social Inequality*. New York: Wiley.

Bourdieu, Pierre, and Jean-Claude Passeron. 1964. *Les Héritiers*. Paris.

———. 1977. *Reproduction in Education, Society and Culture*. Beverly Hills: Sage Publications.

Bracey, Gerald. 1996. 'International comparisons and the condition of American education'. *Educational Researcher* 25(1): 5–11.

Breisach, Ernst. 1983. *Historiography: Ancient, Medieval and Modern*. Chicago: The University of Chicago Press.

Brereton, J. L. 1944. *The Case for Examinations*. London: Cambridge University Press.

Broaded, Montgomery, C. 1994. 'Social origins, ability group placement and educational outcomes in urban Taiwan'. Paper presented at CIES Annual Meetings. San Diego: California.

Budgetary Accounting & Statistics Executive Yuan and Council for Economic Planning and Development Executive Yuan, Republic of China. 1994. *Report on the Manpower Utilization Survey Taiwan Area, Republic of China, 1993*. Taipei.

Caillois, Roger. 1959. *Man and the Sacred*. Translated by Meyer Barash. Westport, Conn.: Greenwood Press.

Carroll, John Bissell. 1963. 'A model of school learning'. *Teachers College Record*. 64: 723–33.

Carroll, John Bissell, and Donald Spearritt. 1967. 'A study of a "model of school learning"'. Cambridge, Mass.: Center for Research and Development on Educational Differences, Harvard University.

Case, S. M., and S. M. Downing. 1989. *Performance of Various Multiple Choice Item Types on Medical Specialty Examinations: Types A, B, C, K, and X.* Philadelphia.

Chan, Wing-tsit. 1953. *Religious Trends in Modern China.* New York: Columbia University Press.

Chang, Hui-Wen. 1932. *The Development of the Civil Service Examination System in China Since 1911.* PhD dissertation, Stanford University.

Cho, Hae-Joang. 1922. 'Children in the examination war in South Korea – a cultural analysis'. Paper presented at the World Conference, 'Children At Risk', Bergen, Norway. The Norwegian Center for Child Research.

Chong, Mian-yoon, Eng-koon Yeh and Jung-kwang Wen. 1992. 'Suicidal behavior in Taiwan'. Chapter 5, pp. 69–82 in *Suicidal Behavior in the Asia-Pacific Region*, edited by Peng, Kok Lee, and Wen-Shing Tseng. Singapore: Singapore University Press.

Cogley, John. 1968. *Religion in a Secular Age: The Search for Final Meaning.* New York: Praeger.

Cohen, Myron L. 1992. *Columbia Project on Asia in the Core Curriculum: Case Studies in the Social Sciences.* Armonk, NY: East Gate.

Cole, M., and J. S. Bruner. 1971. 'Cultural differences and inferences about psychological processes'. Pp. 23–46 in *Culture and Cognition: Readings in Cross-Cultural Psychology.* edited by Berry, J. W., and P. R. Dasen. London: Methuen & Company.

Coleman, James S. 1990. *Foundations of Social Theory.* Cambridge, Mass.: Harvard University Press.

Coleman, James Samuel, *et al.* 1966. *Equality of Educational Opportunity.* Washington: US Department of Health, Education, and Welfare, Office of Education.

Collins, Randall. 1971. 'Functional and conflict theories of educational stratification'. *American Sociological Review* 36: 1002–19.

——. 1979. *The Credential Society: A Historical Sociology of Education and Stratification.* New York: Academic Press.

Condon, John C., and Saito, Mitsuko. 1974. *Intercultural Encounters with Japan: Communication – Contact and Conflict.* Tokyo: The Simul Press.

Confucius (English translation). See Legge, 1992.

Cooper, H. M. 1989. 'Synthesis of research on homework'. *Educational Leadership* 47(3): 85–91.

Crocker, Linda, and James Algina. 1986. *Introduction to Classical & Modern Test Theory.* Orlando, Florida: Holt, Rinehart and Winston.

Cronbach, Lee J. 1960. *Essentials of Psychological Testing.* New York: Harper.

Crump, Thomas. 1991. *The Death of an Emperor*. Oxford University Press.

Cummings, William K. 1980. *Education and Equality in Japan*. Princeton, NJ: Princeton University Press.

Cummings, William K., Ikuo Amano, and Kazuyuki Kitamura. 1979. *Changes in the Japanese University: A Comparative Perspective*. New York. Praeger.

Davis, Philip J., and Reuben Hersh. 1986. *Descartes' Dream: The World According to Mathematics*. Boston: Houghton Mifflin.

Delfs, Robert. 1992. 'All work and no play: cram schools keep alive education nightmare'. *The Far Eastern Economic Review* (12 March): 21–3.

De Maio, Domenico, Franca Carandente, and Claudio Riva. 1982. 'Evaluation of circadian, circaseptan and circannual periodicity of attempted suicides'. *Chronobiologia* 9: 185.

Deuchler, Martina. 1992. *The Confucian Transformation of Korea: A Study of Society and Ideology*. Cambridge, Mass.: Harvard University Press.

De Vos, George A. 1973. *Socialization for Achievement*. Berkeley: University of California Press.

DiMaggio, Paul J., and Walter W. Powell. April 1983. 'The iron cage revisited: institutional isomorphism and collective rationality in organizational fields'. *American Sociological Review* 48: 147–60.

Dong, Wonmo. 1973. 'Assimilation and social mobilization in Korea'. Pp. 146–82 in *Korea Under Japanese Colonial Rule: Studies of the Policy and Techniques of Japanese Colonialism*, edited by Nahm, Andres C. Kalamazoo, Mich.: The Center for Korea Studies, Western Michigan University.

Dore, R. P. 1965. *Education in Tokugawa Japan*. Berkeley: University of California Press.

——. 1975. *The Diploma Disease: Education, Qualification and Development*. Berkeley: University of California Press.

——. 1990. Foreword to *Education and Examination in Modern Japan*, by Ikuo Amano. Tokyo: University of Tokyo Press.

Dorfman, Cynthia, ed. 1987. *Japanese Education Today: A Report from the U.S. Study of Education in Japan*. Washington, DC: US Government Printing Office.

Durkheim, Emile. 1938. *L'Evolution pédagogique en France*. Paris: Presses Universitaires de France. Quoted in *The Evolution of Educational Thought*, translated by Peter Collins. London: Routledge & Kegan Paul. 1979.

——. 1958. *Suicide: A Study in Sociology*. Translated by John A. Spaulding and George Simpson. Glencoe, Illinois: Free Press.

——. 1965. *The Elementary Forms of the Religious Life*. Translated by Joseph W. Swain. New York: Free Press.

Easthope, Gary. 1974. *A History of Social Research Methods*. London: Longman.

Eckert, Carter J., Ki-baik Lee, Young Ick Lew, Michael Robinson, and Edward W. Wagner. 1990. *Korea: Old and New, A History*. Cambridge, Mass.: Harvard University Press.

Eckstein, Max A., and Harold J. Noah. 1992. *Examinations: Comparative and Inter-national Studies*. Oxford: Pergamon Press.

——. 1993. *Secondary School Examinations: International Perspectives on Policies and Practice*. Yale University Press.

Elliott, David L., and Arthur Woodward. 1990. *Textbooks and Schooling in the United States*. Chicago: University of Chicago Press.

Elliott, Emerson J. 1993. *A Preliminary Report of National Estimates from the National Assessment of Educational Progress 1992 Mathematics Assessment*. Washington, DC: National Center for Education Statistics, US Dept. of Education.

Fägerlind, Ingemar, and Lawrence J. Saha. 1989. *Education and National Development: A Comparative Perspective*. Oxford: Pergamon.

Fairbank, J. K., ed. 1968. *The Chinese World Order*. Cambridge, Mass.: Harvard University Press.

Farber, Maurice. 1968. *Theory of Suicide*. New York: Funk and Wagnalls.

Fei, John C., Gustav Ranis, and Shirley W. Kuo. 1979. *Growth with Equity: The Taiwan Case, A World Bank Research Publication*. New York: Oxford University Press.

Feiler, B. S. 1991. *Learning to Bow: An American Teacher in a Japanese School*. New York: Ticknor and Fields.

Foreign Press Center. 1993. *Facts and Figures of Japan*. Tokyo: Foreign Press Center.

Frost, Peter. 1992. 'Tinkering with hell: efforts to reform current Japanese university entrance examinations'. Pp. 25–32 in *Examinations: Comparative and International Studies*, edited by Eckstein, Max A., and Harold J. Noah. Oxford: Pergamon Press.

Fyans, Leslie, Jr., ed. 1980. *Achievement Motivation: Recent Trends in Theory and Research*. New York: Plenum Press.

Gambetta, Diego. 1987. *Were They Pushed or Did They Jump?* Cambridge: Cambridge University Press.

Gardner, Howard. 1983. *Frames of Mind: The Theory of Multiple Intelligences*. New York: Basic Books.

Gardner, John W. 1984. *Excellence: Can We Be Equal and Excellent Too?* New York: W. W. Norton & Company.

Geertz, Clifford. 1973. *The Interpretation of Cultures: Selected Essays*. New York: Basic Books.

Gibney, Frank. 1992. *The Pacific Century: America and Asia in a Changing World*. New York: Charles Scribner's Sons.

Godlove, Terry, Jr. 1989. *Religion, Interpretation, and Diversity of Belief.* Cambridge: Cambridge University Press.

Greeley, Andrew M. 1982. *Religion: A Secular Theory.* New York: Free Press.

Greenfield, Karl T. 1994. *Speed Tribes: Days and Nights with Japan's Next Generation.* New York: HarperCollins.

Haladyna, T. M. 1986. 'Context-dependent item sets'. Pp. 21–5 in *Educational Measurement: Issues and Practices*, edited by National Council on Measurement in Education. Washington, DC: National Council on Measurement in Education.

Halbwachs, Maurice. 1978. *The Causes of Suicide.* Translated by Harold Goldblatt. London: Routledge & Kegan Paul.

Hall, Ivan P. 1973. *Mori Arinori.* Cambridge, Mass.: Harvard University Press.

Hall, John W., and Richard K. Beardsley. 1965. *Twelve Doors to Japan.* New York: McGraw-Hill.

Halliday, Jon, and Gavan McCormack. 1973. *Japanese Imperialism Today.* New York: Monthly Review Press.

Halsey, A. H. 1992. 'An international comparison of access to higher education' in *Lessons of Cross-National Comparison in Education*, edited by Phillips, David. Wallingford, Oxfordshire: Triangle Books.

Hansen, David, Aziz Saleh, William Flinn, and Lawrence Hotchkiss. 1989. 'Determinants of access to higher education in Indonesia'. *Comparative Education Review* 33(3) August: 317–33.

Hanson, F. Allan. 1993. *Testing, Testing: Social Consequences of the Examined Life.* Berkeley: University of California Press.

Hart, Diane. 1994. *Authentic Assessment: A Handbook for Educators.* Menlo Park, Calif.: Addison-Wesley.

Headley, Lee A. 1983. *Suicide in Asia and the Near East.* Berkeley: University of California Press.

Hedges, Harry V., Richard D. Laine, and Rob Greenwald. 1994. 'Does money matter: a meta-analysis of studies of the effects of differential school inputs on student outcomes' *Educational Researcher* 23(3) April: 5–14.

Hendin, Herbert. 1985. 'Suicide among the young: psychodynamics and demography' Pp. 19–38 in *Youth Suicide*, edited by Peck, Michael, Norman Farberow, and Robert Litman. New York: Springer.

———. 1995. *Suicide in America.* New York: W. W. Norton & Company.

Herrnstein, Richard J., and Charles Murray. 1994. *The Bell Curve: Intelligence and Class Structure in American Life.* New York: Free Press.

Heyneman, Stephen P., and Ingemar Fägerlind, eds. 1988. *University Examinations and Standardized Testing: Principles, Experience, and Policy Options.* Washington, DC: World Bank.

Hill, Clifford and Kate Parry, eds. 1994. *From Testing to Assessment: English As An International Language*. London: Longman.

Ho, Ping-ti. 1964. *The Ladder of Success in Imperial China*. New York: Columbia University Press.

Hori, Victor Sogen. 1996. 'Teaching and learning in the Rinzai Zen monastery'. In *Teaching and Learning in Japan*, edited by Rohlen, Thomas P. and Gerald K. LeTendre. Cambridge, England: Cambridge University Press.

Horio, Teruhisa. 1988. *Educational Thought and Ideology in Modern Japan: State Authority and Intellectual Freedom*. Edited and translated by Steven Platzer. Tokyo: University of Tokyo Press.

Huang, Shiqi. 1992. 'The restoration of national unified college entrance examinations in the People's Republic of China and current policy issues'. Pp. 33–57 in *Examinations: Comparative and International Studies*, edited by Eckstein, Max A., and Harold Noah. Oxford: Pergamon Press.

Iga, Mamoru. 1986. *The Thorn in the Chrysanthemum: Suicide and Economic Success in Modern Japan*. Berkeley: University of California Press.

Inkeles, Alex, and David Smith. 1974. *Becoming Modern*. Cambridge, Mass.: Harvard University Press.

Ishida, Hiroshi. 1993. *Social Mobility in Contemporary Japan*. Stanford, Calif.: Stanford University Press.

James, Estelle, and Gail Benjamin. 1988. *Public Policy and Private Education in Japan*. London: Macmillan Press.

Jansen, Marius B., and Gilbert Rozman. 1986. *Japan in Transition from Tokugawa to Meiji*. Princeton, NJ: Princeton University Press.

Japan External Trade Organization. 1992. *U.S. and Japan in Figures II*. Tokyo: Japan External Trade Organization.

Japan Management and Coordination Agency. 1988. *Annual Report on the Family Income and Expenditure Survey*. Tokyo: Japan Management and Coordination Agency.

Japanese Ministry of Education. 1963. *Japan's Growth and Education: Educational Development in Relation to Socio-economic Growth*. Tokyo: Ministry of Education.

——. 1964, 1975. *Educational Standards in Japan*. Tokyo: Ministry of Education.

——. 1980. *Japan's Modern Educational System: A History of the First Hundred Years*. Tokyo: Printing Bureau of Finance Ministry.

——. 1992. *National Center for University Entrance Examination 1991*. Tokyo: National Center for University Entrance Examinations.

——. 1994. *Education in Japan: A Graphic Presentation*. Tokyo: Gyosei.

Jayasuriya, J. E. 1983. *Education in Korea: A Third World Success Story*. Seoul: Korean National Commission for UNESCO.

Jencks, Christopher S., Marshall Smith, Henry Acland, Mary Jo Bane, David Cohen, Herbert Gintis, Barbara Heyns, and Stephan Michelson. 1972. *Inequality: A Reassessment of the Effect of Family and Schooling in America.* New York: Basic Books.

Jensen, Arthur R. 1980. *Bias in Mental Testing.* New York: Free Press.

Joe, Wanne J. 1981. *Traditional Korea: A Cultural History.* Seoul: Chung'ang University Press.

Kazuya, Yoshimatsu. 1992. 'Suicidal behavior in Japan'. Pp. 15–40 in *Suicidal Behavior in the Asia-Pacific Region,* edited by Peng, Kok Lee and Wen-Shing Tseng. Singapore: Singapore University Press.

Keith, T. 1982. 'Time spent on homework and high school grades: a large-sample path analysis'. *Journal of Educational Psychology* 74(2): 248–53.

Kendall, Laurel. 1992. 'Changing gender relations: the Korean case'. Pp. 168–83 in *Columbia Project on Asia in the Core Curriculum: Case Studies in the Social Sciences,* edited by Cohen, Myron L. Armonk, NY: East Gate.

Kim, Kwang-woong, and Yong-duck Jung, eds. 1993. *Korean Public Administration and Policy in Transition.* Vol. 1, *Governmental Institutions and Policy Process.* Seoul: The Korean Association for Public Administration and Jangwon Publishing.

Kim, Young-hwa. 1990. 'Consequences of higher educational expansion in Korea: trends in family background and regional effects on higher educational attainment, 1967–1984'. Seoul: Korea Educational Development Institute.

———. 'Conflicts and choices in educational policy formation: implications for the role of educational policy in the industrialization of Korea'. Paper presented at the Conference on 'Education and Development in the Asian Pacific Rim' held at the Chinese University of Hong Kong, 17–19 June, 1993.

Kitamura, Kazuyuki. 1986. 'The decline and reform of education in Japan: a comparative perspective'. Pp. 153–70 in *Educational Policies in Crisis: Japanese and American Perspectives,* edited by Cummings, William K. *et al.* New York: Praeger.

Kokusai Bunka Shinkokai. 1972. *Higher Education and the Student Problem in Japan.* Tokyo: Kokusai Bunka Shinkokai.

Korea Educational Development Institute. 1993. *Educational Indicators in Korea.* Seoul: Korea Educational Development Institute.

Korea Unified Association of *Hakwon.* 1992. *A Study of the History of the Korea's Hakwon.* Seoul: Korea Unified Association of *Hakwon.*

Korean Ministry of Education. 1994. *Education in Korea 1993–1994.* Seoul: Korean Ministry of Education.

———. 1992a. *Korea Handbook of Education Statistics.* Seoul: Korean Ministry of Education.

———. 1992b. *Entrance Examination Policy for Colleges and Universities in Korea.* Seoul: National Board of Education Evaluation.

Korean Overseas Information Service. 1993. *A Handbook of Korea*. Seoul: Korean Overseas Information Service.

Kracke, Edward A. 1953. *Civil Service in Early Sung China, 960–1067, with Particular Emphasis on the Development of Controlled Sponsorship to Foster Administrative Responsibility*. Cambridge, Mass.: Harvard University Press.

Kubota, Akira. 1969. *Higher Civil Servants in Postwar Japan: Their Social Origins, Educational Backgrounds, and Career Patterns*. Princeton, NJ: Princeton University Press.

Kwak, Byong-sun. 1991. '"Examination hell" in Korea revisited'. *Koreana* (Seoul) 5(2): 45–55.

Leach, Edmund, ed. 1967. *The Structural Study of Myth and Totemism*. London: Tavistock Publications.

Lee, Chung H., and Ippei Yamazawa. 1990. *The Economic Development of Japan and Korea: A Parallel with Lessons*. New York: Praeger.

Lee, Hwa-Wei. 1964. *Education Development in Taiwan Under the Nationalist Government, 1945–1962*. PhD Dissertation, University of Pittsburgh.

Lee, Sungho. 1989. 'The emergence of the modern university in Korea'. *Higher Education* 18: 87–116.

Lee, Thomas H. C. 1985. *Government Education and Examinations in Sung China*. New York: St Martin's Press.

Leestma, Robert, and Herbert Walberg. 1992. *Japanese Educational Productivity*. Ann Arbor, Mich.: Center for Japanese Studies, The University of Michigan.

Legge, James, trans. 1991. *The Chinese/English Four Books*. Changsha: Hunan Chubanshe.

Lenski, Gerhard E. 1966. *Power and Privilege*. New York: McGraw-Hill.

LeTendre, Gerald. 1996. 'Shidô: the concept of guidance'. Pp. 275–94 in *Teaching and Learning in Japan*, edited by Rohlen, Thomas P. and Gerald LeTendre. Cambridge: Cambridge University Press.

Levin, Henry M. 1980. 'Educational production theory and teacher inputs'. Chapter 5, pp. 203–31 in *The Analysis of Educational Productivity*, vol. II, edited by Bidwell, Charles E. and Douglas M. Windham. Cambridge, Mass.: Ballinger Publishing.

Lukacs, Gyoergy. 1971. *History and Class Consciousness*. Cambridge, Mass: MIT Press.

Lynn, Richard. 1988. *Educational Achievement in Japan*. Basingstoke, Hampshire: Macmillan Press.

MacLeod. Roy M. 1982. *Days of Judgment: Science, Examinations and the Organization of Knowledge in Late Victorian England*. Driffield, N. Humberside: Nafferton Books.

Magnussen, Olav. 1975. 'The cost and finance of post-secondary education'. Pp. 171–227 in *Toward Mass Higher Education*, edited by Organization for

Economic Cooperation and Development (OECD). Paris: Organization for Economic Cooperation and Development (OECD).

Mannheim, Karl. 1936. *Ideology and Utopia: An Introduction to the Sociology of Knowledge*. New York: Harcourt, Brace and Company.

Martz, Geoff, John Katzman, and Adam Robinson. 1992. *Cracking the System: The GMAT*. New York: Villard Books.

Mashiko, Ellen. 1989. *Japan: A Study of the Educational System of Japan and a Guide to the Academic Placement of Students in Educational Institutions of the United States*. Washington, DC: American Association of Collegiate Registrars and Admission Officers.

McFarland, H. Neill. 1987. *Daruma: The Founder of Zen in Japanese Art and Popular Culture*. Tokyo: Kodansha International.

McGinn, Noel F. 1980. *Education and Development in Korea*. Cambridge, Mass.: Council on East Asian Studies, Harvard University: distributed by Harvard University Press.

Medrich, Elliott A., and Jeanne E. Griffith. 1992. *International Mathematics and Science Assessments: What Have We Learned?* Washington, DC: US Department of Education, Office of Educational Research and Improvement, National Center for Education Statistics.

Menzel, Johanna M. 1963. *The Chinese Civil Service: Career Open to Talent?* Boston: Heath.

Miyazaki, Ichisada. 1976. *China's Examination Hell: The Civil Service Examinations of Imperial China*. New York: Weatherhill.

Monroe, Paul, ed. 1931. *A Cyclopaedia of Education*. New York: The Macmillan Company.

Mouer, Ross, and Yoshio Sugimoto. 1990. *Images of Japanese Society: A Study in the Social Construction of Reality*. London: Kegan Paul International.

Myers, H. Ramon, and Mark R. Peattie. 1984. *The Japanese Colonial Empire, 1895–1945*. Princeton, NJ: Princeton University Press.

Nahm, Andrew C. 1973. *Korea Under Japanese Colonial Rule: Studies of the Policy and Techniques of Japanese Colonialism*. Kalamazoo, Mich.: The Center for Korea Studies, Western Michigan University.

Nakauchi, Toshio, Hajime Tajima, Eiichi Ameda, and Toshihiko Saito. 1986. *The Modernization of Japanese Education*. Tokyo: International Society for Educational Information.

National Assessment of Educational Progress. 1990. *America's Challenge: Accelerating Academic Achievement, A Summary of Findings from 20 Years of NAEP*. Washington, DC: US Department of Education.

National Education Goals Panel. 1992. *The National Education Goals Report: Building A Nation of Learners, 1992*. Washington, DC: The US Government Printing Office.

Nihon Shiritsu Daigaku Renmei (Japan Association of Private Colleges and Universities). 1987. *Japan's Private Colleges and Universities: Yesterday, Today and Tomorrow*. Translated by Simul International Inc. Tokyo: Nihon Shiritsu Daigaku Renmei.

Ogura, Yoriko. 1987. 'Examination: Japanese education's most serious problem'. *The College Board Review*. 144: 8–11 and 26–30.

Orrù, Marco, Nicole W. Biggart, and Gary G. Hamilton. 1991. 'Organizational isomorphism in East Asia'. Pp. 361–89 in *The New Institutionalism in Organizational Analysis*, edited by Powell, Walter W. and Paul J. DiMaggio. Chicago: The University of Chicago Press.

Parsons, Talcott. 1970. 'Equality and inequality in modern society, or social stratification revisited'. Pp. 13–72 in *Social Stratification*, edited by Laumann, E. O. Indianapolis: Bobbs-Merrill.

Paschal, R. A., T. Weinstein, and H. Walberg. 1984. 'The effect of homework on learning: a quantitative synthesis'. *Journal of Educational Research* 78(2):97–104.

Passin, Herbert. 1965. *Society and Education in Japan*. New York: Bureau of Publications, Teachers College, Columbia University.

Passow, H., H. Noah, M. Eckstein, and J. Mallea. 1976. *The National Case Study: An Empirical Comparative Study of Twenty One Educational Systems*. Stockholm: Almqvist & Wiksell International.

Peak, Lois. 1988. *Learning to Go to School in Japan*. Berkeley: University of California Press.

Peck, Michael L., Norman L. Farberow, and Robert E. Litman, eds. 1985. *Youth Suicide*. New York: Springer.

Peng, Kok Lee, and Wen-Shing Tseng. 1992. *Suicidal Behavior in the Asia-Pacific Region*. Singapore: Singapore University Press.

Pettersen, Larry. 1993. 'Japan's "cram schools"'. *Educational Leadership* 50(5) February: 56–8.

Phillips, David, ed. 1992. *Lessons of Cross-National Comparison in Education*. Wallingford, Oxfordshire: Triangle Books.

Phillips, Denis C. 1987. 'Validity in qualitative research: why the worry about warrant will not wane'. *Education and Urban Society* 20(1) November: 9–24.

Pinguet, Maurice. 1993. *Voluntary Death in Japan*. Translated by Rosemary Morris. Cambridge: Polity Press.

Powell, Walter W., and Paul J. DiMaggio. 1991. *The New Institutionalism in Organizational Analysis*. Chicago: The University of Chicago Press.

Przeworski, Adam, and Henry Teune. 1970. *The Logic of Comparative Social Inquiry*. New York: Wiley-Interscience.

Ragin, Charles C. 1987. *The Comparative Method: Moving Beyond Qualitative and Quantitative Strategies*. Berkeley: University of California Press.

Raivola, Reijo. 1986. 'What is comparison? Methodological and philosophical considerations'. Pp. 261–73 in *New Approaches to Comparative Education*. edited by Altbach, Philip G., and Gail P. Kelly. Chicago: The University of Chicago Press.

Ramirez, Francisco O., and John Boli. 1987. 'The political construction of mass schooling: European origins and worldwide institutionalization'. *Sociology of Education* 60 (January): 2–17.

Ramirez, Francisco O., and John Meyer. 1981. 'Comparative education: synthesis and agenda'. Pp. 215–38 in *The State of Sociology: Problems and Prospects*, edited by Short, James. Newbury Park, Calif.: Sage.

Rapp, Friedrich. 1981. *Analytical Philosophy of Technology*. Translated by Stanley R. Carpenter and Theodore Langenbruch. Dordrecht, Holland: D. Reidel.

Ravitch, Diane. 1995. 'Revise, but don't abandon, the history standards'. *The Chronicle of Higher Education* 17 (February): A52.

Reader, Ian. 1991. *Religion in Contemporary Japan*. Honolulu, Hawaii: University of Hawaii Press.

Reischauer, Edwin O. 1983. 'The Allied Occupation: catalyst not creator'. Pp. 335–42 in *Japan Examined: Perspectives on Modern Japanese History*, edited by Wray, Harry and Hilary Conroy. Honolulu, Hawaii: University of Hawaii Press.

Robinson, James. 1994. 'Social status and academic success in South Korea'. *Comparative Education Review* 38(4): 506–29.

Robinson, Michael. 1991. 'Perceptions of Confucianism in twentieth-century Korea'. Pp. 204–25 in *The East Asian Region: Confucian Heritage and Its Modern Adaptation*, edited by Rozman, Gilbert. Princeton, NJ: Princeton University Press.

Roden, Donald. 1980. *Schooldays in Imperial Japan: A Study in the Culture of a Student Elite*. Berkeley: University of California Press.

Rohlen, Thomas P. 1977. 'Is Japanese education becoming less egalitarian? Notes on high school stratification and reform'. *The Journal of Japanese Studies* 3(1) Winter: 37–70.

———. 1980. 'The *juku* phenomenon: an exploratory essay'. *The Journal of Japanese Studies* 6(2) Summer: 207–42.

———. 1983. *Japan's High Schools*. Berkeley: University of California Press.

———. 1989. 'Order in Japanese society: attachment, authority, and routine'. *The Journal of Japanese Studies* 15(1) Winter: 5–40.

———. 1992. 'Learning: the mobilization of knowledge in the Japanese political economy'. Pp. 321–63 in *The Political Economy of Japan*, Vol. III, edited by Kumon, Shumpei, and Henry Rosovsky. Stanford, Calif.: Stanford University Press.

Rohlen, Thomas P., and Gerald LeTendre, eds. 1996. *Teaching and Learning in Japan*. Cambridge: Cambridge University Press.

Rokkan, Stein. 1966. 'Comparative cross-national research: the context of current efforts'. Pp. 3–26 in *Comparing Nations*, edited by Merritt, Richard, and Stein Rokkan. New Haven: Yale University Press.

Rosenbaum, James E., and Takehiko Kariya. 1989. 'From high school to work: market and institutional mechanisms in Japan'. *American Journal of Sociology* 94(6) May: 1334–65.

Rotberg, I. 1992. 'I never promised you first place'. *Phi Delta Kappan* 72: 296–303.

Rozman, Gilbert, ed. 1991. *The East Asian Region: Confucian Heritage and Its Modern Adaptation*. Princeton, NJ: Princeton University Press.

Rubinger, Richard. 1982. *Private Academies of Tokugawa Japan*. Princeton, NJ: Princeton University Press.

Russell, Bertrand. 1912. *The Problems of Philosophy*. Oxford: Oxford University Press.

——. 1922. *The Problem of China*. London: George Allen & Unwin.

Sapirstein, Milton. 1955. *Paradoxes of Everyday Life: A Psychoanalyst's Interpretations*. Greenwich, Conn.: Fawcett Publication.

Schiffrin, R. M., and Schneider, W. 1977. 'Controlled and automatic human information process. II: Perceptual learning, automatic attending, and a general theory'. *Psychological Review* 84: 127–90.

Schirokauer, Conrad. 1989. *A Brief History of Chinese and Japanese Civilizations*. New York: Harcourt Brace Jovanovich.

Schoolland, Ken. 1990. *Shogun's Ghost*. New York: Bergin & Garvey.

Schoppa, Leonard. 1991. *Education Reform in Japan: A Case of Immobilist Politics*. London: Routledge.

Sewell, Haller, and Hauser. 1980. In Kerckhoff, ed. *Research in Sociological of Education and Socialization* 1.

Sewell, Haller, and Ohlendorf. 1970. *American Sociological Review* 35.

Sewell, Haller, and Straus. 1957. *American Sociological Review* 22.

Shahabi, S., and Yang, L. 1990. 'A comparison between two variations of multiple choice items and their effects on difficulty and discrimination values'. Paper presented at the Annual Meeting of the NCME, Boston.

Shavit, Yossi, and Hans-Peter Blossfeld. 1993. *Persistent Inequality: Changing Educational Attainment in Thirteen Countries*. Oxford: Westview Press.

Shimahara, Nobuo K. 1979. *Adaptation and Education in Japan*. New York: Praeger.

Shimahara, Nobuo K., and Akira Sakai. 1995. *Learning to Teach in Two Cultures: Japan and the United States*. New York: Garland Publishing.

Shively, Donald H. 1971. *Tradition and Modernization in Japanese Culture*. Princeton, NJ: Princeton University Press.

Smith, Douglas C. 1991. *The Confucian Continuum: Educational Modernization in Taiwan*. New York: Praeger.

Sorensen, Clark W. 1994. 'Success and education in South Korea'. *Comparative Education Review* 38(1) February: 10–35.

Sôrifu (Office of Japanese Prime Minister). 1976. *Annual Report on the Family Income and Expenditure Survey*, quoted in *Public Policy and Private Education in Japan*, edited by James, Estelle, and Gail Benjamin. 1988. London: Macmillan Press.

Spaulding, Robert, Jr. 1967. *Imperial Japan's Higher Civil Service Examinations*. Princeton, NJ: Princeton University Press.

Stedman, Lawrence C. 1994. 'Incomplete explanations: the case of U.S. performance in the International Assessments of Education'. *Educational Researcher* 23(7) October: 24–32.

Sternberg, Robert J., and Joseph A. Horvath. 1995. 'A prototype view of expert teaching'. *Educational Researcher* 24(6): 9–17.

Stevenson, David L., and David P. Baker. 1992. 'Shadow education and allocation in formal schooling: transition to university in Japan'. *American Journal of Sociology* 97(6): 1639–57.

Stevenson, Harold W., S. Y. Lee, and James W. Stigler. 1986. 'Mathematics achievement of Chinese, Japanese, and American children'. *Science* 231: 693–9.

Stevenson, Harold W., and James W. Stigler. 1992. *The Learning Gap: Why Our Schools Are Failing and What We Can Learn From Japanese and Chinese Education*. New York: Summit Books.

Stigler, James W., S. Lee, G. Lucker, and Harold W. Stevenson. 1982. 'Curriculum and achievement in mathematics: a study of elementary school children in Japan, Taiwan and the United States'. *Journal of Educational Psychology* 74: 315–22.

Student Learning Orientations Group. 1987. *Why Do Students Learn? A Six-Country Study of Student Motivation*. Brighton, England: Institute of Development Studies at the University of Sussex.

Swanson, Guy. 1971. 'Frameworks for comparative research: structural anthropology and the theory of action'. Pp. 141–202 in *Comparative Methods in Sociology: Essays on Trends and Applications*, edited by Vallier, Ivan. Berkeley: University of California.

Tadashi, Hidano. 1988. 'Admission to higher education in Japan'. Pp. 9–25 in *University Examinations and Standardized Testing*, edited by Heyneman, Stephen P., and Ingemar Fägerlind. Washington, DC: World Bank.

Tanaka, Stefan. 1993. *Japan's Orient: Rendering Pasts into History*. Berkeley: University of California Press.

Têng, Ssu-yü. 1968. 'Chinese influence on the Western examination system'. Pp. 195–242 in *Studies of Governmental Institutions in Chinese History*, edited by Bishop, John L. Cambridge, Mass.: Harvard University Press.

Theisen, Gary L., Paul P. Achola, and Francis M. Boakari. 1986. 'The under-achievement of cross-national studies of achievement'. Pp. 27–49 in *New*

Approaches to Comparative Education, edited by Altbach, Philip G., and Gail P. Kelly. Chicago: The University of Chicago Press.

Thomas, R. Murray, and T. Neville Postlethwaite, eds. 1983. *Schooling in East Asia: Force of Change: Formal and Nonformal Education in Japan, The Republic of China, South Korea, North Korea, Hong Kong, and Macau*. New York: Pergamon Press.

Toynbee, Arnold J. 1947. *A Study of History*. Oxford: Oxford University Press.

Trainor, Joseph C. 1983. *Educational Reform in Occupied Japan: Trainor's Memoir*. Tokyo: Meisei University Press.

Treiman, Donald. 1970. 'Industrialization and social stratification'. Pp. 207–34 in *Social Stratification*, edited by Laumann, E. Indianapolis: Bobbs-Merrill.

Treiman, Donald, and Kazuo Yamaguchi. 1993. 'Trends in educational attainment in Japan'. Pp. 229–49 in *Persistent Inequality: Changing Educational Attainment in Thirteen Countries*, edited by Shavit, Yossi, and Hans-Peter Blossfeld. Boulder, Col.: Westview.

Tsai, Shu-Ling, and Hei-Yuan Chiu. 1993. 'Changes in educational stratification in Taiwan', Pp. 193–227 in *Persistent Inequality: Changing Educational Attainment in Thirteen Countries*, edited by Shavit, Yossi, and Hans-Peter Blossfeld. Boulder, Col.: Westview.

Tsukada, Mamoru. 1991. *Yobiko Life: A Study of the Legitimation Process Stratification in Japan*. Berkeley: University of California.

Tsurumi, E. Patricia. 1977. *Japanese Colonial Education in Taiwan, 1895–1945*. Cambridge: Mass.: Harvard University Press.

———. 1984. 'Colonial education in Korea and Taiwan'. Chapter 7, pp. 275–311 in *The Japanese Colonial Empire, 1895–1945*, edited by Myers, Ramon H., and Mark R. Peattie. Princeton, NJ: Princeton University Press.

Tuner, R. 1960. 'Sponsored and contest mobility in the school system'. *American Sociological Review* 25: 855–67.

Tversky, Amos, and Daniel Kahneman. 1981. 'The framing of decisions and the rationality of choice'. *Science* 211: 453–8.

Tymms, P. B, and C. T. Fitz-Gibbon. 1992. 'The relationship of homework to A-level results'. *Educational Research* 34(1) Spring: 3–10.

Uguroglu, M., and H. Walberg. 1979. 'Motivation and achievement: a quantitative synthesis'. *American Educational Research Journal* 16(4) Fall: 375–89.

United Nations Educational, Scientific and Cultural Organization. *Statistical Yearbook*. Paris: United Nations Educational, Scientific and Cultural Organization.

US Army Military Government in Korea. 1992. 'History of Bureau of Education from 11 September 1945 to 28 February 1946', Pp. 37–145 in *Historical Documents of Korean Education Under the U.S. Army Military Government in Korea*, edited by Zheng, Taixiu. Seoul: Hongzhiyuan.

US Department of Education, National Center for Education Statistics, International Assessment of Educational Progress. 1992. *International Mathematics and Science Assessments: What Have We Learned?* Washington, DC: US Department of Education.

——. 1993. *Digest of Education Statistics.* Washington, DC: US Department of Education.

Valverde, L. A. 1984. 'Underachievement and underrepresentation of Hispanics in mathematics and mathematics-related careers'. *Journal for Research in Mathematics Education* 15: 123–33.

Vogel, Ezra F. 1971. *Japan's New Middle Class: The Salary Man and His Family in a Tokyo Suburb.* Berkeley: University of California Press.

——. 1979. *Japan As Number One: Lessons for America.* Cambridge, Mass.: Harvard University Press.

Wade, Robert. 1990. *Governing the Market: Economic Theory and the Role of Government in East Asian Industrialization.* Princeton, NJ: Princeton University Press.

Wagatsuma, Hiroshi. 1973. 'Status and role behavior in changing Japan: psychocultural continuities'. Chapter 15, pp. 391–419 in *Socialization for Achievement,* edited by De Vos, George A. Berkeley: University of California Press.

Weber, Max. 1951. *The Religion of China.* Translated and edited by Hans H. Gerth. New York: Free Press.

——. 1958. *The Protestant Ethic and the Spirit of Capitalism.* New York: Charles Scribner's Sons.

Werner, E. T. 1961. *A Dictionary of Chinese Mythology.* New York: The Julian Press.

Westbury, Ian. 1990. 'Instructional materials in the twentieth century'. Pp. 1–22 in *Textbooks and Schooling in the United States,* edited by Elliott, David L., and Arthur Woodward. Chicago: University of Chicago Press.

White, Merry. 1987. *The Japanese Educational Challenge: A Commitment to Children.* New York: Free Press.

Wick, John W. 1973. *Educational Measurement: Where Are We Going and How Will We Know When We Get There?* Columbus, Ohio: Charkes E. Merrill.

Wickelgren, Wayne A. 1977. *Learning and Memory.* Englewood Cliffs, NJ: Prentice-Hall.

Williams, S. Wells. 1848. *Middle Kingdom.* New York: John Wiley.

van Wolferen, Karel. 1990. *The Enigma of Japanese Power.* New York: Vintage Books.

World Bank. 1991. *World Development Report 1991: The Challenge of Development.* Oxford: Oxford University Press.

World Health Organization. *World Health Statistics Annuals.* Geneva: WHO.

Woronoff, Jon. 1990. *Japan As Anything But Number One*. Armonk, NY: M. E. Sharpe.

Wray, Harry, and Hilary Conroy. 1983. *Japan Examined: Perspectives on Modern Japanese History*. Honolulu, Hawaii: University of Hawaii Press.

Wu, Wen-Hsing, Shun-fen Chen and Chen-tsou Wu. 1989. 'The development of higher education in Taiwan'. *Higher Education* 18: 117–36.

Yang, Ch'ing-K'un. 1961. *Religion in Chinese Society: A Study of Contemporary Social Functions of Religion and Some of Their Historical Factors*. Berkeley: University of California Press.

Yoshimatsu, Kazuya. 1992. 'Suicidal behavior in Japan'. Pp. 15–40 in *Suicidal Behavior in the Asia-Pacific Region*, edited by Peng, Kok Lee, and Wen-Shing Tseng. Singapore: Singapore University Press.

Young, Michael D. 1958. *The Rise of the Meritocracy*. London: Penguin.

Zeugner, John F. 1984. 'The puzzle of higher education in Japan'. *Change* January–February: 24–31.

Zheng, Taixiu, ed. 1992. *Historical Documents of Korean Education under the U.S. Army Military Government in Korea*. Seoul: Hongzhiyuan.

References in Chinese

Budgetary Accounting & Statistics Executive Yuan and Council for Economic Planning and Development Executive Yuan, Republic of China. 1994. *Report on the Manpower Utilization Survey Taiwan Area, Republic of China, 1993*. Taipei.

Chen, I-yen. 1972. 'Cong buyi renshi lün beisung buyi jieceng de shehui liudong' (A study of the social mobility for the common people in North Sung China). *Si Yü Yan* 9(44): 244–53.

Chen, Jingpan. 1957. *Kongzi de Jiaojü Sixiang* (Confucius' educational thoughts). Wuhan, Hubei: Hubei Renmin Chubanshe.

Chu, Lishi. 1989. *Hanjian Bian* (The change of Han-gang River). Taiwan: Zhongguo Shibaoshe.

Confucius. 1991. *Han-Ying Sishu* (The Chinese/English Four Books). Hunan: Hunan Publishing House.

Furuno, Naoya. 1994. *Taiwan Jindaihua Mishi* (The secret history of modernization in Taiwan). Translated by K'o Kek-tuun from Japanese into Chinese. Taipei: Diyi Chubanshe.

Gao, Mingshi. 1984. *Tangdai Dongya jiaoyüquan de Xingcheng* (The forming of the East Asian sphere of education during the Tang Dynasty). Taipei: Guoli Bianyiguan.

Guo, Qijia. 1994. *Zhongguo Gudai Kaoshi Zhidu* (The ancient exam system in China). Taipei: Shangwu Yinshuguan.

Huang, Yifan. 1994. *Daixüe Yiuni Wan Sinian* (Play for four years in the university). Zhonghe: Qingshao Wenhua.

Ji, Hongdong. 1992. *Gaolichao Kejüzhidu Shou Tang Sung Kejüzhidu Zhi Yingxiang* (The influence of the *keju* system of Chinese Tang–Sung dynasties upon Koryô *keju* system). Master's thesis. Taipei, Taiwan: National Taiwan Teacher's College.

Jiang, Shao-qing, and Zhao-jian Gong. 1994. 'Nanyangjie Zhetiao Shengxüe zhi Lu' (Nanyang Avenue: a pathway to universities). *Zhongguo Shibao* (The China Daily), 16 September 1994, p. 18.

Jin, Liangdan. 1982. *Zhong-Han Liangguo Shengdaxue Chongkaosheng Chongkao Wenti de Bijiao Fenxi* (A comparison of the repeaters for the university entrance exams in Taiwan and Korea). MA thesis, Taiwan Normal University.

Kuling. 1990. *Yikao Ding Zhongsheng* (Exams determine one's future). Taipei: Sitak Publishing & Book Corp.

——. 1994. *Kaoshi Guo Yisheng* (Spend all one's life in exams). Taipei: Sitak Publishing & Book Corp.

Lan, Bozhou. 1993. *Rijü Shidai Taiwan Xüesheng Yündong* (Taiwanese student movement during the Japanese occupation era). Taipei: Shibao Wenhua.

Leng, Shuo-yi. 1977. *Taibeishi Buxi Jiaoyu de Diaocha yu Fenxi* (A survey and analysis of supplementary education of Taipei City). Taipei: Wenxian Weiyuanui.

Li, He. 1994. *You Jihua de Daxue shenghuo* (Well-planned life in university). Yonghe: Daotian.

Longmen. 1994a. *Lishi Shiti Xiangjie* (History exams: questions and answers with annotated answers). Taipei: Longmen.

——. 1994b. *Shuxüe Shiti Xiangjie* (Math exams: questions and answers with annotated answers). Taipei: Longmen.

Qianlong. 1994. *Zhongguo Minjian Zhushen Zhuan* (Biography of Chinese folk deities). Taipei: Quanyuan Chubanshe.

Sheng, Yenliu. 1958. *Qingdai Kejü Kaoshi Shilu* (History of the civil service examinations in the Qing dynasty). Peking: Beijing Chubanshe.

Shi, Xiaojun. 1992. *Zhong-Ri Liangguo Xianghu Renshi de Bianqian* (The evolving history of mutual understanding between China and Japan). Taipei: Shangwu Yinshujü.

Sun, Guodong. 1980. 'Tangsung zhi ji shehui mendi zhi xiaorong' (The disappearance of social status of hierarchy in Tang–Sung China). Pp. 201–308 in Sun, Guodong, *Tangsung Shi Lüncong* (The essay series on Tang–Sung dynasties). Hong Kong: Lungmen.

Taiwan Bijiao Jiaoyü Xüehui (Comparative Education Association of Taiwan), ed. 1983. *Shijie Geguo Daixüe Ruxüe Zhidu zhi Gaige Dongxiang* (The trend of reform of the entrance exams systems). Taipei: Wunan Tushu.

Taiwan Ministry of Education. 1979. *Daixüe Ruxüe Kaoshi Jianjie* (A brief introduction to the university entrance exams). Taipei: Taiwan Ministry of Education.

——. 1987. *Taiwan Jiaoyü Fazhan Shiliao Huibian: Daizhuan Jiaoyüpian* (The historical documents of educational development in Taiwan: higher education). Taipei: Taiwan Ministry of Education.

——. 1989. *Shengxüe Wenli Duanqi buxiban Jiaoyü Pingjian baogaoshu* (The assessment report of the academic cram school education in Taiwan). Taipei: Taiwan Ministry of Education.

——. 1992. *Daixüe Duoyuan Ruxüe Fang'an* (Multiple university entrance program). Taiwan: Taiwan University Entrance Exam Center.

——. 1993a. *Jiaoyü Tongji Zhibiao* (Education statistical indicators). Taipei: Taiwan Ministry of Education.

——. 1993b. *Taiwan Diqü Gelei Duanqi Buxiban Gaikuang Tongji Diaocha Baogao*. (Report of statistic survey on short-term *buxiban*). Taipei: Taiwan Ministry of Education Statistics Office

——. 1994. *Zhonghuaminguo Jiaoyü Tongji* (Education statistics of the Republic of China). Taipei: Ministry of Education.

Wang, Huanshen. 1983. 'Woguo Daixüe Ruxüe Zhidu Lishi zhi Yiye' (One page in the history of Chinese college entrance examination system). Pp. 13–43 in *Shijie Geguo Daixüe Ruxüe Zhidu zhi Gaige Dongxiang* (The trend of reform of the entrance exams systems), edited by Taiwan Bijiao Jiaoyü Xüehui (Comparative Education Association of Taiwan). Taipei: Wunan Tushu.

Wang, Zhi-ting. 1959. *Taiwan Jiaoyü Shi* (History of education in Taiwan). Taipei: Taiwan Shudian.

Wu, Li-fen. 1993. 'Guoxiao Xüesheng Buxi Zhuangkuang Wenjüan Fenxi' (An analysis of the questionnaire survey of the cramming practice among elementary school students). *Renben Jiaoyü Zhaji* (Journal of humanistic education) 43 (15 January): 12–21.

Wu, Yu-chang. 1977. *Woguo Daixüe Lianzhao Kaosheng Weigui zhi Yanjiu* (A study of the rule violations among the students during the university entrance exams in Taiwan). Taipei: Tiangong.

Xu, Nan-hao. 1993. *Taiwan Jiaoyü Shi* (History of education in Taiwan). Taipei: Shida Shuyuan.

Zhongguo Shibaoshe. *Zhongguo Shibao* (The China Daily). Taipei: Zhongguo Shibaoshe.

Zhongyang Ribaoshe. *Zhongyang Ribao* (The Central Daily). Taipei: Zhongyang Ribaoshe.

References in Japanese

Abe, Munemitsu, Hiroshi Abe, Ikuo Arai, Toshio Kanaya, Gi-on Han, and Manabu Watabe. 1972. *Kankoku to Taiwan no Kyôiku Kaihatsu* (The educational development in Korea and Taiwan). Tokyo: Ajia Keizai Kenkyûjo.

Akaike, Hiroshi. 1994. 'Kikyô kara mita Bunkakei no Daigaku no Hanka'. Pp. 62–75 in *Daigaku Rankingu: 561 Daigaku Daigakkô Sôlan* (University ranking: an overview of 561 colleges and universities), edited by Asahi Shinbunsha. Tokyo: Asahi Shinbunsha.

Akanuma, Shigeru, *et al.* 1986. *Za*Yobiko. Omoshirokunatta Yobiko o Kaibô* (A dissection of the fascinating *Yobiko*). Tokyo: Daisan Shokan.

Amano, Ikuo. 1986. *Shiken to Gakureki* (Examination and credentialism). Tokyo: Kôzaidô.

———. 1993. *Kyôiku no Ima o Yomu* (Scrutinizing education today). Tokyo: Yûshindô.

Aoki, Takehiko. 1977. *Tenjinsama Gôkaku shitai* (Heavenly God: I want to succeed in exams). Tokyo: Keimei Shobô.

Aonuma, Yoshimatsu. 1962. *Shin Chûkan Kaikyû no Shakaiteki Seikaku* (The social characteristics of the new middle class). Sanshokki Monograph no. 171. Tokyo: Keio University.

Arimoto, Akira. 1994. 'Jiko keikyû to gaibu hyôka de tamesareru jidai ga kuru' (The experimenting age is coming to conduct research by oneself and let others evaluate it). Pp. 18–25 in *Daigaku Rankingu: 561 Daigaku Daigakkô Sôlan* (University ranking: an overview of 561 colleges and universities), edited by Asahi Shinbunsha. Tokyo: Asahi Shinbunsha.

Asahi Shinbunsha. 1994a. *Daigaku Rankingu: 561 Daigaku Daigakkô Sôlan* (University ranking: an overview of 561 colleges and universities). Tokyo: Asahi Shinbunsha.

Asahi Shinbunsha. 1994b. 'Juku kayoi: Machimurabu ni Kabudai' (Attending *juku*: an expanding rate in small towns and villages). *Asahi Shinbun*. 19 August.

Asô, Makoto and Morikazu Ushiogi, eds. 1977. *Gakureki Kôyôron* (The utility of academic credentials). Tokyo: Ûhikaku.

Bungei Shunjûsha, ed. 1992. *Nihon no Ronten* (Opinions on Japan). Tokyo: Bungei Shunjûsha.

Chôsen Sôtôkufu Naimubu Gakumukyo (Educational Bureau of the Government-General of Korea). 1926. *Nihon Shokuminchi Kyôiku Seisaku Shiryô Shûsei* (The collection of historical documents on the Japanese colonial policy in Korea). Seoul: Ryûkei Gakusha.

———. 1941. *Chôsen ni okeru Kyôiku no Gaikyô* (Overview of Korean education). Seoul: Chôsen Sôtôkufu Gakumukyoku.

Dai Ichi Kôtô Gakkô, ed. 1939. *Dai Ichi Kôtô Gakkô Rokujûnenshi* (60-year history of the First Higher School). Tokyo: Dai Ichi Kôtô Gakkô.

Daisan Shokan, ed. 1993. *Za*Rônin* (The *rônin*). Tokyo: Daisan Shokan.

Enzan, Kei. 1992. *Kyôsô Genri o koete* (Transcending the principle of competition). Tokyo: Tarôjirôsha.

Fujimori, Yoshiro. 1992. *Imakaradekiru Hensachi o 10 Appu saseru Hô* (The methods to raise *hensachi* grade by 10 points). Tokyo: Shinsei Shuppansha.

Fukutake Shoten Kyôiku Kenkyûjo. *Monografu: Shôgakusei*, Vol. 11-8 (Tokyo: Fukutake Shoten Kyôiku Kenkyûjo, 1991); cited in *Nihon Kodomo Shiryô Nenkan* Vol. 3, edited by Nihon Sôgô Ai'iku Kenkyûjo (Tokyo: Nihon Sôgô Ai'iku Kenkyûjo, 1992).

———. 1993. *Monografu: Chûgakusei no Sekai* (Monograph: the world of middle school students). Vol. 43, *Tsukareteiru Chûgakusei* (Exhausted middle school students). Tokyo: Fukutake Shoten Kyôiku Kenkyûjo.

Futatsugi, Kôzo. 1993. *Kyûteikokudai no Hôkai* (The fall of former imperial universities). Tokyo. WAVE.

Hazama, Shinjirô. 1960. 'Shin Chûkan Kaikyû no Mondai' (The problem of the new middle class). *Nihon Hôgaku* 26(5) December: 27–49.

Higuchi, Teiichi. 1993. *Sentâ Shiken: Keikô to Taisaku: Sûgaku I/II* (Trends and Countermeasures for the Center Test: Mathematics I/II). Tokyo: Obunsha.

Horie, Masanori. 1962. *Nihon no Rôdôsha Kaikyû* (The working class in Japan). Tokyo: Iwanami Shoten.

Ichikawa, Shogo. 1978. *Allocation of Educational Resources in Japan*. Tokyo: National Institute for Educational Research.

Ikeda, Yoshiko, and Fumiko Yabana. 1982. *Daigaku Rônin no Shinri to Byôri* (A psychological and pathological study of the *rônin* for university). Tokyo: Kinko.

Inamura, Hiroshi, and Katsuyuki Ogawa, eds. 1986. *Juku* (The cram school). Tokyo: Kyôritsu.

Inoue, Toshiaki. 1980. *Gakureki no Shinsô Shinri* (The deep-structural mentality of credentialism). Kyoto: Sekai Shisôsha.

Inui, Akio. 1993. *Nihon no Kyôiku to Kigyôshakai* (Japanese education and corporate society). Tokyo: Daigatsu Shoten.

Iwai, Hiromi. 1979a. *Kindai no Daiema* (*Ema* of modern era). Tokyo: Baji Bunka Zaidan.

———. 1979b. *Ema Hishi* (Untold history of *ema*). Tokyo: Nihon Hôsô Kyôkai.

Japan External Trade Organization. 1992. *Nihon to Amerika – Sûji wa kataru: 2* (US and Japan in Figures II). Tokyo: Japan External Trade Organization.

Japan Management and Coordination Agency. 1988. *Annual Report on the Family Income and Expenditure Survey*. Tokyo: Japan Management and Coordination Agency.

Japanese Ministry of Education. 1875. *Mankoku Shiryaku* (A concise history of ten thousand nations). Tokyo: Ministry of Education.

———. 1949. *Shôgakusei no Sansû: Daiyon-nenkyû* (The arithmetic for primary school pupils, Grade 4). Tokyo: JMOE.

——. 1977. *Zenkoku Gakushû Juku no Toi no Jittai*. Tokyo: Monbudaijin, Tokei Kenkyûka.

——. 1978–90. *Daigaku to Gakusei* (University and students). Tokyo: Ministry of Education.

——. 1978–90. 'Gakusei Seikatsu Chôsa Hôkoku' (The report on student life survey). In *Daigaku to Gakusei*, edited by Japanese Ministry of Education. Tokyo: Ministry of Education.

——. 1982. *1982 Shôgakkô Gakushû Shidô Yôryô* (1982 Elementary School Curriculum guideline). Tokyo: Ministry of Education.

——. 1985. *Jidô Seito no Gakkôgai Gakushû Katsudô ni kansuru Jittai Chôsa Hôkokusho* (Survey of the extracurricular activities of children/students). Tokyo: Ministry of Education.

——. 1986. 'Hogosha ga Shishutsu shita Kyôikuhi no Sui'i' (The change in family expenditures on education). Pp. 279–82 in *Kyôiku*, edited by Ministry of Education. Tokyo: Ministry of Education.

——. 1987. 'Kyôiku Sangyô ni kansuru Chôsa: Gakushûjuku Sangyô o Chûshin ni'. Pp. 293–314 in *Kyôiku*. Tokyo: Ministry of Education.

——. 1993. *Mombushô Daigaku Nyûshi Sentâ Yôran* (A guidebook for the National Center for University Entrance Examinations of Ministry of Education). Tokyo: National Center for University Entrance Examinations.

——. 1994a. *Gakusei Hyakunijû-nen Shi* (120-year history of school regulations). Tokyo: Gyosei.

——. 1994b. 'Izen mirareru Nanmon Shuddai' (Too difficult questions are still in the exams). *Monbu Kôhô* (Ministry of Education official report), 15 June, 936: 6.

——. 1994c. *Kokukôritsu Daigaku Nyûgakusha Senbatsu jisshi jyôkyô* (The actual implementation of selecting entrants for national/public universiities). Tokyo: National Center for University Entrance Examinations.

——. 1994d. *Monbu Tôkei Yôran* (Monbushô Statistics Handbook). Tokyo: Ministry of Education.

——. 1995. *Gakushûjuku tô ni kansuru Jittai Chôsa. Hôkokusho* (Report on the survey of the issues related to the academic *juku*). Tokyo: Japanese Ministry of Education.

——. 1996. *Juken Annai* (Information on entrance exams). Tokyo: Daigaku Nyûshi Sentâ.

Jiji Tsûshinsha. 1993 and 1994. *Kyôiku Deta Randdo* (A databook of educational statistics). Tokyo: Jiji Tsûshinsha.

Kagayama, Kôichi. 1990. *Kodomo Pittari no Juku o erabu Hon* (A book that helps to choose the right *juku* for children). Tokyo: Chûkei.

Kaigo, T. 1964. *Nihongo Kyôkasho Daikei* (Complete collection of Japanese textbooks). Vol. 14, *Mathematics (5)*. Tokyo.

Kawai, Takeo. 1973. 'Gendai Nihon no Kaikyû Kôzô no Henka to Howaito-karâ Sô: 1955-nen-1970-nen' (Changes in the class structure of postwar Japan and the white-collar stratum: 1955–1970). *Hôgaku Kenkyû* 46(9) September: 31–85.

Kawaijuku, ed. 1993a. *1993 Daigaku Juken to Gurîn Kôsu no Ankêto Chôsa* (1993 survey on the students in the courses of university entrance exams). Nagoya: Kawaijuku.

———. 1993b. *Kawaijuku Green Course Nyûjuku Yôkô* (The outlined information about registration into Kawaijuku 'Green Course'). Nagoya: Kawaijuku.

Kawaijuku and Tôyô Keizai, ed. 1993. *Nihon no Daigaku* (Japanese universities). Nagoya: Kawaijuku.

Keimei Kenkyûkai. 1987. *Kyôshi no tamei no Data-Bank* (Databook for teachers). Tokyo: Keimei Kenkyûkai.

Kim, Shinil. 1992. 'Kan-Ni kan Kyôiku Senbatsu Seido Hikaku' (A comparison of Korean and Japanese educational selection systems). Paper presented at Seoul National University-Tokyo University Symposium. Seoul: Seoul National University.

Kito, K. *Sûgaku no Bunmei Kaika* (Math: civilization and enlightenment). Tokyo.

Komiyama, Hirohito. 1991. *Kashikoi Gakushûjuku no erabikata* (How to select a good academic *juku*). Tokyo: Shinryôron.

———. 1993. *Gakureki Shakai to Juku* (Credentialistic society and *juku*). Tokyo: Shinryôron.

Kurasawa, Takashi. 1973. *Gakusei no Kenkyû* (The educational ordinance). Tokyo: Kodansha.

Kuroki, Hiroshi. 1994. *Kenshô Daigaku Kaikaku* (Examine the university reform). Tokyo: Ronsôsha.

Kyôgakusha, ed. 1993a. *Daigaku Nyûshi Sentâ Shiken: Eigo* (Questions and annotated answers of the exams given by the National Center for University Entrance Exams: English). Tokyo: Kyôgakusha.

———. 1993b. *Daigaku Nyûshi Sentâ Shiken: Sûgaku* (Questions and annotated answers of the exams given by the National Center for University Entrance Exams: Mathematics). Tokyo: Kyôgakusha.

———. 1994. *Daigaku Nyûshi Sentâ Shiken Mondai Kenkyû: Sekaishi* (Questions and annotated answers of the exams given by the National Center for University Entrance Exams: World History). Tokyo: Kyôgakusha.

Li, Yuanhui. 1970. *Nihon Tôchika ni okeru Taiwan Shotô Kyôiku no Kenkyû* (A study of Taiwan's primary education under the Japanese rule). Taizhong: Taizhong Normal School.

Makino, Tsuyoshi. 1986. *Yobiko ni au: Seishun no Kyôiku* (Meet in the *yobiko*: education of the young). Nagoya: Fûbaisha.

Masuda, Koichi, Masato Tokuyama, and Kanjiro Saito. 1961. *Nyûgaku Shiken Seidoshi Kenkyû* (A study of the history of entrance examination system). Tokyo: Tôyôkan Shuppansha.

Matsumoto, Takai. 1960. *Taihoku dekikoku Daigaku Enkakushi* (The history of the Taipei Imperial University). Translated by Guai Tonglin. Taipei: Taipei University.

Miyazawa, Hiroshi, ed. 1991. *Shizen-Shakai Hen* (Nature and society). Vol. 10, *Illustrated Today's Japan*, edited by Japan Travel Bureau. Tokyo: Japan Travel Bureau.

Mori, Kazio, and Hiroshi Nakasato. 1993. *Sentâ Shiken: Keikô to Taisaku: Nihonshi* (Trends and countermeasures for the Center Test of Japanese history). Tokyo: Obunsha.

Murasaki, Fuyoko. 1991. *Hensachi Nikki* (*Hensachi* diary). Tokyo: Kamakura.

Nakajima, Takeshi. 1994. *Jinja, Buggaku, Gorieki no Ryo* (Beneficiary visits to Shinto shrines and Buddhist temples). Tokyo: Ikuhôsha.

Nakauchi, Toshio, Hajime Tajima, Eiichi Ameda, and Toshihiko Saito. 1986. *The Modernization of Japanese Education.* Tokyo: International Society for Educational Information.

Nihon Hôsô Kyôkai (Japan Broadcasting Corporation). 1983a. *Kyôiku: Hensachi ga Nihon no Mirai o Shihai suru* (Education: *hensachi* shapes Japan's future). Tokyo: Nihon Hôsô Kyôkai.

———. 1983b. *Kyôiku: Nani ga Kôhai shiteiru no ka* (Education: why education is being ravaged). Tokyo: Nihon Hôsô Kyôkai.

———. 1992. *Nihonjin no Seikatsu Jikan 1990* (Japanese' time spent in daily life 1990). Tokyo: Nihon Hôsô Kyôkai.

Nihon Shiritsu Daigaku Renmei (Japan Association of Private Colleges and Universities). 1993. *Nyûshi Seido to Shiritsu Daigaku: Shiridai Nyûshi no Kenjô to Kadai* (Entrance examination system and the private university: the status and issues of the entrance exams for private universities). Tokyo: Nihon Shiritsu Daigaku Renmei.

Nishito, Teisei. 1973. *Tô-Ajia Sekai* (East Asian World). Tokyo: Kôdansha.

O, Tchôn-sôk. 1979. *Kankoku Kindai Kyôiku Shi* (History of modern education of Korea). Translated by Manabu Watanabe and Hiroshi Abe from Korean. Tokyo: Korei Shorin.

Obunsha, ed. *Juken Junhô* (Examination journal). Tokyo: Obunsha.

———. 1936–94. *Nyûgaku Shiken Mondai Shôkai* (Entrance examination questions and annotated answers). Tokyo: Obunsha.

———. 1936–94. *Keisetsu Jidai* (The age of firefly and snow). Tokyo: Obunsha.

———. 1966–94. *Daigaku Nyûgaku Nan'i Rankingu* (The ranking of difficulty scale for entering universities). Tokyo: Obunsha.

———. 1985. *Nihonkoku Juken Yûmâ Gojûgo-nen Shi* (The 55-year history of Japan's humour in exams). Tokyo: Obunsha.

Ogura, K. 1978. *Nihon Sûgaku Kyôiku Shi* (Japanese history of mathematics). Tokyo: Kazama Shobô.

Ohashi, Ryuken. 1971. *Nihon no Kaikyû Kôsei* (The class composition of Japan). Tokyo: Iwanami Shoten.

Oyama, Yoshiaki. 1993. *Sentâ Shiken: Keikô to Taisaku: Kokugo* (Trends and countermeasures for the Center Test of Japanese philology). Tokyo: Obunsha.

Riguchi, Teiichi. 1993. *Sentâ Shiken: Keikô to Taisaku: Sûgaku* (Trends and countermeasures for the Center Test of mathematics). Tokyo: Obunsha.

Saida, Seiichi. 1993. *Sentâ Shiken: Keikô to Taisaku: Ego I & II* (Trends and countermeasures for the Center Test of English I & II). Tokyo: Obunsha.

Sakamoto, Shôfu, and Kômitsu Yamamoto. 1992. *Mombushô no Kenkyô* (A study of Japanese Ministry of Education). Tokyo: San'ichi Shobô.

Sato, Kenichi. 1989. *Sûgaku no Bunmei Kaika* (Maths: civilization and enlightenment). Tokyo: Tokyo : Jiji Tsûsinsha.

Sato, Kenichiro, and Zenjiro Tamura. 1978. *Koema: Inori to Katachi* (Small *ema*: prayer and pattern). Tokyo: Tankôsha.

Sato, Tadashi. 1992. 'Hensachi o Mushi shita "Ichigei Nyûshi Senbatsu" wa Daigaku no Hitei ni tsunagaru' (The one-skill entrance selection is a denial of the university). Pp. 732–9 in *Nihon no Ronten* (Opinions on Japan), edited by Bungei Shunjûsha. Tokyo: Bungei Shunjûsha.

Shimizu, Kazihito. 1994. *Kyôiku Detalando* (A databook of educational statistics). Jiji Tsûshinsha.

Shimizu, Kenni. 1991. *Gakumon no Kamisama* (The gods of scholarship). Tokyo: Kamakura Shinsho.

Shimizu, Yoshiro. 1957. *Shiken* (Examinations). Tokyo: Iwanami Shoten.

Shinohara, Akio. 1989. *Shinkyû Gakushû Shidô Yôryô no Taihi to Kôsatsu: Chûgakkô Shakaika* (The comparison and review of the old and new academic guidances: social science of middle school). Tokyo: Meiji Tosho.

Shuken Asahi. 1994. See Asahi Shinbunsha, 1994a.

Sôrifu (Office of Japanese Prime Minister). 1981. *Kokusai Hikaku: Nihon no Kodomo to Hahaoya* (International comparison: Japanese children and mothers). Tokyo: Sôrifu.

Sundai Yobiko. 1994. 'Shin Daigakusei no Gôkaku Jiko Shindan' (Self-analysis by university freshmen of why they succeeded). *Ascent* 20(4): 3-5.

Suzuki, Kin. *Meiji Ishin* (The Meiji Restoration). 1968. Tokyo: Sekai Bunkasha.

Takahashi, Shirô. 1989. 'Nyûshi Kaikaku no Rekishi to Kadai' (History and themes of the entrance Examination Reform). Pp. 107–44 in *Nyûshi Kaikaku to Shintesto* (Reform of the college entrance examination and the new test), edited by Yomiuri Terebi Hôdôbu (Yomiuri Televised News Department). Tokyo: Kyôdô Shuppansha.

Tokyo University. *Gakunai Kôhô* (The campus report). Tokyo: Tokyo University.

Tomiyama, Yoshiaku. 1994. *Gen'eki Gôkaku no Jikanwari Sakusen* (Time schedule of the at-school students to fight for the exams). Tokyo: Yell Books.

Vandermeersch, Léon. 1987. *Ajia Bunkaken no Jidai* (The epoch of Asian Cultural Sphere). Translated by Fukukama Tadahiro. Tokyo: Daishûkan Shoten.

Yano, Sanawa. 1993. *Kôtô Kyôikuhi no Hiyôfutan ni kansuru Seisaku Kagakudeki Kenkyû* (A study of the policy science concerning the cost of higher education). Tokyo: Tokyo University of Industry.

Yano Keizai Kenkyûsho (Yano Economics Research Institute). 1994. *Kyôiku Sangyô Hakusho* (The White Paper on industry). Tokyo: Yano Keizai Kenkyûsho.

Yell Books, ed. 1994. *Mumeikko kara Watashiwa no Todai Gôkaku Sakusen* (My struggle from an unknown school to Tokyo University). Tokyo: Yell Books.

Yomiuri Terebi Hôdôbu (Yomiuri Televised News Department), ed. 1989. *Nyûshi Kaikaku to Shintesto* (Reform of the college entrance examination and the new Test). Tokyo: Kyôdô Shuppansha.

Yonezawa, Akiyoshi. 1992. 'Kôtô kyôiku Seisaku to Shiritsu Daigaku no Kôdô' (Higher education policy and the behaviour of private universities: expansion and stagnation viewed from the supply side). *Kyôiku Shakaigaku Kenkyû* (Research of Educational Sociology) (Tokyo: Tokyo University Graduate School) 50: 325–344.

References in Korean

Chung, Jae-Chol. 1985. *Iljeui Dae Hankook Sikminji Kyoyuk Chongchaeksa* (History of educational policies of Imperial Japan in colonial Korea). Seoul: Iljisa.

Chung, Tae-Su, ed. 1992. *Migunchonggi Hankook Kyoyuk Jaryojip (Sang)* (Historical documents of Korean education under the US Army Military Government in Korea: first volume). Seoul: Hongjiwon.

Hankook Hakwon Chong Yunhaphwe (Korea Unified Association of *Hakwon*). 1992. *Hankook Hakwonsa Tamgu* (A study of the history of Korea's *Hakwon*). Seoul: Hankook Hakwon Chong Yunhaphwe.

Lee, Jong Seung. 1993. 'Guageo Haegyeolnoryeogeui Yeogsa' (The history of past solution efforts). Pp. 127–54 in *Gyoyugeui Bonyeoneul Chajaseo ibsiwa Ibsigyoyeogeui Gaehyeog* (Restoring Korean education from the bondage of entrance examination education), edited by Chung, Bum Mo, *et al.* Seoul: Nanam.

Shin, Se-Ho, Moo-Sub Kang, Youn-Kee Im, Heung-Ju Kim, and Jae-Woong Kim. 1991. *Kwawe Sueop Siltae Bunseok Yungu* (A study of private tutoring in Korea). Seoul: Korea Education Development Institute.

Index